A·N·N·U·A·L E·D·I·T

PSYCHOLOGY

Thirtieth Edition

00/01

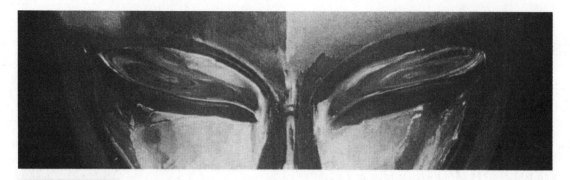

EDITOR

Karen G. Duffy
SUNY College, Geneseo

Karen G. Duffy holds a doctorate in psychology from Michigan State University and is currently a professor of psychology at SUNY at Geneseo. She sits on the executive board of the New York State Employees Assistance Program and is a certified community and family mediator. She is a member of the American Psychological Society and the Eastern Psychological Association.

Dushkin/McGraw-Hill
Sluice Dock, Guilford, Connecticut 06437

Visit us on the Internet
http://www.dushkin.com/annualeditions/

Credits

1. The Science of Psychology
Unit photo—© 1999 by PhotoDisc, Inc.
2. Biological Bases of Behavior
Unit photo—Courtesy of the World Health Organization.
3. Perceptual Processes
Unit photo—© 1999 by PhotoDisc, Inc.
4. Learning and Remembering
Unit photo—© 1999 by Cleo Freelance Photography, Inc.
5. Cognitive Processes
Unit photo—© 1999 by Cleo Freelance Photography, Inc.
6. Emotion and Motivation
Unit photo—© 1999 by Cleo Freelance Photography, Inc.
7. Development
Unit photo—© 1999 by Cleo Freelance Photography, Inc.
8. Personality Processes
Unit photo—© 1999 by Cleo Freelance Photography, Inc.
9. Social Processes
Unit photo—© 1999 by Cleo Freelance Photography, Inc.
10. Psychological Disorders
Unit photo—Courtesy of Dushkin/McGraw-Hill.
11. Psychological Treatments
Unit photo—World Health Organization photo by Jean Mohr.

Cataloging in Publication Data
Main entry under title: Annual Editions: Psychology. 2000/2001.
    1. Psychology—Periodicals. I. Duffy, Karen G., comp.II. Title: Psychology.
BF 149.A58   150'   79-180263   ISBN 0-07-236396-7   ISSN 0272-3794

Thirtieth Edition

Cover image © 2000 PhotoDisc, Inc.

Printed in the United States of America   1234567890BAHBAH543210   Printed on Recycled Paper

Editors/Advisory Board

Staff

To the Reader

In publishing ANNUAL EDITIONS we recognize the enormous role played by the magazines, newspapers, and journals of the public press in providing current, first-rate educational information in a broad spectrum of interest areas. Many of these articles are appropriate for students, researchers, and professionals seeking accurate, current material to help bridge the gap between principles and theories and the real world. These articles, however, become more useful for study when those of lasting value are carefully collected, organized, indexed, and reproduced in a low-cost format, which provides easy and permanent access when the material is needed. That is the role played by ANNUAL EDITIONS.

New to ANNUAL EDITIONS is the inclusion of related World Wide Web sites. These sites have been selected by our editorial staff to represent some of the best resources found on the World Wide Web today. Through our carefully developed topic guide, we have linked these Web resources to the articles covered in this ANNUAL EDITIONS reader. We think that you will find this volume useful, and we hope that you will take a moment to visit us on the Web at **http://www.dushkin.com** to tell us what you think.

Ronnie's parents couldn't understand why he didn't want to be picked up and cuddled as did his older sister when she was a baby. As an infant, Ronnie did not respond to his parents' smiles, words, or attempts to amuse him. By the age of two, Ronnie's parents knew that he was not like other children. He spoke no English, was very temperamental, and often rocked himself for hours. Ronnie is autistic. His parents feel that some of Ronnie's behavior may be their fault; they both work long hours as young professionals and leave both children with an older woman during the week days. Ronnie's pediatrician assures his parents that their reasoning, while logical, probably holds no merit because the causes of autism are little understood and are likely to be physiological rather than parental. What can we do about children like Ronnie? What is the source of autism? Can it be treated or reversed? Can autism be prevented?

Psychologists attempt to answer these and other questions in a specific way. Researchers use carefully planned methods to discover the causes of complex human behavior, normal or not. The scientific results of most psychological research are published in professional journals and therefore may be difficult for the lay person to understand.

Annual Editions: Psychology 00/01 is designed to meet the needs of laypeople and introductory-level students who are curious about psychology. This book provides a vast selection of readable and informative articles, primarily from popular magazines and newspapers. These articles are typically written by journalists, but a few are written by psychologists and retain the excitement of the discovery of scientific knowledge.

The particular articles in this volume were chosen to be representative of the most current work in psychology. They were selected because they are accurate in their reporting and provide examples of the types of psychological research discussed in most introductory psychology classes. As in any science, some of the findings discussed in this collection are startling, while others confirm what we already know. Some entries will invite speculation about social and personal issues; others demand careful thought about potential misuse of the applications of research findings. Readers are expected to make the investment of effort and critical reasoning needed to discuss questions and concerns.

I believe that you will find this edition of *Annual Editions: Psychology 00/01* readable and useful. I suggest that students look at the organization of this book and compare it to the organization of their textbook and course syllabus. By examining the *topic guide* that follows the *table of contents*, you can identify those readings most appropriate for any particular unit of study in your course. The *World Wide Web* sites that follow the topic guide can be used to further explore the topics.

Your instructor may provide some help in assigning certain articles to supplement the text. As you read the selections, try to connect their contents with the principles you are learning from your text and classroom lectures. Some of the articles will help you better understand a specific area of research, while others will help you connect and integrate information from various research areas. Both of these strategies are important in learning about psychology or any other science. It is only through intensive investigation and subsequent integration of the findings from many studies that we are able to discover and apply new knowledge.

Please take time to provide us with feedback to guide the annual revision of this anthology by completing and returning the *article rating form* in the back of the book. With your help, this collection will be even better next year. Thank you.

Karen Grover Duffy

Karen Grover Duffy
Editor

Contents

UNIT 1

The Science of Psychology

Three articles examine psychology as the science of behavior.

UNIT 2

Biological Bases of Behavior

Four selections discuss the biological bases of behavior. Topics include brain functions and the brain's control over the body.

The concepts in bold italics are developed in the article. For further expansion please refer to the Topic Guide, the Glossary, and the Index.

UNIT 3

Perceptual Processes

Four articles discuss the impact of the senses on human perceptual processes.

UNIT 4

Learning and Remembering

Four selections examine how operant conditioning, positive reinforcement, and memory interact during the learning process.

The concepts in bold italics are developed in the article. For further expansion please refer to the Topic Guide, the Glossary, and the Index.

UNIT 5

Cognitive Processes

Four articles examine how social skills, common sense, and intelligence affect human cognitive processes.

UNIT 6

Emotion and Motivation

Five articles discuss the influences of stress, mental states, and emotion on the mental and physical health of the individual.

UNIT 7

Development

Five articles consider the importance of experience, discipline, familial support, and psychological aging during the normal human development process.

UNIT 8

Personality Processes

Four selections discuss a few
of the processes by which
personalities are developed.
Topics include sex differences,
state of mind, and hostility.

UNIT 9

Social Processes

Four selections discuss how the
individual's social development is
affected by genes, stereotypes,
prejudice, and self-help.

UNIT 10

Psychological Disorders

Six articles examine several psychological disorders. Topics include unexpected behavior, the impact of depression on a person's well-being, and physical abuse.

The concepts in bold italics are developed in the article. For further expansion please refer to the Topic Guide, the Glossary, and the Index.

UNIT 11

Psychological Treatments

Four selections discuss a few
psychological treatments, including
psychoanalysis, psychotherapy to
alleviate depression, self-care,
and the use of drugs.

Topic Guide

This topic guide suggests how the selections and World Wide Web sites found in the next section of this book relate to topics of traditional concern to psychology students and professionals. It is useful for locating interrelated articles and Web sites for reading and research. The guide is arranged alphabetically according to topic.

The relevant Web sites, which are numbered and annotated on pages 4 and 5, are easily identified by the Web icon (☺) under the topic articles. By linking the articles and the Web sites by topic, this ANNUAL EDITIONS reader becomes a powerful learning and research tool.

<table>
<tr><th>TOPIC AREA</th><th>TREATED IN</th><th>TOPIC AREA</th><th>TREATED IN</th></tr>
<tr>
<td>Adolescents</td>
<td>28. Rethinking Puberty: The Development of Sexual Attraction
☺ 8, 14, 19, 21, 22, 25</td>
<td>Drugs/Drug Treatment</td>
<td>46. Quest for a Cure
47. New Treatments for Schizophrenia—Part I
☺ 31, 32, 33</td>
</tr>
<tr>
<td>Aging</td>
<td>14. Losing Your Mind?
29. Live to 100? No Thanks
☺ 22</td>
<td>Dysthymia</td>
<td>41. Dysthymia: Treating Mild Depression's Major Effects
☺ 25, 26, 27, 32</td>
</tr>
<tr>
<td>Alzheimer's</td>
<td>14. Losing Your Mind?
☺ 22</td>
<td rowspan="2">Emotions</td>
<td rowspan="2">20. Face It!
21. Emotion in the Second Half of Life
22. Psychology: A Study Finds That among Professions, the Secret Service Is Best at Distinguishing between Lies and Truth
23. Biology of Joy
☺ 20, 22, 23</td>
</tr>
<tr>
<td>Anxiety/Anxiety Disorder</td>
<td>38. Chronic Anxiety: How to Stop Living on the Edge
☺ 25, 26, 27</td>
</tr>
<tr>
<td>Brain</td>
<td>4. Nature, Nuture: Not Mutually Exclusive
7. Split Brain Revisited
8. Senses
☺ 8, 9, 10, 11, 15, 17, 19, 22</td>
<td>Emotional Intelligence</td>
<td>35. What Makes a Leader?
☺ 23</td>
</tr>
<tr>
<td rowspan="2">Children</td>
<td rowspan="2">16. Child Psychologist: Jean Piaget
17. Cognitive Development in Social and Cultural Context
25. Seven Stages of Man
26. Fetal Psychology
27. Do Parents Really Matter? Kid Stuff
☺ 15, 17, 20, 21, 22</td>
<td>Fetus</td>
<td>26. Fetal Psychology</td>
</tr>
<tr>
<td>Friends/ Friendship</td>
<td>34. Friendship and Adaptation across the Life Span
☺ 14, 19, 21</td>
</tr>
<tr>
<td rowspan="2">Cognition</td>
<td rowspan="2">16. Child Psychologist: Jean Piaget
17. Cognitive Development in Social and Cultural Context
19. Penetrating the Barriers to Teaching Higher Thinking
☺ 15, 17, 21, 22</td>
<td>Freud/ Psychoanalysis</td>
<td>30. Who Are the Freudians?
☺ 5, 33</td>
</tr>
<tr>
<td rowspan="2">Genes/Genetics</td>
<td rowspan="2">4. Nature, Nurture: Not Mutually Exclusive
5. What We Learn from Twins: The Mirror of Your Soul
6. Optimizing Expression of the Common Human Genome for Child Development
☺ 8, 9, 10, 11, 22, 23</td>
</tr>
<tr>
<td>Critical Thinking</td>
<td>19. Penetrating the Barriers to Teaching Higher Thinking
☺ 4, 7, 8, 10, 11</td>
</tr>
<tr>
<td>Deafness</td>
<td>9. Deaf Defying
☺ 4</td>
<td>Intelligence</td>
<td>18. Multiple Intelligence Disorder
☺ 15, 16, 17, 18</td>
</tr>
<tr>
<td rowspan="2">Depression</td>
<td rowspan="2">40. Dysthymia: Treating Mild Depression's Major Effects
46. Quest for a Cure
☺ 25, 26, 27, 30, 32</td>
<td>Leadership</td>
<td>35. What Makes a Leader?
☺ 23</td>
</tr>
<tr>
<td rowspan="2">Learning</td>
<td rowspan="2">12. Learning Begins Even before Babies Are Born, Scientists Show
13. What Constitutes "Appropriate" Punishment?
☺ 14, 15</td>
</tr>
<tr>
<td rowspan="2">Development</td>
<td rowspan="2">24. Moral Development of Children
25. Seven Stages of Man
26. Fetal Psychology
27. Do Parents Really Matter? Kid Stuff
28. Rethinking Puberty: The Development of Sexual Attraction
29. Live to 100? No Thanks
☺ 8, 9, 15, 21, 22</td>
</tr>
<tr>
<td>Media</td>
<td>3. How Are Psychologists Portrayed on Screen?
37. Psychologist Links Video Games to Violence</td>
</tr>
<tr>
<td rowspan="2">Memory</td>
<td rowspan="2">14. Losing Your Mind?
15. Traumatic Memory Is Special
☺ 14, 15</td>
</tr>
<tr>
<td>Dreams</td>
<td>11. Night Life
☺ 31, 33</td>
</tr>
</table>

◉ AE: Psychology

The following World Wide Web sites have been carefully researched and selected to support the articles found in this reader. If you are interested in learning more about specific topics found in this book, these Web sites are a good place to start. The sites are cross-referenced by number and appear in the topic guide on the previous two pages. Also, you can link to these Web sites through our DUSHKIN ONLINE support site at *http://www.dushkin.com/online/*.

The following sites were available at the time of publication. Visit our Web site—we update DUSHKIN ONLINE regularly to reflect any changes.

General Sources

1. Mental Health Net
http://mentalhelp.net
This comprehensive guide to mental health online features more than 6,300 individual resources. Information on mental disorders and professional resources in psychology, psychiatry, and social work are presented.

2. Psychnet
http://www.apa.org/psychnet/
Use the site map or search engine to access *APA Monitor*, the American Psychological Association newspaper, APA books on a wide range of topics, PsychINFO, an electronic database of abstracts on scholarly journals, and the HelpCenter.

3. The Psych.com: Internet Psychology Resource
http://www.thepsych.com
Thousands of psychology resources are currently indexed at this site. Psychology Disciplines, Conditions & Disorders, Psychiatry, Assistance, and Self-Development are among the most useful.

4. School Psychology Resources Online
http://www.schoolpsychology.net
Numerous sites on special conditions, disorders, and disabilities, as well as other data ranging from assessment/evaluation to research, are available on this resouce page for psychologists, parents, and educators.

The Science of Psychology

5. Abraham A. Brill Library
http://plaza.interport.net/nypsan/service.html
Containing data on over 40,000 books, periodicals, and reprints in psychoanalysis and related fields, the Abraham A. Brill Library's holdings span the literature of psychoanalysis from its beginning to the present day.

6. American Psychological Society (APS)
http://www.psychologicalscience.org/links.htm
The APS is dedicated to advancing the best of scientific psychology in research, application, and the improvement of human conditions. Links to teaching, research, and graduate studies resources are available.

7. Psychology Research on the Net
http://psych.hanover.edu/APS/exponnet.html
This Net site provides psychologically related experiments. Biological psychology/neuropsychology, clinical psychology, cognition, developmental psychology, emotions, health psychology, personality, sensation/perception, and social psychology are some of the areas covered.

Biological Bases of Behavior

8. Biological Changes in Adolescence
http://www.personal.psu.edu/faculty/n/x/nxd10/biologic2.htm

A discussion of puberty, sexuality, biological changes, cross-cultural differences, and nutrition for adolescents, including obesity and its effects on adolescent development, is presented here.

9. Division of Hereditary Diseases and Family Studies, Indiana University School of Medicine
http://medgen.iupui.edu/divisions/hereditary/
The Department of Medical and Molecular Genetics is primarily concerned with determining the genetic basis of disease. It consists of a multifaceted program with a variety of interdisciplinary projects. The areas of twin studies and linkage analysis are also explored

10. Institute for Behavioral Genetics
http://ibgwww.colorado.edu/index.html
Dedicated to conducting and facilitating research on the genetic and environmental bases of individual differences in behavior, this organized research unit at the University of Colorado leads to Genetic Sites, Statistical Sites, and the Biology Meta Index, as well as to search engines.

11. Serendip
http://serendip.brynmawr.edu/serendip/
Serendip, which is organized into five subject areas (brain and behavior, complex systems, genes and behavior, science and culture, and science education), contains interactive exhibits, articles, links to other resources, and a forum area.

Perceptual Processes

12. Psychology Tutorials
http://psych.hanover.edu/Krantz/tutor.html
Interactive tutorials and simulations, primarily in the area of sensation and perception, are available here.

13. Your Mind's Eye
http://illusionworks.com/html/jump_page.html
This multimedia museum exhibit on illusions will inform (and perhaps delight) about how we think and perceive.

Learning and Remembering

14. The Opportunity of Adolescence
http://www.winternet.com/~webpage/adolescencepaper.html
According to this paper, adolescence is the turning point, after which the future is redirected and confirmed. The opportunities and problems of this period are presented with quotations from Erik Erikson, Jean Piaget, and others.

15. Project Zero
http://pzweb.harvard.edu
The Harvard Project Zero has investigated the development of learning processes in children and adults for 30 years. Today, Project Zero's mission is to understand and enhance learning, thinking, and creativity in the arts and other disciplines for individuals and institutions.

Cognitive Processes

16. Chess: Kasparov v. Deep Blue: The Rematch
http://www.chess.ibm.com/home/html/b.html
Clips from the chess rematch between Garry Kasparov and IBM's supercomputer, Deep Blue, are presented here along with commentaries on chess, computers, artificial intelligence, and what it all means.

17. Cognitive Science Article Archive
http://www.helsinki.fi/hum/kognitiotiede/archive.html
This excellent Finnish source contains articles on various fields of cognitive science.

18. Introduction to Artificial Intelligence (AI)
http://www-formal.stanford.edu/jmc/aiintro/aiintro.html
A description of AI is presented here along with links to other AI sites.

Emotion and Motivation

19. CYFERNET-Youth Development
http://www.cyfernet.mes.umn.edu/youthdev.html
CYFERNET presents many articles on youth development, including a statement on the concept of normal adolescence and impediments to healthy development.

20. Nature vs. Nature: Gergen Dialogue with Winifred Gallagher
http://www.pbs.org/newshour/gergen/gallagher_5-14.html
Experience modifies temperament, according to this TV interview. The author of *I.D.: How Heredity and Experience Make You Who You Are* explains a current theory about temperament.

Development

21. American Association for Child and Adolescent Psychiatry
http://www.aacap.org/factsfam/index.htm
This site is designed to aid in the understanding and treatment of the developmental, behavioral, and mental disorders that could affect children and adolescents. There is a specific link just for families about common childhood problems that may or may not require professional intervention.

22. Behavioral Genetics
http://www.uams.edu/department_of_psychiatry/slides/html/genetics/index.htm
A slide show on Behavioral Genetics, which includes objectives, methods of genetic investigation, family and twin studies, personality, intelligence, mental disorders, and Alzheimer's Disease, is presented on this Web site.

Personality Processes

23. The Personality Project
http://fas.psych.nwu.edu/personality.html
This Personality Project (by William Revelle) is meant to guide those interested in personality theory and research to the current personality research literature.

Social Processes

24. National Clearinghouse for Alcohol and Drug Information
http://www.health.org
Information on drug and alcohol facts that might relate to adolescence and the issues of peer pressure and youth cul-

ture is presented here. Resources, referrals, research and statistics, databases, and related Net links are available.

Psychological Disorders

25. Anxiety Disorders in Children and Adolescents
http://www.adaa.org/4_info/4i_child/4i_01.htm
Anxiety disorders in children and adolescents are reviewed by the Anxiety Disorders Association of America (ADAA). A detailed glossary is included.

26. Ask NOAH About: Mental Health
http://www.noah.cuny.edu/illness/mentalhealth/mental.html
Information about child and adolescent family problems, mental conditions and disorders, suicide prevention, and much more is available here.

27. Mental Health Infosource: Disorders
http://www.mentalhelp.net/dxtx.htm
Presented on this site are hotlinks to psychological disorders pages, which include anxiety, panic, phobic disorders, schizophrenia, and violent/self-destructive behaviors.

28. Mental Health Net: Eating Disorder Resources
http://www.mentalhelp.net/guide/eating.htm
This mental health Net site provides a complete list of Web references on eating disorders, including anorexia, bulimia, and obesity.

29. National Women's Health Resource Center (NWHRC)
http://www.healthywomen.org
NWHRC's site contains links to resources related to women's substance abuse and mental illnesses.

30. Suicide Awareness: Voices of Education
http://www.save.org
This SA/VE suicide site presents data on suicide prevention. It includes symptoms/danger signs, misconceptions, facts, hospitalization, and other details on depression and suicide.

Psychological Treatments

31. JungWeb
http://www.onlinepsych.com/jungweb/
Dedicated to the work of Carl Jung, JungWeb is a comprehensive resource for Jungian psychology with links to Jungian psychology, reference materials, graduate programs, dreams, and multilingual sites.

32. Knowledge Exchange Network (KEN)
http://www.mentalhealth.org
Information about mental health (prevention, treatment, and rehabilitation services), is available via toll-free telephone services, an electronic bulletin board, and publications.

33. Sigmund Freud and the Freud Archives
http://plaza.interport.net/nypsan/freudarc.html
Internet resources related to Sigmund Freud, which include a collection of libraries, museums, and biographical materials, as well as the Brill Library archives, can be found here.

We highly recommend that you review our Web site for expanded information and our other product lines. We are continually updating and adding links to our Web site in order to offer you the most usable and useful information that will support and expand the value of your Annual Editions. You can reach us at:
http://www.dushkin.com/annualeditions/.

www.dushkin.com/online/

Unit Selections

1. **Science and Pseudoscience,** *APS Observer*
2. **Research in the Psychological Laboratory: Truth or Triviality?** Craig A. Anderson, James J. Lindsay, and Brad J. Bushman
3. **How Are Psychologists Portrayed on Screen?** Scott Sleek

Key Points to Consider

❖ Which area of psychology do you think is the most valuable and why? Many people are most aware of clinical psychology by virtue of having watched films and television. Is this the most valuable area of the discipline? About which other areas of psychology do you think the public ought to be informed? Does Hollywood do a good job portraying psychology as it is really practiced?

❖ How do you think psychology is related to other scientific disciplines, such as sociology, biology, and human medicine? Are there other disciplines to which psychology might be related, for example, philosophy and mathematics? How so?

❖ Do you think psychologists will ever be able to piece together a single grand theory of human psychology? Do you have your own theory of human behavior? If yes, on what do you base your theory, your own observations? In developing a theory of human behavior, should psychologists rely exclusively on research?

❖ Why is research important to psychology? What kinds of information can be gleaned from psychological research? What is validity? What is external validity? Can you provide an example of each? Why are these concepts important to psychological research? What types of problems are inherent in poorly designed research? How can psychological research be improved? At what general conclusion do Anderson, Lindsay, and Bushman arrive regarding laboratory research? Regarding field research?

 **Links**   **www.dushkin.com/online/**

5. **Abraham A. Brill Library**
   http://plaza.interport.net/nypsan/service.html
6. **American Psychological Society (APS)**
   http://www.psychologicalscience.org/links.htm
7. **Psychology Research on the Net**
   http://psych.hanover.edu/APS/exponnet.html

These sites are annotated on pages 4 and 5.

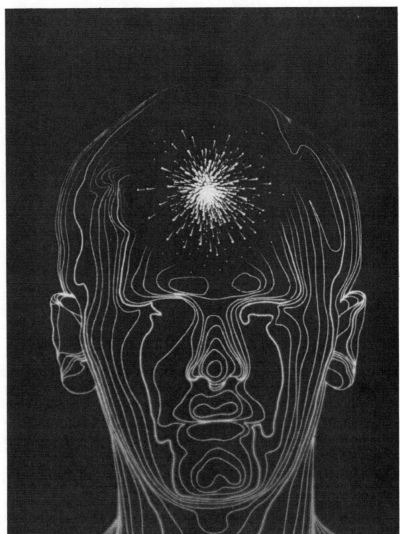

Little did Wilhelm Wundt realize his monumental contribution to science when in 1879, in Germany, he opened the first psychological laboratory to examine consciousness. Wundt would barely recognize today's science of psychology, so much has it changed from how he practiced it.

Contemporary psychology is defined as the science or study of individual mental activity and behavior. This definition reflects the two parent disciplines from which psychology emerged: philosophy and biology. Compared to its parents, psychology is very much a new discipline. Some aspects of modern psychology are particularly biological, such as neuroscience, perception, psychophysics, and behavioral genetics. Other aspects are more philosophical, such as the study of personality. Still others approximate sociology, as does social psychology.

Today's psychologists work in a variety of settings. Many psychologists are academics, teaching and researching psychology on university campuses. Others work in applied settings such as hospitals, mental health clinics, industry, and schools. Most psychologists specialize after some graduate training. Industrial psychologists deal with in human performance in organizational settings. Clinical psychologists are concerned about the assessment, diagnosis, and treatment of individuals with a variety of mental disorders.

Some psychologists think that psychology is still in its adolescence and that the field is experiencing some growing pains. Since its establishment, the field has expanded to many different areas. As mentioned above, some areas are very applied; others emphasize theory and research. The growing pains have resulted in some conflict over what the agenda of the first national psychological association, the American Psychological Association, should be. Because academics perceived this association as mainly serving practitioners, academics and researchers established their own competing association, the American Psychological Society. But, despite its varied nature and growing pains, psychology remains a viable and exciting field. The first unit of this book is designed to introduce you to the nature and history of psychology.

In the first article, "Science and Pseudoscience," experts in psychology debate what science really is. They conclude that science has different meanings, depending upon the constituency. Lay people, for example, often embrace as science simple anecdotal observations. Examples of science and anecdote are given.

The next article also pertains to psychological science. The authors ask a cogent question. Is research conducted in psychology, whether in the laboratory or in the field, trivial or worthwhile? The primary question they ask is about validity. Can psychological research in the laboratory, for example, inform us about human behavior in the "real" world? After reviewing a multitude of studies, the authors conclude that psychological research is sound (valid) and that both laboratory and field studies provide useful and parallel information about human behavior.

The third introductory article on psychology is about public perception of psychologists. Much of the public's notion of what a psychologist does is derived from the media. The American Psychological Association, mentioned in the preface to this section, performs a watchdog function over the portrayal of psychologists, especially therapists, in the media. The good news is that the portrayal of psychologists in the media is becoming more and more accurate.

The Science of Psychology

Science and Pseudoscience

What makes something science? How do we identify what isn't science?

And how do we prevent that pseudoscience from being accepted and promoted as science?

These and other equally loaded questions were taken on at the APS Convention's Presidential Symposium, coordinated this year by then-APS President and current APS Past President Elizabeth Loftus, of the University of Washington.

"We live in a land transformed by science, and yet pseudoscientific ideas are rampant," said Loftus. "Many of these beliefs concern topics that have benefitted from widespread study by psychological scientists. Science and rationality are continually under attack and threatened by a rise of pseudoscience, so I organized this year's Presidential Symposium to illuminate these problems in hopes of fostering critical thinking, educating the public, and ourselves."

Loftus invited several well-known researchers and scholars in the field to help her in her quest, including:

1. Yale University's Robert Steinberg, who spoke on "How more and more research can tell you less and less until finally you know much less than when you started";
2. Carol Tavris, who gave her perspective on "Power, politics, money, and fame: Sources of pseudoscience in research and therapy"; and
3. Ray Hyman, of the University of Oregon, who served as the discussant for these intriguing concepts.

In the Beginning...

Loftus kicked off the symposium discussing the tendency of humans, throughout their existence, to find some kind of explanation for the mysteries of the universe, natural events, and life itself. Loftus favorably mentioned and then paraphrased from a book—*Mind Myths: Exploring popular assumptions about the mind and brain*, edited by Sergio Della Sala—that, she said, captured the paradox:

"The changing seasons, growth and decay, storms, floods, droughts, and good and bad fortune, for example, were all attributed to supernatural beings, to famous ancestors, or ancient heroes," she said. "We now have a better understanding of, for instance, thunder and lightning and they don't terrify us as much, but in the absence of this kind of understanding of the mechanisms of the mind, the brain, and the effects of diseases on the mind and brain, we tackle mysteries still by focusing on divine intervention or we take shelter in simplistic superstition."

Loftus then gave a number of examples of how, even today, pseudoscience and misinformation abounds.

"Educated people have been known to recently express beliefs in alien abduction, fire walking, possession, creationism, and even that 90 percent of handicapped people have parents who were not virgins when they married," said Loftus, who then referred to a survey she conducted with her colleagues of non-psychology graduate students that indicated a good percentage of them believed that therapeutic techniques could be used to remember prenatal accounts.

"One problem here is that the books written by believers—full of enchanting anecdotes that are mistaken for science—sell like hot cakes, while books by skeptics trying to debunk these beliefs don't sell as well or at all," she said.

Loftus cited another example of a self-described "personologist" who has written a book on using a person's facial features to determine their personality and nature.

"Why do people persist in believing in impossible or improbable things?" asked Loftus, who turned the podium over the Steinberg, who explored the phenomenon of quasi-science and challenged the assumption that the more data collected about a phenomenon indicates the more we know about that phenomenon.

This assumption is flat out wrong, says Steinberg, who argues that scientists tend to build in certain limited assumptions in collecting data. The results, he says, is that scientists keep getting the same wrong or limited result and then gain confidence in that result so that they eventually become more confident of something that is not true.

"If you misplace your confidence in your quasi-scientific results, you can end up doing more and more research on a topic and know less and less," he said. "In collecting data, we always build in certain limited assumptions. For example, we may limit the participants we test. Or we may limit the kinds of test materials we use. Or we may limit the situations in which we test people."

The result, said Steinberg, is that we keep getting the same wrong, or at least limited, result and gain confidence in it.

"We are thus becoming more and more confident of something that is not true," he said and gave as a case study the example of intelligence. "Hundreds of studies reviewed by Carroll, Jensen, Brand, and others appear to show that there is a general factor. They are right—but only under the assumptions of these studies."

Steinberg presented data that showed that when one expands the range of participants (e.g., to participants in various African and Asian countries, or even culturally diverse populations in the United States), the range of materials used to test intelligence (not just academic-analytical kinds of problems, but creative and practical ones as well), and the kinds of situations in which testing is done (e.g., getting outside classrooms or psychologists' testing rooms), the "G"

factor disappears. Nor do such tests provide very good prediction of real-world performance, he said.

"The punch line is that continued heavy reliance on IQ-based measures, including the SAT, GRE, LSAT, GMAT, and so forth, depends on reliance on a narrow base of assumptions in research," he said. "Because people do not realize they are making these assumptions and because the assumptions often benefit them, they are blind to the assumptions. But these assumptions are there nevertheless, distorting the conclusions that are drawn. We need a broader conception of intelligence and, more generally, we have to be careful to collecting more data does not tell us less rather than more."

You Know It When You See It

Tavris then presented her perspective on "Power, Politics, Money, and Fame: Sources of pseudoscience in research and therapy" in which she assessed what qualifies as science, what qualifies as pseudoscience, how to tell the difference, and why it matters.

Pseudoscience, said Tavris, is like pornography: we can't define it, but we know it when we see it.

"But what we are arguing about here and what remains a source of confusion for the public is: what is science?" she said. "Philosophers of science have been arguing this for a long time. Some define science by its goal; it is the search for permanent universal laws of behavior. Others define science by its tools; a PET scan is science, an interview is not. Others define it by its subject; a brain is a tangible thing you can study scientifically, whereas love and wisdom and other intangible psychological states are not science. Science for me is one thing: it is an attitude of questioning received wisdom combined with the deepest and most entrenched human cognitive bias—the conformational bias."

Tavris went on to define pseudoscience as the determined pursuit of confirmation of one's beliefs.

"Pseudoscience wears the veneer of science but lacks its central infusing spirit of inquiry and the willingness to come up wrong," she said. "More than ever, I think psychological science has a role to play in counteracting its influence in our culture. Of course, pseudoscience flourishes everywhere in the world and always has. It is a human predilection and not uniquely an American one, however there are two aspects of the American culture that I think foster its particular incarnation in America."

The first aspect, said Tavris, is the American culture's need for certainty. Pseudoscience is popular because it confirms what we believe, she said. The second aspect of our culture that fosters pseudoscience, added Tavris, is the capitalistic quick fix.

"We love instant cures and tonics for what ails us," she said. "From chubbiness to the blues, from serious problems to tragedies. 'We can fix you' is the American credo, and we can fix you especially fast if you take this magic pill or use this magic technology."

These forces, she argues, foster the pseudoscientific effect in research.

"The harmony now between drug researchers and the pharmaceutical industry is stronger and more worrisome than people tend to recognize. Drug companies set up their own research institutes. They sponsor seminars and conferences," she said. "I went to one on new advances in the treatment of depression. All of the advancements were—guess what—antidepressants. So increasingly, biomedical research, even if it is well done, is only giving us part of the story. The public rarely hears the rest—the rest being done by psychological scientists. For example, in the case with the antidepressants, the public rarely hears that upwards of 75 percent of the effectiveness of antidepressants is due to the placebo effect."

Critics of science, said Tavris, are right to remind scientists that they must now assume they have the truth.

"We won't ever have the truth, but, unlike pseudoscience, science give us the ability to be critically demanding," she said. "Demand evidence. Resist the confirmation bias. There are tools that can help us get closer to the answers. Maybe, sometimes, even close enough."

Science In Another Dimension

Discussant Hyman examined how learned scientists can sometime engage in and fall victim to, pseudoscience.

"I have always been fascinated by the scientist who recognizes good science in one area while at the same time is considered to be doing pseudoscience in another area," he said. "This raises a variety of interesting issues."

Hyman has had extensive experience in debunking pseudoscientific issues. For example, earlier in the decade, he was appointed to a blue ribbon panel to evaluate previously secret programs of psychic spying conducted by the CIA over the past 20 years. In addition, he appears frequently on television shows presenting the skeptical views of various paranormal claims. He is also a founding member of the Committee of Scientific Investigation for the Claims of the Paranormal and serves on the editorial board of the journal the *Skeptic Inquirer.* He conducts an annual workshop titled "The Skeptics Toolbox," that is intended to provide participants with the knowledge and tools to property evaluate paranormal claims.

Hyman used as an example, the case of a recognized astrophysicist who published a book in which he claimed to have proven the existence of the fourth dimension from his investigations of a spiritualistic medium.

"Here we have a person who has earned his credentials and reputation in a recognized field of science," said Hyman. "He then develops and supports a theory that his colleagues categorize as pseudoscience. If this is true, then the same person can practice both science and pseudoscience."

Research in the Psychological Laboratory: Truth or Triviality?

Craig A. Anderson,[1] James J. Lindsay, and Brad J. Bushman

Department of Psychology, University of Missouri–Columbia, Columbia, Missouri (C.A.A., J.J.L.), and Department of Psychology, Iowa State University, Ames, Iowa (B.J.B.)

Abstract

This article examines the truism that studies from psychological laboratories are low in external validity. Past rational and empirical explorations of this truism found little support for it. A broader empirical approach was taken for the study reported here; correspondence between lab and field was compared across a broad range of domains, including aggression, helping, leadership style, social loafing, self-efficacy, depression, and memory, among others. Correspondence between lab- and field-based effect sizes of conceptually similar independent and dependent variables was considerable. In brief, the psychological laboratory has generally produced psychological truths, rather than trivialities. These same data suggest that a companion truism about field studies in psychology—that they are generally low on internal validity—is also false.

Keywords

external validity; metaanalysis; philosophy of science

Are you happy with current rates of violent crime in the United States? How about the U.S. ranking in achievement test scores in science, compared with other industrialized nations? Do recent increases in smoking rates among U.S. teens bother you? Do the continuing problems of high rates of "unsafe sex" practices and the resulting incidence of AIDS seem to cry out for a solution?

Constant attention to the problems of modern U.S. society by the mass media, politicians, and concerned citizens may seem to indicate a generally pessimistic worldview. Paradoxically, though, this focus on problems actually reflects a fundamentally optimistic view that as a society we can and should solve these problems. This same optimism drives modern psychology as well. The whole point of the science of psychology is to learn so that we can improve "things."

THE DEBATE ABOUT EXTERNAL VALIDITY

This functionalist view gives rise to a long-running and frequently counterproductive debate about the value of theory-oriented laboratory research versus application-oriented field research.

This article addresses a very specific question from this debate: Does the psychological laboratory yield truths or trivialities? Since Campbell (1957) clearly distinguished between *internal* and *external validity*, a common truism has been that laboratory studies are typically high on internal validity but low on external validity.[2] That is, laboratory studies are good at telling whether or not some manipulation of an independent variable causes changes in the dependent variable, but many scholars assume that these results do not generalize to the "real world." Hence, application-oriented scholars sometimes deride the psychological laboratory as a place where only trivial facts are to be found.[3] In essence, the charge is that (some, most, or all) research from the psychological laboratory is externally invalid, and therefore pointless.

One domain where this debate periodically arises concerns aggression (Anderson & Bushman, 1997). Consider obvious differences in surface characteristics between real-world versus laboratory aggression. Assault typically involves two or more people who know each other, arises from an escalating cycle of provocation, and results in serious physical injury. Aggression in the lab, however, typically involves one person (who only thinks that he or she is interacting with an unknown person via computer, or notes, or message boards of one kind or another), in a session that may last only 50 min, and involves the attempted delivery of noxious stimuli such as electric shock or blasts of noise.

But the charge that psychological laboratory research lacks external validity is not unique to the study of aggression. Recent years have seen similar debates in the study of personnel selection (e.g., Schmitt, 1996), leadership (e.g., Wolfe & Roberts, 1993), management (e.g., Griffin & Kacmar, 1991), and human memory (e.g., Banaji & Crowder, 1989; Neisser, 1978). For instance, in one early laboratory study of context-dependent memory. Dallett and Wilcox (1968) asked participants in one condition to study word lists while standing with their heads inside an oddly shaped box that contained flashing lights of several different colors; other participants studied the word lists without putting their heads inside the box. Participants later recalled the lists either with or without the box, and were most successful when the study and recall conditions were the same. As is obvious, these conditions have no counterpart in the "real" world, thus inviting complaints about external validity.

It is easy to see why nonexperts frequently charge that lab studies are trivial, artificial, and pointless, and easy to ignore such complaints as reflections of ignorance. But when the charge comes from experts—other psychological researchers who presumably share goals, training, and perspective—a thoughtful response is required. Such responses have also been forthcoming.

RESPONSES TO LABORATORY CRITICISMS

Embracing Invalidity

One particularly elegant response, by Mook (1983), celebrates external *in*validity. He described four cases in which the artificial lab setting is not only acceptable but actually preferred to the real-world setting:

First, we may be asking whether something can happen, rather than whether it typically does happen. Second, our prediction may . . . specify something that ought to happen in the lab. . . . Third, we may demonstrate the power of a phenomenon by showing that it happens even under unnatural conditions that ought to preclude it. Finally, we may use the lab to produce condi-

tions that have no counterpart in real life at all. . . . (p. 382)

Mook's main point is that the goal of most laboratory research is to discover theoretical relations among conceptual variables that are never sufficiently isolated in the real world to allow precise examination.

What Is Supposed to Generalize?

A second (and related) response is to note that usually researchers are interested in generalization of theoretical relations among conceptual independent and dependent variables, not the specific instantiations of them. The same scandalous joke will mean something different in church than it does in the men's locker room. In one case it may create embarrassment, whereas in the other it may create humor. If one were interested in the effects of humor on thought processes, one would be foolish to use the same joke as an experimental manipulation of "humor" in both settings. The lack of a manipulation's generalizability constitutes an external validity problem only if one intends specific instantiations of conceptual variables to generalize across radically different contexts, but most laboratory research is concerned only with generalizability of the conceptual variables.

The General Problem With Generalization

A third response begins with the observation that generalization is, generally, risky business. Inductive reasoning, at least in absolute terms, is never wholly justified. Even though every time you have dropped a hammer it has fallen, you cannot know for certain that it will fall the next time. Perhaps the laws of nature will change, or perhaps you will enter a location where your understanding of the laws of nature is revealed to be incomplete. Thus, generalizing from one situation to another, or from one participant population to another, is as problematic for field research as it is for lab research. So, the argument goes, why single out lab research for criticism? At least the lab makes it somewhat easier to satisfy concerns about internal validity, and without internal validity there is nothing to generalize anyway.

But, people do generalize from specific instances to general concepts, then from these general concepts to new situations involving different instances of the general concepts. A justification for such generalization can be readily found both at the level of species survival and at the level of scientific and technological

advances: In both cases, generalization works much of the time.

Past Empirical Approaches

If what psychologists expect (hope?) to generalize are systematic relations among conceptual variables (i.e., theories), and if we grant that attempting to make generalizations is acceptable as long as it occasionally works, then another response to the external validity challenge becomes feasible. The challenge becomes an empirical question. Three different empirical approaches have been used: single-study tests, single-phenomenon tests, and single-domain tests.

Single-study tests examine a specific laboratory finding in other contexts or with other populations. For example, Godden and Baddeley (1975) successfully generalized the context-dependent memory effect using scuba divers as subjects. Word lists that had been studied underwater were better recalled underwater, whereas lists studied on dry land were better recalled on dry land. Such single-study tests of external validity abound in psychology. Many "work," though of course some do not. Though these tests answer the generalization question for a particular case, they do not adequately answer the broader question concerning the external validity of a given laboratory phenomenon.

Single-phenomenon tests examine the external validity of a whole empirical phenomenon rather than one specific laboratory finding. For example, do laboratory-based effects of anonymity on aggression generalize to field settings? Questions like this can be investigated by using *meta-analytic* techniques. That is, one could statistically average all of the research results from lab and field studies that have tested the relation between anonymity and aggression. We performed such a meta-analysis (Anderson & Bushman, 1997) and found comparable anonymity effects in lab and field settings. Similar tests of the generalizability of a specific laboratory phenomenon can be found in numerous additional areas of psychology. Many of these single-phenomenon tests show comparable effects for the psychological laboratory and field studies. But failures to generalize also occur.

Single-domain tests further broaden the generalizability question to a whole research domain. For example, do most aggression findings from the psychological laboratory generalize to field studies? In other words, do the effects of key independent variables—such as alcohol, anonymity, and media violence—have the same effects in lab and field studies of aggression? If laboratory studies from a given domain are inherently invalid and those from field studies are valid, then lab and field studies in that domain should fail to show any correspondence. We (Anderson & Bushman, 1997; Bushman & Anderson, 1998) used meta-analytic techniques to ask this broad question in the aggression domain, and found considerable correspondence between lab and field.

A CROSS-DOMAIN EMPIRICAL APPROACH

We extend the single-domain approach by examining the comparability of findings from lab and field across several domains. Basically, we asked whether the effects of the same conceptual independent variables on the same conceptual dependent variables tended to be consistent in lab and field settings across several psychological domains.

Method

Using the PsycINFO database, we conducted a literature search for the following journals: *Psychological Bulletin, Journal of Applied Psychology, Journal of Personality and Social Psychology,* and *Personality and Social Psychology Bulletin.* We searched with the keyword phrases "meta-analysis" and "quantitative review," and with the combined keyword phrases "meta-analysis" with "field studies" and "meta-analysis" with "laboratory." This selection of journals was intentionally biased toward social psychology because many of the most vociferous criticisms of the psychological laboratory have focused on the social psychological lab. Our search yielded 288 articles.

Many articles were subsequently eliminated because they were methodological in nature, did not include separate tabulations for lab and field settings, or overlapped with a more recent meta-analytic review.[4] The final data set represents 38 pairs of lab and field effects.

Results and Discussion

We used the standardized mean difference, denoted by *d,* as the indicator of effect size. This index shows the size of the difference between two groups, and does so in terms of the standard deviation. For instance, if Group 1 has a mean of 6 and Group 2 has a mean of 5, and the standard deviation is 2, the effect size *d* would be $(6 - 5)/2 = 0.5$. According to Cohen (1988), a "large" *d* is 0.8, a "medium" *d* is 0.5, and a "small"

d is 0.2. Effect sizes for correlations can easily be converted to *d*s, which we did to allow direct comparisons across different types of studies (Hedges & Olkin 1985). Effect-size averages were weighted by sample size and used pooled standard deviations in most cases, but in a few cases we were unable to determine the weights from the original reports. Table 1 and Figure 1 summarize the results.[5]

Figure 1 plots the value of *d* for the lab and field studies for each domain studied. The figure reveals considerable consistency between laboratory and field effects. That is, across domains, the *d*s for lab and field studies tended to be similar. The correlation, $r = .73$, is considerably higher than the gloomy picture that sometimes emerges from the external validity debate. Some readers might wonder whether the disproportionate number of the data points coming from comparisons of gender effects (6 out of 38) biased the results. However, the plot and correlation look much the same with these 6 data points eliminated ($r = .75$). Similarly, one might wonder about the possible nonindependence of some of the attributional-style data points (the results from Sweeney, Anderson, & Bailey, 1986). Dropping all but the two overall "attribution and depression" effects for positive and negative outcomes again yields essentially the same correlation ($r = .73$). All three of these correlations are considerably larger than Cohen's (1988) conventional value for a large correlation ($r = .5$). Furthermore, an *r* of .73 is equivalent to a *d* of 2.14, a huge effect.

Two complementary questions arise from these results, one asking why the correspondence is so high, the other asking why it is not higher. First, consider some limitations on correspondence between lab and field results. One limitation concerns internal validity problems of field studies. Sometimes field studies "discover" relations between independent and dependent variables that are false, and at other times they fail to discover true relations. Both types of internal invalidity reduce correspondence between field and lab, and hence artificially depress the correlation seen in Figure 1. A second limitation concerns the primary reason for studying psychological phenomena in the lab—to improve one's ability to detect relatively subtle phenomena that are difficult or impossible to isolate in the field. Laboratory studies typically accomplish this by focusing on one or two theoretically interesting independent variables while restricting the action or range of other independent variables. This focus can increase the estimated effect size of experimentally manipulated independent

variables while decreasing the effects of individual difference variables. For example, using only college students as experimental participants restricts the range of individual differences in intelligence and antisocial personality, thereby reducing their effects on dependent variables associated with them. Therefore, reducing the effects of individual differences in the lab also reduces variance due to chance or measurement error and thus increases the estimated effect size of manipulated variables, relative to the estimated effect sizes generated from similar field studies without the (intentional) range restriction on subject variables. Thus, both internal validity problems of field studies and the range restriction of lab studies artificially decrease the lab-field correspondence displayed in Figure 1. Now consider the other question, about factors that helped make the correspondence in Figure 1 so high. First, meta-analytically derived indicators of effect size wash out idiosyncratic effects of individual studies. That is, random or idiosyncratic factors that artificially increase an effect in some studies and decrease it in others tend to balance out when averaged across many studies, in much the way that increasing sample size increases the accuracy of the results in a single study. Second, and perhaps more important, we investigated only research domains that have had sufficient research attention to allow meta-analyses. These would usually be successful research domains, where underlying theories and methods are accurate enough to produce a line of successful studies. Such successful lines of investigation are relatively likely to concern true (internally valid) relations between the key independent and dependent variables.

CONCLUSIONS

The obvious conclusion from Figure 1 is that the psychological laboratory is doing quite well in terms of external validity; it has been discovering truth, not triviality. Otherwise, correspondence between field and lab effects would be close to zero.

A less obvious conclusion concerns internal validity of field studies. A second part of the broader debate between theory-oriented laboratory researchers and application-oriented field researchers is the truism that field studies generally lack internal validity. If this second truism were accurate, however, the correspondence between lab and field effects could not have been so positive. Thus, field studies in psychology must be doing a pretty

Table 1. *Mean effect sizes and confidence intervals for topics studied in the lab and field*

Source, independent and dependent variables, and setting	Number of samples	Effect size	95% confidence interval
Ambady and Rosenthal (1992)			
Observation time and outcoming ratings—lab	21	0.87	—
Observation time and outcome ratings—field	17	0.98	—
Anderson and Bushman (1997)			
Gendere and physical aggression—lab	37	0.31	0.23–0.38
Gender and physical aggression—field	6	0.40	0.25–0.55
Gender and verbal aggression—lab	18	0.13	0.03–0.24
Gender and verbal aggression—field	3	0.03	−0.15–0.22
Bushman and Anderson (1998)			
Anonymity and aggression—lab	18	0.57	0.45–0.69
Anonymity and aggression—field	4	0.44	0.25–0.63
Trait aggressiveness and aggression—lab	13	0.49	0.18–0.29
Trait aggressiveness and aggression—field	16	0.93	0.38–0.47
Type A personality and aggression—lab	9	0.34	0.18–0.49
Type A personality and aggression—field	3	0.97	0.71–1.23
Carlson, Marcus-Newhall, and Miller (1990)			
Weapons and aggression—lab	16	0.21	0.01–0.41
Weapons and aggression—field	5	0.17	−0.05–0.39
Eagly and Crowley (1986)			
Gender and helping—lab	16	−0.18	−0.28–0.09
Gender and helping—field (on and off campus)	36+47= 83	0.27	—
Eagly and Johnson (1990)			
Gender and leadership style—lab	17	0.22	—
Gender and leadership style—organizations	269	−0.00	—
Eagly and Karau (1991)			
Gender and leader emergence—lab	50	0.45	0.40–0.51
Gender and leader emergence—natural settings	24	0.10	0.02–0.17
Eagly, Karau, and Makhijani (1995)			
Gender and leader effectiveness—lab	20	0.07	−0.06–0.20
Gender and leader effectiveness—organizations	56	−0.03	−0.06–0.01
Gordon (1996)			
Ingratiation and evaluations—university (lab)	54	0.38	0.33–0.43
Ingratiation and evaluations—field	15	−0.07	−0.13– −0.00
Karau and Williams (1993)			
Social loafing—lab	140	0.47	0.43–0.51
Social loafing—field	23	0.25	0.16–0.35
Kraiger and Ford (1985)			
Race of ratee and performance ratings—lab	10	0.07	−0.41–0.56
Race of ratee and peformance ratings—field	64	0.39	0.06–0.75
Kubeck, Delp, Haslett, and McDaniel (1996)			
Age (continuous) and job-training mastery—lab	17	−0.61	−1.67–0.12
Age (continuous) and job-training mastery—field	31	−0.52	−1.19–0.02
Age and time to finish training—lab	3	0.70	0.08–1.58
Age and time to finish training—field	2	1.35	1.35–1.35
Age (dichotomous) and job-training mastery—lab	9	−0.96	−1.44– −0.47
Age (dichotomous) and job-training mastery—field	2	−0.38	−0.38– −0.38
Lundeberg and Fox (1991)			
Expectancies and recall—essay tests—lab	41	0.60	0.53–0.67
Expectancies and recall—essay tests—class	11	0.33	0.17–0.49
Expectancies and recognition tests—lab	41	−0.07	−0.13– −0.01
Expectancies and recognition tests—class	14	0.28	0.14–0.42
Mento, Steel, and Karren (1987)			
Goal difficulty and performance—lab	47	0.62	—
Goal difficulty and performance—field	23	0.44	—
Mullen and Hu (198)			
Group membership and similarity of group members—artificially created groups	2	0.43	0.04–0.90
Group membership and similarity of group members—real groups	2	0.47	−0.14–1.16
Narby, Cutler, and Moran (1993)			
Authoritarianism and trial verdict—video, written, audio trials	23	0.30	—
Authoritarianism and trial verdict—live trials	3	0.49	—
Paik and Comstock (1994)			
Media violence and aggression—lab	586	0.87	—
Media violence and aggression—field	556	0.42	—
Peters, Hartke, and Pohlman (1985)			
Leadership style and performance, negative octants—lab	30	−0.28	—

(Continued)

Table 1. *(Continued)*

Source, independent and dependent variables, and setting	Number of samples	Effect size	95% confidence interval
Leadership style and performance, negative octants—field	20	−0.90	—
Leadership style and performance, positive octants—lab	20	0.51	—
Leadership style and performance, positive octants—field	15	0.45	—
Sagie (1994)			
Decision-making participation and productivity—lab	—	−0.06	—
Decision-making participation and productivity—field	—	−0.02	—
Sweeney, Anderson, and Bailey (1986)			
Attribution and depression, negative outcomes—lab	25	0.52	—
Attribution and depression, negative outcomes—hospital	8	0.32	—
Attribution and depression, positive outcomes—lab	16	−0.24	—
Attribution and depression, positive outcomes—hospital	5	−0.28	—
Ability and depression, negative outcomes—lab	16	0.63	—
Ability and depression, negative outcomes—hospital	3	1.15	—
Ability and depression, positive outcomes—lab	13	−0.12	—
Ability and depression, positive outcomes—hospital	3	−0.12	—
Effort and depression, negative outcomes—lab	13	0.10	—
Effort and depression, negative outcomes—hospital	2	0.49	—
Effort and depression, positive outcomes—lab	11	−0.02	—
Effort and depression, positive outcomes—hospital	2	−0.04	—
Luck and depression, negative outcomes—lab	14	−0.30	—
Luck and depression, negative outcomes—hospital	3	−0.61	—
Luck and depression, positive outcomes—lab	10	0.43	—
Luck and depression, positive outcomes—hospital	3	0.63	—
Task difficulty and depression, negative outcomes—lab	14	−0.26	—
Task difficulty and depression, negative outcomes—hospital	2	−0.14	—
Task difficulty and depression, positive outcomes—lab	9	−0.20	—
Task difficulty and depression, positive outcomes—hospital	2	0.61	—
Tubbs (1986)			
Goal specificity and performance—lab	34	0.57	0.14–1.01
Goal specificity and performance—field	14	0.43	−0.09–0.94
Goal-setting participation and performance—lab	13	−0.03	−0.86–0.80
Goal-setting participation and performance—field	4	0.12	−0.34–0.59

Note. All effect-size estimates have been converted to *d*—the average effect size in standard deviation units, weighted by sample size whenever sufficient information was available to do so. If the exact same sampling and methodological procedures were used to gather new data to estimate *d*, and if this were done a large number of times, we should expect that 95% of the time, the new ,ld estimates would fall within the range indicated by the 95% confidence interval.

good job when it comes to internal validity.

In the interests of clarity and space, we have oversimplified the lab-field debate on validity. Obviously, studies in either setting may be high or low on internal and external validity. As long as scholars in both settings keep in mind the complementary pitfalls of too little control over extraneous variables (leading to low internal validity) and of overgeneralizing from the specific features of a specific study (leading to low external validity), we believe the psychological research enterprise will continue to succeed.

Finally, failure to find high correspondence between lab and field studies in a given domain or with a specific phenomenon should not be seen as a failure of the researchers in either setting. Instead, such inconsistencies should be seen as an indicator that further conceptual analysis and additional empirical tests are needed to discover the source of the discrepancy. Perhaps there are psychological processes operating in one context but not the other, or perhaps the relative strength of different causal factors differs in the two contexts (see Anderson & Anderson, 1998, for an example involving the positive relation between uncomfortably hot temperatures and aggressive behavior). In any case, the discrepancy sets the stage for further theoretical and (eventually) practical advances. And in the end, that's what we all are working for, isn't it?

Recommended Reading

Anderson, C.A., & Bushman, B.J. (1997). (See References)

Banaji, M.R. & Crowder, R.G. (1989). (See References)

Berkowitz, L., & Donnerstein, E. (1982). External validity is more than skin deep: Some answers to criticism of laboratory experiments. *American Psychologist, 37,* 245–257.

Kruglanski, A.W. (1975). The human subject in the psychology experiment: Fact and artifact. In L. Berkowitz (Ed.), *Advances in*

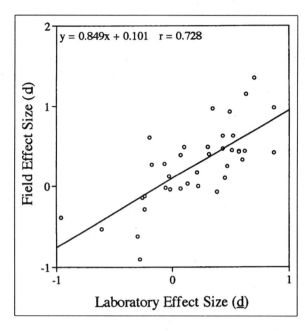

Fig. 1. Relation between effect sizes in the laboratory and field. Each point represents the value of *d* for the lab and field studies in a particular meta-analysis.

experimental social psychology (Vol. 8, pp. 101–147). New York: Academic Press.

Mook, D.G. (1983). (See References)

Acknowledgements—We thank Bruce Bartholomew and Anne Powers for comments on an earlier version. This article is based in part on an invited address delivered by the first author at the May 1998 meeting of the American Psychological Society in Washington, D.C.

Notes

1. Address correspondence to Craig A. Anderson, Department of Psychology, Iowa State University, W112 Lagomarcino Hall, Ames, IA 50011–3180.

2. Internal validity refers to the degree to which the design, methods, and procedures of a study allow one to conclude that the independent variable caused observable differences in the dependent variable. External validity refers to the degree to which the relationship between the independent and dependent variables found in a study generalizes to other people, places, and times.

3. The companion truism, held by some scholars with a more theoretical orientation, is that field studies on "real" phenomena are so plagued by methodological confounds that they lack internal validity, and, hence, fail to say anything at all about the phenomenon under study.

4. For example, the Wood, Wong, and Cachere (1991) analysis of the effects of violent media on aggression overlaps with Paik and Comstock's (1994) analysis.

5. Two additional meta-analyses also demonstrated considerable lab–field correspondence, but did not report separate effect sizes. Kraus's (1995) review of the consistency between attitude and behavior and Kluger and DeNisi's (1996) review of the effects of feedback on performance both coded effects by the lab-field distinction, and both reported a nonsignificant relationship between this distinction and effect size.

References

Ambady, N., & Rosenthal, R. (1992). Thin slices of expressive behavior as predictors of interpersonal consequences: A meta-analysis. *Psychological Bulletin, 111,* 256–274.

Anderson, C.A., & Anderson, K.B. (1998). Temperature and aggression: Paradox, controversy, and a (fairly) clear picture. In R. Green & E. Donnerstein (Eds.), *Human aggression: Theories, research, and implications for social policy* (pp. 247–298). San Diego: Academic Press.

Anderson, C.A., & Bushman, B.). (1997). External validity of "trivial" experiments: The case of laboratory aggression. *Review of General Psychology, 1,* 19–41.

Banaji, M.R., & Crowder, R.G. (1989). The bankruptcy of everyday memory. *American Psychologist, 44,* 1185–1193.

Bushman, B.J., & Anderson, C.A. (1998). Methodology in the study of aggression: Integrating experimental and nonexperimental findings. In R. Green & E. Donnerstein (Eds.), *Human aggression: Theories, research, and implications for social policy* (pp. 23–48). San Diego: Academic Press.

Campbell, D.T. (1957). Factors relevant to validity of experiments in social settings. *Psychological Bulletin, 54,* 297–312.

Carlson, M., Marcus-Newhall, A., & Miller, N. (1990). Effects of situational aggression cues: A quantitative review. *Journal of Personality and Social Psychology, 58,* 622–633.

Cohen, J. (1988). *Statistical power analysis for the behavioral sciences* (2nd ed.). Hillsdale, NJ: Erlbaum.

Dallett, K., & Wilcox, S.G. (1968). Contextual stimuli and proactive inhibition. *Journal of Experimental Psychology, 78,* 475–480.

Eagly, A.H., & Crowley, M. (1986). Gender and helping behavior: A meta analytic review of the social psychological literature. *Psychological Bulletin, 100,* 283–285.

Eagly, A.H., & Johnson, B.T. (1990). Gender and leadership style: A meta-analysis. *Psychological Bulletin, 108,* 233–256.

Eagly, A.H., & Karau, S.J., (1991). Gender and emergence of leaders: A meta-analysis. *Journal of Personality and Social Psychology, 60,* 685–710.

Eagly, A.H., Karau, 5.J., & Makhijani, M.G. (1995). Gender and the effectiveness of leaders: A meta-analysis. *Psychological Bulletin, 117,* 125–145.

Godden, D., & Baddeley, A. (1975). When does context influence recognition memory? *British Journal of Psychology, 71,* 99–104.

Gordon, R.A. (1996). Impact of ingratiation on judgments and evaluations: A meta-analytic investigation. *Journal of Personality and Social Psychology, 71,* 54–70.

Griffin, R., & Kacmar, M.K. (1991). Laboratory research in management: Misconceptions and missed opportunities. *Journal of Organizational Behavior, 12,* 301–311.

Hedges, L.V., & Olkin, I. (1985). *Statistical methods for meta-analyses.* New York: Academic Press.

Karau, S.J., & Williams, K.D. (1993). Social loafing: A meta-analytic review and theoretical integration. *Journal of Personality and Social Psychology, 65,* 681–706.

Kluger, A.N., & DeNisi, A. (1996). Effects of feedback on performance: A historical review, a meta-analysis, and a preliminary feedback intervention theory. *Psychological Bulletin, 119,* 254–284.

Kraiger, K., & Ford, J.K. (1985). A meta-analysis of ratee race effects in performance ratings. *Journal of Applied Psychology, 70,* 56–75.

Kraus, S.J. (1995). Attitudes and the prediction of behavior: A meta-analysis of the empirical evidence. *Personality and Social Psychology Bulletin, 21,* 58–75.

Kubeck, J.E., Delp, N.D., Haslett, T.K., & McDaniel, M.A. (1996). Does job-related training performance decline with age? *Psychology and Aging, 11,* 92–107.

Lundeberg, M.A., & Fox, P.W. (1991). Do laboratory findings on test expectancy generalize to classroom outcomes? *Review of Educational Research, 61,* 94–106.

Mento, A.J., Steel, R.P., & Karren, R.J. (1987). A meta-analytic study of the effects of goal setting on task performance: 1966–1984. *Organizational Behavior & Human Decision Processes, 39,* 52–83.

Mook, D.G. (1983). In defense of external invalidity. *American Psychologist, 38,* 379–387.

Mullen, B., & Hu, L. (1989). Perceptions of ingroup and outgroup variability: A meta-analytic integration. *Basic and Applied Social Psychology, 10,* 233–252.

Narby, D.J., Cutler, B.L., & Moran, G. (1993). A meta-analysis of the association between authoritarianism and jurors' percep-tions of defendant culpability. *Journal of Applied Psychology, 78,* 34–42.

Neisser, U. (1978). Memory: What are the important questions? In M.M. Gruneberg, P.E. Morris, & R.N. Sykes (Eds.), *Practical aspects of memory* (pp. 3–24). London: Academic Press.

Paik, H., & Comstock, G. (1994). The effects of television violence on antisocial behavior: A meta-analysis. *Communication Research, 21,* 516–546.

Peters, L.H., Hartke, D.D., & Pohlman, J.T. (1985). Fiedler's contingency theory of leadership: An application of the meta-analysis procedures of Schmidt & Hunter. *Psychological Bulletin, 97,* 274–285.

Sagie, A. (1994). Participative decision making and performance: A moderator analysis. *Journal of Applied Behavioral Science, 30,* 227–246.

Schmitt, N. (1996). Validity generalization. In R. Barrett (Ed.), *Fair employment strategies in human resource management* (pp. 94–104). Westport, CT: Quorum Books.

Sweeney, P.D., Anderson, K., & Bailey, S. (1986). Attributional style in depression: A meta-analytic review. *Journal of Personality and Social Psychology, 50,* 974–991.

Tubbs, M.E. (1986). Goal setting: A meta-analytic examination of the empirical evidence. *Journal of Applied Psychology, 71,* 474–483.

Wolfe, J., & Roberts, C.R. (1993). A further study of the external validity of business games: Five-year peer group indicators. *Simulation & Gaming, 24,* 21–33.

Wood, W., Wong, F.Y., & Cachere, J.G. (1991). Effects of media violence on viewers' aggression in unconstrained social interaction. *Psychological Bulletin, 109,* 371–383.

How are psychologists portrayed on screen?

An APA committee hopes to help Hollywood more accurately depict therapists.

By Scott Sleek
Monitor staff

It's not that psychologist Harriet T. Schultz didn't enjoy the movies "Tin Cup" and "The First Wives' Club." In fact, she found both films entertaining. But there on the big screen, she was also seeing her profession being portrayed in the worst possible way. Therapists were becoming "unethical boundary violators," as she puts it, by getting romantically involved with their patients.

Schultz is among several psychologists who lament the negative stereotypes of therapists displayed on the big and small screens and who worry even more that the public views these depictions as normal therapist behavior.

In response, Schultz, a Houston practitioner, and other members of APA's Div. 46 (Media) have joined a special panel called the Media Watch Committee to examine the way therapists are portrayed in movies, television shows and books.

The group, assembled and chaired by Baltimore practitioner Shirley Glass, PhD, hopes eventually to develop regular contacts with Hollywood producers, screenwriters and directors so that committee members can help those professionals foster more accurate depictions of therapists and the psychotherapy process.

The group is particularly concerned that many fictional on-screen therapists whose actions violate the APA Code of Ethics, are portrayed as brilliant and even noble, Glass says.

Examples include therapists played by Barbra Streisand in "Prince of Tides" and Robin Williams in "Good Will Hunting." Both characters made great therapeutic inroads with their patients but crossed ethical boundaries in the process. Streisand's character began an affair with her patient's brother—who himself became her patient—while Williams discussed his own personal issues with his patient and at one point physically threatened him.

There's more to come. Warner Bros. next July will release a film "Eyes Wide Shut," a story about two troubled psychologists who are also husband and wife. Details of the film are sketchy, but reportedly the therapists, played by Tom Cruise and Nicole Kidman, have extramarital affairs with their patients and shoot morphine.

Glass said she was inspired to inaugurate the committee because she was so distressed by the depictions of patient-therapist sexual relationships in film and television. (Glass was formerly chair of Maryland's psychology board and a member of a statewide task force that is examining sexual exploitation by health providers.)

"I get very concerned with a lot of the messages conveyed to the public about what good therapy is," says Glass. "A lot of times it's the therapist who oversteps the boundaries who is seen as the super-wonderful therapist."

A rating system

Media Watch plans initially to develop a rating system that ranks the different ways psychologists are portrayed. The rankings will gauge the overall imagery of therapists being presented in the media.

Schultz, who has been studying psychologists in the movies, has already developed several categories of therapist stereotypes on the screen. The first three were developed by psychiatrist Irving Schneider, MD, but others she labeled herself. They include:

- "Dr. Dippy," who is crazier or zanier than his patients. Examples are Mel Brooks in "High Anxiety" or TV's Frasier Crane.
- "Dr. Evil," usually a corrupt mind-controller or homicidal maniac like Hannibal Lecter in "Silence of the Lambs."
- "Dr. Wonderful," the warm, caring, competent therapist who has endless time to devote to patients and often cures them by uncovering a single traumatic event. Examples are the psychiatrists in

"Ordinary People" and "Three Faces of Eve."
- "Dr. Rigid," who stifles joy, fun and creativity. The spoilsport psychologist who tries to have Santa Claus committed as a lunatic in "Miracle on 34th Street" is an illustration of this stereotype.
- "Dr. Line-Crosser," who becomes romantically involved with a patient, like Streisand in "Prince of Tides."

The public's perceptions

The images may indeed be affecting public perceptions, Schultz says. She and colleague Susan Dickson

---

"I get very concerned with a lot of the messages conveyed to the public about what good therapy is."

Shirley Glass
Baltimore practitioner

---

recently conducted a survey of 504 people—mostly college students—to see if they recognized certain therapist violations in the movies and to see if they hold stereotypes of therapists. Schultz and Dickson discovered that 90 percent of the respondents

know romantic relationships between therapist and patient are wrong, but about 70 percent thought it fine for therapists to have business or social relationships with patients once treatment has ended.

Males more than females held stereotypes of therapists, particularly the "dippy" and "rigid" stereotypes, they found. And males were more likely than females to view the line-crossing behaviors as acceptable.

The misperceptions also occur among film critics. Mary Banks Gregerson, PhD, a Media Watch member and Alexandria, Va., therapist, recently studied all the reviews of last year's film "Good Will Hunting." She found that while critics had a variety of descriptions of the psychologist Sean McGuire—one described him as "brilliant," another as "troubled"—only one of the more than 250 reviews she examined even questioned the "professionalism" of his actions. Some even describe the scene in which McGuire (played by Williams) angrily chokes Will Hunting (played by Matt Damon) as only "rocky" or "abrasive."

Media Watch wants to educate the public about ethical and competent therapist behaviors so that people can better identify inappropriate actions by therapists.

For serious films, the group hopes to advise Hollywood producers and screenwriters about how to portray a therapist as competent and ethical without sacrificing dramatic or comedic impact. Movies or films could, for example, depict a therapist struggling with strong feelings for a patient, but

ultimately resisting temptation, Schultz suggests.

The committee is especially concerned about presentations of psychologists' sexual behavior. Several psychologists have had an Internet dialogue about the Fox sitcom "Getting Personal." The season premiere included a scene in which a psychologist initiates a sexual encounter with a client. (The show has since been cancelled due to low ratings.)

In response, Media Watch is collaborating with an America Online feature called "Electra" (www.electra. com), a feature web page for women, to cast light on the program. Electra recently ran an article written by Amherst, Mass., psychologist Keri Heitner, PhD, criticizing the episode. And Glass, who serves as relationship columnist for the online feature, also helped Electra set up a poll to ask readers about their thoughts on the media's portrayal of psychologists and psychotherapy.

Meanwhile, Gregerson's writings on her "Good Will Hunting" research recently appeared on the practitioner page of "Psychwatch," an online information service for psychologists at www.psychwatch.com.

But Media Watch members also want to keep a sense of humor. They plan to recognize lampoonery as lampoonery, says Glass.

"We want to be careful not to get too critical of things that are obviously satire," she says. "Then we would come across as too self-centered and rigid. When the film is making fun of everybody, therapist included, we shouldn't act overly offended.

Unit Selections

Key Points to Consider

❖ What do you think contributes most to our psychological makeup and behaviors: the influence of the environment, the expression of genes, or the functioning of the nervous system? Do you believe that perhaps some combination of these factors accounts for psychological characteristics and behaviors? How are these various contributors to behavior studied? Do you think the importance of the environment changes over the course of development?

❖ What is genetic research? How is it done? How much of human behavior are genes responsible for? Give some examples of the influence of genes on human behavior. How does such research help experts in psychology and medicine predict and treat various disorders? What environmental factors affect genetic expression?

❖ How do twins contribute to research on nature and nurture? What types of twins are there; how does each type help us understand the development of human behavior?

❖ How does the brain relate to human behavior and psychological characteristics? What functions does the brain control? What behaviors does each brain hemisphere control? Are these hemispheres really two different brains; that is, are they independent of one another? How do we study the brain? What are some of the types of brain disorders and their symptoms? How do these disorders develop? Are any disorders reversible?

 **Links**   **www.dushkin.com/online/**

8. **Biological Changes in Adolescence**
   http://www.personal.psu.edu/faculty/n/x/nxd10/biologic2.htm
9. **Division of Hereditary Diseases and Family Studies, Indiana University School of Medicine**
   http://medgen.iupui.edu/divisions/hereditary/
10. **Institute for Behavioral Genetics**
    http://ibgwww.colorado.edu/index.html
11. **Serendip**
    http://serendip.brynmawr.edu/serendip/

These sites are annotated on pages 4 and 5.

As a child, Nancy vowed that she did not want to turn out like either of her parents. Nancy's mother was very passive and acquiescent about her father's drinking. When Dad was drunk, Mom always called his boss to report that Dad was "sick" and then acted as if there was nothing wrong at home. Nancy's childhood was a nightmare. Her father's behavior was erratic and unpredictable. If he drank just a little bit, he was happy. If he drank a lot, which was usually the case, he often became belligerent.

Despite vowing not to become like her father, as an adult Nancy found herself in the alcohol rehabilitation unit of a large hospital. Her employer could no longer tolerate her on-the-job mistakes or her unexplained absences from work, and he referred her to the clinic for help. As Nancy pondered her fate, she wondered whether her genes preordained her to follow in her father's inebriated footsteps or whether the stress of her childhood had brought her to this point in her life. After all, being the child of an alcoholic is not easy.

Just like Nancy, psychologists are concerned with discovering the causes of human behavior. Once the cause is known, treatments for problematic behaviors can be developed. In fact, certain behaviors might even be prevented when the cause is known. But for Nancy, prevention was too late.

One of the paths to understanding humans is to understand the biological underpinnings of their behavior. Genes and chromosomes, the body's chemistry (as found in hormones, neurotransmitters, and enzymes), and the central nervous system (comprised of the brain, spinal cord, and nerve cells) are all implicated in human behavior. All represent the biological aspects of behavior and ought, therefore, to be worthy of study by psychologists.

Physiological psychologists and psychobiologists are often the ones who examine the role of biology in behavior. The neuroscientist is especially interested in brain functioning; the psychopharmacologist is interested in the effects of various psychopharmacological agents or psychoactive drugs on behavior.

These psychologists often utilize one of three techniques to understand the biology-behavior connection. One technique is animal studies, as reviewed in the first unit, involving manipulation, stimulation, or destruction of certain parts of the brain. A second technique includes the examination of unfortunate individuals whose brains are defective at birth or damaged later by accidents or disease.

We can also use animal models to understand genetics; with animal models we can control reproduction and develop various strains of animals if necessary. Such tactics with humans would be considered extremely unethical. However, the third technique, studying an individual's behavior in comparison to both natural and adoptive parents or by studying identical twins reared together or apart,

allows psychologists to begin to understand the role of genetics versus that of environment in human behavior.

This unit is designed to familiarize you with the knowledge that psychologists have gleaned by using these techniques as well as others to study physiological processes and mechanisms in human behavior. I believe that each article will interest you and make you more curious about the role of biology in human endeavors.

The first selection in this unit reviews almost all aspects of the biological and environmental bases of behavior. In "Nature, Nurture, Not Mutually Exclusive," Beth Azar reviews how genes and the environment interact to affect us. She instills in the reader an understanding that human behavior is probably the complex interplay of many factors related to both nature and nurture.

The next selection examines the role of genes in human behavior. The article, "What We Learn from Twins: The Mirror of Your Soul," reviews why psychologists study twins—to examine the effects of genetics and compare them to environmental effects. The selection does a good job of differentiating between identical and fraternal twins, explaining how each type of twin allows us to understand aspects of the nature/nurture debate. Such twin research is not without controversy.

In the next article, Bernard Brown covers basic information about genetics. Genes underpin much of the rest of our physiology and therefore our behaviors. This article covers factors that affect genetic expression and, consequently, individual differences. Such factors include but are not limited to stress, nutrition, and the endocrine system.

The last article concerns the human brain, which is the most significant part of the central nervous system and therefore plays a large role in our psychological makeup. In "The Split Brain Revisited" Michael Gazzaniga discusses the role of the two hemispheres of the cerebral cortex. Even though both hemispheres seem to play different roles in influencing behavior, there is some communication between the two sides. Gazzaniga also makes it clear that there are marked individual differences in how our brains influence us.

Nature, nurture: not mutually exclusive

Studies on twins have established that most traits and behaviors are partially influenced by genes.

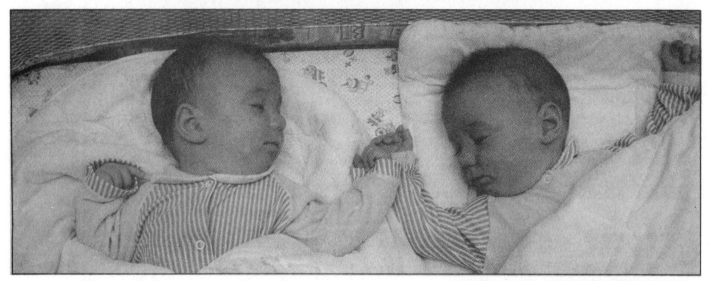

Elizabeth Crews/The Image Works

Beth Azar
Monitor staff

Psychologist Robert Plomin, PhD, would like to see the nature versus nurture debate end. Most human behaviors are not influenced by nature *or* nurture but by nature *and* nurture, he says.

Studies over the past 20 years on twins and adopted children have firmly established that there is a genetic component to just about every human trait and behavior, including personality, general intelligence and behavioral disorders such as schizophrenia and autism.

But the genetic influence on these traits and behaviors is only partial: Genetics account, on average, for half of the variance of most traits. That means the environment accounts for the rest, said Plomin.

"Twin and adoption studies have established that most traits and behaviors are partially influenced by genes," said Thomas Bouchard, PhD, of the University of Minnesota. "Now, using the same techniques, we can ask a lot more detailed and searching questions about the interaction between genes and the environment, between nature and nurture."

Such studies are painting a much more complex picture of development than psychologists had previously conceived. Researchers are finding that the balance between genetic and environmental influences on certain traits change as people age. They also find that genes not only influence behavior directly but may also influence the environment. In other words, our experiences may be influenced in part by our genetic propensities—people may react to us in certain ways because of a genetically influenced personality and we may choose certain experi-

ences because they fit best with our innate preferences.

Such findings imply that the only valid way to study environmental influences on human development is to use genetically sensitive designs, say many researchers.

"If we want to understand things like how the relationships between parents and children affect development, we must conduct genetically informed studies," said psychologist Nathan Brody, PhD, of Wesleyan University. "I'm a generalist, not a behavioral geneticist, but I find that knowing some behavioral genetics is essential as a way of addressing the field."

Increasing inheritance

One way researchers can study the development of traits and behaviors is to measure the influence of genetics

 From *APA Monitor,* May 1997, pp. 1, 28. © 1997 by the American Psychological Association. Reprinted by permission.

Dolly helps researchers underscore importance of environment

The announcement last winter that researchers successfully cloned a sheep and two monkeys brings up countless ethical conundrums regarding the potential to clone humans.

But it also gives behavioral geneticists an ideal opportunity to emphasize the ultimate importance of the environment to human development.

"As the public is exposed to all this information about cloning and molecular genetics, they may realize, as we have, that while genetics is important, the environment really plays a big role," said Christopher Cunningham, PhD, of the Oregon Health Sciences University. "As soon as the cells of an embryo are implanted [into a surrogate mother], it's unique because its experiences are different."

"The data are in and the environment is important to how people develop," adds psychologist Thomas Bouchard, PhD, of the University of Minnesota. As head of the Minnesota Study of Twins Reared Apart, he's spent most of his career studying twins—a natural study of cloning.

While research has established beyond a doubt that many aspects of human behavior are partly inherited (see article), the same work also affirms the critical importance of environment in shaping who we are, said Bouchard. By environment, researchers are referring to everything from the prenatal environment to the home environment. A person's clone would be more different from him or her than two identical twins are from one another because they would not share such environments, said Robert Plomin, PhD, of the Institute of Psychiatry in London. "Although identical twins are in effect clones,

AP Photo/Paul Clements

Dolly, the cloned sheep, is fueling the nature v. nurture debate.

they're only about 50 percent concordant on most traits" indicating that the environment accounts for the other 50 percent, he said. "That means that real clones will also not be identical—they grow up in a different time with different parents and should be even less similar than identical twins."

Even though genes may influence people's personality and social preferences, in the end, individual experiences will affect which niches they drop into and, in effect, who they become, said Bouchard.

—Beth Azar

throughout the life span. When they do, they find that the genetic influence on several traits increases as people age, said Plomin.

This phenomenon is most apparent in studies of general cognitive ability. The Colorado Adoption Project, for example, found that the resemblance on general cognitive ability between adopted children and their birth parents increased dramatically from ages 3 to 16. In contrast, there was no relationship between the IQ of adopted children at age 16 and their adoptive parents, indicating that the general rearing environment has little impact on IQ, said John DeFries, PhD, a principal investigator on the project.

"This is a striking result," said DeFries, director of the University of Colorado at Boulder's Institute for Behavioral Genetics. "Although early on

there is a small correlation between adoptive parents and their adopted children, this resemblance fades. I'm convinced that parents do have an impact on their children beyond their genes but such environmental influences do not seem to be correlated with cognitive ability."

Defining the Environment

The results also highlight a distinction behavioral geneticists make between two major sources of environmental influence:

- Shared environmental factors, which are common to children reared together and cause similarities in their behavior; and

- Nonshared environmental factors, which are unique to children

reared together and cause differences in their behavior.

For example, parents with two unrelated adopted children provide a common rearing environment—a shared environment that should make the unrelated siblings similar in some respects. But the children also have unique interactions with their parents and distinct perceptions of family encounters that may influence each sibling in different ways.

Behavioral genetics research shows that nonshared environment accounts for most of the environmental influence on children's personalities and moods. The most psychologically relevant environmental influences are those that make children in a family different from, not similar to, one another, said Plomin.

To evaluate which aspects of non-shared environment contribute to child adjustment, several years ago David Reiss, MD, of George Washington University, and several colleagues including Plomin and E. Mavis Heatherington, PhD, of the University of Virginia, began the Nonshared Environment and Adolescent Development (NEAD) project, which included twins as well as full siblings, half-siblings and step-siblings. They expected to pin down some general principles of nonshared environment that affect all people in a similar way. For example, children whose fathers treated them roughly but treated their siblings nicely might all suffer similar developmental problems.

Indeed, the research team found that if parents direct more negative attention toward one child than another, that child is more likely to experience adjustment difficulties, measured as depressive symptoms and antisocial behavior.

However, the correlation between parental treatment and child adjustment virtually disappeared when the researchers accounted for genetic influences on how parents treat their children. Parents' behavior seemed to be highly influenced by each child's genetic propensities, said Reiss, who, along with his co-investigators, just completed a draft of a book detailing their conclusions about the role of nonshared environment in child development.

This finding—that a seemingly environmental measure such as parental behavior is influenced by genetics—is called "the nature of nurture" and is supported by other recent studies.

For example, the Colorado Adoption Project has found that genetics partially mediate relationships between children's home environment and their psychological development, language development and general cognitive ability.

Several researchers have described three types of gene-environment correlations:

- A passive correlation may occur because parents transmit genes that promote a certain trait and also construct the rearing environment, which will likely support a child's genetic propensities. For example, if we assume musical ability is genetic, musically gifted children will likely have musically inclined parents who provide them with genes and an environment that promotes the development of musical ability.
- An evocative correlation may occur because genetically distinct people evoke different reactions from parents, peers and others.

For example, teachers may select musically talented children for special opportunities.

- And an active correlation may occur because people may actively select experiences that fit with their genetically influenced preferences. For example, musically gifted children may seek out musical friends and opportunities.

This does not mean that there are no purely environmental effects on behavior. Ken Kendler, MD, of the Medical College of Virginia/Virginia Commonwealth University, and his colleagues found that loss of a parent during childhood is directly correlated with alcoholism in women.

However, if researchers are ever going to unravel the effect of the environment, shared and nonshared, on human traits and behaviors, they must account for the large influence of genes on both behaviors and the environment, said Plomin.

"Research must address the notion that environment is important but, in large measure, may not be independent of genetics," said Reiss. "Developmental researchers must link their work with genetics—it should be a central part of the developmental psychology curriculum, to be used as a fundamental tool."

WHAT WE LEARN FROM TWINS

The mirror of your soul

Familiar question: Are we shaped by our genes, or by what life does to us?
Possible new answer: It isn't as simple as that makes it sound

BARBARA HERBERT, a former council worker living in southern England, discovered after the death of the woman she had thought was her mother that in fact she had been adopted. Among her assumed mother's papers, she found a name and address in Finland. When that produced no answer, she contacted the local newspaper in Finland. A reporter dug up the story. Her real mother had been sent to England, two months pregnant, in 1939. She had given birth, been sent back to Finland, and committed suicide at the age of 24.

Mrs Herbert had a feeling the story was not over. She seemed to recall somebody saying, "There was another one." So she contacted Hammersmith Hospital, where she was born; and, sure enough, there had been twins. The Registrar-General refused to help her contact her twin. She took the Registrar-General to court, and won. That is how she found her sister.

They met at King's Cross station in London. "We just said 'Hi' and walked off together, leaving our husbands standing there," says Mrs Herbert. "It seemed so natural." Mrs Herbert is a bit fatter than her sister, but she can think of no other important difference between them. Their intelligence quotients (IQs) were one point apart. They were tested again a year later; they scored ten points higher, but still only one point apart.

Mrs Herbert and her sister Daphne are gold dust to geneticists. Unlike fraternal twins, who are the product of separate eggs fertilized by different sperm, identical twins are natural clones, produced when a fertilized egg splits in two shortly after conception. Such twins, when separated after birth, are thus a scientific experiment designed jointly by nature and by society. They have the same genes but have been brought up in different environments.

These curiosities are getting rarer. Until the 1960s, twins offered for adoption in the West were often separated at birth, on the argument that two babies would be too much for one mother. That no longer happens. Since only one birth in 300 produces identical twins, and separated pairs are increasingly hard to find, people like Barbara Herbert and her sister are much sought after by scientists eager to study the relative importance of nature and nurture.

These studies provide some of the best clues to the question of how we become who we are—a question which fascinates people in different ways. Ordinary people wonder about the source of their failings and virtues, and would like to know whether they can make their children better, cleverer and happier than they themselves have been. Scientists are gripped, and still largely baffled, by how the human brain and personality are formed. And, in politics, the nature-nurture question lies at the centre of the argument about "social intervention". If our intelligence and our personalities are written into our genes, there is not much that governments can do to improve us.

Since the study of twins generally seems to support the nature side of the argument, it is triumphantly saluted by hereditarians as evidence for their case. "Twins have been used to prove a point, and the point is that we don't become. We are." So writes Lawrence Wright in his new book, "Twins: Genes, Environment and the Mystery of Human Identity". The environmentalists, on the other hand, condemn most studies of twins as methodologically flawed and even dishonest. Actually, what such studies show may be more interesting and mysterious than either side yet realises.

It was Francis Galton, Charles Darwin's cousin, who in the late 19th century first thought of using twins to investigate the differences between people. Galton, who coined the term "eugenics", correctly suggested that twins who looked alike came from one egg, and that those who did not came from different eggs. From that, he worked out a way of using twins to estimate the impact of genes. Look, he suggested, at the similarities between identical twins and those between ordinary ones (who genetically are no more similar than any children of the same parents). Those characteristics which identical twins share more than other twins will, he reasoned, be more caused by the genes the pair brought into the world.

This process, and the study of separated identical twins, are the two main ways of using twins to study the effects of nature and nurture. Galton carried out the first systematic study of twins. The results convinced him of the pre-eminence of genes in human make-up.

Eugenics in disgrace

The idea of eugenics captivated people on both the left and the right of politics in the first half of the 20th century. Fabian social reformers such as Sidney and Beatrice Webb were delighted to think that they would be able to breed a better working class. Josef Mengele, on the other hand, wanted to breed a better race for Hitler.

As Robert Jay Lifton recounts in "The Nazi Doctors", Mengele was obsessed with twins. When a new group of prisoners arrived in the concentration camp at Auschwitz, Mengele would run out to meet them shouting, "Twins out!" Twins lived in a separate block, and were allowed to keep their clothes and their hair. Mengele gave them sweets, and called them his little friends. He weighed them, measured them and logged the colour of their hair and their eyes. And he gave them diseases, to see how long they took to die.

The Nazis' enthusiasm for genetics did the subject no good at all. The left forgot it had ever had any interest in the matter. So did most academics. For a time it became fashionable, instead, to assume that people are chiefly the result of their environment, what they experience after they have been born. This rival view fitted neatly into the social-engineering optimism of most of the world's post-1945 governments.

The posthumous scandal over the work of Cyril Burt seemed to confirm this change of mind. Burt was the main proponent of hereditarian ideas in Britain. His evidence came from studies of separated identical twins. After his death in 1971, it was claimed that much of this evidence had been fabricated. His defenders' attempts to rescue his reputation have been less than conclusive. At best, he was a sloppy scientist; at worst, a fraud.

Still, despite its embarrassments, the hereditarian school began to reassert itself. In 1969 the Harvard Educational Review published an article by Arthur Jensen called "How much can we boost IQ and scholastic achievement?". Mr Jensen's answer: Not much, because IQ is highly hereditary; so money spent on preschool programmes for poor children is wasted. As Adrian Wooldridge, of *The Economist,* puts it in his book "Measuring the Mind": "The hereditarians felt that the environmentalists had turned into a decadent establishment, smugly self-satisfied but intellectually sloppy."

Hereditarians ascendant

The new hereditarians were assailed, in print and in person; but they were not squashed. Their research won support from, and gave support to, conservative politicians keen to roll back the costly welfare policies of the post-1945 years. "The Bell Curve", by Charles Murray and Richard Herrnstein, published in 1994, is a powerful expression of this alliance. It argues that, since IQ is largely inherited, and people marry people like themselves, the difference between the intelligence of races and classes is liable to grow steadily wider.

The study of twins provided much of the ammunition for the hereditarian counter-attack. Some of it emerged from the first large scale post-Burt study of separated identical twins, run by Thomas Bouchard, a professor at the University of Minnesota. Mr Bouchard saw an article on a pair of reunited identical twins, and decided to make a study of them. It was fun, says Mr Bouchard. Much research work by psychologists involves grumpy students, doing it for the money. The twins, delighted to be reunited, were a pleasure to work with. Mr Bouchard now has a register of 8,000 pairs of twins, some identical, some not, some separated, most reared together.

Another American scientist, Robert Plomin, has been working with 25,000 pairs of identical and non-identical twins in Sweden. Mr Plomin has also set up a study working with 10,000 pairs of identical and non-identical twins in Britain. He now works at the Social, Genetic and Developmental Psychiatry Research Centre at Britain's Institute of Psychiatry.

Over the past couple of decades there has been a clear shift in science's view of the hereditarian argument. These days, no respectable scientist denies the role of genes in forming our brains and characters. The question over which argument continues to rage is just how big that role is.

Studies of twins have examined a range of physical and psychological traits to try to estimate how large a contribution genes make. Some of the work looks at illnesses such as cancer, schizophrenia and alcoholism. Finding the cause of these could help in learning how to cure or contain them. If, for instance, schizophrenia is something you can inherit, then it may be susceptible to gene therapy.

Some of the studies are curiosities. David Lykken, a colleague of Mr Bouchard's, has inquired into the origins of happiness. He concludes that happiness bears almost no relation to wealth, professional standing or marital status, and is 80% inherited. Some other studies have made sceptics' eye brows rise because they appear to show that political conservatism and religious fundamentalism have a genetic basis.

But the most contentious work of all is on IQ. Mr Bouchard's studies suggest that the level of one's intelligence is, in the jargon, "69–78% heritable"—heritability being the proportion of the difference between people that is acquired through the genes, not life itself. Burt's disputed figure is within that range.

Some critics, such as Marcus Feldman, a professor of population genetics at Stanford University, says the work on twins is tainted by politics. The Minnesota research is financed by the Pioneer Fund, a foundation set up in 1937 to help research into heredity and eugenics, including racial differences. The fund has financed work by such controversial figures as Philippe Rushton on the relative size of the genitals and brains of different races. It is accused of, but strongly denies, racist motives.

Mr Lykken has played into the critics' hands by arguing that women should be licensed to have children and that children produced by unlicensed breeders should be compulsorily adopted. Mr Bouchard defends Mr Lykken's intellectual freedom. He says he is uneasy about the source of his cash, but insists that the Pioneer Fund has never tried to influence what he does.

What matters in the end, assuming that most of the people involved in this work do it in a properly detached way, is what they find out. It is striking that studies of twins regularly come up with higher levels of heritability than do other sorts of studies. Mr Bouchard's estimate runs up to 78%. That compares with studies of adopted children, and of first- and second-degree relations, which produce figures as low as 30%, and at the highest 50%. A task force of the American Psychological Association, trawling through all the available studies, including those on non-twins, has come up with an average of 50%.

This disparity has led to questions about the reliability of twins studies. One problem is that separated identical twins do not actually provide a perfect nature versus-nurture template. For a start, they do at one time share the same environment—in the womb. If, as some scientists now believe, those nine months are important in deciding how the brain is wired, this would help to explain why non-identical twins, who are no more genetically alike than any brother and sister, have IQS more like each other's than ordinary siblings do. It would also undermine the claims of the separated-twins studies to offer conclusive proof of what genes do.

Moreover, separated identical twins are rarely separated at the moment of birth, and some of them are then reunited before they come under the scientists' eye. If the first six months of a child's life matter as much as most people think they do, then spending even that short time together could influence the result of a twins study. And, when grown-up twins are reunited, they will naturally pay special attention to what they have in common; they may, the professors explain, "mythologise" their relationship. The twins in the Minnesota study had an average of five months together before they were separated, and nearly two years together after their reunion before Mr Bouchard got hold of them.

A subtler concern—voiced by Mr Feldman, himself a father of identical twins—is that the dichotomy between genes and environment is a false one. His own twins, he says, share professions, ideas and friends; their environments, in other words, are much closer than those of most non-identical twins. Maybe Galton's classic twins study was invalid: perhaps you cannot look at the similarities between identical twins, and those between non-identical ones, and conclude that the difference must necessarily be due to genes.

Chickens, eggs and babies

Mr Plomin, the student of those 35,000 pairs of twins, does not deny this. One of the ways in which genes work, he says, is through our tendency to select and design a particular environment. A baby, for instance, may be born happy;

its happiness may make its mother show it more affection; that may reinforce its cheerfulness. Even though that virtuous circle may have originated with the child's genetic tendency, it can be strengthened by what happens after the baby is born. If the child is taken away from its mother and dumped in a children's home, it may not stay happy. Or, if a child with a tendency to be miserable gets an unswervingly affectionate mother, it may cheer up.

And, just as our genes can affect our environment, so our environment may shape the expression of our genes. Height, for instance, is now around 90% heritable in rich countries. In the past the figure was lower because not everybody was well-nourished enough for their genes to express themselves properly. Heritability, in other words, is not a constant; it is affected by whether life is giving people's natural tendencies a chance to flower properly.

Turn the results of the heritability studies on their heads, and there is further cause for reflection. If IQ is 50% or so heritable, then up to another 50% is determined by something other than genes. The same applies to many other parts of our makeup, the figures for which are roughly of the same order of magnitude. But some things seem to be markedly less genetic. Despite the talk of a "breast cancer gene", for instance, this disease seems rarely to be the result of genetic programming. When one identical twin gets breast cancer, the other gets it in only 12% of cases.

Look, too, at sexual orientation. Some studies have suggested that homosexuality is around 50% heritable. Yet a recent study of Australian identical twins who had grown up apart from each other appeared to show that homosexuality was only 20% heritable in men and 24% in women.

So where, if these figures are right, does homosexuality mainly come from? Not, apparently, from growing up in the same family. Across a whole range of measures, including the tendency to homosexuality, if you look at separated identical twins and identical twins who have been brought up together you will find that they are pretty much alike. Belonging to the same family does not, on this evidence, have much effect. This seems to be confirmed by an examination of adopted children, born of different parents, who have been brought up in the same family.

Do they have much more in common with each other than they do with the kids next door? They do not.

There's something else

But that is daft, most people will instinctively say. The experiences we had in our parents' house were surely of vital importance in shaping our lives. The families we grew up in—and the families we ourselves are now creating—cannot be irrelevant to the character of the children they produce. Yet, if this scientific work is to be believed, belonging to the same family apparently has little effect on the way people turn out.

To some extent, of course, the explanation is that parents do not treat their various offspring in the same way. Mr Plomin cites a study which compares parents' and children's accounts of whether one child got the same treatment as his brother or sister. Not surprisingly, the children reported a greater level of difference than did the parents. Yet it is hard to believe that parents commonly treat identical twins so differently that one becomes a homosexual and one a heterosexual.

The bigger part of the explanation may be that except in special cases—the loving mother who manages to warm her genetically miserable child into real-life happiness—what our parents do is not decisively important to the way we grow up. That is the view of Sandra Scarr, a controversial professor of psychology at the University of Virginia. She offers the idea of "good enough" parenting. So long as a child has parents, and so long as they are not seriously brutal, she reckons, one set of parents is just as good as another.

If that is so, the really important variable may be chance. Perhaps it is the small, random event—the instant romance by the swings, the bullying in the corner of the playground—that shifts us imperceptibly towards widely different ends. Or maybe, for those who look at the universe in a different light, it is some higher power. Anyway, those who had feared that the scientists would soon have us neatly dissected on their laboratory tables can take new heart. How we become who we are seems as mysterious as ever. Thank God.

Optimizing Expression of the Common Human Genome for Child Development

Bernard Brown[1]

Abstract

Molecular biology has moved the gene-environment issue in behavior genetics to how and when expression of the human genome is triggered and maintained. How does environment influence gene expression? How many genes are expressed in producing a given behavior? The genome is a data bank and does not automatically create a working brain. The body and brain grow well when (a) endocrine hormones initiate and promote the expression of genes, (b) nutrition is sufficient to sustain the production of proteins, and (c) stress does not suppress gene expression. The growth of brain synapses also requires appropriate neural stimulation. To study gene expression, it is essential to view the complex biology of the cell from a system context that includes the entire genome plus the biological and psychological environments. Optimizing gene expression for child growth can be achieved by a balance of medicine, nutrition, and appropriate physical, educational, and psychological environments.

Keywords

gene expression; molecular biology; environment; development

The nature-versus-nurture debate is now informed by current research on molecular biology that moves the question from which factor is more important to how and when expression of the human genome is triggered and maintained. The basic behavior genetics issue has become how environment influences gene expression. How do human physiology and biochemistry, which react to the external environment, affect gene expression? Can facilitated gene expression enhance children's development, physical and mental health, and cognitive ability or rehabilitate brain injury and inadequate nurture?

WHAT IS A GENE?

The human cell can be viewed as a protein factor in which genes transmit

From *Current Directions in Psychological Science*, April 1999, pp. 37-41. © 1999 by the American Psychological Society. Reprinted by permission of Blackwell Publishers.

molecular messages to ribosomes to produce protein from amino acids. A gene is a small unit of the DNA molecule that contains information for building a single protein. The genome is the equivalent of a database in a computer ROM memory. Located in the DNA molecule, a long string of genes shaped like a double helix, the genome contains codes that prescribe the structure and function of the cell. A gene is activated when the external environment asks the genome to supply information. The information from the activated gene is then processed by the body's basic operating system, the DNA-ribosome protein factory. The ROM's information is essential for the operation of the protein factory, but it is only information, a blueprint, and not otherwise part of the control system that regulates the factory's production of protein. A vast array of biological structures is built from the information in the human genome's 50,000 to 100,000 genes (Lewin, Siliciano, & Klotz, 1997).

In a critical number of cells affecting human growth, the genetic machinery of the cell does not by itself issue instructions to assemble proteins from the genetic blueprint. Rather, gene expression is triggered by hormones, messenger proteins secreted by endocrine glands. Hormone levels are influenced by biological and psychological environments. Many structural genes that code for proteins remain quiescent until the environment gives rise to hormones and chains of molecules created by hormones, such as steroids, that signal cells to activate genes. An activated gene's structure is copied (transcribed) to produce a new molecule, a messenger RNA molecule, which is then sent to tell a ribosome to produce a protein. To get the messages across the bridge from gene to ribosome, the cell requires biochemical promoters and inhibitors, as well as certain biochemical and physiological conditions within the cell, such as sufficient levels of energy and nutrients (Lewin et al., 1997).

GROWTH AND DIFFERENTIATION

Stress, nutrition, health, endocrine hormones, and the psychological environment all affect the rate and magnitude of brain growth, information processing and storage, and competition among neural networks. The rate at which the brain absorbs, processes, and consolidates information depends on the neural stimulation it receives and on its biochemical resources for processing and absorbing information.

Homeostasis is an organism's tendency to preserve its state. The body is a multiply redundant failsafe system controlled by multiple feedback loops in which genes play a protective role, ensuring function under adverse conditions and survivability across generations. Genes conserve the organism's form, sequence of development, and function, supplying mechanisms for adapting to the environment. Even when severe stress, malnutrition, or lack of stimulation slows the growth of brain structures, the order of gene expression is conserved. Each stage of brain growth follows its predecessor, and the genetic plan still unfolds, albeit more slowly and less perfectly.

After an early period of exponential growth, human children grow in stages of differentiation; simple cells and tissues specialize into more complex forms and functions. The genome specifies the order in which genes are expressed and provides sets of contingency plans for the different conditions the organism may encounter. Hundreds of genes that eventually affect behavior are expressed in each of hundreds of differentiation waves. A child's development reflects a series of genetically programmed steps that start at different ages. As the steps progress, old and newly expressed genes interact with successive environments. In brain growth, neurons (nerve cells) increase in the early stages and connecting tissues (axons and dendrites) increase and organize in later stages. Brain plasticity, the capacity of the brain to change as a result of experience, concerns changes in the number and size of synapses and synaptic networks. When sufficient electrical signals are sent from a neuron through an axon to a synapse (a small attachment point on the dendrite of a second neuron) and the biological environment of the synapse is supportive, the synapse will grow. The brain grows in cycles of synaptic growth and pruning (elimination). If a door opens on a favorable microenvironment, synapses tend to form and neural networks grow. But if the door opens on an unfavorable microenvironment, synapses are more likely to be pruned.

TRIGGERING AND MAINTAINING GENETIC ACTION

Hormones secreted by the endocrine glands are the primary source of genetic action. Stress has a major impact on which hormones are secreted and hence on how children grow. The influence of hormones and neural stimulation on

brain growth also depends on nutrition at the cellular level.

The Endocrine System

As a child grows, the endocrine system —under the influence of its biochemical, biophysical, and psychological environments—generates many hormones, chemicals that signal body cells to change the rates of chemical reactions. Levels of hormones change with nutrition, stress, illness, medication, and mood (Wilson & Foster, 1985). The hormones, in turn, trigger the expression of tens of thousands of genes. Hormonal levels influence the growth and function of the brain at many levels (Kuhn & Shanberg, 1984).

Thyroid hormones trigger gene transcription and accelerate the functional maturation of the brain. Too much thyroid hormone produces adverse effects, such as over-rapid growth. When thyroid hormone levels are insufficient, brain growth slows and cell division persists past the normal time of termination. There are reductions in cell size, synaptic density, and density of brain cell connections, and delayed functional development. Gene expression is slowed, impairing production of proteins and decreasing RNA content and T3 thyroid hormone receptors (Kuhn & Shanberg, 1984).

Steroids, the molecular end products of the thyroid hormone chemical chain, which is activated by stress, profoundly suppress growth in all tissues. Large doses of steroids suppress brain growth. Stress, medication, and some illnesses raise levels of cortisol, the thyroid chain's final end product, delaying development and suppressing DNA synthesis. Steroids affect nervous system plasticity (McEwen, 1992).

Growth hormone directly affects the rate at which genes transcribe their messages to produce proteins. Growth hormone is necessary for normal body and brain development.

Stress

Stress is universal, and children must learn to cope with normal stressful events; however, continuing, uncontrolled stress slows mental growth (Brown & Rosenbaum, 1985). Stress has strong effects on endocrine function (Chrousos & Gold, 1992). High stress-related cortisol levels damage the brain's hippocampus (Sapolsky, 1996) and slow body growth (Wilson & Foster, 1985). Meerson (1984) found that stressed rats increased cellular weight and had higher levels of DNA, RNA, and protein synthesis. The diversion of energy and cellular resources toward the buildup of large stress-resisting cellular structures clearly competes with growth.

Nutrition

The role of nutrition in physical growth and brain growth is well established (Brown, 1972). For example, Bogin (1988) found Guatemalan children raised in the United States gain greater stature than their fathers and children in Guatemala. For optimum gene expression, it is essential to provide nutrients that maintain cellular energy and sufficient cellular concentrations of amino acids (basic protein components; Chan & Hargrove, 1993).

ASPECTS OF GENETIC ACTION

The 19th century saw tremendous scientific progress as physics and biology moved beyond global analysis and examined small subsystems. Developmental biology, influenced by Mendel, adapted a mechanistic model that separated the inside of the body from the outside environment. In Mendelian genetics, the gene was conceptualized as unitary, independent, and the determinant of the final state of the developing organism (Lewontin, 1994). However, molecular biology now shows that gene expression is more complex.

Gene expression has often been measured in terms of the number of gene copies found in a chromosome, a section of the DNA helix. Although relating the number of copies of a gene in a chromosome to the color of peas worked well in Mendel's context, inherited traits are not a simple function of the number of gene copies. Within the various chromosomes of DNA, there are many copies and reverse copies of genes, as well as psuedogenes, all of which may look like true copies but will not be expressed. The alternative to measuring the number of gene copies, and the only sure way to study the likelihood that a given gene has been expressed, is to test for the presence of a specific messenger RNA.

Often, gene expression is measured inadequately in terms of copies of receptor genes. Receptors are molecules, created from receptor genes, that sit on membranes (e.g., the surfaces of cells) and act as entry portals. When a receptor recognizes an incoming molecule and binds to it, a chain of chemical reactions that leads to gene expression (production of a protein) begins. A receptor gene is not the same as the gene of the molecule that binds to it. Both the receptor and the molecule that binds to it are needed to create a chemical pathway leading to the creation of a protein. Moreover, the number of receptors will change with tissue needs. Hormonal changes can increase the density of receptors at a site by a factor of 10.

The D4DR dopamine receptor gene is an important and well-known gene that has been associated with sensation seeking, risk taking, substance abuse, attention deficit hyperactivity disorder (ADHD), dyslexia, delinquency, and antisocial behavior (Hamer & Copeland, 1998). Practitioners treat these conditions with nutritional regimes, biofeedback, behavior modification, cognitive therapy, and various medications such as ritalin.

The D4DR receptor is part of a larger system that regulates behavior. Many neurons produce the neurotransmitter dopamine. Dopamine is transmitted from a neuron to a synapse on a second neuron and then binds to the second neuron's receptor, delivering the first neuron's message. But the D4DR receptor is only one of many dopamine receptors that sit on the surface of some neurons. Once the dopamine is delivered to the receptor, dopamine transporters return the dopamine across the synapse to the first neuron, to be used again. Mutations in transporter genes can cause the dopamine secreted by the synapse to be returned before it binds to the dopamine receptor and delivers its message. Behavior problems attributed to D4DR may instead result from the level of dopamine; from different kinds of neurons, synapses, receptors, or molecular agents; or from their various combinations. In the brain, synaptic growth and function depend on complex biochemical systems that regulate many different kinds of molecules that act as neurotransmitters, receptors, release agents, and promotors, inhibitors, modulators, and integrators of the chemical reactions that lead to gene transcription and protein production.[2]

Although Mendel viewed both parents as the source of inheritance, molecular pathways are more complex. Lamond and Earnshaw (1998) showed that the cell nucleus (in which DNA resides) has a dynamic structure. Genes are generally kept in inactive nuclear regions, but the most recently activated genes are located at nuclear processing sites in the best position to be processed again if there is an environmental trigger. Human female XX chromosomes, for example, have been observed with one X chromosome (from one parent) in an active region and the other (from the other parent) in an inactive region, potentially increasing the influence of one parent over the other. The elevated reaction probability of genes in activated nuclear regions may explain many aspects of learning. Mitochondria, the cellular energy sources, are inherited only from the mother. The tiny mitochondrion has a small DNA-like strand with genes for 37 energy-generating molecules. There are about 100 mitochondria per cell. Genetic disorders stemming from mitochondria may be involved in many energy-related behavior problems, especially in the aged (Wallace, 1997). Stressed or malnourished mothers may develop low mitochondrial density and pass the environmental condition on to their children through their ova.

OPTIMIZING GENETIC EXPRESSION

Genes are not destiny. There are many places along the gene-behavior pathway where genetic expression can be regulated. Environmental factors such as temperature; nutrition; light level; the timing, pace, and intensity of stimuli; and effective coping skills can promote or inhibit the expression of specific genes and proteins that lead to specific behaviors. Treatment of a single factor may be too weak to effect change. It is important to use system thinking as treatments for behavior problems are combined and optimized.

Medicine

Physicians use thousands of drugs that alter biochemical pathways to reduce or remove genetically related illness and dysfunction. Some drugs modify physiological pathways through which genes are expressed; many target gene products, proteins. The use of drugs to promote learning in schools has become commonplace. New generations of psychoactive drugs regulate receptor function. Some regulate neurotransmitters in synapses, such as serotonin and dopamine. More than 20 antidepressant drugs, such as Prozac, are regularly prescribed to increase serotonin concentrations in synapses. Benzodiazipines are now used to treat anxiety, insomnia, and seizures. The enormous progress in molecular biology may lead to drugs that improve cognitive ability and cure schizophrenia.

Nutrition

Alternative medicine is developing wellness models, as opposed to deficit models, to meet growth-retarded and ADHD children's nutritional needs. One current approach is a learning-nutrition discipline that adjusts diets to optimize energy and levels of amino acids, vitamins, gene-promoting enzymes, and minerals.

Physical Environment

Physical environment involves factors such as light, temperature, noise, humidity, wind, space, and air pressure. Genes determine the eye's iris color and retinal pigmentation. Children with dark eyes may need more light for optimum visual performance than other children. They would have no problem if school lighting met prescribed standards and teachers did not draw the shades and turn off the lights at 2:00, as children taking ritalin become less tractable because their medicine wears off. This real genetic problem has a simple practical solution. Another example of the relationship between light and behavior concerns the use of high light levels. Intense light is used to treat depression by changing levels of the neurotransmitter serotonin and to regulate daily body rhythms by changing levels of melatonin.

Regulation of home and school temperatures is important. High temperature, which can cause sleepiness in hot classrooms, shunts blood away from the brain into the peripheral vascular system, reducing the energy and nutrient supply needed for gene expression.

Psychological Environment

In child development, gene expression responds to love; security; effective role models; stimulating language and cognitive environments; a positive family environment including support, discipline, values, and positive directions; education; and appropriate management of stress and anxiety. These psychological factors modulate genetic expression through the endocrine system and the brain, and when deficient can be improved through psychotherapy.

Providing stress-coping skills and controlling the intensity, frequency, and duration of stress are essential for optimizing gene expression. Mind-body therapies such as biofeedback and progressive relaxation promote relaxation, improving health and performance.

Adverse psychological environment can slow gene expression, leading to slower mental growth, especially when a child is subject to malnutrition, stress, illness, or suboptimal physical environments. Psychological environment also plays a role in the origins and outcomes of known brain disorders with genetic components, including stress-induced dysfunction of the amygdala and hippocampus, substance abuse, and some disorders of sleep, metabolism, vision, hearing, and speech. In addition to psychotherapy and pharmacology, education has played a vital role in the treatment of these disorders.

Genetic Differences Between the Sexes

Sex, the most obvious genetic difference, has received too little study. When scaled tests are used to measure cognitive differences, the selection of test items to ensure equal responses by males and females obscures male-female differences. Hanlon (1996) found dramatic sex differences in brain growth and in the areas at which brain activity occurs. Young girls are more verbal than young boys, who show better spatial and gross motor ability. Are boys taught to read before genes for reading are expressed? Would the Swedish approach to education, which delays reading instruction, reduce boys' reading disabilities in the United States? Some day genetic testing may help determine when a child is ready for a given educational program.

CONCLUSION

The gene is as a framed canvas, an invariant plane on which the organic environment molds a variegated hormonal surface, upon which the psychological environment paints a person.

The genome gives rise to an enormous, complex array of balanced chemical subsystems highly resistant to change. Regulatory pathways often overlap. Exciting or inhibiting one pathway can affect a series of pathways, sometimes leading to side effects. A single gene by itself may not be sufficiently strong to affect the system. A gene may be present, but there may not be a trigger to express the gene. A gene may lead to dysfunction in one environment yet produce exceptional function in another environment.

To optimize gene expression, it is essential to adopt a multidisciplinary system approach that takes into account the entire genome plus the biological and psychological environments. Even if a gene is the direct source of a behavior problem, there may be ways to alter its expression or to bypass it by promoting alternative genetic pathways. Treatment needs to balance medicine, nutrition, and physical, educational, and psychological environments and must be sensitive to gender differences. A narrow focus on a given gene, a given condition, or a single treatment is not likely to change the system. From the viewpoint of molecular biology, growth involves very complex and continuing interaction of genes and environment. But within the complexity lies a vast number of possibilities for improving children's growth.

Recommended Reading

Bogin, B. (1988). (See References)

Diamond, M.C. (1988). *The impact of the environment on the anatomy of the brain.* New York: Free Press.

Hamer, D.H., & Copeland, P. (1998). (See References)

Notes

1. Address correspondence to Bernard Brown, 182 New Mark Esplanade, Rockville, MD 20850; e-mail: berniebr@ erols.com.
2. Genome database projects now provide excellent information on most gene sequences and protein products. Functional information about what each protein does in the cell and what its metabolic and regulatory pathways are is available on the World Wide Web from the Kyoto University database, www.genome.ad.jp/kegg/. The CMS Molecular Biology Resources database can be visited at www.sdsc.edu/restools/cmshp.html. It is a functional listing of public-domain biological research tools.

References

Bogin, B. (1988). *Patterns of human growth.* Cambridge, England: Cambridge University Press.

Brown, B. (1972). *Growth retardation: A systems study of the educational problems of the disadvantaged child.* Unpublished doctoral dissertation, American University, Washington, DC.

Brown, B., & Rosenbaum, L. (1985). Stress and competence. In J.H. Humphrey (Ed.), *Stress in childhood* (pp. 127–154). New York: AMS Press.

Chan, D.K.-C., & Hargrove, J.L. (1993). Effects of dietary protein on gene expression. In C.D. Berdanier & J.L. Hargrove

(Eds.), *Nutrition and gene expression* (pp. 353–375). Boca Raton, FL: CRC.

Chrousos, G. P., & Gold, P.W. (1992). The concepts of stress and stress system disorders: Overview of physical and behavioral homeostasis. *Journal of the American Medical Association, 267,* 1244–1252.

Hamer, D.H., & Copeland, P. (1998). *Living with our genes.* New York: Doubleday.

Hanlon, H. (1996). Topographically different regional networks impose structural limitations on both sexes in early post-natal development. In K.H. Pribram & J. King (Eds.), *Learning as self-organization* (pp. 311–376). Hillsdale, NJ: Erlbaum.

Kuhn, C., & Shanberg, S. (1984). Hormones and brain development. In C.B. Nemeroff & A.D. Dunn (Eds.), *Peptides, hormones and behavior* (pp. 775–821). New York: SP Medical and Scientific Books.

Lamond, A.I., & Earnshaw, W.C. (1998). Structure and function in the nucleus. *Science, 280,* 547–553.

Lewin, B., Siliciano, P., & Klotz, M. (1997). *Genes VI.* Oxford, England: Oxford University.

Lewontin, R.C. (1994). *Inside and outside: Gene, environment and organism.* Worcester, MA: Clark University.

McEwen, B.S. (1992). Effects of the steroid/thyroid hormone family on neural and behavioral plasticity. In C.B. Nemeroff (Ed.), *Neuroendocrinology* (pp. 333–351). Boca Raton, FL: CRC.

Meerson, F.Z. (1984). *Adaptation, stress and prophylaxis.* New York: Springer-Verlag.

Sapolsky, R.M. (1996). Why stress is bad for your brain. *Science, 273,* 749–750.

Wallace, D.C. (1997). Mitochondrial DNA in aging and disease. *Scientific American, 277,* 40–47.

Wilson, J.D., & Foster, D.W. (1985). *Williams textbook of endocrinology* (7th ed.). Philadelphia: Saunders.

The Split Brain Revisited

Groundbreaking work that began more than a quarter of a century ago has led to ongoing insights about brain organization and consciousness

by Michael S. Gazzaniga

About 30 years ago in these very pages, I wrote about dramatic new studies of the brain. Three patients who were seeking relief from epilepsy had undergone surgery that severed the corpus callosum—the superhighway of neurons connecting the halves of the brain. By working with these patients, my colleagues Roger W. Sperry, Joseph E. Bogen, P. J. Vogel and I witnessed what happened when the left and the right hemispheres were unable to communicate with each other.

It became clear that visual information no longer moved between the two sides. If we projected an image to the right visual field— that is, to the left hemisphere, which is where information from the right field is processed— the patients could describe what they saw. But when the same image was displayed to the left visual field, the patients drew a blank: they said they didn't see anything. Yet if we asked them to point to an object similar to the one being projected, they could do so with ease. The right brain saw the image and could mobilize a nonverbal response. It simply couldn't talk about what it saw.

The same kind of finding proved true for touch, smell and sound. Additionally, each half of the brain could control the upper muscles of both arms, but the muscles manipulating hand and finger movement could be orchestrated only by the contralateral hemisphere. In other words, the right hemisphere could control only the left hand and the left hemisphere only the right hand.

Ultimately, we discovered that the two hemispheres control vastly different aspects of thought and action. Each half has its own specialization and thus its own limitations and advantages. The left brain is dominant for language and speech. The right excels at visual-motor tasks. The language of these findings has become part of our culture: writers refer to themselves as left-brained, visual artists refer to themselves as right-brained.

In the intervening decades, split-brain research has continued to illuminate many areas of neuroscience. Not only have we and others learned even more about how the hemispheres differ, but we also have been able to understand how they communicate once they have been separated. Split-brain studies have shed light on language, on mechanisms of perception and attention, and on brain organization as well as the potential seat of false memories. Perhaps most intriguing has been the contribution of these studies to our understanding of consciousness and evolution.

The original split-brain studies raised many interesting questions, including ones about whether the distinct halves could still "talk" to each other and what role any such communication played in thought and action. There are several bridges of neurons, called commissures, that connect the hemispheres. The corpus callosum is the most massive of these and typically the only one severed during surgery for epilepsy. But what of the many other, smaller commissures?

Remaining Bridges

By studying the attentional system, researchers have been able to address this question. Attention involves many structures in the cortex and the subcortex—the older, more primitive part of our brains. In the 1980s Jeffrey D. Holtzman of Cornell University Medical College found that each hemisphere is able to direct spatial attention not only to its own sensory sphere but also to certain points in the sensory sphere of the opposite, disconnected hemisphere. This discovery suggests that the attentional system is common to both hemispheres—at least with regard to spatial information—and can still operate via some remaining interhemispheric connections.

Holtzman's work was especially intriguing because it raised the possibility that there were finite attentional "resources." He posited that working on one kind of task uses certain brain resources; the harder the task, the more of these resources are needed—and the more one half of the brain must call on the subcortex or the other hemisphere for help. In 1982 Holtzman led the way again, discovering that, indeed, the harder one half of a split brain worked, the harder it was for the other half to carry out another task simultaneously.

Recent investigations by Steve J. Luck of the University of Iowa, Steven A. Hillyard and his colleagues at the University of California at San Diego and Ronald Mangun of the University of California at Davis show that another aspect of attention is also preserved in the split brain. They looked at what happens when a person searches a visual field for a pattern or an object. The researchers found that split-brain patients perform better than normal people do in some of these visual-searching tasks. The intact brain appears to inhibit the search mechanisms that each hemisphere naturally possesses.

The left hemisphere, in particular, can exert powerful control over such tasks. Alan Kingstone of the University of Alberta found that the left hemisphere is "smart" about its search strategies, whereas the right is not. In tests where a person can deduce how to search efficiently an array of

similar items for an odd exception, the left does better than the right. Thus, it seems that the more competent left hemisphere can hijack the intact attentional system.

Although these and other studies indicated that some communication between the split hemispheres remains, other apparent interhemispheric links proved illusory. I conducted an experiment with Kingstone, for instance, that nearly misled us on this front. We flashed two words to a patient and then asked him to draw what he saw. "Bow" was flashed to one hemisphere and "arrow" to the other. To our surprise, our patient drew a bow and arrow! It appeared as though he had internally integrated the information in one hemisphere; that hemisphere had, in turn, directed the drawn response.

We were wrong. We finally determined that integration had actually taken place on the paper, not in the brain. One hemisphere had drawn its item—the bow—and then the other hemisphere had gained control of the writing hand, drawing its stimulus—the arrow—on top of the bow. The image merely looked coordinated. We discovered this chimera by giving less easily integrated word pairs like "sky" and "scraper." The subject did not draw a tall building; instead he drew the sky over a picture of a scraper.

The Limits of Extrapolation

In addition to helping neuroscientists determine which systems still work and which

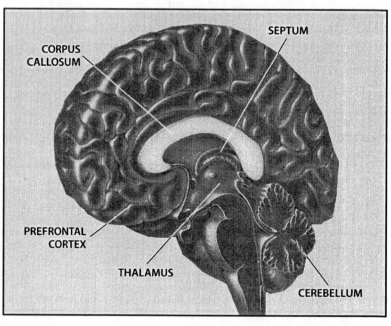

BRAIN WIRING is, in many cases, contralateral. The right hemisphere processes information from the left visual field, whereas the left hemisphere processes data from the right visual field. For hand movement as well, the right hemisphere controls the hand and fingers of the left arm; the left hemisphere controls the right. Both hemispheres, however, dictate the movement of the upper arms. The two hemispheres are connected by neuronal bridges called commissures. The largest of these, and the one severed during split-brain operations, is the corpus callosum (right).

SEPTUM

CORPUS CALLOSUM

PREFRONTAL CORTEX

THALAMUS

CEREBELLUM

JOHN W. KARAPELOU

are severed along with the corpus callosum, studies of communication between the hemispheres led to an important finding about the limits of nonhuman studies. Humans often turn to the study of animals to understand themselves. For many years, neuroscientists have examined the brains of monkeys and other creatures to explore the ways in which the human brain operates. Indeed, it has been a common belief—emphatically disseminated by Charles Darwin—that the brains of our closest relatives have an organization and function largely similar, if not identical, to our own.

Split-brain research has shown that this assumption can be spurious. Although some structures and functions are remarkably alike, differences abound. The anterior commissure provides one dramatic example. This small structure lies somewhat below the corpus callosum. When this commissure is left intact in otherwise split-brain monkeys, the animals retain the ability to transfer visual information from one hemisphere to the other. People, however, do not transfer visual information in any way. Hence, the same structure carries out different functions in different species—an illustration of the limits of extrapolating from one species to another.

Even extrapolating between people can be dangerous. One of our first striking findings was that the left brain could freely process language and speak about its experience. Although the right was not so free, we also found that it could process some language. Among other skills, the right hemisphere could match words to pictures, do spelling and rhyming, and categorize objects. Although we never found any sophisticated capacity for syntax in that half of the brain, we believed the extent of its lexical knowledge to be quite impressive.

Over the years it has become clear that our first three cases were unusual. Most people's right hemispheres cannot handle even the most rudimentary language, contrary to what we initially observed. This finding is in keeping with other neurological data, particularly those from stroke victims. Damage to the left hemisphere is far more detrimental to language function than is damage to the right.

Testing for Synthesis

Ability to synthesize information is lost after split-brain surgery, as this experiment shows. One hemisphere of a patient was flashed a card with the word "bow"; the other hemisphere saw "arrow." Because the patient drew a bow and arrow, my colleagues and I assumed the two hemispheres were still able to communicate with each other—despite the severing of the corpus callosum—and had integrated the words into a meaningful composite.

The next test proved us wrong. We flashed "sky" to one hemisphere, "scraper" to the other. The resulting image revealed that the patient was not synthesizing information: sky atop a comblike scraper was drawn, rather than a tall building. One hemisphere drew what it had seen, then the other drew its word. In the case of bow and arrow, the superposition of the two images misled us because the picture appeared integrated. Finally, we tested to see whether each hemisphere could, on its own, integrate words. We flashed "fire" and then "arm" to the right hemisphere. The left hand drew a rifle rather than an arm on fire, so it was clear that each hemisphere was capable of synthesis.

—*M.S.G.*

LEFT HEMISPHERE   RIGHT HEMISPHERE

ARROW   BOW

DRAWING

LEFT HEMISPHERE   RIGHT HEMISPHERE

SCRAPER   SKY

DRAWING

LEFT HEMISPHERE   RIGHT HEMISPHERE

FIRE

ARM

DRAWING

LAURIE GRACE

Nevertheless, there exists a great deal of plasticity and individual variation. One patient, dubbed J.W., developed the capacity to speak out of the right hemisphere—13 years after surgery. J.W. can now speak about information presented to the left or to the right brain.

Kathleen B. Baynes of the University of California at Davis reports another unique case. A left-handed patient spoke out of her left brain after split-brain surgery—not a surprising finding in itself. But the patient could *write* only out of her right, nonspeaking hemisphere. This dissociation confirms the idea that the capacity to write need not be associated with the capacity for phonological representation. Put differently, writing appears to be an independent system, an invention of the human species. It can stand alone and does not need to be part of our inherited spoken language system.

Brain Modules

Despite myriad exceptions, the bulk of split-brain research has revealed an enormous degree of lateralization—that is, specialization in each of the hemispheres. As investigators have struggled to understand how the brain achieves its goals and how it is organized, the lateralization revealed by split-brain studies has figured into what is called the modular model. Research in cognitive science, artificial intelligence, evolutionary psychology and neuroscience has directed attention to the idea that brain and mind are built from discrete units—or modules—that carry out specific functions. According to this theory, the brain is not a general problem-solving device

whose every part is capable of any function. Rather it is a collection of devices that assists the mind's information-processing demands.

Within that modular system, the left hemisphere has proved quite dominant for major cognitive activities, such as problem solving. Split-brain surgery does not seem to affect these functions. It is as if the left hemisphere

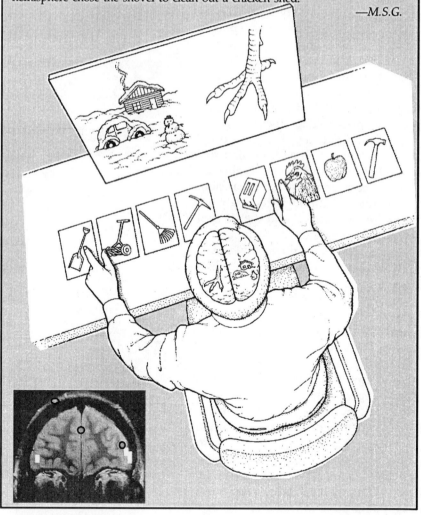

Finding False Memory

False memories originate in the left hemisphere. As this MRI image indicates (see insert), a region in both the right and left hemispheres is active when a false memory is recalled *(white)*; only the right is active during a true memory *(circled areas)*. My colleagues and I studied this phenomenon by testing the narrative ability of the left hemisphere. Each hemisphere was shown four small pictures, one of which related to a larger picture also presented to that hemisphere. The patient had to choose the most appropriate small picture.

As seen below, the right hemisphere—that is, the left hand—correctly picked the shovel for the snowstorm; the right hand, controlled by the left hemisphere, correctly picked the chicken to go with the bird's foot. Then we asked the patient why the left hand—or right hemisphere—was pointing to the shovel. Because only the left hemisphere retains the ability to talk, it answered. But because it could not know why the right hemisphere was doing what it was doing, it made up a story about what it could see—namely, the chicken. It said the right hemisphere chose the shovel to clean out a chicken shed.

—M.S.G.

MICHAEL B. MILLER   JOHN W. KARAPELOU has no need for the vast computational power of the other half of the brain to carry out high-level activities. The right hemisphere, meanwhile, is severely deficient in difficult problem solving.

Joseph E. LeDoux of New York University and I discovered this quality of the left brain almost 20 years ago. We had asked a simple question: How does the left hemisphere respond to behaviors produced by the silent right brain? Each hemisphere was presented a picture that related to one of four pictures placed in front of the split-brain subject. The left and the right hemispheres easily picked the correct card. The left hand pointed to the right hemisphere's choice and the right hand to the left hemisphere's choice [see illustration, "Finding False Memory"].

We then asked the left hemisphere—the only one that can talk—why the left hand was pointing to the object. It really did not know, because the decision to point to the card was made in the right hemisphere. Yet, quick as a flash, it made up an explanation. We dubbed this creative, narrative talent the interpreter mechanism.

This fascinating ability has been studied recently to determine how the left hemisphere interpreter affects memory. Elizabeth A. Phelps of Yale University, Janet Metcalfe of Columbia University and Margaret Funnell, a postdoctoral fellow at Dartmouth College, have found that the two hemispheres differ in their ability to process new data. When presented with new information, people usually remember much of what they experience. When questioned, they also usually claim to remember things that were not truly part of the experience. If split-brain patients are given such tests, the left hemisphere generates many false reports. But the right brain does not; it provides a much more verdical account.

This finding may help researchers determine where and how false memories develop. There are several views about when in the cycle of information processing such memories are laid down. Some researchers suggest they develop early in the cycle, that erroneous accounts are actually encoded at the time of the event. Others believe false memories reflect an error in reconstructing past experience: in other words, that people develop a schema about what happened and retrospectively fit untrue events—that are nonetheless consistent with the schema—into their recollection of the original experience.

The left hemisphere has exhibited certain characteristics that support the latter view. First, developing such schemata is exactly what the left hemisphere interpreter excels at. Second, Funnell has discovered that the left hemisphere has an ability to determine the source of a memory, based on the context or the surrounding events. Her work indicates that the left hemisphere actively places its experiences in a larger context, whereas the right simply attends to the perceptual aspects of the stimulus. Finally, Michael B. Miller, a graduate student at Dartmouth, has demonstrated that the left prefrontal regions of normal subjects are activated when they recall false memories.

These findings all suggest that the interpretive mechanism of the left hemisphere is always hard at work, seeking the meaning of events. It is constantly looking for order and reason, even when there is none—which leads it continually to make mistakes. It tends to overgeneralize, frequently constructing a potential past as opposed to a true one.

The Evolutionary Perspective

George L. Wolford of Dartmouth has lent even more support to this view of the left hemisphere. In a simple test that requires a person to guess whether a light is going to appear on the top or bottom of a computer screen, humans perform inventively. The experimenter manipulates the stimulus so that the light appears on the top 80 percent of the time but in a random sequence. While it quickly becomes evident that the top button is being illuminated more often, people invariably try to figure out the entire pattern or sequence—and they deeply believe they can. Yet by adopting this strategy, they are correct only 68 percent of the time. If they always pressed the top button, they would be correct 80 percent of the time.

Rats and other animals, on the other hand, are more likely to "learn to maximize" and to press only the top button. It turns out the right hemisphere behaves in the same way: it does not try to interpret its experience and find deeper meaning. It continues to live only in the thin moment of the present—and to be correct 80 percent of the time. But the left, when asked to explain why it is attempting to figure the whole sequence, always comes up with a theory, no matter how outlandish.

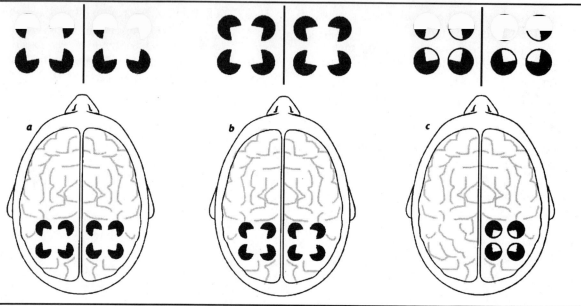

LAURIE GRACE

This narrative phenomenon is best explained by evolutionary theory. The human brain, like any brain, is a collection of neurological adaptations established through natural selection. These adaptations each have their own representation—that is, they can be lateralized to specific regions or networks in the brain. Throughout the animal kingdom, however, capacities are generally not lateralized. Instead they tend to be found in both hemispheres to roughly equal degrees. And although monkeys show some signs of lateral specialization, these are rare and inconsistent.

For this reason, it has always appeared that the lateralization seen in the human brain was an evolutionary add-on—mechanisms or abilities that were laid down in one hemisphere only. We recently stumbled across an amazing hemispheric dissociation that challenges this view. It forced us to speculate that some lateralized phenomena may arise from a hemisphere's losing an ability—not gaining it.

In what must have been fierce competition for cortical space, the evolving primate brain would have been hard-pressed to gain new faculties without losing old ones. Lateralization could have been its salvation. Because the two hemispheres are connected, mutational tinkering with a homologous cortical region could give rise to a new function—yet not cost the animal, because the other side would remain unaffected.

Paul M. Corballis, a postdoctoral fellow at Dartmouth, and Robert Fendrich of Dartmouth, Robert M. Shapley of New York University and I studied in many split-brain patients the perception of what are called illusory contours. Earlier work had suggested that seeing the well-known illusory contours of Gaetano Kanizsa of the University of Trieste was the right hemisphere's specialty. Our experiments revealed a different situation.

We discovered that both hemispheres could perceive illusory contours—but that the right hemisphere was able to grasp certain perceptual groupings that the left could not. Thus, while both hemispheres in a split-brain person can judge whether the illusory rectangles are fat or thin when no line is drawn around the openings of the "Pacman" figures, only the right can continue to make the judgment after the line has been drawn [see illustration, "Looking for Illusions"]. This setup is called the amodal version of the test.

What is so interesting is that Kanizsa himself has demonstrated that mice can do the amodal version. That a lowly mouse can perceive perceptual groupings, whereas a human's left hemisphere cannot, suggests that a capacity has been lost. Could it be that the emergence of a human capacity like language—or an interpretive mechanism—chased this perceptual skill out of the left brain? We think so, and this opinion gives rise to a fresh way of thinking about the origins of lateral specialization.

Our uniquely human skills may well be produced by minute and circumscribed neuronal networks, And yet our highly modularized brain generates the feeling in all of us that we are integrated and unified. How so,

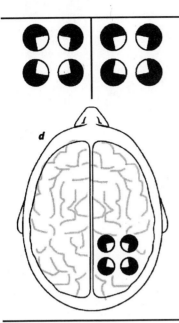

Looking for Illusions

Illusory contours reveal that the human right brain can process some things the left cannot. Both hemispheres can "see" whether the illusory rectangles of this experiment are fat (a) or thin (b). But when outlines are added, only the right brain can still tell the difference (c and d). In mice, however, both hemispheres can consistently perceive these differences. For a rodent to perform better than we do suggests that some capabilities were lost from one hemisphere or the other as the human brain evolved. New capabilities may have squeezed out old ones in a race for space.

—*M.S.G.*

conscious, the left brain's consciousness far surpasses that of the right. Which raises another set of questions that should keep us busy for the next 30 years or so.

The Author

MICHAEL S. GAZZANIGA is professor of cognitive neuroscience and director of the Center for Cognitive Neuroscience at Dartmouth College. He received his Ph.D. at the California Institute of Technology, where he, Roger W. Sperry and Joseph E. Bogen initiated split-brain studies. Since then, he has published in many areas and is credited with launching the field of cognitive neuroscience in the early 1980s.

given that we are a collection of specialized modules?

The answer may be that the left hemisphere seeks explanations for why events occur. The advantage of such a system is obvious. By going beyond the simple observation of events and asking why they happened, a brain can cope with these same events better, should they happen again.

Realizing the strengths and weaknesses of each hemisphere prompted us to think about the basis of mind, about this overarching organization. After many years of fascinating research on the split brain, it appears that the inventive and interpreting left hemisphere has a conscious experience very different from that of the truthful, literal right brain. Although both hemispheres can be viewed as

Further Reading

HEMISPHERIC SPECIALIZATION AND INTERHEMISPHERIC INTEGRATION. M. J. Tramo, K. Baynes, R. Fendrich, G. R. Mangun, E. A. Phelps, P. A. Reuter-Lorenz and M. S. Gazzaniga in *Epilepsy and the Corpus Callosum*. Second edition. Plenum Press, 1995.

HOW THE MIND WORKS. Steven Pinker. W. W. Norton, 1997.

THE MIND'S PAST. Michael S. Gazzaniga. University of California Press, 1998.

THE TWO SIDES OF PERCEPTION. Richard B. Ivry and Lynn C. Robertson. MIT Press, 1998.

Unit 3

Key Points to Consider

❖ Why are psychologists be interested in studying sensations and perceptions, which are ordinarily the domain of biologists and physicians? Try to rank the senses, that is, place them in a hierarchy of importance. Justify your rankings.

❖ What role does the brain play in sensation and perception? Can you give specific information about the role of the brain in each of the senses? Are some senses "distant" senses and some "near" senses in terms of how we perceive a stimulus, whether the stimulus be physical or social? Can you think of other ways to categorize the various senses?

❖ Describe deafness and some of its causes. What role do genes play in deafness? What are the hair cells in the ear and how are they related to deafness? What are the newest methods for overcoming deafness?

❖ Is the sense of taste important? Why do some people intensely experience taste while others can barely taste differences among three brands of cola? How does our experience of taste affect our health? How do age and gender affect our ability to perceive various tastes?

❖ What is REM sleep? What are some of the problems dream researchers encounter? Was Freud correct that dreams are repressed wishes that we want to forget? Or are dreams events we would rather remember? Besides dreaming, describe any other parapsychological phenomena or altered states of consciousness that you know. How could you research them? If they exist, what does it mean for the individual who is able to experience them?

 **Links**   **www.dushkin.com/online/**

These sites are annotated on pages 4 and 5.

Susan and her roommate have been friends since freshmen year. Because they share so much in common, they decided to become roommates in their sophomore year. They both want to travel abroad one day. Both date men from the same fraternity, major in education majors, and want to work with young children after graduation. Today they are at the local art museum. As they walk around the galleries, Susan is astonished at her roommate's taste in art. Whatever her roommate likes, Susan hates. The paintings and sculptures that Susan admires are the very ones at which her roommate turns up her nose. "How can our tastes in art be so different?" Susan wonders.

What Susan and her roommate are experiencing is a difference in perception, or the interpretation of the sensory stimulation provided by the artwork. Perception and its sister area of psychology, sensation, are the focus of this unit.

For many years in psychology, it was popular to consider sensation and perception as two distinct processes. Sensation was defined in passive terms as the simple event of some stimulus energy (i.e. a sound wave) impinging on the body or on a specific sense organ that then reflexively transmits appropriate information to the central nervous system. Both passivity and simple reflexes were stressed in this concept of sensation. Perception, on the other hand, was defined as an integrative and interpretive process that the higher centers of the brain accomplish based on sensory information and available memories for similar events.

The Gestalt psychologists, early German researchers, were convinced that perception was a higher order function than sensation. They believed that the whole stimulus was more than the sum of its individual sensory parts and that this statement was made true by the process of perception.

For example, when you listen to a song, you hear the words, the loudness, and the harmony as well as the main melody. However, you do not really hear each of these separately; what you hear is a whole song. If the song is pleasant to you, you may say that you like it. If the song is raucous to you, you may perceive that you do not like it. However, even the songs that you do not like on first hearing may become likable after repeated exposure. Hence perception, according to these early Gestalt psychologists, is a more advanced and complicated process than sensation.

This dichotomy of sensation and perception is no longer widely accepted. The revolution came in the mid-1960s when a psychologist published a then-radical treatise in which he reasoned that perceptual processes included all sensory events, which he saw as directed by a searching central nervous system. Also, this view provided that certain perceptual patterns, such as recognition of a piece of artwork, may be species-specific. That is, all humans, independent of learning history, should share some of the same perceptual repertoires. This unit on perceptual processes is designed to further your understanding of these complex and interesting processes.

The first article, "The Senses," introduces one of the main topics of this unit and reviews many of the dominant senses in the human being. The author concludes that when we understand the senses, we also understand the brain.

One of the dominant senses in humans is audition or hearing. In the next article, "Deaf Defying," the topic of deafness is covered, including a discussion of the special role that genetics and the fragile hair cells in the ear play in deafness. New research on deafness is helping scientists find artificial means to improve our hearing.

What would our daily lives be like if we couldn't taste a delicious pizza or smell freshly baked bread? Taste and smell are intimately related to each other and to our nutrition and diet. In "The Importance of Taste," Beatrice Hunter reveals that some of us are super-tasters; that is, we are ultrasensitive to taste. Such individuals may have different nutritional and health statuses because of their ability to experience taste more intensely.

The final selection in this unit relates to an altered state of perception or consciousness, something outside of normal sensation and perception. Such altered states include extrasensory perception and dreaming. This last article is about dreaming, something we all do and something that fascinates most individuals. By studying sleep, especially dream or REM sleep, researchers are beginning to understand why we dream and why we don't remember all of our dreams. Scientists are also examining the effects of quality of sleep as well as quantity of sleep.

THE SENSES

They delight, heal, define the boundaries of our world. And they are helping unlock the brain's secrets

To the 19th-century French poet Charles Baudelaire, there was no such thing as a bad smell. What a squeamish, oversensitive bunch he would have deemed the denizens of 20th-century America, where body odors are taboo, strong aromas are immediately suppressed with air freshener, and perfume—long celebrated for its seductive and healing powers—is banned in some places to protect those with multiple chemical sensitivities.

Indeed, in the years since Baudelaire set pen to paper, civilization has played havoc with the natural state of all the human senses, technology providing the ability not only to tame and to mute but also to tease and overstimulate. Artificial fragrances and flavors trick the nose and tongue. Advertisers dazzle the eyes with rapid-fire images. Wailing sirens vie with the beeping of pagers to challenge the ears' ability to cope.

Yet even as we fiddle with the texture and scope of our sensibilities, science is indicating it might behoove us to show them a bit more respect. Growing evidence documents the surprising consequences of depriving or overwhelming the senses. And failing to nurture our natural capabilities, researchers are discovering, can affect health, emotions, even intelligence. Hearing, for example, is intimately connected to emotional circuits: When a nursing infant looks up from the breast, muscles in the middle ear reflexively tighten, readying the child for the pitch of a human voice. The touch of massage can relieve pain and improve concentration. And no matter how we spritz or scrub, every human body produces a natural odor as distinctive as the whorls on the fingertips—an aroma that research is showing to be a critical factor in choosing a sexual partner.

Beyond their capacity to heal and delight, the senses have also opened a window on the workings of the human brain. A flood of studies on smell, sight, hearing, touch and taste in the last two decades have upended most of the theories about how the brain functions. Scientists once believed, for example, that the brain was hard-wired at birth, the trillions of connections that made up its neural circuits genetically predetermined. But a huge proportion of neurons in a newborn infant's brain, it turns out, require input from the senses in order to hook up to one another properly.

Similarly, scientific theory until recently held that the sense organs did the lion's share of processing information about the world: The eye detected movement; the nose recognized smells. But researchers now know that ears, eyes and fingers are only way stations, transmitting signals that are then processed centrally. "The nose doesn't smell—the brain does," says Richard Axel, a molecular biologist at Columbia University. Each of our senses shatters experience into fragments, parsing the world like so many nouns and verbs, then leaving the brain to put the pieces back together and make sense of it all.

In labs across the country, researchers are drafting a picture of the senses that promises not only to unravel the mysterious tangle of nerves in the brain but also to offer reasons to revel in sensuous experience. Cradling a baby not only feels marvelous, scientists are finding, but is absolutely vital to a newborn's emotional and cognitive development. And the results of this research are beginning to translate into practical help for people whose senses are impaired: Researchers in Boston last year unveiled a tiny electronic device called a retinal chip that one day may restore sight to people blinded after childhood. Gradually, this new science of the senses is redefining what it means to be a feeling and thinking human being. One day it may lead to an understanding of consciousness itself.

SIGHT

Seeing is believing, because vision is the body's top intelligence gatherer, at least by the brain's reckoning. A full quarter of

SIGHT

Cells in the retina of the eye are so sensitive they can respond to a single photon, or particle of light.

the cerebral cortex, the brain's crinkled top layer, is devoted to sight, according to a new estimate by neuroscientist David Van Essen of Washington University in St. Louis—almost certainly more than is devoted to any other sense.

It seems fitting, then, that vision has offered scientists their most powerful insights on the brain's structure and operations. Research on sight "has been absolutely fundamental" for understanding the brain, says neurobiologist Semir Zeki of University College in London, in part because the visual system is easier to study than the other senses. The first clues to the workings of the visual system emerged in the 1950s, when Johns Hopkins neurobiologists David Hubel and Torsten Wiesel conducted a series of Nobel Prize–winning experiments. Using hair-thin electrodes implanted in a cat's brain, they recorded the firing of single neurons in the area where vision is processed. When the animal was looking at a diagonal bar of light, one neuron fired. When the bar was at a slightly different angle, a different nerve cell responded.

Hubel and Wiesel's discovery led to a revolutionary idea: While we are perceiving a unified scene, the brain is dissecting the view into many parts, each of which triggers a different set of neurons, called a visual map. One map responds to color and form, another only to motion. There are at least five such maps in the visual system alone, and recent work is showing that other senses are similarly encoded in the brain. In an auditory map, for example, the two sets of neurons that respond to two similar sounds, such as "go" and "ko," are located near each other, while those resonating with the sound "mo" lie at a distance.

Though we think of sensory abilities as independent, researchers are finding that each sense receives help from the others in apprehending the world. In 1995, psycholinguist Michael Tanenhaus of the University of Rochester videotaped people as they listened to sentences about nearby objects. As they listened, the subjects' eyes flicked to the objects. Those movements—so fast the subjects did not realize they'd shifted their gaze—helped them under-

stand the grammar of the sentences, Tanenhaus found. Obviously, vision isn't required to comprehend grammar. But given the chance, the brain integrates visual cues while processing language.

The brain also does much of the heavy lifting for color vision, so much so that some people with brain damage see the world in shades of gray. But the ability to see colors begins with cells in the back of the eyeball called cones. For decades, scientists thought everyone with normal color vision had the same three types of cone cell—for red, green and blue light—and saw the same hues. New research shows, however, that everybody sees a different palette. Last year, Medical College of Wisconsin researchers Maureen Neitz and her husband, Jay, discovered that people have up to nine genes for cones, indicating there may be many kinds of cones. Already, two red cone subtypes have been found. People with one type see red differently from those with the second. Says Maureen Neitz: "That's why people argue about adjusting the color on the TV set."

HEARING

Hearing is the gateway to language, a uniquely human skill. In a normal child, the ears tune themselves to human sounds soon after birth, cementing the neural connections between language, emotions and intelligence. Even a tiny glitch in the way a child processes sound can unhinge development.

About 7 million American children who have normal hearing and intelligence develop intractable problems with language, reading and writing because they cannot decipher certain parcels of language. Research by Paula Tallal, a Rutgers University neurobiologist, has shown that children with language learning disabilities (LLD) fail to distinguish between the "plosive" consonants, such as b, t and p. To them, "bug" sounds like "tug" sounds like "pug." The problem, Tallal has long argued, is that for such kids the sounds come too fast. Vowels resonate for 100 milliseconds or more, but

HEARING

At six months, a baby's brain tunes in to the sounds of its native tongue and tunes out other languages.

plosive consonants last for a mere 40 milliseconds—not long enough for some children to process them. "These children hear the sound. It just isn't transmitted to the brain normally," she says.

Two years ago, Tallal teamed up with Michael Merzenich, a neurobiologist at the University of California–San Francisco, to create a set of computer games that have produced stunning gains in 29 children with LLD. With William Jenkins and Steve Miller, the neurobiologists wrote computer programs that elongated the plosive consonants, making them louder—"like making a yellow highlighter for the brain," says Tallal. After a month of daily three-hour sessions, children who were one to three years behind their peers in language and reading had leaped forward a full two years. The researchers have formed a company, Scientific Learning Corp., that could make their system available to teachers and professionals within a few years. (See their Web site: *http://www.scilearn.com* or call 415-296-1470.)

An inability to hear the sounds of human speech properly also may contribute to autism, a disorder that leaves children unable to relate emotionally to other people. According to University of Maryland psychophysiologist Stephen Porges, many autistic children are listening not to the sounds of human speech but instead to frightening noises. He blames the children's fear on a section of the nervous system that controls facial expressions, speech, visceral feelings and the muscles in the middle ear.

These muscles, the tiniest in the body, allow the ear to filter sounds, much the way muscles in the eye focus the eyeball on near or distant objects. In autistic children, the neural system that includes the middle ear is lazy. As a result, these children attend not to the pitch of the human voice but instead to sounds that are much lower: the rumble of traffic, the growl of a vacuum cleaner. In the deep evolutionary past, such noises signaled danger. Porges contends that autistic children feel too anxious to interact emotionally, and the neural system controlling many emotional responses fails to develop.

Porges says that exercising the neural system may help autistic kids gain language and emotional skills. He and his colleagues have begun an experimental treatment consisting of tones and songs altered by computer to filter out low sounds, forcing the middle ear to focus on the pitches of human speech. After five 90-minute sessions, most of the 16 children have made strides that surprised even Porges. Third grader Tomlin Clark, for example, who once spoke only rarely, recently delighted his parents by getting in trouble for talking out of turn in school. And for the first time, he shows a sense of humor. "Listening to sounds seems so simple, doesn't it?" says Porges. "But so does jogging."

TOUCH

The skin, writes pathologist Marc Lappé, "is both literally and metaphorically 'the body's edge' . . . a boundary against an inimical world." Yet the skin also is the organ that speaks the language of love most clearly—and not just in the erogenous zones. The caress of another person releases hormones that can ease pain and clear the mind. Deprive a child of touch, and his brain and body will stop growing.

This new view of the most intimate sense was sparked a decade ago, when child psychologist Tiffany Field showed that premature infants who were massaged for 15 minutes three times a day gained weight 47 percent faster than preemies given standard intensive care nursery treatment: as little touching as possible. The preemies who were massaged weren't eating more; they just processed food more efficiently, says

TOUCH

People with "synesthesia" feel colors, see sounds and taste shapes.

Field, now director of the University of Miami's Touch Research Institute. Field found that massaged preemies were more alert and aware of their surroundings when awake, while their sleep was deeper and more restorative. Eight months later, the massaged infants scored better on mental and motor tests.

SIXTH SENSES
Wish you had that nose?

Folklore abounds with tales of animals possessing exceptional sensory powers, from pigs predicting earthquakes to pets telepathically anticipating their owners' arrival home. In some cases, myth and reality are not so far apart. Nature is full of creatures with superhuman senses: built-in compasses, highly accurate sonar, infrared vision. "Our worldview is limited by our senses," says Dartmouth College psychologist Howard Hughes, "so we are both reluctant to believe that animals can have capabilities beyond ours, and we attribute to them supernatural powers. The truth is somewhere between the two."

In the case of Watson, a Labrador retriever, reality is more impressive than any fiction. For over a year, Watson has reliably pawed his owner, Emily Ramsey, 45 minutes before her epileptic seizures begin, giving her time to move to a safe place. Placed by Canine Partners for Life, Watson has a 97 percent success rate, according to the Ramsey family. No one has formally studied how such dogs can predict seizure onset consistently. But they may smell the chemical changes known to precede epileptic attacks. "Whatever it is," says Harvard University neurologist Steven Schachter, "I think there's something to it."

Scientists have scrutinized other animals for decades, trying to decipher their sensory secrets. Birds, bees, moles and some 80 other creatures are known to sense magnetic fields. But new studies indicate birds have two magnetic detection systems: One seems to translate polarized light into visual patterns that act as a compass; the other is an internal magnet birds use to further orient themselves.

Dolphin sonar so intrigued government researchers that they launched the U.S. Navy marine Mammal Program in 1960, hoping it would lead to more-sophisticated tracking equipment. But the animals still beat the machines, says spokesman Tom LaPuzza. In a murky sea, dolphins can pinpoint a softball two football fields away. A lobe in their forehead focuses their biosonar as a flashlight channels light, beaming 200-decibel clicks.

It took night-vision goggles for humans to replicate the infrared vision snakes come by naturally: A cameralike device in organs lining their lips lets them see heat patterns made by mammals. And humans can only envy the ability of sharks, skates and rays to feel electric fields through pores in their snouts—perhaps a primordial skill used by Earth's earliest creatures to scout out the new world.

BY ANNA MULRINE

SMELL

A woman's sense of smell is keener than a man's. And smell plays a larger role in sexual attraction for women.

Being touched has healing powers throughout life. Massage, researchers have found, can ease the pain of severely burned children and boost the immune systems of AIDS patients. Field recently showed that office workers who received a 15-minute massage began emitting higher levels of brain waves associated with alertness. After their massage, the workers executed a math test in half their previous time with half the errors.

While such findings may sound touchy-feely, an increasing volume of physiological evidence backs them up. In a recent series of experiments, Swedish physiologist Kerstin Uvnas-Moberg found that gentle stroking can stimulate the body to release oxytocin, sometimes called the love hormone because it helps cement the bond between mothers and their young in many species. "There are deep, deep, physiological connections between touching and love," Uvnas-Moberg says. Oxytocin also blunts pain and dampens the hormones release when a person feels anxious or stressed.

For the babies of any species, touch signals that mother—the source of food, warmth and safety—is near. When she is gone, many young animals show physiological signs of stress and shut down their metabolism—an innate response designed to conserve energy until she returns. Without mother, rat pups do not grow, says Saul Schanberg, a Duke University pharmacologist, even when they are fed and kept warm. Stroking them with a brush in a manner that mimics their mother licking them restores the pups to robust health. "You need the right kind of touch in order to grow," says Schanberg, "even more than vitamins."

SMELL

Long ago in human evolution, smell played a prominent role, signaling who was ready to mate and who ready to fight. But after a while, smell fell into disrepute. Aristotle disparaged it as the most animalistic of the senses, and Immanuel Kant dreamed of losing it. Recent research has restored the nose to some of its former glory. "Odor plays a far more important role in human behavior and physiology than we realize," says Gary Beauchamp, director of Philadelphia's Monell Chemical Senses Center.

A baby recognizes its mother by her odor soon after birth, and studies show that adults can identify clothing worn by their children or spouses by smell alone. In 1995, Beauchamp and colleagues at Monell reported that a woman's scent—genetically determined—changes in pregnancy to reflect a combination of her odor and that of her fetus.

The sense of smell's most celebrated capacity is its power to stir memory. "Hit a tripwire of smell, and memories explode all at once," writes poet Diane Ackerman. The reason, says Monell psychologist Rachel Herz, is that "smells carry an emotional quality." In her latest experiment, Herz showed people a series of evocative paintings. At the same time, the subjects were exposed to another sensory cue—an orange, for example—in different ways. Some saw an orange. Others were given an orange to touch, heard the word "orange" or smelled the fruit. Two days later, when subjects were given the same cue and were asked to recall the painting that matched it, those exposed to the smell of the orange recalled the painting and produced a flood of emotional responses to it.

Herz and others suspect that an aroma's capacity to spark such vivid remembrances arises out of anatomy. An odor's first way station in the brain is the olfactory bulb, two blueberry-sized lumps of cortex from which neurons extend through the skull into the nose. Smell molecules, those wafting off a cinnamon bun, for example, bind to these olfactory neurons, which fire off their signals first to the olfactory bulb and then to the limbic system—the seat of sexual drive, emotions and memory. Connections between the olfactory bulb and the neocortex, or thinking part of the brain, are secondary roads compared to the highways leading to emotional centers.

Scientists once thought all smells were made up of combinations of seven basic odors. But in an elegant series of experiments, research teams led by Columbia's Axel and Linda Buck of Harvard have shown the mechanics of smell to be much more complicated. In 1991, the scientists discovered a family of at least 1,000 genes corresponding to about 1,000 types of olfactory neurons in the nose. Each of these neuronal types responds to one—and only one—type of odor molecule.

The average person, of course, can detect far more than 1,000 odors. That's because a single scent is made up of more than one type of molecule, perhaps even dozens. A rose might stimulate neurons A, B and C, while jasmine sets off neurons B, C and F. "Theoretically, we can detect an astronomical number of smells." says Axel—the

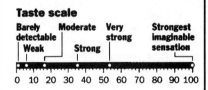
equivalent of 10 to the 23rd power. The brain, however, doesn't have the space to keep track of all those possible combinations of molecules, and so it focuses on smells that were relevant in evolution, like the scent of ripe fruit or a sexually receptive mate—about 10,000 odors in all.

Axel and Buck have now discovered that the olfactory bulb contains a "map," similar to those the brain employs for vision and hearing. By implanting a gene into mice, the researchers dyed blue the nerves leading

TASTE

Human beings are genetically hard-wired to crave sweetness; sugar on the lips of a newborn baby will bring a smile.

from the animals' olfactory bulbs to their noses. Tracing the path of these neurons, the researchers discovered that those responsible for detecting a single type of odor molecule all led back to a single point in the olfactory bulb. In other words, the jumble of neurons that exists in the nose is reduced to regimental order in the brain.

Smell maps may one day help anosmics, people who cannot smell. Susan Killorn of Richmond, Va., lost her sense of smell three years ago when she landed on her head while in-line skating and damaged the nerves leading from her nose to her brain. A gourmet cook, Killorn was devastated. "I can remember sitting at the dinner table and begging my husband to describe the meal I'd just cooked," she says. Killorn's ability to detect odors has gradually returned, but nothing smells quite right. One possibility, says Richard Costanzo, a neurophysiologist at Virginia Commonwealth University, is that some of the nerves from her nose have recovered or regenerated but now are hooked up to the wrong spot in her smell map.

Though imperfect, recoveries like Killorn's give researchers hope they may one day be able to stimulate other neurons to regenerate—after a spinal cord injury, for example. Costanzo and others are searching for chemicals made by the body that can act as traffic cops, telling neurons exactly where to grow. In the meantime, Killorn is grateful for every morsel of odor. "I dream at night about onions and garlic," she says, "and they smell like they are supposed to."

TASTE

Human beings will put almost anything into their mouths and consider it food, from stinging nettles to grubs. Fortunately, evolution armed the human tongue with a

set of sensors to keep venturesome members of the species from dying of malnutrition or poison. The four simple flavors—sweet, salty, bitter and sour—tell human beings what's healthy and what's harmful. But as researchers are finding, the sense of taste does far more than keep us from killing ourselves. Each person tastes food differently, a genetically determined sensitivity that can affect diet, weight and health.

In a quest for novelty, people around the world have developed an affinity for foods that cause a modicum of pain. "Humans have the ability to say, 'Oh, that didn't really hurt me—let me try it again,'" says Barry Green, a psychologist at the John B. Pierce Laboratory in New Haven, Conn. Spicy food, Green has found, gives the impression of being painfully hot by stimulating the nerves in the mouth that sense temperature extremes. The bubbles in soda and champagne feel as if they are popping inside the mouth; in reality, carbon dioxide inside the bubbles irritates nerves that sense pain.

One person's spicy meatball, however, is another's bland and tasteless meal. Researchers have long known that certain people have an inherited inability to taste a mildly bitter substance with a tongue-twisting name: propylthiouracil, or PROP, for short. About a quarter of Caucasians are "nontasters," utterly insensitive to PROP, while the vast majority of Asians and Africans can taste it. Now, researchers at Yale University led by psychologist Linda Bartoshuk have discovered a third group of people called "supertasters." So sensitive are supertasters' tongues that they gag on PROP and can detect the merest hint of other bitter compounds in a host of foods, from chocolate and saccharin to vegetables such as broccoli, "which could explain why George Bush hates it," Bartoshuk says. She has recently discovered that supertasters have twice as many taste buds as nontasters and more of the nerve endings that detect the feel of foods. As a consequence, sweets taste sweeter to supertasters, and cream feels creamier. A spicy dish can send a supertaster through the roof.

In an ongoing study, Bartoshuk's group has found that older women who are nontasters tend to prefer sweets and fatty foods—dishes that some of the supertasters find cloying. Not surprisingly, supertasters also tend to be thinner and have lower cholesterol. In their study, the researchers ask subjects to taste cream mixed with oil, a combination Bartoshuk confesses she finds delicious. "I'm a nontaster, and I'm heavy," she says. "I gobble up the test." But tasting ability is not only a matter of cuisine preference and body weight. Monell's Marcia

RESULTS OF TASTE TEST ON PREVIOUS PAGE		
	SUPER-TASTERS	NON-TASTERS
No. of taste buds	25 on average	10
Sweet rating	56 on average	32
Tabasco rating	64 on average	31

Average tasters lie in between. Bartoshuk and Lucchina lack the data to rate salt.

Pelchat and a graduate student recently completed a study indicating that nontasters also may be predisposed to alcoholism.

The human senses detect only a fraction of reality: We can't see the ultraviolet markers that guide a honeybee to nectar; we can't hear most of the noises emitted by a dolphin. In this way, the senses define the boundaries of mental awareness. But the brain also defines the limits of what we perceive. Human beings see, feel, taste, touch and smell not the world around them but a version of the world, one their brains have concocted. "People imagine that they're seeing what's really there, but they're not," says neuroscientist John Maunsell of Baylor College of Medicine in Houston. The eyes take in the light reflecting off objects around us, but the brain only pays attention to part of the scene. Looking for a pen on a messy desk, for example, you can scan the surface without noticing the papers scattered across it.

The word "sentience" derives from the Latin verb *sentire,* meaning "to feel." And research on the senses, especially the discovery of sensory mapping, has taken scientists one step further in understanding the state we call consciousness. Yet even this dramatic advance is only a beginning. "In a way, these sexy maps have seduced us," says Michael Shipley, director of neurosciences at the University of Maryland–Baltimore. "We still haven't answered the question of how do you go from visual maps to recognizing faces, or from an auditory map to recognizing a Mozart sonata played by two different pianists." The challenge for the 21st century will be figuring out how the brain, once it has broken the sensory landscape into pieces, puts them together again.

BY SHANNON BROWNLEE
WITH TRACI WATSON

Deaf defying

Geneticists and physiologists are disentangling the causes of deafness and beginning to glimpse ways of doing something about it

HAIR cells are tiny—about fifteen-thousandths of a millimetre long. If you are lucky, they are also abundant. An average human ear contains some 16,000 of them scattered over the surface of a snail-shaped organ called the cochlea. But if you are unlucky, and that number is reduced, you will be partly or completely deaf. And there are many ways to destroy a hair cell.

Some of these ways are genetic. So far, more than a dozen genes that affect hearing when they fail to work have been identified. Almost all of these failing genes have been found to induce deafness by reducing the number or the effectiveness of the hair cells rather than, say, damaging the auditory nerve that runs from the ear to the brain. Hair cells can also be damaged by environmental factors: they react badly to excessive pressure and can thus be destroyed by loud noises. And sometimes deafness is just the result of *anno domini*: as people age, their hair cells tend to wither away. Unfortunately—and this is the key point—once a hair cell is gone, it is gone for ever.

For years, therefore, the only remedy for deafness has been an artificial hearing aid of one sort or another. But now a small group of researchers is addressing the problem of deafness directly. These people are trying to understand the different ways in which hair cells may go wrong and, if their wildest dreams come true, to work out how to stimulate the growth of new and healthy ones to replace those that no longer work, or have never worked properly in the first place.

Hair today, gone tomorrow

Hair cells are delicate beasts. They seem to react to biochemical difficulties that other cells shrug off without even noticing. For example, Eric Lynch of the University of Washington, in Seattle, and Pedro Leon of the University of Costa Rica, in San Jose, recently showed that malfunctions of a gene known as *diaphanous*—after its effects on the wings of fruit flies, the species in which it was first identified—also cause deafness in people.

Diaphanous has a role in the assembly of a protein called actin. But actin is a ubiquitous molecule. It helps to form cytoskeletons—the networks of proteinaceous filaments that give shape and stiffness to almost all cells. And, though it comes in various forms, not all of which are affected by a malfunction of the *diaphanous* gene, the form that is affected exists in brains, hearts, lungs and kidneys. A malfunctioning *diaphanous* gene might therefore be expected to cause all sorts of difficulties in these organs, but it does not. The tissues involved scarcely seem to notice the loss.

Mutations affecting the production of actin's cytoskeletal partner, myosin, also cause deafness—as Karen Steel at Britain's Institute of Hearing Research in Nottingham has demonstrated. Cytoskeletal filaments are usually composed of both actin and myosin, and tension within them is adjusted by the two proteins sliding past each other. This suggests that the correct degree of stiffness is critical to a hair cell's function—which is not surprising as its job is to detect vibrations. (When correctly stimulated, hair cells give out small electrical impulses which are carried to the brain by the auditory nerve.) Perhaps that is why minor genetic malfunctions of the cytoskeletal elements are so significant: if a cell has the wrong tension it will not respond correctly to sound waves.

Hair cells, then, are highly specialised and very sensitive structures. And, in mammals, cells that are this highly differentiated (nerve and muscle cells, for instance) are usually created in the womb and expected to last a lifetime. They do not naturally regenerate themselves.

The idea that hair cells might be artificially stimulated to regenerate was first conceived by Jeffrey Corwin. Dr Corwin now works at the University of Virginia, Charlottesville, but he once did a stint at the University of Hawaii in Honolulu studying the local sharks. There, he discovered that the ears of adult sharks have hundreds of thousands more hair cells than do those of juveniles. Sharks, it turns out, continue to produce hair cells throughout their lives.

Dr Corwin's discovery in sharks led him to wonder if hair-cell regeneration was possible in species more closely related to humanity. A couple of years ago Douglas Cotanche, one of Dr Corwin's collaborators who now works at Boston University, found that it was.

Dr Cotanche decided to look at birds instead of fish. He found that if the hair cells of chickens are killed with gentamicin (one of several antibiotics that can also have this effect in people) or by exposing them to punishingly loud noise, new cells form from the so-called supporting cells of the cochlea. These supporting cells, as their name suggests, surround and support hair cells, giving them extra rigidity and helping them do their job.

Dr Cotanche's finding is now being followed up elsewhere. Last year, for example, Carl Oberholtzer and his colleagues at the University of Pennsylvania, in Philadelphia, reported that the supporting cells of healthy chicken cochleas (ie, ones with full complements of hair cells) can be induced to divide and grow into hair cells by treating them with forskolin—a chemical used in the laboratory to boost levels of a substance called cyclic AMP.

This is an exciting discovery. It is not particularly surprising that cyclic AMP causes supporting cells to divide, because it is a signalling molecule that helps to control the "cell cycle" (the series of events which takes place when one cell becomes two). That the result of such a division is two hair cells is, however, surprising. Although Dr. Cotanche's work showed that supporting cells have the potential to divide into hair cells, some extra external trigger resulting from an insufficiency of existing hair cells might have been expected to be part of the process.

Dr Oberholtzer's study suggests this is not the case. The relevant molecular switches already seem to have been thrown, and the supporting cells,

at least in chickens, are thus primed to go down the hair-cell path when they receive the signal to divide.

What those molecular switches are, and how they might be thrown in mammals, is the subject of yet another piece of research, this time on America's other coast. In their laboratory at the University of California, San Diego, Linda Erkman, Allen Ryan and Michael Rosenfeld have created a colony of mice that lack a gene known as *Brn-3.1*. This gene carries the blueprint for a transcription factor—a protein that switches other genes into life. Without this transcription factor mouse embryos fail to develop hair cells in the first place.

Though Dr Ryan and his colleagues have only just begun to explore which genes are switched on by the newly discovered transcription factor, there is a reasonable chance that they will turn out to be the collective elixir of

biochemical life for hair cells. Indeed, Dr Ryan suspects that almost all of the genes which, when they fail to work properly, cause deafness (such as those discovered by Drs Lynch, Leon and Steel) will turn out to be under the conductor's baton wielded by *Brn-3.1*. A preliminary comparison of the genes active in hair cells and those active in the surrounding supporting cells suggests that the distinctions between the two are the consequence of *Brn-3.1*'s activities.

What can be made of such knowledge remains to be seen. It may be that switching on the *Brn-3.1* gene in supporting cells will be enough to persuade them to differentiate into hair cells. Or a drug that mimics the effect of the transcription factor might be developed. But it looks as though Dr Ryan and his team may have hit on the key to the problem. The days of the hearing aid may be numbered.

The importance of *taste*

Beatrice Trum Hunter

Are you a non-taster? A medium taster? Or a super-taster? Your classification may have relevance to your nutritional status and health.

Scientists at Yale University are investigating the genetic variation in individual tasting ability. They devised a taste test, using a bitter substance, PROP (6-n-propylthiouracil) to investigate the relationships between taste and nutrition. A dye, applied to the tongue, can make taste-bud pores visible and countable. It was found that non-tasters have few taste buds; medium tasters have more; and super-tasters have many.

Super-tasters perceive tastes more intensely. For example, bitter-flavored substances such as caffeine, quinine, and alcohol taste more bitter to them than to other people. Sweet-flavored substances such as sugar and saccharin taste sweeter, and the oral burning sensation from capsaicin (the active ingredient in chili peppers) inflicts greater pain intensity.

Gender may play a role. Research shows that females are more likely to be super-tasters than males. The liking for sweets by prepubertal girls and post-menopausal women is thought to be related to their ability to taste PROP. Those who find PROP to be the most bitter have the most taste buds and like sweets the most. However, this liking for sweets may reverse for women in their childbearing years. Those who taste PROP as the most bitter dislike sweets the most during these years. A burning mouth syndrome, experienced by postmenopausal women, is thought to be a mechanism of the interaction of taste and trigeminal nerves (cranial nerves having sensory and motor functions in the face, teeth, mouth, and nasal cavity).

Taste components such as PROP receptors may be estrogen-sensitive, and decline after menopause when estrogen declines. Currently, researchers are examining variations in taste ability, and the number of taste buds related to variations in sex hormones. Also, drugs, hormone levels, and other physiological factors related to taste can influence nutritional intake significantly, and can complicate pharmaceutical treatment.

Super-tasters may avoid nutritious vegetables and fruits that contain bitter principles. In a recent study, Adam Drewnowski, Ph.D. at the University of Michigan at Ann Arbor, noted that "the bitter taste of many vegetables and fruit is aversive to some consumers, particularly children." Low acceptance of bitter cruciferous vegetables such as Brussels spouts, and bitter fruit such as grapefruit (which is rich in PROP), may prevent some people from following diets consistent with the recommended dietary guidelines. Studies show that only 9% to 32% of Americans consume fruits and vegetables regularly. Drewnowski found that 40% of the women he tested could taste PROP, and 28% of them were super-tasters.

Zinc deficiency has been associated with a loss of taste, termed hypogeusia. Zinc deficiency is common in America, regardless of economic level. Contributing factors include the common practice of refining grains and stripping them of zinc and other nutrients. The decline in consumption of red meats, a reliable source of zinc, may be another factor.

As people age, the senses of taste and smell usually decline. More than three-quarters of Americans over 80 years of age have significant taste and smell impairment, according to Susan Schiffman, a psychologist at Duke University. Reduced sensory perceptions may result in decreased eating pleasure, accidental poisoning, poor eating habits, and malnutrition. In turn, malnutrition impairs taste bud reproduction, which intensifies the problems of impaired sense of taste and smell. Poor eating habits also can reduce levels of important immune system components such as T-cells and B-cells. At present, no treatment exists to restore lost taste and smell perceptions.

Scientists at the Hershey Medical Center at Pennsylvania State University found that elderly women who had a good ability to taste PROP had a low risk for cardiovascular diseases.

During the past decade, progress has been made in understanding the nature of changes that occur in the sense of taste as people age. Formerly, it was difficult to establish a connection between taste and nutrition because of the presence of taste disorders. The sense of taste can be altered temporarily by common medical problems such as colds, ear infections, or mild head injuries. The sense of taste can be impaired, too, by grave conditions such as cancer.

Taste plays an important role in regulating our food and beverage consumption. Any deficit of the four basic *taste* perceptions of sweet, sour, bitter, and salty, can lead to serious problems by affecting our desire to consume certain nutrients. For example, an impaired ability to taste saltiness may lead to a habit of oversalting food. Excessive sodium craving has been related to certain diseases or disorders, including obesity, head trauma, diabetes, and cancer.

The relationship of taste to nutritional status and health is being researched by funds from the National Institute on Deafness and Other Communication Disorders (NIDCD). This institute conducts and supports biomedical and behavioral research on normal and disordered processes of hearing, balance, smell, taste, voice, speech, and language that affect some 46 million Americans. The NIDCD supports efforts to create devices that substitute for lost or impaired sensory and communication functions. Also, it conducts and supports research related to disease prevention through a wide range of research performed in its own laboratories, as well as research grants to individuals and institutions. Some of the research described in this article has been conducted with NIDCD funding. The research on taste and its relationship to nutrition provides new understandings of the factors that can influence nutritional intake, and how it can complicate clinical treatment of health problems.

Night Life

Dreams are our built-in entertainment as well as a porthole to the inner workings of our minds. New findings show they are a form of creative insanity than the brain uses for everything from mood regulation to learning, memory—maybe even messages from beyond.

by Jill Neimark

Ten years ago, in New Mexico, I had a startling dream. I'd made an appointment by phone to see an acupuncturist, and the night before my visit, I dreamed about him. "Listen," my dream-self said, "I'm still adjusting to the altitude here and need an unusually gentle treatment, or I'll get sick."

When I walked into his office the next day, he was exactly the man of my dream, down to each fine detail of his wavy brown hair and boyish face. I told him so, and he replied that he believed in precognition. He gave me a gentle treatment.

That dream was a small anomaly, but one that ripped opened my perspective: if in a dream I could know what someone looked like before I actually met him, then the dreaming mind is capable of spectacular range. That is the only precognitive dream I've ever had, but, like most of us, I've found my dreams to be deep and shallow, beautiful, nutty, mysterious, chaotic, and sometimes meaningful enough to trigger big life decisions.

From the Australian aborigines, who believe that the dreaming and waking worlds are equally real, to Freud, who felt dreams were a braid of repressed wishes; from Jung, who saw dreams as stories dipped in our collective unconscious, to Nobel-prize-winning scientist Francis Crick, who has suggested dreams are just the brain's way of forgetting, a sloughing-off of each day's meaningless events; from the cognitive neuroscientists who have discovered that dreams and REM sleep are linked to our ability to learn and remember, to those who believe dreaming is the meaningless and random sputtering of nerve cells, dreams are the sphinx-like riddle we keep trying to solve.

Robert Stickgold, Ph.D., a Harvard neuroscientist, has his own fascinating description: "The mind becomes clinically insane while dreaming." Stickgold says we're so comfortable with dreaming "that we don't realize how strange it is to lie in bed hallucinating patently impossible things without ever noticing that these things might be impossible."

"You're delusional and hyper-emotional and you might even suddenly wonder, 'Is this a dream?' but nine times out of ten you'll decide it's definitely real." Even stranger, Stickgold observes, is the fact that "for every person in the world, the same brain that works one way during the day shifts into a completely different mode at night."

According to Stickgold, dreams are proof that "the mechanism for producing insanity is present in all of us." The only questions are: "How do we throw that switch every night?" and "Why do we bother to do it at all?" He and others are now beginning to sketch out some intriguing answers.

Do we dream to forget? Or to remember? The answer seems to lie in the new findings about REM sleep and its unique biological function. First, however, let's shatter a myth. Dreams and rapid-eye-movement (REM) sleep are not one and the same. We dream throughout the night, sometimes while in deep sleep—the sleep marked by slow EEG waves, during which the body repairs itself, releasing growth hormone. REM sleep, in contrast, is a violently "awake" sleep; the muscles are at rest but the brain and nervous system are highly active.

The brain cycles through REM sleep about four to six times a night, each time marked by irregular breathing, increased heart rate and brain temperature, general physiological arousal, and, in men, erections. Arousal is such that ulcer sufferers secrete twenty times more stomach acid in REM than in non-REM sleep.

The first REM cycle follows ninety minutes of slow-wave deep sleep and lasts about ten minutes. REM cycles lengthen through the night and the dreams in them get more bizarre and detailed, like wacky movies. REM dreams tend to be uniformly more emotional and memorable than non-REM ones. One of the most interesting aspects of REM sleep is that, for its duration, we are paralyzed from the neck down, and our threshold for sensory input is raised, so that external stimuli rarely reach and wake us. The brain is soaked in acetylcholine, which seems to stimulate nerve cells while it strips muscles of tone and tension. At the same time, serotonin levels plummet. The changes are swift and global. It's as if during these cycles we are functioning with a different brain entirely.

Because we are literally paralyzed while we dream, we do not act out our nightly hallucinations. Otherwise, we might gesticulate, twitch, and actually stand up and play out our dreams. It's interesting that our eye muscles do not become paralyzed, and researchers have speculated that nature did not bother to develop a mechanism to paralyze our eye muscles simply because eye movement is a kind of gratuitous detail—it doesn't have much impact on the dreamer. Whatever the reason, REM has been a boon to dream researchers, since it's a clear indication that we've slipped into that particular phase of sleep.

As the biology of dreams is being pieced together, the theories of Freud have begun to seem more improbable. Dreams are likely *not* the eruptions of the repressed primal self, disguised in clever puzzles that only your psychoanalyst can decipher at $180 an hour. The first blow to this theory was dealt in 1977, when Harvard's J. Allan Hobson, Ph.D., proposed that dreams are a kind of narrative structure we impose on the random firing of neurons in the brainstem. The neocortex, our meaning-maker, creates stories out of this neuronal chaos—just as it does of waking life.

Those stories may indeed be clues to our inner selves. But when brains are scanned during dreaming, researchers find that the frontal lobes, which integrate information, are shut down, and the brain is driven by its emotional centers. Just last year, researchers Allen R. Braun, M.D., of the National Institutes of Health, and Thomas J. Balkin, M.D., of the Walter Reed Army Institute, scanned the brain in both slow-wave and REM sleep and found that during the latter, the visual cortex and frontal lobes were both shut down. That deals yet another blow to Freud: if dream content were being monitored, with unconscious wishes being actively repressed and disguised, the frontal lobes would have to be active.

What is the purpose of the neural chaos of dreaming? Scientists are still puzzling that out. In 1983, Nobelist Francis Crick, of the Salk Institute in La Jolla, suggested that the brain was actually "reverse learning," that REM sleep allows the neurons to spew out each day's spurious and extra stimuli, cleansing the brain. "We dream to forget," Crick wrote, to enormous outcry. In 1986, he revised the hypothesis, noting that perhaps we dream to reduce fantasy and obsession—that dreams are a way of forgetting material that might otherwise needlessly intrude on everyday life.

Then, in 1994, two researchers showed that our ability to learn seems dependent on REM sleep. Scientists Avi Karni and Dov Sagi, at Israel's Weitzman Institute, found that if someone is trained in a task and allowed a normal night's sleep, they will show improvement the next day. But if sleep is interrupted in each REM cycle, they show no improvement at all.

And the particular cycle of REM that gets interrupted is crucial. It's REM sleep in the last quarter of the night that counts. Bob Stickgold trained 57 individuals in a task and then tested them 3, 6, 9, or 12 hours later the same day, or overnight after an interval of 13, 16, or 22 hours. The task involved visual discrimination: a subject looks for diagonal lines against a background of horizontal lines.

The time interval had no influence on performance; the amount of sleep did. "If they had less than six hours of sleep, they did not improve," says Stickgold.

One might simply conclude that people need a lot of sleep in order to learn. The truth seems to be: they need certain cycles of sleep, and when awakened before their last REM cycle, the brain is unable to consolidate the memory of the task. But Stickgold and his colleagues found that more than REM cycles were at stake.

"A student of mine did another experiment and found that the amount of slow-wave sleep in the first two hours of the night is highly correlated with the amount of learning as well." How might the two sleep cycles— REM and deep slow-wave sleep—work together? There may be a two-step process of memory enhancement. "We know that levels of acetylcholine are high in REM sleep and low in slow-wave sleep. Perhaps as you cycle from one to the other, you're passing information back and forth between different parts of the brain. It's as if the brain is holding a conversation with itself and identifying exactly what it needs to know."

Stickgold thinks REM sleep may have yet another purpose: to actually alter intrusive experiences and memories from the day. "I was putting my son, who is ten, to bed after a day of skiing together. We were lying there with our eyes closed and I said, 'I feel I'm back on the ski slope.' He said, 'Really? I'm on the ski lift.'" There's a tendency to have an intrusive replay of novel experiences when you go to sleep, says Stickgold, especially ones that involve the vestibular system of the brain, which plays a role in balance. "If I fall asleep, go through one REM cycle, and wake two hours later, the feeling is gone. I can't reproduce it. Something has happened to that memory in those two hours."

Stickgold is looking at this effect in people who play the computer game Tetris, which requires rotating small blocks that float down the screen. "More than one person has told me that the day they first got hooked on the game, they went to bed, closed their eyes, and could see these blocks floating. It's gone the next day. Something in your brain in that first two hours has taken a memory that at sleep onset is incredibly intrusive and altered it so that it no longer behaves that way."

Rosalind Cartwright, Ph.D., the doyenne of dream research, has also found that sleep softens intrusive experiences, especially depressing feelings and moods. Director of the sleep disorders service and head of psychology at Chicago's Rush Presbyterian-St. Luke's Medical Center, she has evidence that dreams help regulate and stabilize mood, defusing negative feelings.

· By observing sixty normal and seventy clinically depressed adults, Cartwright found that among those who had a mildly unpleasant day or experience, dreams were negative at the beginning of the night and became pleasant by the end. Among the clinically depressed, dreams were bland at the beginning

and negative by night's end. "Normal individuals wake up in a better mood after a depressing day," she says. "Depressed individuals wake up feeling worse."

Cartwright adds a coda. "I'll tell you the kicker: a few of the depressed people showed the opposite pattern. Their dreams got more positive across the night. And those were the ones who got over their depression. You could predict it from a single night of dreaming."

Dreams, Cartwright believes, are our "internal therapist"; they offer an emotional information processing system. When that therapist isn't functioning—if, for example, you suffer from post-traumatic stress disorder manifested by recurrent nightmares—you may actually be able to lend it some help. Recently, researchers in Canada have found that consciously changing your dream in any direction while awake may stop the recurrence.

Tony Zadra, Ph.D., of the Dream and Nightmare Laboratory at the University of Montreal, studied six cases of recurrent nightmares—"and all got better," he says. The technique? While awake, the dreamers were taken on a guided visualization into the nightmare, and, at an emotional moment in the dream, were asked to visualize a simple task, such as looking at their hands. Then they were asked to respond differently—say, confront an aggressor or otherwise create a positive outcome.

After rehearsing the new ending while awake, the dreamers go to sleep as usual. And then an interesting thing happens: "Some people actually remember to look at their hands at the right moment, and then become aware that they are dreaming and that they can consciously carry out their dream differently. Others don't remember to look at their hands, but they dream the new dream they created while awake."

Either way, the nightmares stop. Says Zadra: "Some studies show that you can change absolutely anything in the nightmare, rehearse that change, and the nightmare will get better." It's the change that counts—it dismantles the dream and pries loose its hold on the dreamer.

It seems that dreams are many-purposed. They invite us into the truly interesting frontier of the mind. That may be why Stickgold says, "I love dreaming. And I love dreams."

Unit Selections

Key Points to Consider

❖ What is learning? What is memory? How are the two linked? Are they necessarily always linked to each other?

❖ Can fetuses learn? If yes, what is it that they learn? By what mechanisms would unborn children learn? Is this type of learning important? Do you think the types of learning they do are different from the learning older children experience?

❖ What is operant conditioning? What principles of learning have we gleaned from the study of operant conditioning and other forms of simple learning? What is reinforcement? What is punishment? Why is it better to reinforce than punish behaviors? How can operant principles be practiced or put into effect in everyday life?

❖ Why is memory important? What is forgetting? Why do psychologists want to know about mechanisms that underlie learning and remembering? To what use can we put this information? Do we learn and remember like a computer does? Why do we forget? What methods can we use to improve memory? Can you give an example of each?

❖ What types of memory lapses are normal? What memory lapses signal problems? How do memory lapses normally unfold with age? What is Alzheimer's disease? What other disorders besides Alzheimer's can cripple memory? Do people remember things that did not happen? Why is this problematic? Is memory distorted by the emotional tone of the event? Does trauma distort our memory; if so, how?

 **Links**   **www.dushkin.com/online/**

These sites are annotated on pages 4 and 5.

Do you remember your first week of classes at college? There were so many new buildings to recognize and people's names to remember. And you had to recall accurately where all your classes were as well as your professors' names. Just remembering your class schedule was problematic enough. For those of you who lived in residence halls, the difficulties multiplied. You had to remember where your residence was, recall the names of individuals living on your floor, and learn how to navigate from your room to other places on campus, such as the dining halls and library. Then came examination time. Did you ever think you would survive college exams? The material in terms of difficulty level and amount was perhaps more than you thought you could manage.

What a stressful time you experienced when you first came to campus! Much of what created the stress was the strain on your learning and memory systems, two complicated processes. Still, most of you survived just fine and with your memories, learning strategies, and mental health intact.

The processes you depended on when beginning college were learning and memory, two of the processes studied the longest by psychologists. Today, with their sophisticated experimental techniques, psychologists have detected several types of memory processes and have discovered what makes learning more complete so that subsequent memory is more accurate. We also discovered that humans aren't the only organisms capable of these processes. All types of animals can learn, even an organism as simple as an earthworm or an amoeba.

Psychologists know, too, that rote learning and practice are not the only forms of learning. For instance, at this point in time in your introductory psychology class, you might be studying operant and classical conditioning, two simple but nonetheless important forms of learning of which both humans and simple organisms are capable. Both types of conditioning can occur without our awareness or active participation in them. The processes of learning and remembering (or its reciprocal, forgetting) are examined here in some detail.

The unit begins with a look at learning even before life begins. In "Learning Begins Even before Babies Are Born, Scientists Show," Beth Azar discovers that the fetus can indeed learn about sounds and flavors. Such learning comes from experiences of the mothers. Researchers have, with difficulty, discovered clever methods for studying fetal learning in utero.

The second article looks at simple learning—operant conditioning. In "What Constitutes

'Appropriate' Punishment?" Paul DeVito and Ralph Hyatt examine reinforcement and punishment, whose principles derive from the study of operant conditioning. The authors conclude that because punishment is often used, it needs to be applied appropriately. They detail the conditions under which punishment is best used. They conclude that it is better for parents and teachers to reinforce prosocial behaviors than to continually punish negative behaviors.

While the first few articles pertain to learning in its various forms, the remaining articles relate to memory, the process triggered as an adjunct to learning. The next article, "Losing Your Mind," focuses on the opposite of remembering—forgetting. Memory lapses are common in everyone. This article helps differentiate normal lapses from more serious memory problems, one of the most severe of which is found in Alzheimer patients.

The article that follows is also about memory. Freud was one of the first psychologists to suggest that trauma alters (represses) our memory. In "Traumatic Memory Is Special," Lynn Nadel and Jake Jacobs review the scientific literature on the effects of trauma on memory. They find that traumatic events indeed are stored differently in memory than are other events.

Learning and Remembering

Learning begins even before babies are born, scientists show

The prenatal environment

The fetus learns to interpret sounds, flavors and vibrations, studies have found.

By Beth Azar
Monitor staff

The old metaphor of children as blocks of unmolded clay has lost its relevance over the decades. Research reveals not only that newborns have many genetically based preferences, but some of those preferences may also be the result of fetal learning.

Newborns remember certain aspects of their fetal environment, researchers argue. And research in animals and humans finds that the fetus is capable of rudimentary forms of learning.

This is not to say that parents should start trying to teach their children prenatally, say researchers. Rather, it confirms the importance of prenatal care during a time when the human fetus is developing not only physically but also cognitively. The research may also provide clinicians with a measure they can use to evaluate infant health prenatally.

A memory for sounds

There's no evidence that playing Mozart to an unborn child will encourage musical aptitude, but research does confirm that newborns enter the world with a preference for certain sounds from the fetal world. That world is dominated by two sounds: the mother's heartbeat and her voice. According to research by Columbia University psychologist William Fifer, PhD, and his colleagues, newborns prefer their mother's voice to the voice of other women. They also prefer her voice when it's electronically altered to sound as it did in the uterus, compared with her voice outside the uterus.

In contrast, infants don't prefer their father's voice over the voices of other men, indicating that they have a particular preference for prenatal sounds, not just familiar sounds, says Fifer.

It's likely that it is the cadences, and not the specific words, that the newborns recognize, he adds. One study found that newborns recognize the cadences of rhymes that they heard their mother say repeatedly during the last few weeks of pregnancy, but not the specific words themselves.

"These studies show that there is a mechanism for longterm memory available to the fetus," says Fifer.

The fetus may also have the capacity to remember food flavors available in utero, says Julie Mennella, PhD, of the Monell Chemical Senses Center in Philadelphia. She's found that the fetus has access to flavors, such as garlic, that become present in the amniotic fluid. This flavor transfer from mother to infant can continue after birth as many flavors from the mother's diet are integrated into her breast milk. These early experiences with flavors may form the basis of some food preferences as the child ages, says Mennella, who is beginning experiments to test that theory.

Habituation

Further evidence of fetal learning comes from studies of habituation—the process through which an animal learns, over repeated episodes of stimulation, to give less attention to an increasingly familiar stimulus. To test habituation in the human fetus, researchers apply a stimulus—often a vibrating device—to a pregnant woman's abdomen. By 26 weeks of gestation, a human fetus will reliably move in response to such a stimulus, researchers find. And, after repeated stimulation, a fetus will stop responding, having habituated to the stimulus. However, if a new stimulus is used, the fetus will once again respond.

There's no evidence that playing Mozart to an unborn child will encourage musical aptitude, but research does confirm that newborns enter the world with a preference for certain sounds from the fetal world.

Some researchers argue that habituation is a measure of learning that can predict later cognitive abilities, says psychologist Eugene K. Emory of Emory University.

In particular, Leo Leader, PhD, believes that clinicians can use fetal habituation to evaluate the health and development of the fetus. He's conducted several studies that correlate habituation with later development. Other researchers aren't convinced it's time to start making predictions, but they don't rule out the possibility in the near future.

The National Institute on Child Health and Human Development, which funds much of the fetal research, has hosted two meetings of fetal researchers to discuss the possibility of using data from basic research to begin to inform clinicians.

Fetal learning

Animal researchers can study more specific forms of learning because they can manipulate the fetus in ways impossible to attempt in humans. In rats, researchers can remove an individual pup from its mother's uterus and, keeping it attached to the umbilical cord, keep it alive in small dishes filled with a temperature-regulated water bath that mimics amniotic fluid. The pups can be kept inside the amniotic sac or removed.

Binghamton University psychologist William T. Smotherman, PhD, has taken the lead in fetal learning studies. He's designed a standard conditioned-learning paradigm that he can manipulate to examine specific

questions about fetal learning, including the molecular mechanisms that control it. The paradigm involves one aspect of feeding behavior—learning to respond to a nipple in a way to promote feeding, a behavior we assume is instinctive but that may partly involve learning. Smotherman places an artificial nipple close to the fetus' mouth, and if the fetus grasps the nipple, it receives a squirt of mother's milk into its mouth.

He finds that by around 21 days gestation—equivalent to early in the ninth month of a human pregnancy—the fetuses easily and quickly learn to respond to the nipple as if they were going to receive milk from it.

When researchers examine this response at the molecular level, they find that the milk triggers the release of certain neuropeptides in the brain of the rat fetus, which work to reinforce early feeding behaviors such as suckling. For example, the milk triggers a release of opiates into the fetuses' brains, which reinforces the pups' behavior. When Smotherman and his colleagues block this opiate release, the fetuses no longer become conditioned to the artificial nipple, indicating that the chemicals are necessary for learning.

He's also found that if he exposes fetuses to the nipple and the milk, but not paired in time, they don't become conditioned to respond to the nipple. They have the equivalent amount of experience with the crucial stimuli—the milk and the nipple—but because the two stimuli aren't coupled in time, learning doesn't occur.

This may have implications for premature infants who are fed either intravenously or through a feeding tube. Like the rat fetuses that receive the milk without access to the nipple, these infants may not learn to associate eating with suckling. It may be helpful to pair feeding with some type of non-nutritive suckling, says Smotherman.

Working for warmth

Indiana University psychologist Jeffery Alberts, PhD, agrees that fetal experiences and early newborn experiences help shape early development. Research by him and research scientist April Ronca, PhD, finds that the physical pressures put on the fetus just before and during labor are critical for developmental success and that, after birth, environment can shape early learning.

In one study, the Indiana researchers found that day-old rat pups will work to gain access to heat. Postdoctoral fellow Cynthia Hoffman, PhD, designed an operant conditioning paradigm, taking advantage of the fact that young, immobile pups periodically move their heads from side to side. When the pups in the experiment randomly turned their heads to the left, Hoffman rewarded them with 20 seconds of belly warming—she ran warm water under the plates the pups were lying on. They quickly learned to turn their heads to the left to elicit the belly warming, says Alberts.

"This research shows us how environmental factors, like warmth, can quickly shape behavior very early in life," he says.

Further reading

"Fetal Development: A Psychobiological Perspective," by J. P. Lecanuet, W. Fifer, N. A. Krasnegor, W. Smotherman (Lawrence Erlbaum Associates, Inc., 1995).

**Paul L. DeVito
and Ralph Hyatt**

What Constitutes "APPROPRIATE" PUNISHMENT?

Although Americans insist that anti-social behavior must be controlled, they are ambivalent about methods to do so.

TAKE A FEW moments to test your philosophy of punishment. Read each of the following situations and write out your responses to the questions that follow them.

• Poverty-stricken teenagers Joey and Art had been dreaming about the rock concert for months, and now that it was in town they only could continue to dream, for they did not have the entrance fee. In desperation, Art sneaked into the kitchen and snatched several dollars from his mother's hiding place in the cupboard. That evening, Joey's father cracked him across the face and accused him of stealing the money. Art, his supposed friend, had lied to his parents and implicated Joey. Art's father complained to Joey's father about the felony. After Joey screamed out the truth, Joey's father angrily approached Art, grasped him around the throat, and quickly got a confession. Art was confined to his room for a week by his parents.

a) Did Joey deserve his whacking?

b) Should Art have been choked?

c) Were Art's parents too lenient?

• Pennsylvania has a unit called "super-max" in its maximum security prisons. This unit houses chronic troublemakers, who totally are segregated from the other inmates. They are given one hour daily of isolated exercise out of their small cells. Many have spent years in super-max.

a) Is it humane to isolate troublesome maximum security prisoners? For such long periods of time?

b) Is this program consistent with rehabilitation?

c) Does the death penalty make more sense?

• Autistic children, although often quite intelligent, do not develop in expected ways. They may be overly active, speech can be delayed, and they do not establish normal human attachments. Many gesture in strange ways and do not make good eye contact. At times, they can be destructive to themselves and others. Some professionals believe that physical restraint is necessary to get their attention as well as a means of helping them to release their pent-up anger. Aversion therapy, a group of methods for treating such individuals, includes paddling and mild electric shock. This mode of treatment also has been used with some success with drug addicts, sexual deviants, and people demonstrating extremely violent behavior.

Dr. DeVito is chairman, Department of Psychology, Saint Joseph's University, Philadelphia, Pa. Dr. Hyatt, Psychology Editor of USA Today, is professor emeritus of psychology, Saint Joseph's University.

a) Should aversion therapy be used as a form of treatment or banned by law?

b) How about physical restraint?

These situations and questions were given to a variety of people on an informal, non-scientific basis. It is safe to say that your particular response—or any of them—is included among those of the group. Respondents replied with a yes, no, and everything in-between to each question. Those at the extremes invariably qualified their answers if additional conditions were to exist. This should come as no surprise since those interviewees who were psychologists, attorneys, correctional employees, and school counselors also had no pat answers.

Recent events bear out the uncertainties people have about meting out punishment, some praying for mercy and forgiveness, others demanding justice—and often blood. Take the caning of Michael Fay, the 18-year-old American visiting Singapore, who was accused of spray-painting and tossing eggs at automobiles, among other acts of vandalism. Prior to his punishment of four cane strokes, which was "mercifully" reduced from six, American sentiment, as revealed by a series of polls, was pro-caning by a large majority. Even Fay's emotional denials of any wrong-doings other than removing some street signs did not soften their hearts.

Americans, it was hypothesized, had had it up to their eyeballs with teenage social irresponsibility, lack of respect, and gun toting crime. "He deserves it" and "He should have known better" generally expressed their exasperation. Yet, in his hometown in Ohio, 90 days of incarceration and a $750 fine would have taken care of the matter.

It is worth recalling that, in the 1960s, flogging was a form of legal punishment in Delaware. The whipping post still was being used there in 1952. American colonists brought with them and promulgated their array of European penalties—imprisonment, banishment, mutilation, branding, flogging, and execution—despite the forbiddance of "cruel and unusual punishment" in the Constitution!

Many who advocate the death penalty maintain that it could terminate concerns about too few prisons, the cost of incarceration, and the entire mess of rehabilitation and what that means. Yet, the fact is that the death penalty never has succeeded as a deterrent to heinous acts, nor have stiffer sentences.

"The increased severity of the penalties has not reduced crime, it has only increased the prison population," writes former Common Pleas Court judge Lois G. Forer in her book, *A Rage to Punish*. Her non-mandatory sentencing approach runs head-on into Pres. Clinton's "Three strikes and you're out" solution, which throws away the key after a felon's third violent crime. She argues that the crime rate "has not risen materially since 1980 while the prison population and numbers of inmates on death row have soared." She believes in the full use of restitution, fines, education, and counseling. Prior to O.J. Simpson's trial, Americans were in disagreement regarding the appropriateness of the death penalty for him. This occurs in a society that presumes innocence unless proven guilty beyond reasonable doubt.

Defining wrongdoing and setting penalties

There is little wonder that everyone has opinions about punishment. People are subjected to it from the moment they slide out of the womb into a new environment full of strange sounds, temperatures, and pressures. Painful feelings continue from that experience onward: delay in feeding when hungry, soaked diapers, restraint when dressed, scraped knees, sibling rivalry, etc. We are not sure an infant perceives these events as punishment (although "Why is all this happening to me?" may be going through his or her mind), but the concept develops quickly when something like a hot stove is touched: Do the wrong thing and a penalty (pain) follows. Confusion occurs, research has shown, when a penalty does not directly follow wrongdoing or follows it erratically.

The conceptual riddle begins when we try to define "wrong" and "penalty." Wrongdoing, in the first place, may be real or perceived. Someone may believe you did something wrong when, actually, you didn't. Or he or she may accuse you of wrongdoing just to do you in. Also, one can wrong people, property, and God.

Penalties are no less universally agreed upon. There are tongue-lashing, restriction of freedoms, and corporal and capital punishment, not to omit condemnation to hell of sinners. Depending on the occasion, and given a choice, the offender may rather have one form than the other. For example, a kid may prefer to have his rear end smacked in public than hear his mother scream, "Do it again and I'll tell everyone you're a bed-wetter!" Then there is the judgment of how little is little and how big is big. One person's "little" smack is another's "big" one. Is a judge's verdict of one to three years incarceration short or long? What quantity of penalty does a child's "big mouth" deserve? What type of penalty, if any, is suitable for an infant? For doing how much of what?

Insights do not become any less confusing by remembering Proverbs: 13-2: "He that spareth the rod hateth his own son." If one can assume that autistic behaviors such as inattention, aggression, and destructiveness can be improved or eradicated by the use of corporal punishment, should it be permissible? Suppose parents strongly request such "teaching" or "therapeutic" procedures for their autistic child?

Psychologist B.F. Skinner, who condemned the overutilization of punishment, wrote about this issue: "If brief and harmless aversive stimuli, made precisely contingent over self-destructive behavior, suppress the behavior and leave the children free to develop in other ways, I believe it can be justified. When taken out of context, such stimuli may seem less than humane, but they are not to be distinguished from the much more painful stimuli sometimes needed in dentistry and various medical practices. To remain satisfied with punishment without exploring non-punitive alternations is the real mistake."

There is something about punishment that relates it to evil. Do wrong and you get punished; do right and you don't. Does that principle apply to God? Rabbi Harold Kushner's best-seller, *Why Bad Things Happen to Good People*, grapples with that question from a theological perspective. He argues that much of what happens to us—the good and the bad—occurs purely by chance. God does not manage our each and every action, punishing some and rewarding others.

Thomas Hobbes, the 17th-century philosopher, believed that humans are basically solitary, selfish, and practical. They accept socialization primarily to satisfy their needs for safety and protection; otherwise, they wantonly would murder, rape, and pillage. Given the condition of today's world—most prominently in Rwanda, Serbia, and Chechnya, to name a few trouble spots—one is hard put to wave away this negative view, which squarely places Homo sapiens among all other creatures in the universe. Naturalist Charles Darwin, in *Origin of the Species*, espoused the evolutionary theory that solidly links human emotions to lowly organisms.

Sigmund Freud's id theory postulates a self-seeking pleasure instinct in everyone. The superego, an internalized conscience which evolves from early parental scolding and spanking, continually battles the id in order to keep people socialized. Thus, evils lurk inside and outside of individuals, and must be tamed by punishment of some sort.

There are, of course, philosophies and research which deem that humans are basically good. Psychologists have found, for instance, that effective nurturing and love are products of healthy, well-adjusted individuals, not those who are bestial. Kind and helpful children are popular with their peers and self-confident, not isolated and fearful. However, few philosophers, if any, deny the potential malevolence in all people. The enduring question is: What are the most effective methods for socializing humans?

Skinner noted, "We have not yet discovered adequate non-punitive practices to replace the aversive part of our genetic endowment. For example, we are far from abandoning the use of force in international relations or in maintaining domestic order. People living closely together, and that includes teachers and students, therapists and clients, can seldom avoid all forms of punishment."

According to contemporary psychological theory, punishment is included under the domain of behavior modification. Psychologists define it as any procedure that reduces or suppresses an undesirable behavior. The behavior is *not* eradicated or forgotten—just not expressed as it was before. There are both positive and negative forms. "Positive punishment," popularly known as corporal punishment, is exemplified by a child receiving a hand slap after biting his mother's leg. "Negative punishment" is applied, for instance, when a teenager who receives a poor report card is grounded for three weeks. The U.S. criminal justice system largely is based on this form—that is, when one is guilty of some crime, punishment usually is a monetary fine or incarceration. Something painful is applied in positive punishment, whereas something attractive is taken away in negative punishment. Both can have the effect of suppressing an unwanted response.

The alternative is known as reinforcement, where the objective is to increase the likelihood of some desired behavior. As with punishment, there are positive and negative approaches. When Johnny mows the lawn and is told "What a great job!" that is positive reinforcement. He probably will be less resistant to mowing the lawn again. A classic example of negative reinforcement is nagging. When you nag so much that your spouse yields in order to shut you up, that is negative reinforcement. Skinner was a champion of positive reinforcement, and his students coined the phrase "Spare the rod, use behavior mod!"

Experimental studies of positive and negative punishment, with both human and animal subjects, unequivocally demonstrate the effectiveness of these procedures in eliminating unacceptable behaviors. A serious problem, though, is that, in addition to suppressing the behavior, negative punishment often produces undesirable side effects. In a 1953 study, hungry spider monkeys were trained to press a switch for food. Once this response was learned, the experimenters placed a snake in the monkeys' cage whenever they reached for food. This was certain punishment since monkeys are terrified of snakes. After a few such experiences, the monkeys completely stopped pressing the switch for food. However, numerous side effects soon became apparent, including disturbances in eating behavior (loss of 15–25% of body weight), sexual disorders, and a breakdown in social relationships. Most of the monkeys began to develop classic human neurotic and psy-

chotic symptoms, including asthma, facial and muscular tics, and hallucinations.

Do you know a parent who has not experienced a temper tantrum from his or her child? To stop such shenanigans, children have been restricted to their rooms, had cold water thrown in their faces, been yelled at, slapped, ignored, and exposed to countless other "creative" remedies. In a newspaper column, pediatrician T. Berry Brazelton counseled: "Parents are likely to feel manipulated by this kind of behavior, but they miss the purpose of these episodes if they feel they must either eliminate them or punish the child for them. Tantrums are expressions of the child's inner struggle for self-control. It is up to the child to work it out—not the parent." What if the child is throwing hard metal toys against the dining room furniture, though? Or hitting the parents with a stick? Or kicking out the window in the kitchen door? Should he or she be allowed to "work it out"?

The last few decades have shown a rise of disobedience along with violence among children and adolescents. In their vernacular, they seem to be "losing it." Psychologists have become more sensitive to this acting out, and label it "loss of impulse control" when it becomes extreme. One way or another, anti-social behavior must be curbed.

Confusion about punishment reigns in part because of semantics. "Abuse" means unwarranted, inhuman punishment. Child sexual abuse probably has few dissenters in terms of definition, but that is not to say that differences of opinion do not exist. Unless there is a sadomasochistic relationship, spouse abuse also presents relatively few problems in definition. Prisoner abuse, no matter how severe, probably would elicit the fewest disagreements. Discipline, on the other hand, typically evokes multiple meanings and the greatest debates—even between parents.

Are physical restriction, isolation to a room, and being screamed at forms of punishment? Is the current popular technique of "time out," when a child must sit quietly in some corner of the room for an unspecified time, not to be considered punishment? Does anything change when the procedure is described as a lesson in listening? Suppose the child refuses to go into time out, what then? Is the prisoner in super-max being punished or disciplined?

A recent op-ed column in a large city newspaper espoused corporal punishment in the classroom because "using the rod early can help keep some youths from more serious trouble later." The writer continued: "Of course, people warped by the Benjamin Spock school hyperventilate at the slightest mention of paddling. They still believe the Socratic method can be applied to youthful Al Capones. The object lesson for kids is that as they approach adulthood, violation of others' property or property

rights results in punishments much worse than minor taps on the tush."

Children should not grow up with a set of models—parents, teachers, etc.—who are abusive. There is absolutely no argument with that. It is known that the abused tend to become abusers, in turn. The major objective is never to hurt or uncontrollably release anger, but, rather, to curb unacceptable behavior and teach methods of altering it. Infants must *never* be given corporal punishment. Toddlers should be distracted by showing them attractive toys and objects or playing simple games, not slapped.

No matter what it is called—discipline or punishment—good judgment is required. By definition, however, judgment is an opinion, an estimate. It can not be measured or weighed with any scientific accuracy. The hope is that judges, teachers, parents, and others in authority will have sufficient information and self-control to make judgments that are fair, proper, and good. Ordinarily, assessment of their judgments is made after the fact, often when it is too late to alter. Society's task is to make adequate provisions for the training and education of those who are given the responsibility to judge.

Dispensing discipline effectively

Although the following guidelines denote parent-child relationships, the principles apply to all situations: employer-employee, correctional officer-inmate, teacher-student, etc.

• Accentuate the positives. Youngsters should learn behaviors that are acceptable, rather than constantly being told what to avoid. Example: Rather than "Stop yelling," say "Please use a quiet voice."

• Do not label your child. Eliminate name-calling and generalizations. Be specific. Behavior is undesirable, not people. Example: Rather than "You're a liar," say "If you do not tell the truth about going to the movies, your brother no longer will trust you."

• Discipline should follow the unacceptable behavior as closely as possible. *Each* spouse has equal responsibility for disciplining his or her child.

• Setting reasonable limits reflects your values and love. Limits provide the basis of your offspring's self-confidence throughout his or her lifetime.

• When setting limits, ask yourself the following questions:

a) Are they understood? Ask the youngster to state the limit and why it was set.

b) Are they appropriate in this situation?

c) Have too many been set lately?

d) Is the child confused by mixed messages, sometimes having a limit set for a particular misbehavior; at other times, not?

e) Are you ready to enforce a violation of the limit reasonably?

• Discipline is a learning process, never purely a coercive experience to prove your mastery and control.

Losing Your Mind?

Memory lapses are usually normal, but some may signal deeper problems

By Wray Herbert

Polly Van Benthusen was known to her colleagues as "the archivist"—the repository of institutional memory in the Northern California Social Security Administration offices where she worked for more than two decades. She could recall volumes of technical details from cases that had been processed years before, and if anyone needed a legal citation or the location of a regulatory document, the refrain in the corridors was always the same: "Ask Polly. Polly will remember that."

Then all that changed. When she was 42, Van Benthusen began to notice that she no longer had the agency's history at her fingertips. Worse, she found that she couldn't give a simple presentation without detailed note cards, and she was once very embarrassed when she completely forgot about an important board meeting. By age 45, Van Benthusen found herself fretting: "Well, I really am losing my mind. This is how it happens, in little bits and stages." She would wake up at night wondering, "Am I going to remember my son's first footsteps?"

Anxious boomers. Polly Van Benthusen's story might belong to many members of her generation. In her case, the memory problems were diagnosed as a likely consequence of early menopause, and estrogen-replacement therapy did help with her mental fogginess. But menopause is just one of many triggers for age-related memory loss. Indeed, some 10,000 Americans are turning 50 every day, and as they do, many begin experiencing—or at least noticing more acutely—signs of memory impairment. What's more, the baby boom generation now entering midlife is the first to have

grown up fully aware of the ravages of Alzheimer's disease, which their parents knew more benignly as senility or "hardening of the arteries." Faced with that awful prospect, boomers feel great anxiety about even the slightest loss of cognitive function. Is blanking on an acquaintance's name or misplacing the car keys an early sign of encroaching dementia? Worried Americans are spending billions of dollars each year on memory enhancement aids, in the form of books, tapes, and mnemonics courses, not to mention aggressively marketed (but largely unproven) food supplements such as ginkgo biloba.

The federal government is anxious about memory loss as well, and is investing millions of dollars in projects aimed at defining "normal" age-related memory loss, and sorting it out from the more sinister declines that accompany serious brain disease. Alzheimer's disease alone costs American society at least $100 billion a year in lost productivity and long-term care, so any insights that might halt the progression of mild memory impairment have become a pressing concern for both scientists and social planners. The questions they are asking range from psychological to neurological, from practical to philosophical, including: Do mild memory problems foreshadow trouble? What's broken when memory fails? And can memory be enhanced, even in people whose memory loss is considered normal?

Trouble ahead? The "worried well"—that's what scientists and clinicians label 50-to-60-year-olds who come in complaining of memory problems but who test in normal ranges on standard measures of memory. Richard Mitlyng is a

perfect example. The 63-year-old Minnesotan had worked for years in a manufacturing plant near Rochester, Minn., but when he retired a year and a half ago, he started noticing memory lapses. He would head out to do two or three errands and come home having completed only one. Mitlyng became worried that these lapses might predict Alzheimer's disease, so he took himself into the Mayo Clinic, also in Rochester, where he was given a battery of cognitive tests, including tests of both short- and long-term memory. The diagnosis: normal. The clinicians sent him home with the advice that he needed to concentrate a bit more and write things down—and return in a year for another evaluation.

What the clinicians at Mayo were testing Mitlyng for is a newly recognized diagnosis called "mild cognitive impairment," or MCI. The concept grew out of a long-term study by Mayo's Ronald Petersen, who for years has been observing the natural course of aging in his Rochester community. In the course of that study, Petersen identified a subgroup of people who had significant memory problems yet were not demented; indeed, they were otherwise healthy and functional. When he studied these people over time, he found that about 12 percent a year developed Alzheimer's disease—a high rate of conversion compared with the 1 or 2 percent of people in the general population who develop that degenerative disorder. Petersen speculates that ultimately 80 percent of those with MCI will go on to develop Alzheimer's—he calls the condition "Alzheimer's in evolution." The National Institute on Aging has just launched a major, $20 million study of MCI and its relationship to both dementia and normal aging, in an effort to prevent the onset of debilitating memory disorders.

But there's a puzzle with mild cognitive impairment: the 20 percent of people with MCI who don't seem to get progressively worse. Aging experts want to find out if those people will deteriorate given a long enough life span, or whether they have a fairly stable condition related to normal aging. Researchers at dozens of labs around the country are using a battery of tests to sort out different kinds of memory failure, in an effort to determine which types may predict worse things ahead. Their findings so far are hopeful. For example, one of the most common memory complaints is the inability to remember names. But according to memory experts, this should be one of the least worrisome changes. First of all, forgetting names is not uncommon, even at younger ages. Names are completely arbitrary; the brain has evolved as much for forgetting as for remembering—it would be disabling if we stored too much irrelevant information—and names often lack both context and emotional power, the two aspects that make new information memorable. Further, memory researchers say, most people who experience trouble calling up names or other similar information really have a problem with speed of retrieval. It's not that the memories are fading or disintegrating in the brain's memory banks; it just takes a bit more time to activate the circuits. This is what accounts for the familiar "tip of the tongue" sensation, which researchers identify as an indicator of a healthy memory search.

Aha! Another telling indicator of whether a memory lapse is benign or worrisome is what Harvard University neuropsychologist Marilyn Albert calls the "aha! phenomenon": Healthy people who blank on a word temporarily, then call it up, experience a sense of, "Oh, yeah. That's what I was searching for." Victims of severe brain disorders experience neither the "tip of the tongue" sensation nor such a sense of recollection.

Indeed, much of normal, age-related memory loss has to do with loss of processing speed. This can be seen not only with memory retrieval but with memory storage as well. For example, given a test where they have to learn a list of

① When middle-aged people are concerned about memory lapses, clinicians ask them to assess their everyday memory.

MEMORY SELF-EVALUATION

Have you experienced any of the following problems during the past six months?

	YES	NO
1. Forgetting the name of a friend or family member (such as a grandchild).	☐	☐
2. Difficulty finding the right word while speaking.	☐	☐
3. Problems doing things that were once done easily (balancing a checkbook, preparing a meal, shopping).	☐	☐
4. Becoming confused about the month or season.	☐	☐
5. Forgetting addresses and phone numbers that were familiar.	☐	☐
6. Forgetting what happened only a day or two ago.	☐	☐
7. Problems remembering what you just said or heard.	☐	☐
8. Forgetting previous conversations.	☐	☐
9. Confusing recent with past events.	☐	☐
10. Awakening during the night confused as to where you are.	☐	☐

SCORE

Add up the number of "yes" boxes checked. A score of 2 or 3 indicates significant problems, according to psychologist Thomas Crook. He cautions, however, that subjective concerns about memory often do not match objective measures. Therefore, the self-evaluation score should be considered in relation to scores on objective tests, such as the Name-Face Association Test that follows.

Source: Psychologix Inc.

new words, older people often take longer than younger people to master the list; but with a bit more time and effort they usually can memorize the list. This stands in sharp contrast to the victims of Alzheimer's disease, who have terrible trouble getting new information into storage. Neither time nor cues appear to help.

Even given these differences, however, it's not always easy to distinguish normal aging from dementia—especially in the earliest stages. For one thing, normal aging does often bring with it certain declines in attention, which can be mistaken for loss of memory skill. In particular, says neurologist Guy McKhann of Johns Hopkins University, it's fairly common to experience some difficulty with "set shifting"—trying to concentrate on more than one activity at once, or to concentrate on one conversation with another conversation taking place nearby. So people often think they've forgotten something that they never really acquired—or "encoded"—in the first place.

Healthy aging and dementia resemble each other in other ways as well. For instance, long-term memory seems to remain fairly intact even in Alzheimer's patients, so in the early stages of the disease they can appear quite normal. Similarly, what's called "procedural memory"—skills with a large motor component—are generally preserved even in later stages of dementia. People who once knew how to play golf or skipper a sailboat don't lose these skills, so on this measure, too, they can appear much like healthy aging adults. And with memory for names and words—"semantic memory"—the differences are more a matter of degree, at least in the early stages of disease. As the disease progresses, however, victims of dementia lose ground rapidly, while the deficits of aging either do not progress or progress very slowly over time.

One kind of memory deficit that does seem to be a bad omen has to do with what researchers call "executive functioning." This is the kind of memory required for fairly complicated tasks that involve a sequence of steps—an oral presentation at the office, for example, or preparing a multicourse Thanksgiving dinner. Even perfectly healthy people may have to pause to remember what step comes next, the cranberry sauce or the potatoes, but serious disruption of such memory often indicates something could be seriously awry.

What's broken? All memory loss takes place in the brain, whether it's the end stages of Alzheimer's or "senior moments" like misplacing one's eyeglasses for half an hour. But researchers are finding that just as senior moments and dementia *look* qualitatively different, the underlying neurology is also different. Indeed, over the past few years there has been a revolution in thinking about memory loss and the brain.

The old thinking was that all memory loss was caused by the death of neurons. For decades, the prevailing theory was that all people begin losing brain cells in their 20s and lose more and more each decade as they age—until they reach some kind of demented condition as a result of lack of processing capacity. But increasingly sophisticated instruments—including magnetic resonance imaging, or MRI—have allowed scientists a much more accurate view of the brain, both its anatomy and its physiology. It turns out that much of the "neuron death" theory is wrong, and the new view is much more complicated.

Researchers have long known from autopsies of Alzheimer's victims that the disease is characterized by lesions in the brain. These lesions—called "plaques" and "neurofibrillary tangles"—tend to be found in a seahorse-shaped section deep in the brain called the hippocampus. Brain scanning has confirmed that this region atrophies as the disease progresses. Recently, however, with the use of better scanners, scientists have been able to pinpoint neuronal loss. Specifically, the atrophy appears to begin in an area called the entorhinal cortex—the "gateway" to the hippocampus—and then spread through an elaborate brain circuit. This circuit is a pathway for a chemical messenger called acetylcholine, which has long been implicated in memory and memory decline. Preliminary studies indicate that people with healthy memories and atrophy in this hippocampal region are likely to progress to mild cognitive impairment. The hippocampus is the brain structure that's responsible for the laying down of new memories, and that is the structure—and the function—that's the first to go with dementia. But it's not the only thing to go, new studies reveal. As dementia progresses, an area called the anterior cingulate also begins to lose nerve cells. This region is responsible

② *By far the most common memory problem of middle age is learning the names of new acquaintances, according to psychologist Thomas Crook. Here's a typical memory assessment.*

NAME-FACE ASSOCIATION TEST

Starting at the top and going left to right, take a few seconds to study each face and the name under it. On a following page you will see the faces again, but in a different order and without the names. You will be asked to write the name that corresponds to each face.

Roger

Michelle

Andrea

Gary

Mark

Joan

■ *Delayed recall of new information is one of the most sensitive measures of memory acuity. The test of these name-face associations can be found on Page 65, but take some time between studying and testing yourself.*

Source: Psychologix Inc.

for executive functioning, and the nerve loss is the cause of dysfunctions such as being unable to manage that Thanksgiving dinner. Neuronal loss is irreversible, which is why there is no known treatment for Alzheimer's disease. Once learning and executive functioning are gone, they're gone for good.

Severe diseases like Alzheimer's are not the only things that can harm the hippocampus or interfere with its functioning. A large body of research indicates that stress can also wreak havoc with memory, and that it does so through the hippocampus, which is rich in receptors for the stress hormone cortisol. Cortisol actually improves memory when it circulates briefly through the brain—that's why we have "flashbulb memories" of emotionally charged events—but if stress hormone levels stay elevated, the effects reverse. Neurons in the hippocampus begin to function poorly and become more vulnerable to damage. Chronic stress actually causes cell death in the brain's memory circuits.

Chronic stress has many sources. Depression, for example, can keep the body in a persistent state of stress reaction, skewing the normal interplay of neurochemicals and hormones. Indeed, a recent study of women who had suffered from depression revealed significant atrophy in the hippocampus. According to George Washington University psychiatrist Gene Cohen, a reliable indicator of clinical depression is when someone complains of memory problems that others haven't noticed. Typically, people with depression express physical complaints when they are younger, but as they get older their complaints tend to focus on memory and thinking.

Poor and stressed. Chronic stress can also result from the wear and tear of everyday living—the body's physiological response to untoward events. This is why society's less privileged tend to report more memory problems, says Rockefeller University neuroscientist Bruce McEwen. A whole cluster of factors associated with being poor and less educated—hostility, lack of control, a general sense of being disenfranchised—all work to keep such people stressed out, which in turn interferes with mental functioning, including memory. In an intriguing animal study, McEwen found that newborns who experience a lot of stress show lifelong mental impairment, including memory deficits; their brains in effect "age

The spectrum of memory

Mild cognitive impairment is a new category of memory disorder that falls between normal memory loss and dementia. Not everyone progresses through these stages, but those who do are apt to experience these symptoms:

NORMAL	MILD COGNITIVE IMPAIRMENT	ALZHEIMER'S DISEASE
■ Misplacing keys, checkbook	■ Difficulty learning new names	■ Forgetting close relatives' names
■ Blanking on a new acquaintance's name	■ Missing important appointments	■ Inability to plan and execute a meal
■ Trouble reading with the TV on	■ Repeating the same question to your spouse	■ Trouble with dressing and hygiene

faster," says McEwen, while newborns with calm early days retain age-appropriate function.

Barring the presence of depression or other stressful conditions, however, the picture of normal aging is quite different—and encouraging. The most dramatic difference is that—in contrast to early theory—age-related memory loss does *not* appear to involve neuron loss. There does appear to be some loss of dendrites, the spiny extensions of neurons, and of synapses, but the loss is minimal and not really important, researchers say. The only real age-related atrophy is in tiny structures deep within the brain, known as nuclei. The nuclei are a source of the brain's neurochemicals, so age-related memory loss is more of a physiological disorder than an anatomical one. The machinery of memory is still intact, it's just lacking fuel.

All of this is very good news, says Albert, because it points to two conclusions: First, since age-related memory loss is a chemical problem, there is at least the possibility that drugs might be developed that could ameliorate it. And second, age-related memory loss may be preventable, through lifestyle changes that might keep the brain's chemistry from going awry in the first place.

Good news, bad news. The potential for treating age-related memory loss with new drugs is the good news. The bad news is that they don't yet exist. Says George Washington University's Cohen: "All the magic bullets are blanks." That appears to be the consensus among those who study memory enhancement. Nevertheless, there are some intriguing theories about what *might* work—and some suggestive early findings, mostly from animal studies.

The most promising research focuses on the brain's neurotransmitter systems involved in memory and memory loss. The most obvious target is acetylcholine, because of its well-documented

role in Alzheimer's disease. In fact, acetylcholine-boosting drugs have been shown to delay the symptoms of dementia by several months. The role of this chemical messenger in normal aging and memory is less clear, although at least one recent study—by Richard Wurtman, a neuroscientist at the Massachusetts Institute of Technology—has demonstrated that an acetylcholine booster is capable of restoring some memory function in animals. In a National Institute on Aging study, rats were given acetylcholine boosters while pregnant, and their offspring had no age-related cognitive decline. Similarly, dopamine, another neurotransmitter, is involved in the chemical process that makes a memory potent enough to move from short- to long-term memory. A recent study by Eric Kandel, a neuroscientist at Columbia University, has shown that a dopamine-like drug can restore certain kinds of memory lost as a result of normal aging. NIH is very interested in neurotransmitters and memory; part of the recently launched investigation of mild cognitive impairment is a study of the effectiveness of Aracept—an acetylcholine booster—in preventing the progression of MCI to Alzheimer's.

The other substance under investigation as part of the federal study of mild cognitive impairment is vitamin E. The theory behind vitamin E supplements is that they act as an antioxidant, mopping up tissue-damaging chemicals called free radicals. It's not known for sure whether age-related memory loss has anything to do with free radicals, but a number of animal studies offer intriguing hints that they might. For example, a National Institute on Aging study has demonstrated that vitamin E, strawberry extract, and spinach extract all help forestall age-related cognitive decline (spinach was the most effective); a related study showed that strawberry and spinach extract both actually reverse cognitive impairment in old animals.

Brain boosters? These supplements, says Molly Wagster, chief of research on aging and memory at the National Institute on Aging, are all antioxidants, but they also have anti-inflammatory properties and are thought to increase the fluidity of cell membranes. Both inflammation and loss of membrane fluidity are suspected in dementia. A naturally occurring fat called phosphatidylserine, or PS, is being marketed in supplement stores as a memory booster, in part because it helps keep cell membranes flexible. Some preliminary studies of this soy derivative—sold as "Brain Gum" and in other forms—produced modest results, but most memory researchers remain skeptical.

A potential memory enhancer that has recently attracted attention is the sex hormone estrogen, the one that helped Polly Van Benthusen regain some of her lost acuity. Nobody knows its precise mechanism, but according to neuropsychologist Claire Warga, author of *Menopause and the Mind,* the revelation that estrogen—known for its role in reproduction—is also found in the thinking parts of the brain is in itself suggestive. Preliminary studies have shown that women on estrogen-suppressing drugs do suffer cognitive losses, including deficits in verbal memory; memory is restored at least in part by estrogen supplements. Such estrogen-related memory loss is not an inevitable result of aging, of course, though Warga argues that it's a far more common consequence of menopause than has been recognized. Estrogen replacement also brings with it certain risks—including increased risk for uterine cancer—so memory researchers remain tentative in their enthusiasm for estrogen as a memory booster.

Oddly, one of the most popular memory boosters on the market is one of the least well documented. Ginkgo biloba, a derivative of the ginkgo tree, is being promoted as a remedy for everything from Alzheimer's and age-related memory loss to varicose veins and impotence, and Americans are spending about $350 million a year on it. Its claim to efficacy is vague—usually something having to do with improved circulation—but the consensus of experts, including a review by the Center for Science in the Public Interest, is that there is no evidence it improves memory in healthy people. Because ginkgo is sold as a food supplement rather than a drug, there is no incentive to conduct rigorous tests of its effectiveness. The National Center for Complementary and Alternative Medicine, part of NIH, is about to launch a clinical trial of ginkgo's effectiveness in preventing cognitive decline in the elderly, but the results are at least three years away.

Lacking magic bullets, then, what's a 55-year-old to do when it seems that memory is failing? One alternative is mental calisthenics—promoted under such names as "neurobics." These exercises—brushing one's teeth with the nondominant hand, for instance, or varying the route of one's daily commute—are designed to boost the production of brain chemicals called neurotrophins, which enrich neuronal connections. None of these calisthenics has been rigorously studied, but experts say there is little downside risk in trying them, and the basic theory—that a more active brain is a healthier brain—has been well documented in animal studies.

Exercising the mind. Physical fitness appears to translate into mental fitness as well. One National Institute on Aging study of rats found that regular exercise did boost the production of cell-protecting neurotrophins in the brain. And in an article published in this month's *Journal of the American Medical Association,* researchers reported that people with poor cardiovascular health were three times more likely than healthy elderly to have loss of cognitive function. Indeed, when 60-year-old restaurateur Robert Wattel and his wife, Rosalind Wattel, 58, became concerned about mild memory lapses and went to a University of Chicago clinic, the advice they got from internist Michael Roizen had nothing to do with mental

③ *You were introduced to these six people half an hour ago at a cocktail party. Now you have to introduce them to someone who just arrived. See how well you do.*

NAME-FACE ASSOCIATION TEST

Take a look at these six faces. Then think back and write the name that you associate with each of them.

SCORE

Check against the previous test. Scores generally decline with age, as follows:

Age	Average Score
18-29	6
30-39	5
40-49	4
50-59	3
60-69	2-3
70 plus	1-2

Source: Psychologix Inc.

calisthenics. What he prescribed was a regimen of diet and exercise to keep their arteries healthy; according to Roizen, healthy arteries are the best guarantor of acute memory. "We've been very health conscious for a long time," says Rosalind Wattel. "Our diet and exercise are meant to prevent sinister problems in the future." All this is consistent with a 10-year-long MacArthur Foundation study of people 65 years old and older, which found that the only predictors of healthy memory over time were physical fitness, mental fitness, and sense of control.

This sense of control intrigues researchers and points to another alternative to drugs and herbs: memory training. This is the route that Lynn Troyka took. An English professor at New York's Queensborough Community College, the 61-year-old Troyka recently found her memory slipping; she was no longer able to remember her students' names, something she had always done effortlessly over her 30-year career. So she enrolled in a class at Mount Sinai Medical Center and studied memory techniques—creating visual associations with names, for example. But the most important result of the training, Troyka says, was the assurance she gained that her memory loss was normal. "I just stopped worrying about the fact that I didn't have every student's name memorized," she says. Her experience is consistent with one study of memory training, which found that gains in memory ability were often lost over months, but that confidence in one's memory—sense of control—remained high.

The best memory classes are very practical in their approach. The one Troyka attended, for example—designed and run by psychologist Cynthia Green—teaches techniques that can be used in different circumstances, but it also promotes a lifestyle that minimizes the need for gimmickry. There is no need, for example, to commit a grocery list to memory, Green notes, when a simple list will do. Indeed, memory experts are big fans of pencil and paper, and point out that writing was invented as a mnemonic device. Green likes to quote Confucius: "The strongest memory is not as strong as the weakest ink."

Traumatic Memory Is Special

Lynn Nadel and W. Jake Jacobs[1]

Department of Psychology, University of Arizona, Tucson, Arizona

Does the brain represent and store memories for traumatic events differently than memories for everyday autobiographical events (cf. the June 1997 Special Issue of *Current Directions)?* Laboratory evidence is central to answering this question, and hence to understanding clinical trauma. An answer would provide a guide to how "recovered" memories should be interpreted, and would also have implications for treating victims of trauma. In this article, we consider empirical data concerning the neurobiological nature of multiple memory systems, and how stress and trauma affect these systems, and then we briefly discuss the implications of these facts for the clinical issues.

EMPIRICAL DATA

On the basis of several decades of empirical work, most investigators distinguish between at least two types of memory (e.g., explicit and implicit; see Schacter & Tulving, 1994, for a variety of multiple-memory-systems approaches). Going beyond a simple dichotomy, more recent research establishes that each major class of memory encompasses more than one form of memory, and the concomitant in-

volvement of more than one underlying neural substrate. Consider explicit memory, which refers to any and all forms of recollection entering awareness. This sort of memory is most often associated with the medial temporal lobe, an area of the brain that includes the amygdala, rhinal cortex, parahippocampal gyrus, and hippocampal formation. Although there has been a tendency to think of these structures as parts of a larger medial temporal lobe memory system, recent work indicates that each is responsible for different aspects of explicit memory. In the present context, it is particularly important to attend to these distinctions, because stress has differential impact on them.

• *Amygdala.* This structure is thought to be essential in memory for emotionally charged events. Studies in rats, monkeys, and humans have now shown that (a) damage to the amygdala interferes with learning about fearful or unpleasant stimuli (Adolphs, Tranel, Damasio, & Damasio, 1994; Davis, 1992; LeDoux, 1995; McGaugh, Cahill, & Roozendaal, 1996); (b) neurons in the amygdala of experimental animals are activated by stimuli with motivational or emotional import (e.g., Rolls, 1982); and (c) the human amygdala is activated when a person is exposed to emotion-

provoking stimuli or events (Morris et al., 1996). By contrast, other regions in the medial temporal lobe are apparently not involved, in any general way, with such stimuli.

• *Rhinal cortex.* This structure is thought to be central to recognition memory, the process by which an organism determines it has, or has not, had prior experience with a particular stimulus or event. A prominent demonstration of this function concerns the laboratory task known as delayed matching (or nonmatching) to sample. In this widely used paradigm, the experimental subject is exposed briefly to a *sample* stimulus, and then after a variable delay, allowed to choose between the sample and another, new, stimulus. In the more commonly used nonmatching case, the subject must choose the new stimulus in order to receive reward. Monkeys, and rats, with damage to the rhinal cortex are severely impaired at this task at a wide range of delay intervals (Mumby, & Pinel, 1994; Murray, Gaffan, & Flint, 1996; Zola-Morgan, Squire, Amaral, & Suzuki, 1989). By contrast, subjects with damage to the hippocampus or amygdala are either not impaired at all or impaired only under a narrow range of as yet poorly understood conditions (e.g., Gaffan, 1994). In addition to the

From *Current Directions in Psychological Science,* October 1998, pp. 154-157. © 1998 by the American Psychological Society. Reprinted by permission of Blackwell Publishers.

evidence from such behavioral studies, electrophysiological analyses of the rhinal area have shown that its neuronal activity reflects recognition memory (e.g., Brown, 1996).

• *Parahippocampal gyrus.* This brain region is now thought to play an important role in some forms of spatial cognition. Thus, this area in humans is activated in circumstances in which individuals are thinking about moving around in space (e.g., Maguire, Frackowiak, & Frith, 1996). In people with damage to the parahippocampal region, learning about the spatial layout of a test environment is severely impaired (e.g., Bohbot et al., 1998).

• *Hippocampal formation.* This region has long been implicated in spatial learning and memory (O'Keefe & Nadel, 1978) and in memory for episodes (Kinsbourne & Wood, 1975; Milner, 1962). How best to characterize its precise role in memory function has been a matter of intense debate in recent years. Many investigators (Metcalfe & Jacobs, 1998; Moscovitch, 1995; Nadel, Willner, & Kurz, 1985; Squire, Cohen, & Nadel, 1984; Teyler & DiScenna, 1985) agree that the hippocampus plays a role "binding" together the elements of an episode, which themselves are represented in dispersed brain systems. That is, the hippocampus provides a mechanism by which disaggregated bits of information making up an episode can be kept in touch with one another (Jacobs & Nadel, in press). There is general agreement that the hippocampus is essential to this function for recent memories; its role in the retrieval of remote memories is a matter of considerable current debate (cf. Moscovitch & Nadel, 1998; Nadel & Moscovitch, 1997).

A key point of this proposal is that various aspects of an episode memory are represented and stored in dispersed brain modules (cf. O'Keefe & Nadel, 1978, p. 100). Also, each module interconnects with the hippocampal complex, so that the collection of representations of the features of an episode can activate within the hippocampal complex an ensemble encoding that episode. This creation of a hippocampal ensemble (or "cognitive map"; O'Keefe & Nadel, 1978) occurs rapidly, through the mechanism of long-term synaptic potentiation (a form of neural plasticity thought by many to underlie learning and memory) within the relevant hippocampal connections. An act of episode retrieval can be accomplished in two ways: first, by activating the relevant hippocampal ensemble, which then activates dispersed extrahippocampal features, or second, by activating some subset of these dispersed features, which then activate the hippocampal ensemble. In both cases, the hippocampal component is essential to accurate reconstruction of the episodic memory.

STRESS AND MEMORY SYSTEMS

These distinctions among types of explicit memory, and their neural substrates, must be taken into account in any consideration of the ways in which stress affects memory. The data suggest that within physiological limits, stress enhances the function of the amygdala, and consequently strengthens those aspects of explicit memory subserved by this structure (cf. Metcalfe & Jacobs, 1998). The data also firmly establish that high levels of stress or the high levels of the hormone corticosterone (cortisol in humans) typically resulting from stress impair the function of the hippocampus, weakening or totally disrupting those aspects of spatial and explicit memory subserved by this structure. A number of studies, with both humans and animals, have demonstrated this now well-accepted fact (e.g., Bodnoff et al., 1995; de Quervain, Roozendaal, & McGaugh, 1998; Diamond & Rose, 1994; Foy, Stanton, Levine, & Thompson, 1987; Luine, Villegas, Martinez, & McEwen, 1994). For example, Luine et al. (1994) induced stress levels of corticosterone in rats by restraining them in Plexiglas containers in their home cages for 6 hr/day for 21 days. When tested on an eight-arm radial maze, a widely used spatial memory task, these rats were impaired compared with nonstressed control rats (see also Kállai, Kóczán, Szabó, Molnár, & Varga, 1995; Kirschbaum, Wolf, May, Wippich, & Hellhammer, 1996; Lupien et al., 1998, for related studies in humans).

Intriguingly, abnormally low levels of corticosterone, produced by removal of the adrenal glands, can also impair spatial learning (e.g., Conrad & Roy, 1995; Vaher, Luine, Gould, & McEwen, 1994). We, and others, have concluded that the relation between corticosterone and hippocampal function is U-shaped; that is, circulating levels of corticosterone within some optimal range yield normal function. Too little or too much corticosterone impairs function.

Thus, the laboratory data show that the relation between stress and the function of neural structures important for explicit memory is quite complex. Within a certain range, stress could enhance all forms of explicit memory, but high levels of stress could enhance some aspects of explicit memory while impairing others.

And here is the critical point: When stress is high enough to impair the function of the hippocampus, resulting memories will be different from those formed under more ordinary circumstances. These empirical data suggest that memories of trauma may be available as isolated fragments rather than as coherently bound episodes (e.g., van der Kolk & Fisler, 1995). This hypothesis contrasts with the position espoused by Shobe and Kihlstrom (1997), who did not take into account the differential effects of stress on the various memory modules.

CLINICAL IMPLICATIONS

We (Jacobs & Nadel, in press) have argued that these differential effects of stress on the various components of episode memory account for several of the unusual features of memories formed under stress. Traumatic stress can cause amnesia for the autobiographical context of stressful events, but stronger than normal recall for the emotional memories produced by them. That such *emotional hypermnesia* may result from traumatic stress is consistent with early reports (e.g., Charcot, 1887; Janet, 1889). Even in the context of extensive autobiographical amnesia, intrusive emotions or images associated with the trauma (and related events) may appear (Jacobs, Laurance, Thomas, Luzcak, & Nadel,

Recommended Reading

Jacobs, W.J., & Nadel, L. (1985). Stress induced recovery of fears and phobias. *Psychological Review, 92,* 512–531.

LeDoux, J.E. (1994). Emotion, memory and the brain. *Scientific American, 270,* 50–57.

Lupien, S.J., & McEwen, B.S. (1997). The acute effects of corticosteroids on cognition: Integration of animal and human model studies. *Brain Research Reviews, 24,* 1–27.

Sapolsky, R.M. (1998). *Why zebras don't get ulcers: An updated guide to stress, stress-related diseases, and coping.* New York: W.H. Freeman.

Schacter, D. (1996). *Searching for memory: The brain, the mind, and the past.* New York: Basic Books.

1996). Intrusions appear in the context of grief, anxiety disorders, mood disorders, and dissociative disorders (syndromes involving disturbances in identity, memory, or consciousness; Brewin, Hunter, Caroll, & Tata, 1996; Gibbs, 1996; Horowitz, 1986; Howe, Courage, & Peterson, 1995), and can also be elicited in the laboratory (van der Kolk, 1994). What distinguishes these intrusive memory states is the absence of the time-and-place contextual information that typically characterizes autobiographical episode memory.

Van der Kolk and Fisler (1995) showed that after an initial phase when traumatic memories are experienced as fragmentary, an autobiographical memory eventually emerges. We have suggested that this emergence reflects a process of "inferential narrative smoothing," whereby disembodied fragments are knit together into a plausible autobiographical episode (Jacobs & Nadel, in press).

The present analysis suggests that at least some memories "recovered" during therapy should be taken seriously. Although such memories may contain emotional experiences accumulated across multiple stressful events, some of this emotional content could be veridical. The narratives associated with these memories are less likely to be veridical in their entirety. These narratives may be composites of real fragments of experience and the emotions elicited by those experiences, filled out by tacit knowledge and logic available to the individual, and shaped by interlocutors such as friends and therapists.

Notes

1. Address correspondence to Lynn Nadel, Department of Psychology, University of Arizona, Tucson, AZ 85721.

References

Adolphs, R., Tranel, D., Damasio, H. & Damasio, A. (1994). Impaired recognition of emotion in facial expressions following bilateral damage to the human amygdala. *Nature, 372,* 669–672.

Bodnoff, S.R., Humphreys, A.G., Lehman, J.C., Diamond, D.M., Rose, G.M., & Meaney, M.J. (1995). Enduring effects of chronic corticosterone treatment on spatial-learning, synaptic plasticity, and hippocampal neuropathology in young and mid-aged rats. *Journal of Neuroscience, 15,* 61–69.

Bohbot, V., Kalina, M., Stepankova, K., Spackova, N., Petrides, M., & Nadel, L. (1998). Spatial memory deficits in patients with lesions to the right hippocampus and to the right parahippocampal cortex. *Neuropsychologia, 36,* 1217–1238.

Brewin, C.R., Hunter, E., Caroll, F., & Tata, P. (1996). Intrusive memories in depression: An index of schema activation? *Psychological Medicine, 26,* 1271–1276.

Brown, M.W. (1996). Neuronal responses and recognition memory. *Seminars in the Neurosciences, 8,* 23–32.

Charcot, J.M. (1887). *Lecons sur les maladies du système nerveux faites a la Salpêtrière* [Lessons on the illnesses of the nervous system held at Salpetriere] (Vol. 3). Paris: Progres Medical en A. Delahye & Lecorsnie.

Conrad, C.D., & Roy, E.J. (1996). Dentate gyrus destruction and spatial learning impairment after corticosteroid removal in young and middle-aged rats. *Hippocampus, 5,* 1–15.

Davis, M. (1992). The role of the amygdala in fear and anxiety. *Annual Review of Neuroscience, 15,* 353–375.

de Quervain, D.J.-F., Roozendaal, B., & McGaugh, J.L. (1998). Stress and glucocorticoids impair retrieval of long-term spatial memory. *Nature, 394,* 787–790.

Diamond, D.M., & Rose, G.M. (1994). Stress impairs LTP and hippocampal-dependent memory. *Annals of the New York Academy of Sciences, 746,* 411–414.

Foy, M.R., Stanton, M.E., Levine, S., & Thompson, R.F. (1987). Behavioral stress impairs long-term potentiation in rodent hippocampus. *Behavioral and Neural Biology, 48,* 138–149.

Gaffan, D. (1994). Dissociated effects of perirhinal cortex ablation, fornix transection and amygdalectomy: Evidence for multiple memory systems in the primate temporal lobe. *Experimental Brain Research, 99,* 411–422.

Gibbs, N.A. (1996). Nonclinical populations in research on obsessive-compulsive disorder—A critical-review. *Clinical Psychology Review, 16,* 729–773.

Horowitz, M.J. (1986). *Stress response syndromes* (2nd ed.). New York: Jason Aronson.

Howe, M.I., Courage, M.I., & Peterson, C. (1995). Intrusions in preschoolers' recall of traumatic childhood events. *Psychonomic Bulletin & Review, 2,* 130–134.

Jacobs, W.J., Laurance, H.E., Thomas, K.G.F., Luzcak, S.E., & Nadel, L. (1996). On the veracity and variability of recovered traumatic memory. *Traumatology, 2*(1) [Online]. Available: http://rdz.stjohns.edu/trauma/traumaj.html.

Jacobs, W.J., & Nadel, L. (in press). Neurobiology of reconstructed memory. *Psychology of Public Policy and Law.*

Janet, P. (1889). *L'automatisme psychologique.* Paris: Alcan.

Kállai, J., Kóczán, G., Szabó, I., Molnár, P., & Varga, J. (1995). An experimental study to operationally define and measure spatial orientation in panic agoraphobia subjects, generalized anxiety and healthy control groups. *Behavioural and Cognitive Psychology, 23,* 145–152.

Kinsbourne, M., & Wood, F. (1975). Short-term memory processes and the amnesic syndrome. In D. Deutsch & J.A. Deutsch (Eds.), *Short-term memory* (pp. 258–291). New York: Academic Press.

Kirschbaum, C., Wolf, O.T., May, M., Wippich, W., & Hellhammer, D.H. (1996). Stress- and treatment-induced elevations of cortisol levels associated with impaired declarative memory in healthy adults. *Life Sciences, 58,* 1475–1483.

LeDoux, J.E. (1995). Emotion: Clues from the brain. *Annual Review of Psychology, 46,* 209–235.

Luine, V., Villegas, M., Martinez, C., & McEwen, B.S. (1994). Repeated stress causes reversible impairments of spatial memory performance. *Brain Research, 639,* 167–170.

Lupien, S.J., de Leon, M., de Santi, S., Convit, A., Tarshish, C., Nair, N.P.V., Thakur, M., McEwen, B.S., Hauger, R.L., & Meaney, M.J. (1998). Cortisol levels during human aging predict hippocampal atrophy and memory deficits. *Nature Neuroscience, 1,* 69–73.

Maguire, E.A., Frackowiak, R.S.J., & Frith, C.D. (1996). Learning to find your way: A role for the human hippocampal formation. *Proceedings of the Royal Society of London, 263,* 1745–1750.

McGaugh, J.L., Cahill, L., & Roozendaal, B. (1996). Involvement of the amygdala in memory storage—Interaction with other brain systems. *Proceedings of the National Academy of Sciences, USA, 93,* 13508–13514.

Metcalfe, J., & Jacobs, W.J. (1998). Emotional memory: The effects of stress on 'cool' and 'hot' memory systems. In D.L. Medin (Ed.), *The psychology of learning and motivation: Vol. 38. Advances in research and theory* (pp. 187–222). San Diego: Academic Press.

Milner, B. (1962). Les troubles de la memoire accompagnant les lesions hippocampiques bilaterales. In P. Passouant (Ed.), *Physiologie de l'hippocampe* (pp. 257–272). Paris: Centre National de la Recherche Scientifique.

Morris, J.S., Frith, C.D., Perrett, D.I., Rowland, D., Young, A.W., Calder, A.J., & Dolan, R.J. (1996). A differential neural response in the human amygdala to fearful and happy facial expressions. *Nature, 383,* 812–815.

Moscovitch, M. (1995). Recovered consciousness: A hypothesis concerning modularity and episodic memory. *Journal of Clinical and Experimental Neuropsychology, 17,* 276–290.

Moscovitch, M., & Nadel, L. (1998). Consolidation and the hippocampal complex revisited: In defense of the multiple-trace model. *Current Opinions in Neurobiology, 8,* 297–300.

Mumby, D.G., & Pinel, J.P.J. (1994). Rhinal cortex lesions and object recognition in rats. *Behavioral Neuroscience, 108,* 11–18.

Murray, E.A., Gaffan, E.A., & Flint, R.W., Jr. (1996). Anterior rhinal cortex and amygdala: Dissociation of their contributions to memory and food preference in rhesus monkeys. *Behavioral Neuroscience, 110,* 30–42.

Nadel, L., & Moscovitch, M. (1997). Memory consolidation, retrograde amnesia and the hippocampal formation: A re-evaluation of the evidence and new model. *Current Opinions in Neurobiology, 7,* 217–227.

Nadel, L., Willner, J., & Kurz, E.M. (1985). Cognitive maps and environmental context. In P. Balsam & A. Tomie (Eds.), *Context and learning* (pp. 385–406). Hillsdale, NJ: Erlbaum.

O'Keefe, J., & Nadel, L. (1978). *The hippocampus as a cognitive map.* Oxford, England: Oxford University Press.

Rolls, E.T. (1982). Neuronal mechanisms underlying the formation and disconnection of associations between visual stimuli and reinforcement in primates. In C.C. Woody (Ed.), *Conditioning* (pp. 363–373). New York: Plenum Press.

Schacter, D.L., & Tulving, E. (1994). *Memory systems 1994* (pp. 369–394). Cambridge, MA: MIT Press.

Shobe, K.K., & Kihlstrom, J.F. (1997). Is traumatic memory special? *Current Directions in Psychological Science, 6,* 70–74.

Squire, L.R., Cohen, N.J., & Nadel, L. (1984). The medial temporal region and memory consolidation: A new hypothesis. In H. Weingartner & E.S. Parker (Eds.), *Memory consolidation: Psychobiology of cognition* (pp. 185–210). Hillsdale, NJ: Erlbaum.

Teyler, T.J., & DiScenna, P. (1985). The role of the hippocampus in memory: A hypothesis. *Neuroscience and Biobehavioral Reviews, 9,* 377–389.

Vaher, P., Luine, V., Gould, E., & McEwen, B. (1994). Effects of adrenalectomy on spatial memory performance and dentate gyrus morphology. *Brain Research, 656,* 71–76.

van der Kolk, B. (1994). The body keeps the score: Memory and the evolving psychobiology of posttraumatic stress. *Harvard Review of Psychiatry, 5,* 253–265.

van der Kolk, B., & Fisler, R. (1995). Dissociation and the fragmentary nature of traumatic memories: Overview and exploratory study. *Journal of Traumatic Stress, 8,* 505–525.

Zola-Morgan, S., Squire, L.R., Amaral, D.G., & Suzuki, W.A. (1989). Lesions of perirhinal and parahippocampal cortex that spare the amygdala and the hippocampal formation produce severe memory impairment. *Journal of Neuroscience, 9,* 4355–4370.

Unit Selections

Key Points to Consider

❖ Why study cognition? Why study the development of cognitive abilities; why would this be of interest to psychologists? What exact role does the brain play in cognitive abilities, for example, language processing? What role does experience play in cognitive development? Can you describe Piaget's stage theory of cognitive development?

❖ How does culture play a role in cognition? What aspects of culture most influence how we process incoming information about our world?

❖ What is intelligence? How are learning and thinking central to our concepts of intelligence? What are the various types of intelligence described by Howard Gardner? Why is traditional IQ testing controversial? Can you think of people whom you would call "bright" by standards other than the traditional definitions of intelligence? What are some of the myths (and are they true) surrounding the theory of multiple intelligences? How can intelligence be enhanced by education?

❖ What is critical thinking? Can you provide some examples of it? Why is it important to develop critical thinking skills? What can teachers do to stimulate more advanced thinking processes in their students?

 **Links** | **www.dushkin.com/online/**

These sites are annotated on pages 4 and 5.

As Rashad watches his 4-month-old baby, he is convinced that the infant possesses a degree of understanding of the world around her. In fact, Rashad is sure he has one of the smartest babies in the neighborhood. Although he is indeed a proud father, he keeps these thoughts to himself rather than alienate his neighbors whom he perceives as having less-intelligent babies.

Jack lives in the same neighborhood as Rashad. However, Jack doesn't have any children, but he does own two fox terriers. Despite Jack's most concerted efforts, the dogs never come to him when he calls them. In fact, the dogs have been known to run the opposite way on occasion. Instead of being furious, Jack accepts his dogs' disobedience because he is sure the dogs are just dumb beasts and do not know any better.

These vignettes illustrate important ideas about cognition or thought processes. In the first, Rashad ascribes cognitive abilities and high intelligence to his child; in fact, he perhaps ascribes too much cognitive ability to his 4-month-old. In the other case, Jack assumes that his dogs are incapable of thought, more specifically incapable of premeditated disobedience, and therefore he forgives them.

Few adults would deny the existence of their cognitive abilities. Some adults, in fact, think about thinking, something which psychologists call metacognition. Cognition is critical to our survival as adults. But are there differences in mentation in adults? And what about other organisms? Can children think? If they can, do they think like adults? And what about animals; can they think and solve problems? These and similar questions are related to cognitive psychology and cognitive science, which is showcased in this unit.

Cognitive psychology has grown faster than most other specialties in psychology in the past 20 years in response to new computer technology as well as to the growth of psycholinguistics. Computer technology has prompted an interest in artificial intelligence, the mimicking of human intelligence by machines. Similarly the study of psycholinguistics has prompted the examination of the influence of language on thought and vice versa.

While interest in these two developments has eclipsed interest in more traditional areas of cognition such as intelligence, we cannot ignore these traditional areas in this anthology. With regard to intelligence, one persistent problem has been the difficulty of defining just what intelligence is. David Wechsler, author of several of the most popular intelligence tests in current clinical use, defines intelligence as the global capacity of the individual to act purposefully, to think rationally, and to deal effectively with the environment. Other psychologists have proposed more complex definitions. The definitional problem arises when we try to develop tests that validly and reliably measure such concepts. Edward Boring once suggested that we define intelligence as whatever it is that an intelligence test measures.

The first article in this unit offers the reader an introduction to the complex relationship between cognition and development. Specifically, this article describes the child and the development of cognition as outlined in Jean Piaget's landmark theory of cognitive development. The child develops language, logic, and other cognitive skills in systematic ways due to maturation and experience in the environment.

With the first article as an introduction, we continue with a discussion of cognitive development. No child grows up free of cultural influences. The study of culture and its impact on human behavior is fascinating. In "Cognitive Development in Social and Cultural Context," Mary Gauvain discusses how the values and goals of a culture influence cognitive development. She asserts that one cannot study how the mind functions without also studying the influence of culture.

The third article offers a new look at intelligence, which underpins problem solving, decision making, and other cognitive abilities. However, this article takes a new and broader approach to intelligence. Howard Gardner's theory of multiple intelligences is critiqued. Gardner suggests that the traditional definition of intelligence is too narrow and should be expanded to include other measures. The article continues with a discussion of what schools and parents can do to enhance the various forms of intelligence once they have accepted Gardner's theory.

Almost all schools and universities stress critical thinking in today's students. Critical thinking involves deeper processing than just learning or remembering material. It involves, for example, integration, analysis, and interpretation of information. In "Penetrating the Barriers to Teaching Higher Thinking," Viola Supon discusses critical thinking and suggests classroom practices that promote advanced cognitive processing of information.

CHILD PSYCHOLOGIST

JEAN PIAGET

He found the secrets of human learning and knowledge hidden behind the cute and seemingly illogical notions of children

BY SEYMOUR PAPERT

ARCHIVES JEAN PIAGET

PIAGET IN '23: REVERED BY GENERATIONS OF TEACHERS

Jean Piaget, the pioneering Swiss philosopher and psychologist, spent much of his professional life listening to children, watching children and poring over reports of researchers around the world who were doing the same. He found, to put it most succinctly, that children don't think like grownups. After thousands of interactions with young people often barely old enough to talk, Piaget began to suspect that behind their cute and seemingly illogical utterances were thought processes that had their own kind of order and their own special logic. Einstein called it a discovery "so simple that only a genius could have thought of it."

Piaget's insight opened a new window into the inner workings of the mind. By the end of a wide–ranging and remarkably prolific research career that spanned nearly 75 years—from his first scientific publication at age 10 to work still in progress when he died at 84—Piaget had developed several new fields of science: developmental psychology, cognitive theory and what came to be called genetic epistemology. Although not an educational reformer, he championed a way of

BORN *Aug. 9, 1896, in Switzerland*
1907 Publishes first paper at age 10
1918 Obtains doctorate in zoology, studies psychoanalysis
1920 Studies children's intelligence in Paris
1923 First of nearly 60 scholarly books published
1929 Appointed director, International Bureau of Education
1955 Establishes Center for Genetic Epistemology
1980 Dies in Geneva

PIAGET FAMILY/ARCHIVES JEAN PIAGET

PIAGET'S SUBJECTS INCLUDED HIS OWN THREE CHILDREN

thinking about children that provided the foundation for today's education-reform movements. It was a shift comparable to the displacement of stories of "noble savages"

> ## "[He is] one of the two towering figures of 20th century psychology."

JEROME BRUNER, Founder of the Harvard Center for Cognitive Studies

and "cannibals" by modern anthropology. One might say that Piaget was the first to take children's thinking seriously.

Others who shared this respect for children—John Dewey in the U.S., Maria Montessori in Italy and Paulo Freire in Brazil—fought harder for immediate change in the schools, but Piaget's influence on education is deeper and more pervasive. He has been revered by generations of teachers inspired by the belief that children are not empty vessels to be filled with knowledge (as traditional pedagogical theory had it) but active builders of knowledge—little scientists who are constantly creating and testing their own theories of the world. And though he may not be as famous as Sigmund Freud or even B.F. Skinner, his contribution to psychology may be longer lasting. As computers and the Internet give children greater autonomy to explore ever larger digital worlds, the ideas he pioneered become ever more relevant.

Piaget grew up near Lake Neuchâtel in a quiet region of French Switzerland known for its wines and watches. His father was a

From *Time*, March 29, 1999, pp. 104-107. © 1999 by Time Inc. Magazine Company. Reprinted by permission.

professor of medieval studies and his mother a strict Calvinist. He was a child prodigy who soon became interested in the scientific study of nature. When, at age 10, his observations led to questions that could be answered only by access to the university library, Piaget wrote and published a short note on the sighting of an albino sparrow in the hope that this would influence the librarian to stop treating him like a child. It worked. Piaget was launched on a path that would lead to his doctorate in zoology and a lifelong conviction that the way to understand anything is to understand how it evolves.

After World War I, Piaget became interested in psychoanalysis. He moved to Zurich, where he attended Carl Jung's lectures, and then to Paris to study logic and abnormal psychology. Working with Théodore Simon in Alfred Binet's child-psychology lab, he noticed that Parisian children of the same age made similar errors on true-false intelligence tests. Fascinated by their reasoning processes, he began to suspect that the key to human knowledge might be discovered by observing how the child's mind develops.

Back in Switzerland, the young scientist began watching children play, scrupulously recording their words and actions as their minds raced to find reasons for why things are the way they are. In one of his most famous experiments, Piaget asked children, "What makes the wind?" A typical Piaget dialogue:

Piaget: What makes the wind?

Julia: The trees.

P: How do you know?

J: I saw them waving their arms.

P: How does that make the wind?

J (waving her hand in front of his face): Like this. Only they are bigger. And there are lots of trees.

P: What makes the wind on the ocean?

J: It blows there from the land. No. It's the waves . . .

Piaget recognized that five-year-old Julia's beliefs, while not correct by any adult criterion, are not "incorrect" either. They are entirely sensible and coherent within the framework of the child's way of knowing. Classifying them as "true" or "false" misses the point and shows a lack of respect for the child. What Piaget was after was a theory that could find in the wind dialogue coherence, ingenuity and the practice of a kind of explanatory principle (in this case by referring to body actions) that stands young children in very good stead when they don't know enough or have enough skill to handle the kind of explanation that grownups prefer.

Piaget was not an educator and never enunciated rules about how to intervene in such situations. But his work strongly suggests that the automatic reaction of putting the child right may well be abusive. Practicing the art of making theories may be more valuable for children than achieving meteorological orthodoxy; and if their theories are always greeted by "Nice try, but this is how it really is . . . " they might give up after a while on making theories. As Piaget put it, "Children have real understanding only of that which they invent themselves, and each time that we try to teach them something too quickly, we keep them from reinventing it themselves."

Disciples of Piaget have a tolerance for—indeed a fascination with—children's primitive laws of physics: that things disappear when they are out of sight; that the moon and the sun follow you around; that big things float and small things sink. Einstein was especially intrigued by Piaget's finding that seven-year-olds insist that going faster can take more time—perhaps because Einstein's own theories of relativity ran so contrary to common sense.

Although every teacher in training memorizes Piaget's four stages of childhood development (sensorimotor, preoperational, concrete operational, formal operational), the better part of Piaget's work is less well known, perhaps because schools of education regard it as "too deep" for teachers. Piaget never thought of himself as a child psychologist. His real interest was epistemology—the theory of knowledge—which, like physics, was considered a branch of philosophy until Piaget came along and made it a science.

Piaget explored a kind of epistemological relativism in which multiple ways of knowing are acknowledged and examined nonjudgmentally, yet with a philosopher's analytic rigor. Since Piaget, the territory has been widely colonized by those who write about women's ways of knowing, Afrocentric ways of knowing, even the computer's ways of knowing. Indeed, artificial intelligence and the information-processing model of the mind owe more to Piaget than its proponents may realize.

The core of Piaget is his belief that looking carefully at how knowledge develops in children will elucidate the nature of knowledge in general. Whether this has in fact led to deeper understanding remains, like everything about Piaget, controversial. In the past decade Piaget has been vigorously challenged by the current fashion of viewing knowledge as an intrinsic property of the brain. Ingenious experiments have demonstrated that newborn infants already have some of the knowledge that Piaget believed children constructed. But for those, like me, who still see Piaget as the giant in the field of cognitive theory, the difference between what the baby brings and what the adult has is so immense that the new discoveries do not significantly reduce the gap but only increase the mystery.

M.I.T. professor Seymour Papert, creator of the Logo computer language, worked with Piaget in Geneva

Cognitive Development in Social and Cultural Context

Mary Gauvain[1]
Department of Psychology, University of California at Riverside,
Riverside, California

Abstract

The development of thinking is discussed from a sociocultural perspective. Three features of the social and cultural context that play important roles in organizing and directing cognitive development are presented and illustrated empirically: (a) activity goals and values of the culture, (b) material and symbolic tools for satisfying cultural goals and values, and (c) higher level structures that instantiate cultural goals and values in everyday practices. The article concludes with a discussion of the utility of this approach for advancing understanding of human intellectual growth.

Keywords

cognitive development; sociocultural influences; sociohistorical approach

In all societies throughout the world, most children grow up to be competent members of their communities. This impressive phenomenon—and indeed it is impressive—relies on some inherent human ability to develop intellectual and social skills adapted to the circumstances in which growth occurs. It also relies on social and cultural practices that support and maintain desired patterns of development. This article focuses on two questions pertaining to this process. First, how do children develop the skills and knowledge to become competent members of their community? Second, how are cultures uniquely suited to support and lead this development? To address these questions, I discuss culturally devised ways for supporting the development and maintenance of valued cultural skills. Several areas of research are foundational to the ideas presented here.

The first influence is a cultural-practice view of cognition (Chaiklin & Lave, 1996), which includes research on situated learning, everyday cognition and practical intelligence. This work takes as

a starting point the idea that people learn to think in specific contexts in which human activity is directed toward practical goals. An important contribution of this work is attention to the coordination between the thinker and the actions performed. The main limitation for present purposes is that it concentrates on learning rather than development. A second influence is the sociohistorical tradition (Cole, 1996), which emphasizes the role of material, symbolic, and social resources in organizing and supporting mental growth. The primary contribution of this approach is attention to the opportunities and constraints for cognitive development provided by the cultural community in which growth occurs. A practical limitation is that this idea, to date, has been broad in conception, touching on many aspects of psychological development. An organizational framework that links this approach more systematically to contemporary domains of research is needed for further examination and incorporation into the field. A final influence is the concept of the *developmental niche* (Super & Harkness,

1986), which characterizes the psychological structure of the human ecosystem that guides children's development. The central idea is that it is not only the organism that provides structure and direction to development; rather, culture also possesses structure and direction, and it is through the conjoining of these two organized systems that human development unfolds. Super and Harkness proposed three subsystems of the developmental niche, physical and social settings, customs of child care, and psychology of the caregiver. These subsystems concentrate on social development. In this review, I extend this basic framework to the study of cognitive development.

THREE COGNITIVE SUBSYSTEMS OF THE DEVELOPMENTAL NICHE

Three subsystems of the developmental niche that connect cognitive development to culture are the activity

From *Current Directions in Psychological Science*, December 1998, pp. 188-192. © 1998 by the American Psychological Society.
Reprinted by permission of Blackwell Publishers.

goals and values of the culture and its members; historical means for satisfying cultural goals and values, especially the material and symbolic tools that support thinking and its development; and higher level structures that instantiate cultural goals and values in everyday practice and through which children become participants in the intellectual life of their community. These subsystems are hierarchically organized, from the microanalytic level (i.e., the level of individual psychological activity) to the broader social circumstances of development. A key point is the range of human experience represented: Culture penetrates human intellectual functioning and its development at many levels, and it does so through organized individual and social practices.

Activity Goals and Values of the Culture

Human behavior and thinking occur within meaningful contexts as people conduct purposeful, goal-directed activities (Vygotsky, 1978). The developmental implication is that children learn about and practice thinking in the course of participating in goal-directed activities—activities defined and organized by the cultural community in which development occurs. Much psychological research has focused on the organized, goal-directed nature of human activity (e.g., Duncker's classic studies of functional fixedness[2] and Bartlett's studies of memory), so this basic idea is not new. However, a cultural psychological approach offers two unique contributions: (a) an emphasis on the connection between activity structures (the means and goals that define human action) and the cultural practices from which they stem and (b) an examination of the relations among activity structures, cultural practices, and cognitive growth.

Research on children's everyday mathematics illustrates this linkage. Studies of the mathematical skills of Brazilian children who sell candy in the street (Carraher, Carraher, & Schliemann, 1985) indicate that mental activity reflects the practices that individuals engage in, that these practices are defined by cultural convention and routine, and that mathematical activities are handled differently, and more successfully, when the goal of the calculation is meaningful than when it is not. Another example is found in how intelligent behavior changes following social reorganization. Inkeles and Smith (1974) observed industrialization in non-Western communities and found that one behavioral change was greater concern with time and planning activities in advance. The point is not that Western-

ers plan and non-Westerners do not. What occurred was a reorganization of cultural practices that, in turn, led to the reorganization of a cognitive behavior, planning.

The main point is that activities and the goals that guide them are expressions of culture. Focusing on the cultural context of human activity may advance understanding of how the human mind is organized over the course of development to fit with the requirements and opportunities of the culture. Incidentally, this point may offer insight into the issue of transfer or generalization of cognitive skills across different task contexts, a topic that has vexed psychologists for generations. Psychologists have often sought transfer by focusing on isomorphic tasks (i.e., tasks that are very similar in structure). However, the key psychological linkage supporting transfer may not be task properties per se, but may instead be the meaning and goals of an activity and how a culture has devised ways, such as problem-solving routines, to achieve these goals and connect human action over time and space.

Material and Symbolic Tools

Material and symbolic tools, or artifacts (Cole, 1996), are developed and used by cultural communities to support mental activity. Such tools not only enhance thinking but also transform it, and in so doing, they channel cognitive development in unique ways. Involvement with more experienced cultural members, who demonstrate and convey the use of these tools, is a critical part of this process. Through the use of such "tools for thinking," a person's mental functioning acquires an organized link to sociohistorically formulated means of thinking transmitted through these tools.

Research on the use of particular cultural tools and the development of mathematical thinking illustrates this point. Children who are skilled at using the abacus employ a "mental abacus" when calculating solutions in their heads (Hatano, Miyake, & Binks, 1977), and this skill enhances mental calculation. Historical examination lends further insight into this process (Swetz, 1987). Late in the 12th century, a book by Leonardo of Pisa, who was also known as Fibonacci, introduced Hindu-Arabic notation and described the commercial applications of this system. This idea was picked up by Italian merchants in the next century and led to changes in conventions of calculating. At the time, Roman numerals were used, and large calculations were executed on the counting board, a form of abacus. These

boards were very large, hard to transport, and difficult to use. Extensive training was needed to reach competence, and only a few people could do the calculations or check them for correctness. Hindu-Arabic numerals were entirely different. Far less equipment was needed to calculate with this system—ink and paper sufficed. This equipment was easy to transport, and, more important, it was easy to teach and learn. In a brief period of time, the long-established form of calculation was replaced. Although the Hindu-Arabic system limited the need for mental calculation, it helped lay the foundation for further developments in mathematics, especially in areas like number theory, in that calculations can be represented on paper and reexamined for patterns and structure (Swetz, 1987).

How does this historical case relate to the findings about skilled abacus users? Think again about mental calculation, a cognitive process that research indicates is aided by skill with the abacus. What this history tells us is that the shift from Roman to Hindu-Arabic numerals made mental calculation largely obsolete, as well as less valued, because calculating on paper allowed people to demonstrate their solution steps. It appears that differential skill of people who do and do not use the abacus may have origins in the notation shift introduced in the 13th and 14th centuries. The mathematical skills of experts are consistent with the requirements of the apparatus and the practice their notation systems afford.

The main point is that cultural tools and the thinking they support are not independent but merged. To describe thinking by concentrating on one and not the other is to ignore part of the problem-solving process. Too often in psychological research when tools of thinking are described, they are treated as entities outside the head, and therefore not part of, or at least not central to, the cognitive process being investigated. However, such thinking tools, both material and symbolic, are constituent elements of cognition and its development. The historical example suggests that many of the concepts considered fundamental to human cognition in the domains in which artifacts play important roles have not always been in place, at least not in the way they are conceptualized today. Certain tools of thought came into being at various points during human history, and these influenced thinking in extraordinary ways. These historical "changes of mind" may be illuminating for scholars interested in cognitive development. Although historical analysis is of limited use to psychologists for many reasons, such cases may be helpful for demonstrating an organized link among artifacts, social processes, and the mind that is often difficult to see in the more local, contemporary circumstances in which psychologists usually do their research.

Higher Level Structures and Practices

Organized social practices or conventions allow people to share their knowledge with one another. These structures help connect members of a community to each other and to a shared system of meaning. Examples of the connection between cognitive development and cultural ways of organizing and communicating knowledge exist in the developmental literature. Research on scripts, which are "outlines" of common, recurrent events (Nelson & Gruendel, 1981), treats the acquisition of culturally organized knowledge as a critical developmental achievement. Research on the development of other pragmatic conventions, such as skill at describing large-scale space (Gauvain & Rogoff, 1989) as if one is being taken on an imagined walk through it (a "mental tour"), also suggests that one important aspect of development is the increasing alignment of knowledge with the conventions of the community in which development occurs.

An intriguing question is whether these conventional forms influence the process of thinking and its development. There is far less data on this question. However, an interesting series of studies by Levinson (1996) in an Australian Aboriginal community, the Guugu Yimithirr, is relevant. To describe spatial location, the language used in this community does not rely on relativistic terms, like left and right, but on absolute or fixed directional terms, like north, south, windward, and upstream. How do these speakers encode spatial information? In one study, objects were positioned on a table in a windowless, nondescript room. Each participant studied these placements, was then taken to a similar room that was oriented differently, and asked to place the same set of objects on a table so as to duplicate the placements in the first room. Participants placed the items in ways that respected the cardinal directions of the original placements (i.e., an object placed on the north side of the table was placed on the north, even though this would mean that it would be on the "other side" of an object to an observer using relative position as a guide). Although these results do not specify the cognitive processes underlying this behavior, they suggest that performance on tasks involving spatial

cognition involves the coordination of visual and linguistic encoding in ways related to practices of the cultural community.

Another set of higher level structures related to the development of thinking appears in practices of social interaction. In recent years, there has been extensive research on the influence of social interaction on cognitive development, with much of this work based on Vygotsky's (1978) notion of the zone of proximal development, which is defined as the distance between an individual's attained level of development and the individual's potential level of development that may be reached by guidance and support from others (see Rogoff, 1990). Results from this research support the claim that intelligence, especially in the early years, develops largely through social experiences. For example, when Tessler and Nelson (1994) tested the recall of 3- to 3-1/2-year-old children about a visit they took to a museum with their mothers, none of the children recalled any information that they had seen in the museum but not discussed with their mothers. Dyadic interaction with adults or peers is only one form of social exchange that may determine young children's opportunities for cognitive development in social context. Parents also influence children's learning via the practical routines they adopt to organize children's behaviors and by regulating the composition of children's social groups. Beyond the family and peer group, cognitive development is influenced by children's participation in more formal social institutions, especially school, and by opportunities to observe more competent cultural members as they engage in cognitive activities, a process Lave and Wenger (1991) call legitimate peripheral participation.

The point is that cognitive development occurs in and emerges from social situations. Conventions for organizing and conveying knowledge, as well as social practices within which knowledge is displayed and communicated, are an inherent aspect of thinking. For research to advance, these social systems need to be connected in a principled way to the developmental processes they help organize, as well as to the cultural system of meaning and practice they represent.

CONCLUSIONS

In summary, a sociocultural view of cognitive development enhances understanding of this psychological process. Dimensions of culture are realized in human action, and it is possible to specify and study these dimensions in relation to psychological development. They can

bring the social and cultural character of intellectual development into relief. Understanding culture and cognitive development can be advanced via research designed for this purpose as well as by reexamining findings extant in the literature.

All this said, many hard questions remain. One concerns how to understand and describe individual skill that emerges in and is displayed in social situations. Psychologists have yet to devise a language for describing thinking that is not entirely in the head of the child or is only partially in place (i.e., evident only in some circumstances). Haith (1997) pointed out that many of the cognitive skills that children develop are defined in dichotomous terms. Consider mental representations. Representations are typically understood as something that a person either has or does not have (i.e., as states of understanding rather than as processes), and rarely as something that is partially or incompletely achieved. Such conceptualization may suffice in describing the mature thinker, though this is an open question. But it is surely inadequate for describing the development of knowledge that appears in the form of "partial understanding," such as that located in social performance. Thus, in order to incorporate the notion of partial or socially contextualized intellectual accomplishments into an understanding of cognitive development, we need a different conceptualization of many cognitive skills.

The analysis of culture in all aspects of psychological functioning is likely to increase dramatically in the next decade. How psychologists, especially those interested in intellectual development, will address this concern is unclear. Perhaps by developing conceptual frameworks, such as the one presented here, in which social and cultural systems of interacting and supporting psychological functions are an inextricable part of human behavior and development, this task may be eased.

Notes

1. Address correspondence to Mary Gauvain, Department of Psychology, University of California at Riverside, Riverside, CA 92521; e-mail: mary.gauvain@ ucr. edu.

2. Functional fixedness is a problem-solving phenomenon in which people have difficulty seeing alternate uses for common objects.

Recommended Reading

Cole, M. (1996). (See References)

Gauvain, M. (1995). Thinking in niches: Sociocultural influences on cognitive development. *Human Development, 38,* 25–45.

Goodnow, J.J. (1990). The socialization of cognition. In J.W. Stigler, R.A. Schweder, & G. Herdt (Eds.), *Cultural psychology* (pp. 259–286). New York: Cambridge University Press.

Nelson, K. (1996). *Language in cognitive development: The emergence of the mediated mind.* Cambridge, England: Cambridge University Press.

Rogoff, B. (1998). Cognition as a collaborative process. In W. Damon (Series Ed.) & D. Kuhn & R.S. Siegler (Vol. Eds.), *Handbook of child psychology: Vol. 2. Cognition, perception, and language* (pp. 679–744). New York: John Wiley and Sons.

References

Carraher, T.N., Carraher, D.W., & Schliemann, A.D. (1985). Mathematics in the streets and in schools. *British Journal of Developmental Psychology, 3,* 21–29.

Chaiklin, S., & Lave, J. (1996). *Understanding practice: Perspectives on activity and context.* Cambridge, England: Cambridge University Press.

Cole, M. (1996). *Cultural psychology.* Cambridge, MA: Harvard University Press.

Gauvain, M., & Rogoff, B. (1989). Ways of speaking about space: The development of children's skill at communicating spatial knowledge. *Cognitive Development, 4,* 295–307.

Haith, M.M. (1997, April). *Who put the cog in infant cognition? Is rich interpretation too costly?* Paper presented at the biennial meeting of the Society for Research in Child Development, Washington, DC.

Hatano, G., Miyake, Y., & Binks, M. (1977). Performance of expert abacus operators. *Cognition, 9,* 47–55.

Inkeles, A., & Smith, D.H. (1974). *Becoming modern.* Cambridge, MA: Harvard University Press.

Lave, J., & Wenger, E. (1991). *Situated learning: Legitimate peripheral participation.* New York: Cambridge University Press.

Levinson, S.C. (1996). Frames of reference and Molyneux's question: Crosslinguistic evidence. In P. Bloom, M.A. Peterson, L. Nadel, & M.F. Garrett (Eds.), *Language and space* (pp. 109–169). Cambridge, MA: MIT Press.

Nelson, K., & Gruendel, J. (1981). Generalized event representations: Basic building blocks of cognitive development. In M.E. Lamb & A.L. Brown (Eds.), *Advances in developmental psychology* (Vol. 1, pp. 131–158). Hillsdale, NJ: Erlbaum.

Rogoff, B. (1990). *Apprenticeship in thinking.* New York: Oxford University Press.

Super, C.M., & Harkness, S. (1986). The developmental niche: A conceptualization at the interface of child and culture. *International Journal of Behavioral Development, 9,* 545–569.

Swetz, F.J. (1987). *Capitalism and arithmetic.* La Salle, IL: Open Court.

Tessler, M., & Nelson, K. (1994). Making memories: The influence of joint encoding on later recall. *Consciousness and Cognition, 3,* 307–326.

Vygotsky, L.S. (1978). *Mind in society.* Cambridge, MA: Harvard University Press.

MULTIPLE INTELLIGENCE DISORDER

Howard Gardner's campaign against logic.

By James Traub

Howard Gardner first realized that he had struck a chord in the national psyche when he gave a speech to private-school administrators on his new theory of "multiple intelligences" and saw the headmasters elbowing each other to get into the hall. That was in 1983. Since that time, Gardner, a Harvard professor who still carries a book bag and wears a ski parka over his tweed jacket, has blossomed into a genuine academic superstar. He has won a MacArthur "genius" grant; his books have been translated into 20 languages; and he gives about 75 talks a year. There are now "M.I. schools" all over the country. His ideas have achieved extraordinary currency in even the most rarefied reaches of the educational world; when the directorship of one of New York's most prestigious private schools recently came open, almost every candidate for the job mentioned Gardner in his or her one-page educational-philosophy statement. In the 15 years since the publication of Gardner's *Frames of Mind*, multiple intelligences has gone from being a widely disputed theory to a rallying cry for school reformers to a cultural commonplace. And, amazingly, it has done so without ever winning over the scientific establishment.

Gardner's central claim is that what we normally think of as intelligence is merely a single aspect, or two aspects, of a much wider range of aptitudes; he has counted eight so far. Thus we have exalted the attribute measured by IQ tests—the hyperlogical style Gardner

half-jokingly calls the "Alan Dershowitz" model of intelligence—and have slighted our creative and interpersonal gifts. Of course, the primary question about this theory is whether or not it's true. But an intriguing secondary question is why it's so wildly popular. "I think the whole intelligence establishment and the psychometric tradition were ready to be attacked by somebody who was credible," Gardner told me the first time I met him, in the midst of a two-day speaking tour in Chicago last December. "We know that kids who do well on tests are smart, but we also know that a lot of kids who don't do well on tests are getting it. The question is not how smart people are but in what ways people are smart." This is, of course, an immensely appealing idea. Gardner has offered an explanation for academic failure in which the problem lies in the system of measurement rather than the student or the teacher; more broadly, he has given intellectual legitimacy to critiques of the test-driven meritocracy and of the high-IQ elite it fosters. Multiple intelligence theory clearly serves many purposes. That makes it powerful, but not necessarily valid.

Psychometrics hasn't changed much since Alfred Binet devised a test at the turn of the century to predict which French children would succeed or fail in school. The instruments we now use to test a child's "intelligence quotient" measure essentially the same aptitudes that Binet did—memory, vocabulary, spatial thinking, the ability to draw analogies and solve puzzles—because these are the aptitudes historically as-

JAMES TRAUB is a contributing writer for *The New York Times Magazine*.

sociated with success in school and in professional life. While psychometricians disagree about the extent to which intelligence is an inherited trait rather than a result of environment and upbringing, there is broad consensus around the idea that intelligence is a single entity that can be measured with fairly great accuracy. The various mental aptitudes are understood as aspects of a single underlying trait called g, for "general intelligence."

Howard Gardner has approached the subject of intelligence from an entirely different angle, one that combines scientific research and speculation with personal experience. Gardner is a polymath, with a breadth of interests unusual in his field. As a boy, he was a serious pianist and a student of composition; as a young scholar at Harvard, where he has spent his entire professional life, he worked with Nelson Goodman, the philosopher of aesthetics. In one of his first books, *The Arts and Human Development*, published in 1973, Gardner noted that the developmental model created by the great Swiss psychologist Jean Piaget applied only to "those mental processes that culminate in scientific thought, an end state that can be expressed in logical terms." Gardner looked instead at the development of the cognitive processes involved in creative work. Several of his subsequent books have explored the thought processes of great artistic figures. Gardner had also begun to study brain-damaged patients at Boston's Veterans Administration Hospital. He found that many of them had suffered devastating damage to a core intellectual function that had nevertheless left other functions intact—so that some aphasics who could barely comprehend speech could nevertheless recognize a metaphor or even tell a joke. This fit with an emerging consensus in neuroscience: namely, that the brain operates in "modular" fashion, with autonomous systems devoted to different mental acts.

Gardner built on these insights in *Frames of Mind*. Rather than accepting that intelligence tests captured intelligence, he drew up a series of criteria from a wide range of disciplines and assigned the title "intelligence" to whatever mental traits satisfied them. In order to make Gardner's final cut, an aptitude had to have been isolated, or spared, in instances of brain damage; had to furnish instances of prodigies or idiots savants; had to have a unique developmental and evolutionary history; and so on. These intelligences were almost wholly independent of one another; there was no master trait—no g. The seven winners were "linguistic" and "logical-mathematical"—the two already recognized by psychometricians—plus "musical," "spatial," "bodily kinesthetic," "intrapersonal," and "interpersonal." Gardner has since added an eighth, the "naturalist intelligence," which is the ability to make distinctions and to form classes among objects. "Existential intelligence" has been a candidate for several years, but Gardner has not yet admitted it to the pantheon.

Gardner failed to persuade his peers. George Miller, the esteemed psychologist credited with discovering the mechanisms by which short-term memory operates, wrote in *The New York Times Book Review* that Gardner's argument boiled down to "hunch and opinion." And Gardner's subsequent work has done very little to shift the balance of opinion. A recent issue of *Psychology, Public Policy, and Law* devoted to the study of intelligence contained virtually no reference to Gardner's work. Most people who study intelligence view M.I. theory as rhetoric rather than science, and they're divided on the virtues of the rhetoric. Steven Ceci, a developmental psychologist at Cornell, praises Gardner as "a wonderful communicator" who has publicized "a much more egalitarian view of intelligence." But he points out that Gardner's approach of constructing criteria and then running candidate intelligences through them, while suggestive, provides no hard evidence—no test results, for example—that his colleagues could evaluate. Ceci adds: "The neurological data show that the brain is modular, but that does not address the issue of whether all these things are correlated or not." Track-and-field athletes, he notes, may have special gifts in one particular event, but they will score better than the average person on every event. Psychological tests show the same kind of correlations.

Gardner describes this conventional view of intelligence as Cartesian rather than Darwinian. Cartesians, he argues, see the mind in strictly rational and ahistorical terms. "The Darwinian view," he says, "is that this is a crazy-quilt group of faculties that we have here, and they've dealt with survival over hundreds of thousands of years in very different environments. Literacy only existed twenty-five hundred years ago. What does it mean to develop a whole theory of intelligence that didn't even exist three thousand years ago? Moreover, given that we now have computers that will do our rational behavior for us, it's an open question what the intelligences are going to be that are valued fifty years from now. It might be artistic; it might be pointless kinds of things." Why should we accept a definition of intelligence that "took a certain scholastic skill—what it meant to be a good bureaucrat a hundred years ago—and make that the quintessence of intelligence"?

But that is, in a way, precisely the problem with Gardner's theory. Intelligence is not a crisp concept but a term of value—indeed, the ultimate term of value. Some in Gardner's corner, like his mentor and colleague Jerome Bruner, say they wish Gardner had employed a more neutral term like "aptitude." But if Gardner hadn't used "intelligence" he wouldn't be the colossal figure he is today. Gardner does not shy away from the "political" dimension of his argument. "My claim that there are seven or eight Xs is not a value judgment," he told me. "It's my best reading of the biological and cultural data. But my decision to call them 'intelligences' is clearly picking a fight with a group that thought it, and it alone, could decide what intelligence was."

There may well be validity to Gardner's claim that core mental aptitudes are more autonomous from one another than psychometricians like to believe. But the reason psychologists don't measure the elements of "bodily kinesthetic" intelligence isn't that they doubt the elements exist—it's that they don't think the elements matter. Some societies may be structured around musical or athletic or spiritual attainments, but ours isn't. This is where Gardner's quarrel lies. Like Robert Coles, the author of *The Moral Intelligence of Children,* and Daniel Goleman, who wrote the wildly popular *Emotional Intelligence,* Gardner believes that we have submitted too much to the tyranny of logic. What he has elaborated over the years is the most scientifically credible and deeply pondered of the various assaults on the hegemony of logic. It's an extraordinary polemic, but it's still a polemic. And so the question it leaves us with is: Are we too preoccupied with cultivating the old-fashioned intellectual gifts, or are we not preoccupied enough?

The psychometric establishment was no match for *Frames of Mind* in the court of public opinion. Gardner had offered a vision of human nature that spoke eloquently to public disillusionment with the scientific, technocratic worldview. Although Gardner had almost nothing to say about the practical applications of his theory, he had provided a paradigm that opened up new vistas for the education of children. From the outset, educators passed *Frames of Mind* around like samizdat. Tom Hoerr, the headmaster of a private school in St. Louis, told me that he bought the book soon after it was published, read it with mounting excitement, and then spent months meeting after school with his faculty to discuss it chapter by chapter. A group of teachers in Indianapolis drove 14 hours to talk with Gardner about creating a school based on his philosophy. Gardner didn't have a philosophy, and yet his reticence about the world of practice had the effect of vindicating almost any departure from the traditional curriculum or traditional pedagogy made in his name.

And so began the astonishing second life of *Frames of Mind* as a template for the transformation of the schools—a transformation much in evidence today. Open up a copy of *Education Week* and you'll see ads for conferences on the "Student at Risk" and "Restructuring Elementary Schools" and "Training for Trainers"—all with presentations on M.I. theory. One progressively minded educator recently told me, "Howard is the guru, and *Frames of Mind* is the bible." Few of the teachers and administrators I talked to were familiar with the critiques of multiple intelligence theory; what they knew was that the theory worked for them. They talked about it almost euphorically. To Dee Dickinson, an educator and consultant in Seattle, *Frames of Mind* offered a "metatheory" that tied together all the effective teaching strategies she had been promoting. "Here was a new way of looking at hu-

man capacities," she said, "and a new way of identifying people's strengths and finding effective ways of helping people use those strengths." Gardner appealed to the teachers' intuitive sense that children learn in different ways, and the teachers responded to Gardner's more explicitly political agenda of democratizing human gifts. Tom Hoerr said that what he learned from Gardner was that "working with other people, working with yourself, knowing other people, is a form of intelligence." Hoerr's own motto is: "Who you are is more important than what you know."

M.I. has now spawned a burgeoning cottage industry of consultants and manuals and videotapes. Several publishers have an entire sideline of Gardneriana, and I sent away for material from several of them. One of the items I received was *Celebrating Multiple Intelligences,* a teachers' guide written by Hoerr and his staff at the New City School, one of the most highly regarded M.I. schools. The book consists of a series of lesson plans in the various intelligences, further divided according to the students' ages. In one exercise designed to stimulate the interpersonal intelligence of students from the first through third grades, children form a circle and throw a ball of string back and forth, each time saying something complimentary about the recipient. The "learner outcome" is: "Children will focus on expressing positive comments to peers who they may or may not know well." Every exercise comes with "M.I. Extensions" designed to stimulate some other intelligence—write songs about the activity, play charades to illustrate the activity, and, above all, talk about how you felt about the activity. The sensitivity toward the variety of children's abilities is connected to a broader preoccupation with diversity. In order to "look at issues of prejudice and discrimination relating to disabilities, race, gender, and religion," the teachers devised an experiment in which "each child spent six hours a day being blindfolded, wearing ear plugs, sitting in a wheelchair, or having limited use of arms and hands." It lasted five days.

Here we come to the heart of the problem with multiple intelligences—not as theory, but as practice. M.I. theory has proved powerful not because it's true but because it chimes with the values and presuppositions of the school world and of the larger culture. When theories escape into the world, they get used in ways that their inventors could scarcely have predicted or even approved. Gardner hasn't been quite sure where his responsibility lies in such matters. He told me that he cannot be the "policeman" of the world he set into motion, though he has, increasingly, been its poster boy. Gardner has begun to speak out against some of the more extreme uses of his theory, and critics like educational historian Diane Ravitch have urged him to do more. When I showed Gardner copies of some of the exercises in *Celebrating Multiple Intelligences,* he scrutinized them carefully, frowned, and said, " The only answer I can give to this is: I would certainly not want to be in a school where a lot of time was spent doing these things."

Gardner himself is a rigorous thinker, and he now takes pains to talk about "the school virtues." He often describes himself as a "disciplinarian," by which he means that he believes in the traditional academic disciplines. The intelligences, he says, are not academic ends in themselves, but means by which legitimate academic ends may be reached. For example, if a child is not particularly strong in "logical-mathematical" intelligence, the math teacher should seek a medium in which the child feels more comfortable—language or even physical movement. In *Multiple Intelligences,* a book of practical advice published in 1993, Gardner writes, "Any concept worth teaching can be approached in at least five different ways that, roughly speaking, map onto the multiple intelligences." The model school that he sketches in the book has much in common with progressive schools generally. Students work with one another as much as with the teacher; they design and carry out long-term projects rather than completing daily assignments; they seek to master concepts rather than absorb information; they spend time in real-world environments. What's different about an M.I. school is that it observes a rigorous equality among the intelligences—no "hierarchizing" of language and logic.

Whether that's desirable or not depends in part on whether you think the schools are turning out too many Dershowitz-like whiz kids or too few. Having visited several dozen schools over the last decade or so, I would suggest the answer is clearly "too few." Maybe in Japan, or even in France, are schools producing students who are too narrow; the problem in the United States is that students are too shallow. M.I. can, in theory, be a means of teaching deeper understanding, but it's at least as likely that it will be used in the service of a specious sense of "breadth." Chester Finn, an educational reformer and former Reagan administration official, describes M.I. pedagogy as the cognitive version of the multiculturalist view that school should offer a celebration of diversity. Harold Stevenson, a psychologist at the University of Michigan, says, "What they're trying to say is, 'You may not be able to do academic things, but you move well, or you're very good at music or spatial intelligence.' " Whatever Gardner himself intends, M.I. theory legitimizes the fad for "self-esteem, " the unwillingness to make even elementary distinctions of value, the excessive regard for diversity, and the decline of diligence.

Gardner and other progressive educators are surely right that traditional pedagogy, at least as it is practiced in most schools, leads to superficial understandings and the confusion of recitation with real knowledge. Good teachers challenge their students at the deepest possible level; they understand that the mastery of facts and dates is a means to an end, not an end in itself. But it's a powerful means. And it may be better for schools to err on the side of too much of it rather than too little.

There are now hundreds of schools that claim to be based in whole or in part on M.I. pedagogy. Educational journals carry glowing accounts of schools "turned around" by M.I. A researcher working for Gardner says that she finds that trivial uses of the pedagogy are giving way to more serious ones. Gardner himself guessed that, if I were to visit 50 M.I. schools, "you'd see a lot more schools that are indistinguishable from other schools than you would schools that are Mickey Mouse"— not exactly a stirring defense. Still, he said, enough schools are using his principles wisely to demonstrate the potential power of M.I.

In the middle of this past school year, I spent a day at the Key Learning Center in Indianapolis, probably the most famous of the M.I. schools. I had expected Key to be one of those schools where kids learn everything in seven or eight ways, jumping up and down in math class and singing their way through English. In fact, the math and science classes I sat in on looked perfectly familiar. Still, M.I.'s influence was as conspicuous as the drawings of the intelligences that line the entrance corridor. Every student spends as much time on music and art as English or social studies. Students are not graded. They receive, instead, "pupil progress reports" in which their academic improvement, their level of motivation, and their "performance along the developmental continuum" are measured in terms that can't be plotted on invidious bell curves.

Peter Reynolds, a bright, mop-haired seventh-grader, was assigned to serve as my "docent." Peter talked about school in a way that I couldn't have imagined doing in seventh grade. What he liked about Key, he said, was the opportunity to "interact" with people, not only other kids, but also the adults in the school. Peter explained that every year, starting in kindergarten, students are expected to devise a project and present it to teachers and peers. In first grade, he had made a study of his pet rats and talked about how they reproduced, how they used their teeth, how they responded to different stimuli. All of the presentations were videotaped, so he had an archive of his work from the age of five.

Peter happened to be presenting his project that day. He had gone to Romania with his father and a friend, and he put a crude oak-tag map up on a stand, showed photographs of the trip, and talked about the people they had met. Most of it was pitched at the level of "it was really nice" and "it was really interesting." On the other hand, I was impressed by what Gardner would have called Peter's interpersonal intelligence. He was calm and forthright, and his classmates listened respectfully and asked questions. The whole school, in fact, had a very civilized and noncompetitive atmosphere; there was none of the waving of hands and shouting "me, me, me" that I remember from junior high. Then again, what's so terrible about a little self-aggrandizing intellectual enthusiasm at age 13?

The school did have a few semi-farcical touches. There was a "flow" room designed to foster the state of unselfconscious engagement that people attain at moments of peak creativity—a practice that rested on a theory devised by Mihaly Csikszentmihalyi, a psychologist who works closely with Gardner. Kids were playing computer games, "Parcheesi, " or "Guess Who?"—the kind of activities I'm happy to have my seven-year-old do at home but wouldn't expect to be part of a curriculum. But the Key school was not absurd in the way that educational traditionalists imagine. It was a serious-minded place, and the kids I met seemed enthusiastic and engaged. On the other hand, if they were engaged in deep understanding, I must have missed it. The eighth-grade "linguistics" class I sat in on read through a passage in *Life On The Mississippi* without getting within hailing distance of its meaning. The school's ambitions almost seemed to be elsewhere—in fostering a sense of personal maturity, in a genuine commitment to music, in making the children conscious of their own strengths.

What the Key school is arguably about is the fostering of a new kind of child and thus of a new kind of person—less linear and more "well-rounded," less competitive and more cooperative. This is a monumental ambition, but it's actually not far from Gardner's own vision. Something grandiose lurks beneath Gardner's modesty and care—that's why he insisted on using that provocative word, "intelligence." Back in Chicago, I heard him tell spellbound special-ed teachers that we are living at the edge of a paradigm shift. "This is a new definition of human beings, cognitively speaking," he said. "Socrates defined man as a rational animal; Freud defined him as an irrational animal; what M.I. theory says is that we are the animal that exhibits the eight and a half intelligences."

Penetrating the Barriers to Teaching Higher Thinking

Viola Supon

Enhancing students' abilities to become critical thinkers continues to be one of education's fundamental purposes. Over the decades, educational researchers, corporate leaders, employers, and parents have constantly urged teachers to help students to develop the ability to think critically (Potts 1994; Howe and Warren 1989), a skill that "involves not only knowledge of content but also concept formation and analysis, reasoning and drawing conclusions, recognizing and avoiding contradiction, and other essential cognitive activities" (Scheinin 1995, 1). The current emphasis on critical thinking can be related to societal factors, such as global economic shifts, massive dissemination of information, and occupational mobility.

Teachers face numerous barriers, however, when they attempt to create thinking classrooms—for example, insecurities about their own abilities to think critically, fear on the part of students that they will be ridiculed by their peers when they share experiences, and teachers' own attachment to the lecture method. The major ways to overcome barriers such as these are as follows: (1) acquisition of a conscious commitment, (2) legitimization of students' experiences, (3) integration of visualizing into the curriculum, (4) use of reflective analysis, and (5) diversification of perspectives. Let us consider each of those steps.

Acquisition of Conscious Commitment

In one recent study, Yildirim (1994) found that teachers feel a responsibility for promoting thinking. Over half the teachers in the study, however, stated they had only adequate skills for improving thinking, and approximately 14 percent did not believe they had even adequate skills.

One way to penetrate this barrier is to foster a change in teacher attitude toward teaching critical thinking. Brookfield (1987) stated emphatically that "there is no Holy Grail of facilitating critical thinking and no one way

---

Viola Supon is an assistant professor of education in the Department of Curriculum and Foundations at Bloomsburg University, Bloomsburg, Pennsylvania.

to instructional enlightenment" (233). Teachers can begin to recognize that with a conscious commitment to having students engage in meaningful and enthusiastic learning, they are contributing to the application of critical thinking efforts. Teachers can begin to hone their instructional skills by reading educational journals and attending seminars and staff development programs on various ways of teaching thinking. When they consciously commit themselves to breaking the pattern of routine teaching and to developing alternative ways of delivering the content, teachers can begin to develop critical thinking skills for themselves and their students.

Researchers have found that critical thinking occurs when teachers' attitudes and methods help students gain the "practical wisdom" necessary to engage in learning (Weinstein 1995; Paul 1990). Higher standards of thinking are achieved when students recognize the relationships between a certain disciplinary or instructional theory and their own immediate concerns. When teachers relate students' personal experiences, concerns, anxieties, and/or successes to a particular lesson, they are penetrating the first barrier to reaching the educational ideal.

Legitimization of Students' Experiences

Teaching higher levels of thinking encompasses various methodologies that legitimize students' experiences and ideas. Legitimizing can be accomplished through collaborative group work and class discussions. Teachers need to recognize that "emphasis is placed on attitudes and dispositions which the teacher must demonstrate in order to create a non-judgmental atmosphere in which critical thinking is fostered" (Gordon 1991, 5). When teachers deliberately integrate the selected content, while embracing and combining students' ideas and experiences, critical thinking capacities are being conditioned. When teachers deliberately incorporate these dimensions into their teaching, they are encouraging students to become aware of their own ideals, behaviors, and values.

From *The Clearing House*, May/June 1998, pp. 294–296. © 1998 by Heldref Publications, 1319 Eighteenth St., NW, Washington, DC 20036-1802. Reprinted by permission.

To legitimize students' experiences, teachers have to establish a classroom of trust. The most direct route to trust is through mutual respect. Although student respect for the teacher may develop slowly, if at all, the teacher fosters it by demonstrating respect toward the students. A teacher must let the students know that caring, understanding, and empathy exist toward each of them. Creating experiences that allow students to share their thoughts with one another and with the teacher opens the door to trust through respect. The encouraging factors that occur in the classroom can prompt students to be open with the experiences they have had. Slowly, the barriers of peer ridicule and fear are broken, and students recognize that their experiences and ideas have validity and worth.

Integration of Visualizing into the Curriculum

It is through visualizing important concepts and facts that students can build knowledge bases. Visualizing, according to Miles (1994), means "creating mental pictures to aid in learning, thinking, and solving" (50). When concepts are organized and visual, students can begin to sharpen their abilities to communicate the information (Hyerle 1996). When teachers oppose the traditional method of lecturing in the middle and secondary classrooms and integrate visuals and visualizing into the class on a regular basis, they have penetrated another barrier. Integrating and exercising visualization results in student enthusiasm and interest (Freseman 1990).

Teachers across all disciplines can begin to emphasize visuals and visualization activities such as writing assignments (using images), role playing, journal writing, brainstorming webs, graphic organizers, and thinking process maps (Miles 1994; Hyerle 1996). Cave (1996) observed that "[i]mages are . . . often more evocative than words, more precise and potent in triggering a wide range of associations, thereby enhancing creative thinking and memory. So why do we bother taking notes without the benefit of images? Sadly, we have a modern emphasis on words as the primary vehicle of information" (2).

In addition to using real objects to stimulate students' inquiry processes, teachers should continue to integrate visuals into their lessons through the standard means of chalkboard, overhead, and computers. Rakes, Rakes, and Smith (1995) emphasized that integrating visuals into the curriculum enhances it because visuals serve as analytical frameworks for teaching and learning. Textbook visuals, as well as student-made visuals, can be effective means of inviting higher levels of thinking.

Use of Reflective Analysis

Wilson (1988) recommended that use of reflective analysis begin with teachers. That reflection should start in the planning stages of the lesson design, specifically with the lesson objective. Teachers should design lessons that are not just the completion of a worksheet but that instead have students reading, writing, comparing, and discussing, all while using a variety of resources. Lesson plans that include those activities encourage critical thinking and higher learning to occur.

For teachers to become critical facilitators, they must analyze their own teaching and thinking with the intention of generating student participation and student questioning. Teachers need to model reflective analysis with their students on a regular basis. In this mode of learning, students become skilled at critical examination and assessment while formulating opinions, practices, and guidelines for improving their lives and the lives of others (Paul and Elder 1997).

According to Yildirim (1994), students are "more comfortable with learning in structured ways and often are not eager and enthusiastic about new ideas and perspectives" (8). However, teachers should deliberately penetrate that barrier and have students compare their thoughts and ideas so they can begin the reflective analysis process for themselves. Only when students are comparing, validating, and reconstructing their own ideas are they constructively engaging in higher thinking.

Diversification of Perspectives

Teachers of higher thinking encourage and motivate learners with educational activities that promote new perspectives. For it is in diversification—in noting ambiguities, similarities, differences, and challenges—that students voice their concerns. With block scheduling, middle and secondary classrooms can provide opportunities for nurturing spontaneity, and it is in a climate of spontaneity that critical thinking evolves.

Teachers of higher thinking are aware that "critical teaching is helping learners to acquire new perceptual frameworks and structures of understanding" (Brookfield 1987, 82). Meyers (1986) suggested that teachers deliberately contrive a problem or challenge for students as they begin each class period and that cooperative group work be employed to solve it. That arrangement will generate critical thinking opportunities where mental mapping and reflection become pronounced.

Conclusion

Middle and high school teachers can promote higher thinking. With a conscious commitment to do so, they can provide opportunities for application of higher-thinking activities. By making that conscious commitment, teachers can expect to develop brand new repertoires of competencies and instructional modes. By legitimizing students' experiences in the curriculum, the teacher strengthens the instructional process. Students learn to raise the "why" question, and thus passivity turns to activity that generates thinking. Also, by integrating visuals in various forms in the curriculum, teachers allow images to become connections to related content. And, when teachers allow time for reflective analysis as well as diversity of thought, students identify real concerns and develop a shared language. All of this begins incrementally and intentionally.

Despite the barriers, teachers who implement higher thinking strategies need to realize that their efforts promote powerful results in and beyond the classroom.

REFERENCES

Brookfield, S. D. 1987. *Developing critical thinkers.* San Francisco: Jossey-Bass.

Cave, C. 1996. *The mind map book.* Retrieved June 19, 1997, from the World Wide Web: http://www.ozemail.com.au/~caveman/Creative/Mindmap/Radiant.html

Freseman, R. D. 1990. Improving higher order thinking of middle school geography students by teaching skills directly. ERIC Document Reproduction Service, ED 320842.

Gordon, B. 1991. *Explicit integration of critical thinking skills into content area instruction.* Retrieved June 30, 1997, from the World Wide Web: http://www/cct/emb.edu/theses/secondar.html

Howe, R. W., and C. R. Warren. 1989. Teaching critical thinking through environmental education. ERIC Document Reproduction Service, ED 324193.

Hyerle, D. 1996. *Visual tools for constructing knowledge.* Alexandria, Va.: Association for Supervision and Curriculum Development.

Meyers, C. 1986. *Teaching students to think critically: A guide for faculty in all disciplines.* San Francisco: Jossey-Bass.

Miles, C. 1994. The fourth "r": Practical thinking for the cautious teacher. *Journal of Developmental Education* 17(3): 50–51.

Paul. R. 1990. *Critical thinking: What every person needs to survive in a rapidly changing world.* Rohnert Park, Calif.: Sonoma State University Center for Critical Thinking and Moral Critique.

Paul, R., and L. Elder. 1997. Critical thinking: Implications for instruction of the stage theory. *Journal of Developmental Education* 20(3): 34–35.

Potts, B. 1994. *Strategies for teaching critical thinking.* Retrieved June 30, 1997, from the World Wide Web: http://www.ed.gov/databases/ERIC_Digests/ed385606.html

Rakes, G. C. T A. Rakes, and L. J. Smith. 1995. Visuals to enhance secondary students' reading comprehension of expository tests. *Journal of Adolescent and Adult Literacy* 39(1): 46–54.

Scheinin, P. M. 1995. *Improving thinking skills.* Retrieved June 27, 1997, from the World Wide Web: http://www.helsinki.fi/~scheinin /abs6.html

Weinstein, M. 1995. *Critical thinking: expanding the paradigm.* Retrieved June 27. 1997. from the World Wide Web: http://www.shss.montclair.edu/inquiry/fall95/weinste.html

Wilson, M. 1988. Critical thinking: Repacking or revolution? *Language Arts* 65(6): 543–51.

Yildirim, A. 1994. Promoting student thinking from the practitioner's point of view: Teachers' attitudes toward teaching. (March) ERIC Documents, 1–20.

FURTHER READING

Allen, D. L. 1994. *Critical and creative thinking in middle/secondary education.* Retrieved June 30, 1997, from the World Wide Web: http://www.cct.umb.edu/theses/secondar.html

Collins, N. D. 1993. *Teaching critical reading through literature.* Retrieved June 30, 1997, from the World Wide Web: http://www.ed.gov/databases/ERIC_Digests/ed363869.html

Elder, L., and R. Paul. 1994. Critical thinking: Why we must transform our teaching. *Journal of Developmental Education* 18(1): 34–35.

———. 1995a. Critical thinking: Content is thinking, thinking is content. *Journal of Developmental Education* 19(2): 34–35.

———. 1995b. Critical thinking: Why teach students intellectual standards, part 1. *Journal of Developmental Education* 18(3): 36–37.

———. 1995c. Critical thinking: Why teach students intellectual standards, part II. *Journal of Developmental Education* 19(1): 34–35.

———. 1996a. Critical thinking: A stage theory of critical thinking, part I. *Journal of Developmental Education* 20(1): 34–35.

———. 1996b. Critical thinking: A stage theory of critical thinking, part II. *Journal of Developmental Education* 20(2): 34–35.

Hamilton, W. V. 1993. *Using and teaching critical thinking.* Retrieved June 30, 1997, from the World Wide Web: http://joe.uwex.edu/test/joe/1993spring/f2.html

Paul, R., and L. Elder. 1994. Critical thinking: Using intellectual standards to assess student reasoning. *Journal of Developmental Education* 18(2): 32–32.

———. 1996a. Critical thinking: Rethinking content as a mode of thinking. *Journal of Developmental Education* 19(3): 2.

———. 1996b. The role of questions in thinking, teaching, & learning. Retrieved from the World Wide Web:http://www.sonoma.edu/Cthink/University/univclass/rolefquest.nclk

Penner, K. 1995. *Teaching critical thinking.* Retrieved June 30, 1997, from the World Wide Web: http://web.ucs.ubc.ca/kpenner/c-think.html

Pool, C. R. 1997. Up with emotional health. *Educational Leadership* 54(8): 12–14.

Ryan, E. 1994. *Teaching thinking in the content area: A workshop for secondary school teachers.* Retrieved June 30, 1997, from the World Wide Web: http://www.cct.umb.edu/theses/secondar.html

See, P. 1996. Ideas in practice: An introspective approach for developing critical thinking. *Journal of Developmental Education* 20(2): 26–33.

Splitter, L. J. 1995. *On the theme of "teaching for higher order thinking skills."* Retrieved June 27, 1997, from the World Wide Web: http://www.shss.montclair.edu/inquiry/summ95/splitter.html

Winocur, S. L. 1995. *Increase maximal performance by activating critical thinking (IMPACT).* Retrieved June 30, 1997, from the World Wide Web: http://www.ed.gov/pubs/EPTW/eptw10/eptw10h.html

Unit 6

Key Points to Consider

❖ From where do emotions originate, nature or nurture? Defend your answer. Do you think a person's level of emotionality or overall personality can change with time or is it somehow fixed early in life? Give examples.

❖ Why is the face the key to understanding another's emotions? Are there any universally expressed facial emotions? What are the problems with studying universal emotions; in other words, does culture play a role in emotional expression?

❖ Are adult emotions similar to or different from emotions of younger individuals? How so? Is it true that adults only experience declines in psychological functions? What strengths, emotional or otherwise, do adults carry into old age with them?

❖ What is a polygraph? Why is this apparatus of interest to psychologists? To professionals in the justice system? Can the polygraph measure lying? If not, what does it measure, if anything? Are there individuals who are better than average at detecting emotions in others? Who are they; what is it that makes them better?

❖ Are various emotions controlled by different factors? For example, is one emotion controlled by the brain while others are controlled by hormones? What other positive emotions do we experience besides joy? Where does joy come from?

❖ Are people born to be good? What is morality? What elements control whether we are moral? How does morality develop? Why is it essential to raise children with a sense of moral consciousness?

 **Links** | **www.dushkin.com/online/**

These sites are annotated on pages 4 and 5.

Jasmine's sister was a working mother and always reminded Jasmine about how exciting her life was. Jasmine's choice was to stay home with her children, 2-year old Min, 4-year-old Chi'Ming, and newborn Mi-may. One day, Jasmine was having a difficult time with the children. The baby, Mi-May, had been crying all day from colic. The other two children had been bickering over their toys. Jasmine, realizing that it was already 5:15 and her husband would be home any minute, frantically started preparing dinner. She wanted to fix a nice dinner so that she and her husband could eat after the children went to bed, then relax together.

This was not to be. Jasmine sat waiting for her no-show husband. When he finally walked in the door at 10:15, she was furious. His excuse, that his boss had invited the whole office for dinner, didn't reduce Jasmine's ire. She reasoned that her husband could have called, could have taken 5 minutes to do that. Jasmine yelled and ranted at her husband. Her face was taut and red with rage and her voice wavered. Suddenly, bursting into tears, she ran into the living room. Her husband retreated to the safety of their bedroom.

Exhausted and disappointed, Jasmine sat alone and pondered why she was so angry with her husband. Was she just tired? Was she frustrated by negotiating with young children all day and did she simply wanted another adult around once in a while? Was she secretly worried and jealous that her husband was seeing another woman and had lied about his whereabouts? Was she combative because her husband's and her sister's lives seemed so much fuller than her own? Jasmine was unsure just how she felt and why she had exploded in such rage at her husband, someone she loved dearly.

This story, while sad and gender-stereotyped, is not unrealistic when it comes to emotions. There are times when we are moved to deep emotion. On other occasions, we expect waterfalls of tears but we find that our eyes are dry or simply a little misty. What are these strange things we call emotions? What motivates us to rage at someone we love?

These questions and others have inspired psychologists to study emotions and motivation. The episode about Jasmine, besides introducing these topics to you, also illustrates why these two topics are usually interrelated in psychology. Some emotions, such as love, pride, and joy are pleasant,

so pleasant that we are motivated to keep them going. Other emotions, such as anger, grief, and jealousy are terribly draining and oppressive, so negative that we hope they will be over as soon as possible. The relationship of emotions and motivation are the focus of this unit.

The first two articles offer general information about emotions. In the first article, the authors discuss research on the face and the use of the face in the detection of emotions by others. The face does signal emotions (both genuine and faked). Some emotions appear to be universal, but culture also influences how emotions are expressed and whether they are indeed expressed at all. The second article, "Emotions in the Second Half of Life," deals specifically with the question of whether emotional expression flattens in the latter half of life. Evidently, social and emotional life in our aging population is quite rich.

According to some people, one way to measure emotions is by using the polygraph or lie detector. Prospective employers, for example, eagerly embraced this apparatus as a scientific way to detect emotionality, particularly emotions related to lying, such as guilt. Research, however, has demonstrated that the polygraph is a very questionable apparatus, in fact, so questionable that it is no longer admissible evidence in a court of law. Given this, are there professionals in our society who are better at detecting lying and other emotions? The answer is "yes." In her article on ability to detect emotions, Susan Campbell reports well-received research demonstrating that Secret Service agents are quite skilled in this area.

The next to last article in this section concerns a specific emotion—joy. In "The Biology of Joy," Jeremiah Creedon discusses joy and pleasure. He delineates the role that endorphins, a type of neurotransmitter, play in our pleasant experiences and emotions.

The last article pertains to motivation, an area akin to the study of emotions. William Damon, in "The Moral Development of Children," explains why children need to be motivated to move from being egocentrically moral to being highly socialized. According to this article, children need to develop a sense of moral conscience that motivates them to develop personal integrity. Then and only then, claims Damon, can children learn to be honest with others.

Face It!

How we make and read the fleeting split-second expressions that slip across our countenances thousands of times each day is crucial to our emotional health as individuals and to our survival as a species. By Deborah Blum

Who hasn't waited for an old friend at an airport and scanned faces impatiently as passengers come hurrying through the gate? You can recognize instantly the travelers with no one to meet them, their gaze unfocused, their expressions carefully neutral; the people expecting to be met, their eyes narrowed, their lips poised on the edge of a smile; the children returning home to their parents, their small laughing faces turned up in greeting. Finally, your own friend appears, face lighting up as you come into view. If a mirror suddenly dropped down before you, there'd be that same goofy smile on your face, the same look of uncomplicated pleasure.

Poets may celebrate its mystery and artists its beauty, but they miss the essential truth of the human countenance. As scientists now are discovering, the power of the face resides in the fleeting split-second expressions that slip across it thousands of times each day. They guide our lives, governing the way we relate to each other as individuals and the way we connect together as a society. Indeed, scientists assert, the ability to make faces—and read them—is vital both to our personal health and to our survival as a species.

Growing out of resurging interest in the emotions, psychologists have been poring over the human visage with the intensity of cryptographers scrutinizing a hidden code. In fact, the pursuits are strikingly similar. The face is the most extraordinary communicator, capable of accurately signaling emotion in a bare blink of a second, capable of concealing emotion equally well. "In a sense, the face is equipped to lie the most and leak the most, and thus can be a very confusing source of information," observes Paul Ekman, Ph.D., professor of psychology at the University of California in San Francisco and a pioneer in studying the human countenance.

"The face is both ultimate truth and fata morgana, declares Daniel McNeill, author of the new book *The Face* (Little Brown & Company), a vivid survey of face-related lore from the history of the nose to the merits of plastic surgery. "It is a magnificent surface, and in the last 20 years, we've learned more about it than in the previous 20 millennia."

Today, scientists are starting to comprehend the face's contradiction, to decipher the importance of both the lie and leak, and to puzzle out a basic mystery. Why would an intensely social species like ours, reliant on communication, be apparently designed to give mixed messages? By connecting expression to brain activity with extraordinary precision, researchers are now literally going beyond "skin deep" in understanding how the face connects us, when it pulls us apart. "The face is a probe, a way of helping us see what's behind people's interactions," explains psychology professor Dacher Keltner, Ph.D., of the University of California-Berkeley. Among the new findings:

• With just 44 muscles, nerves, and blood vessels threaded through a scaffolding of bone and cartilage, all layered over by supple skin, the face can twist and pull into 5,000 expressions, all the way from an outright grin to the faintest sneer.

SMILES, the most recognizable signal of HAPPINESS in the world, are so important that we can SEE them far more clearly than any other EXPRESSION—even at 300 feet, the length of a FOOTBALL field.

• There's a distinct anatomical difference between real and feigned expressions—and in the biological effect they produce in the creators of those expressions.

• We send and read signals with lightning-like speed and over great distances. A browflash—the lift of the eyebrow common when greeting a friend—lasts only a sixth of a second. We can tell in a blink of a second if a stranger's face is registering surprise or pleasure—even if he or she is 150 feet away.

• Smiles are such an important part of communication that we see them far more clearly than any other expression. We can pick up a smile at 300 feet—the length of a football field.

• Facial expressions are largely universal, products of biological imperatives. We are programmed to make and read faces. "The abilities to express and recognize emotion are inborn, genetic, evolutionary," declares George Rotter, Ph.D., professor of psychology at Montclair University in New Jersey.

• Culture, parenting, and experience can temper our ability to display and interpret emotions. Abused children may be prone to trouble because they cannot correctly gauge the meaning and intent of others' facial expressions.

Making FACES

Deciphering facial expressions first entails understanding how they are created. Since the 1980s, Ekman and Wallace Friesen, Ph.D., of the University of California in San Francisco, have been painstakingly inventorying the muscle movements that pull our features into frowns, smiles, and glares. Under their Facial Action Coding System (FACS), a wink is Action Unit 46, involving a twitch of a single muscle, the *obicularis oculi*, which wraps around the eye. Wrinkle your nose (Action Unit 09), that's a production of two muscles, the *levator labii superioris* and the *alaeque nasi*.

The smile, the most recognizable signal in the world, is a much more complex endeavor. Ekman and colleagues have so far identified 19 versions, each engaging slightly different combinations of muscles. Consider two: the beam shared by lovers reunited after a long absence and the smile given by a teller passing back the deposit slip to a bank patron.

The old phrase "smiling eyes" is exactly on target. When we are genuinely happy, as in the two lovers' re-

union, we produce what Ekman and Richard Davidson of the University of Wisconsin-Madison call a "felt" smile. The *zygomatic major* muscles, which run from cheekbone to the corner of the mouth, pull the lips upward, while the *obicularis oculi* crinkle the outer corner of the eyes. In contrast, the polite smile offered by the bank teller (or by someone hearing a traveling salesman joke for the hundredth time) pulls up the lips but, literally, doesn't reach the eyes.

It doesn't reach the brain either. Felt smiles, it seems, trigger a sort of pleasurable little hum, a scientifically measurable activity in their creators' left frontal cortex, the region of the brain where happiness is registered. Agreeable smiles simply don't produce that buzz.

Are we taught to smile and behave nicely in social situations? Well, certainly someone instructs us to say, "Have a nice day." But we seem to be born with the ability to offer both felt and social smiles. According to studies by Davidson and Nathan Fox of the University of Maryland, ten-month-old infants will curve their lips in response to the coo of friendly strangers, but they produce happy, felt smiles only at the approach of their mother. The babies' brains light with a smile, it appears, only for those they love.

Evolution's IMPERATIVE

Why are we keyed in so early to making faces? Charles Darwin argued in his 1872 book, *The Expression of the Emotions in Man and Animals*, that the ability to signal feelings, needs, and desires is critical to human survival and thus evolutionarily based. What if infants could not screw up their faces to communicate distress or hunger? Or if foes couldn't bare their teeth in angry snarls as a warning and threat? And what if we couldn't grasp the meaning of those signals in an instant but had to wait minutes for them to be decoded?

Everything known about early hominid life suggests that it was a highly social existence," observes Ekman, who has edited a just-published new edition of Darwin's classic work. "We had to deal with prey and predators; we had a very long period of child rearing. All of that would mean that survival would depend on our being able to respond quickly to each other's emotional states."

We can move PEOPLE from culture to culture and they KNOW how to make
and read the same basic expressions: anger, fear, sadness, disgust, surprise, and
happiness. The six appear to be HARDWIRED in our brains.
EMBARRASSMENT, some suspect, may be a seventh.

Today, the need is just as great. As Ekman points out, "Imagine the trouble we'd be in, if when an aunt came to visit, she had to be taught what a newborn baby's expression meant—let alone if she was going to be a caretaker." Or if, in our world of non-stop far-flung travel, an expression of intense pain was understood in one society but not in another. "And yet," says Ekman, "we can move people from one culture to another and they just know."

Researchers have identified six basic or universal expressions that appear to be hardwired in our brains, both to make and to read: anger, fear, sadness, disgust, surprise, and happiness. Show photos of an infuriated New Yorker to a high-mountain Tibetan or of a miserable New Guinea tribeswoman to a Japanese worker, and there's no translation problem. Everyone makes the same face—and everyone gets the message.

One of the expressions that hasn't made the universal list but probably should is embarrassment. It reflects one of our least favorite emotions: who doesn't loathe that red-faced feeling of looking like a fool? Yet such displays are far less self-centered than has been assumed. Rather than marking a personal humiliation, contends Keltner, embarrassment seems designed to prompt social conciliation.

Think about it. If we accidentally spill a drink on a colleague, stumble into a stranger in the hall, what's the best way to defuse the tension and avoid an escalation into battle? Often, notes Keltner, even before offering a verbal apology, we appease the injured party by showing embarrassment.

When we're embarrassed, our hands tend to come up, partly covering the face. We rub the side of the nose. We cast our eyes downward. We also try to appear smaller, to shrink into ourselves. These behaviors aren't uniquely ours. In awkward social situations, chimpanzees and monkeys do the same thing—and accomplish the same end. The actions defuse hostility, offer a tacit apology, even elicit sympathy in viewers. (When Keltner first tentatively introduced his chosen topic at research meetings, even jaded scientists let out immediate empathetic "oohs" at the slides of people with red faces).

There are physiological changes associated with this," notes Keltner. "If people see an angry face staring at them, they have a heightened autonomic response—rising stress hormones, speeding pulse—all the signs of fear. When they see an embarrassment response, fear is reduced."

A reddened face and downward glance typically start a rapid de-escalation of hostility among children involved in playground quarrels, says Keltner. Parents go easier on youngsters who show visible embarrassment after breaking a household rule, such as playing handball on the living room wall or chasing the dog up and downstairs throughout the house. Adults also go easier on adults. In one of Keltner's studies, jurors in a hypothetical trial meted out much lighter sentences when convicted drug dealers displayed the classic signs of embarrassment.

Cultural RULES

Expressions aren't dictated by biology alone, however; they are deeply influenced by cultural attitudes. De Paul University psychologist Linda Camras, Ph.D., has been exploring why European-American adults seem so much more willing than Asians to express emotion in public. In one experiment, she studied the reactions of European-American and Asian infants, age 11 months, to being restrained by having one arm lightly grasped by a researcher.

European-American and Japanese babies were remarkably similar in their visible dislike of being held still by a stranger's grip. (The scientists let go if the babies cried for seven seconds straight.) Since infants show no apparent inborn difference in the willingness to publicly express dismay, it stands to reason that they must eventually learn the "appropriate" way to express themselves from their families and the society in which they are reared.

Ekman's work clearly shows how culture teaches us to subdue our instinctive emotional reactions. In one set of studies, he asked American and Japanese college students to watch nature films of streams tumbling down mountainsides and trees rustling in the wind, and also graphic tapes of gory surgeries, including limb amputations. Everyone grimaced at the spurting blood at first. But when a note-taking scientist clad in a white coat—the ultimate authority figure—sat in on watching the films, the Japanese students' behavior altered radically. Instead

> When it comes to READING the subtleties of emotion, women are the stronger SEX. While men almost always correctly recognize happiness in a female face, they pick up DISTRESS just 70% of the time. A WOMAN'S face has to be really sad for men to see it.

of showing revulsion, they greeted the bloody films with smiles.

"No wonder that foreigners who visit or live among the Japanese think that their expressions are different from Americans," says Ekman. "They see the results of the cultural display rules, masking and modifying the underlying universal expressions of emotion."

Blank LOOKS

Mental or physical illness, too, can interfere with the ability to make faces—with profound consequences for relationships, researchers are learning. Neurophysiologist Jonathan Cole, of Poole Hospital at the University of Southampton, Great Britain, and author of the new book *About Face* (MIT Press), points out that people with Parkinson's disease are often perceived as boring or dull because their faces are rigid and immobile.

Consider also depression. As everyone knows, it shuts down communication. But that doesn't mean only that depressed people withdraw and talk less. The normal expressiveness of the face shuts down as well.

In one experiment, psychologist Jeffrey Cohn, Ph.D., of the University of Pittsburgh had healthy mothers mimic a depressed face while holding their infants. The women were told not to smile. Their babies responded with almost instant dismay. At first they tried desperately to recruit a response from their mother, smiling more, gurgling, reaching out. "The fact that the babies were trying to elicit their mother's response shows that at an early age, we do have the beginnings of a social skill for resolving interpersonal failures," Cohn notes.

But equally important, the infants simply could not continue to interact without receiving a response. They stopped their efforts. The experiment lasted only three minutes, but by that time, the babies were themselves withdrawn. "When mothers again resumed normal behavior, babies remained distant and distressed for up to a minute," says Cohn. "You can see that maternal depression, were it chronic, could have developmental consequences."

In fact, children of depressed parents tend to become very detached in their relationships with others. They often fail to connect with other people throughout their life and experience difficulties in romantic relationships and marriage, in large part, researchers suspect, because they have trouble producing and picking up on emo-

tional signals. "We think that the lack of facial animation interferes with forming relationships," says Keltner.

Reading FACES

Displays of emotion are only half the equation, of course. How viewers interpret those signals is equally important. "We evolved a system to communicate and a capacity to interpret," observes Keltner. "But much less is known about the interpreting capacity."

What scientists do know for certain is that we are surprisingly bad at discerning the real emotions or intentions behind others' facial expressions. "One of the problems that people don't realize is how complicated face reading is," notes Pollak. "At first glance, it seems very straightforward. But if you break it down—think of all the information in the face, how quickly the brain has to comprehend and analyze it, memories come in, emotions, context, judgments—then you realize that we really can't do it all."

Or can't do it all well. What we seem to have done during our evolution is to learn shortcuts to face reading. In other words, we make snap judgments. "It's not actually a conscious decision," Pollak explains. "But decisions are being made in the brain—What am I going to pay attention to? What am I going to clue into?"

Most of us are pretty good at the strong signals—sobbing, a big grin—but we stumble on the subtleties. Some people are better than others. There's some evidence that women are more adept than men at picking up the weaker signals, especially in women's faces.

In an experiment conducted by University of Pennsylvania neuroscientists Ruben and Raquel Gur, men and women were shown photos of faces. Both genders did well at reading men's expressions. Men also were good at picking up happiness in female faces; they got it right about 90% of the time. But when it came to recognizing distress signals in women's faces, their accuracy fell to 70%.

"A woman's face had to be really sad for men to see it," says Ruben Gur. The explanation may lie in early human history. Charged with protecting their tribes, men had to be able to quickly read threats from other males, suggests Gur. Women, in contrast, en-

Abused children are so POISED to detect anger that they often will READ it into others' faces even when it isn't there. That tendency may serve them well at HOME, where they need all the self defenses they can muster, but it can lead to TROUBLE outside.

trusted with child-rearing, became more finely-tuned to interpreting emotions.

We may be biologically primed to grasp certain expressions, but our individual experiences and abilities also filter the meaning. Mental disorders, apparently, can swamp the biology of facial recognition. People with schizophrenia, for instance, are notoriously bad at face reading; when asked to look at photographs, they struggle to separate a happy face from a neutral one.

Mistaking CUES

Seth Pollak, Ph.D., a psychologist at the University of Wisconsin-Madison, has been exploring how children who have suffered extreme parental abuse—broken bones, burn scarring—read faces. In his studies, he asks these youngsters and those from normal homes to look at three photographs of faces which display classic expressions of fear, anger, and happiness. Mean-while, electrodes attached to their heads measure their brain activity.

Battered children seem to sustain a damaging one-two punch, Pollak is finding. Overall, they have a subdued level of electrical activity in the brain. (So, in fact, do people suffering from schizophrenia or alcoholism. It seems to be a sign of trouble within.) However, when abused youngsters look at the photo of an angry face, they rapidly generate a rising wave of electrical energy, sharper and stronger than anything measured in children who live in less threatening homes.

When Pollak further analyzed the brain activity readings, he found that abused children generate that panicky reaction even when there's no reason to, misreading as angry some of the other pictured faces. They are so primed to see anger, so poised for it, that when making split-second judgments, they tilt toward detection of rage.

This falls in line with findings from DePaul's Camras and other psychologists, which show that abused children struggle significantly more in deciphering ex-

Face SHAPE

Since ancient times, human beings have been making judgments about each other based not just on the expressions that cross the face but on its very structure. The practice of finding meaning in anatomy is enjoying a remarkable renaissance today.

A plethora of pop books ponder the significance of chins, eye slant, and eyebrows. One popular magazine has even started a new face-reading feature. First to be analyzed: President William Jefferson Clinton. His triangular face apparently indicates a dynamic and—big surprise—sexual personality. Among the theories now being trotted out: heavy eyelids denote jealousy, a rosebud mouth promises fidelity, and a hairy brow line ensures restlessness.

Scientists dismiss these readings as no more than facial astrology. "There is as yet no good data to support this practice," observes Lesley Zebrowitz, professor of psychology at Brandeis University.

While many may regard it as a sort of harmless parlor game, face reading does have a more pernicious effect. Charles Darwin noted that he was almost barred from voyaging on the H.M.S. Beagle because the captain thought his nose suggested a lazy nature. In the 1920s, Los Angeles judge Edward Jones insisted that he could, with over 90% accuracy, determine someone was a "born criminal" by his protruding lips and too-close-together eyes.

Though today no one would make such a blatant assessment of character based on anatomy, facial shape at least subconsciously does appear to figure into our judgments. In her book, *Reading Faces*, Zebrowitz meticulously documents her research showing that baby-faced adults, with big eyes and full cheeks and lips, bring out in the rest of us a nurturing protective response, the kind we give to children.

In one remarkable study, she tracked proceedings in Boston small claims court for more than 500 cases and found that, whatever the evidence, chubby-cheeked plaintiffs were more apt to prevail than claimants with more mature-looking faces. Says Zebrowitz: "Although our judicial system talks about 'blind justice,' it's impossible to control the extra-legal factor of stereotyping based on physical appearance."—D.B.

pression. "Overall, there's a relationship between the expressive behavior of the mother and the child's recognition ability," Camras says. "And it's an interesting kind of a difference."

Identifying negative expressions seems to be essential in human interaction; four of the six universal expressions are negative. In most homes, notes Camras, mothers use "mild negative expressions, little frowns, tightening of the mouth." Children from such families are very good at detecting early signs of anger. But youngsters from homes with raging furious moms have trouble recognizing anger. "If the mom gets really angry, it's so frightening, it's so disorganizing for children that it seems they can't learn anything from it."

The Best DEFENSE

So, out of sheer self-protection, if the children from abusive homes are uncertain about what a face says—as they often are—they'll fall back on anger as the meaning and prepare to defend themselves. "They overdetect rage," says Pollak. Does this create problems in their relationships outside the home? It's a logical, if as yet unproven, conclusion.

What Darwin tells us is that emotions are adaptations," Pollak explains. "If a child is physically abused, I'd put my money on an adaptation toward assuming hostile intent. Look at the cost for these kids of missing a threat. So what happens is, they do better in the short run—they're very acute at detecting anger and threat because unfortunately they have to be. But take them out of those maltreating families and put them with other people and their reactions don't fit."

One of Pollak's long-term goals is to find out if such harmful effects can be reversed, if abused children can regain or reconstruct the social skills—that is, reading faces—that are evidently so critical to our design.

Failure to read signals accurately may also figure in juvenile delinquency. "There are studies that have found that juvenile delinquents who are prone to aggression have trouble deciphering certain expressions," says Keltner. "They're not as good as other kids at it. Is that because they're particularly bad at reading appeasement signals like embarrassment? That's something we'd really like to know."

Truth OR LIES?

One area where *everyone* seems to have trouble in reading faces is in detecting deception. We average between 45 and 65% accuracy in picking up lies—pretty dismal when one considers that chance is 50%. Secret Service agents can notch that up a bit to about 64%; sci-

entists suspect that improvement comes only after years of scanning crowds, looking for the faces of potential assassins.

Con artists, too, seem to be especially adept at reading expressions. The latter are also skilled at faking emotions, a trait they share with actors. Not surprising, since success in both careers depends on fooling people.

We seem to be duped particularly easily by a smile. In fact, we tend to implicitly trust a smiling face, just as we do a baby-faced one. In one experiment, Rotter cut out yearbook photos of college students and then asked people to rate the individuals pictured for trustworthiness. In almost every instance, people chose the students with smiling faces as the most honest. Women with the biggest grins scored the best; men needed only a slight curve of the lips to be considered truthful. "Smiles are an enormous controller of how people perceive you," says Rotter. "It's an extremely powerful communicator, much more so than the eyes."

> **We do a better job of detecting falsehoods if we listen to a voice or examine body stance than if we read a face.**

Incidentally, we aren't suckered only by human faces. We can be equally and easily tricked by our fellow primates. In one classic story, a young lowland gorilla gently approached a keeper, stared affectionately into his face, gave him a hug—and stole his watch. Chimpanzees, too, are famous for their friendly-faced success in luring lab workers to approach, and then triumphantly spraying them with a mouthful of water.

There *are* clues to insincerity. We tend to hold a simulated expression longer than a real one. If we look carefully, a phony smile may have the slightly fixed expression that a child's face gets when setting a smile for a photograph. As we've discussed, we also use different muscles for felt and fake expressions. And we are apt to blink more when we're lying. But not always—and that's the problem. When Canadian researchers Susan Hyde, Kenneth Craig, and Chrisopher Patrick asked people to simulate an expression of pain, they found that the fakers used the same facial muscles—lowering their brows, tightening their lips—as did those in genuine pain. In fact, the only way to detect the fakers was that the expressions were slightly exaggerated and "blinking occurred less often, perhaps because of the cognitive demands to act as if they were in pain," the scientists explain.

We do a better job of finding a falsehood by listening to the tone of a voice or examining the stance of a body than by reading the face, maintains Ekman, who has served as a consultant for police departments, intelligence agencies, and antiterrorist groups. He's even been approached by a national television network—"I can't tell you which one"—eager to train its reporters to better recognize when sources are lying.

Which brings us to perhaps the most provocative mystery of the face: why are we so willing to trust in what the face tells us, to put our faith in a steady gaze, a smiling look? With so much apparently at stake in reading facial cues correctly, why are we so prone to mistakes?

Living SMOOTHLY

Most of us don't pick up lies and, actually, most of us don't care to," declares Ekman. "Part of the way politeness works is that we expect people to mislead us sometime—say, on a bad hair day. What we care about is that the person goes through the proper role."

Modern existence, it seems, is predicated to some extent on ignoring the true meaning of faces: our lives run more smoothly if we don't know whether people really find our jokes funny. It runs more smoothly if we don't know when people are lying to us. And perhaps it runs more smoothly if men can't read women's expressions of distress.

Darwin himself told of sitting across from an elderly woman on a railway carriage and observing that her mouth was pulled down at the corners. A proper British Victorian, he assumed that no one would display grief while traveling on public transportation. He began musing on what else might cause her frown.

While he sat there, analyzing, the woman's eyes suddenly overflowed with tears. Then she blinked them away, and there was nothing but the quiet distance between two passengers. Darwin never knew what she was thinking. Hers was a private grief, not to be shared with a stranger.

There's a lesson in that still, for all of us airport face-watchers today. That we may always see only part of the story, that what the face keeps secret may be as valuable as what it shares.

Emotion in the Second Half of Life

Laura L. Carstensen and Susan Turk Charles[1]

Department of Psychology, Stanford University, Stanford, California

Research on aging has focused primarily on the functional decline people experience as they grow old. Empirical evidence from multiple subdomains of psychology, most notably cognition, perception, and biological psychology, documents reduced efficiency, slowing, and decreased elasticity of basic mental and physical processes with age. Though findings are far more mixed in social aging research, there remains widespread, if tacit, sentiment that the task of gerontological psychology is to assess the ways in which functional declines affect the life of the aging individual.

We assert that the focus on age-related declines in human aging may have steered researchers away from certain questions that, when answered, would paint a more positive picture of old age. Specifically, we argue that changes in the emotion domain challenge models of aging as pervasive loss and point to one central area that is better characterized by continued growth in the second half of life. We posit that old age is marked by greater saliency and improved regulation of emotions, and that emotional well-being, when it does suffer, declines only at the very end of life, when the cognitive and physical disabilities that often precede death in very old age overshadow previously vital areas of functioning (M. M. Baltes, 1998). These ideas are consistent with a curvilinear pattern of findings that document preserved or improved satisfaction with interpersonal relationships in older age groups (Diener & Suh, 1997), despite increased depressive symptoms and functional difficulties among the oldest old (e.g., Smith & Baltes, 1997).

The research we review here is rooted in socioemotional selectivity theory (Carstensen, 1993, 1995, 1998; Carstensen, Gross, & Fung, 1997; Carstensen, Isaacowitz, & Charles, 1999), a psychological model maintaining that limitations on perceived time lead to motivational shifts that direct attention to emotional goals. The theory posits that the resulting increased attention to emotion results in greater complexity of emotional experi-ence and better regulation of emotions experienced in everyday life. One emotional goal that becomes paramount is interacting with individuals who provide emotionally fulfilling interactions. When people are relieved of concerns for the future, attention to current feeling-states heightens. Appreciation for the fragility and value of human life increases, and long-term relationships with family and friends assume unmatched importance. Because of the inextricable association between age and time left in life, the theory maintains that aging is associated with preferences for and increased investment in emotionally close social relationships, as well as increased focus on other less interpersonal emotional goals. This age-related motivational shift leads to alterations in the dynamic interplay between individuals and their environments, so that optimization of socioemotional experience is prioritized in later life.

SELECTIVE SOCIAL INTERACTION ENHANCES EMOTIONAL ASPECTS OF LIFE

The program of research we have pursued over the years began with consideration of the highly reliable decline in social contact evidenced in later life and concern for the potential emotional consequences of this reduction. Because human emotions develop within social contexts, and throughout life the most intense emotional experiences, such as anger, sadness, jealousy, and joy, are intimately embedded within them, do fewer social contacts entail emotional costs?

Early theories in psychology and sociology most definitely presumed that reductions in social contact take a toll on emotional life. Although emotional quiescence was in some theories considered the cause and in others the consequence of reduced social contact, for many years no theories contested the idea that emotional experience suffers in old age. Jung (1933) proposed that emotions become progressively generated from internal sources and detached from external events when he wrote that the "very old person . . . has plunged again into the unconscious, and . . . progressively vanishes within it" (p. 131).

Our research on social networks, however, reveals that even though, overall, social networks are smaller in old age, they continue to include comparable numbers of very close relationships throughout later adulthood (Lang & Carstensen, 1994). The reliable age-related decrease in the size of social networks instead appears to result from circumscribed reductions in relatively peripheral relationships. These reductions are not accounted for by poor physical health or declining cognitive status and are not restricted to particular personality styles (Lang & Carstensen, 1994; Lang, Staudinger, & Carstensen, 1998). Moreover, longitudinal analysis suggests that reduction in contact with acquaintances and selective investment in fewer social relationships begins early in adulthood (Carstensen, 1992). It appears that social networks grow smaller across adulthood and are increasingly focused on fewer but emotionally significant social partners.

Socioemotional selectivity theory views the reduction in social contact as a proactive process associated with the growing desire to have meaningful experiences. We do not regard aging adults as "budding hedonists," directing social interactions solely to those relationships characterized by positive emotions; rather, we argue that the realization that time is limited directs social behavior to experiences that are emotionally meaningful. Moreover, the character of emotional responses changes. Awareness of constraints on time transforms once light-hearted and uniformly positive emotional responses into complex mixtures in which poignancy reigns. Spending time with a close friend, for example, with the awareness that it may be among the last of such occasions inevitably entails sadness along with joy. Our research, along

From *Current Directions in Psychological Science*, October 1998, pp. 144–149. © 1998 by Laura L. Carstensen and the American Psychological Society. Reprinted by permission of Blackwell Publishers.

with other findings concerning terminally ill patients, suggests that the prototypical emotional response to approaching endings is not morbid. On the contrary, people facing the end of life often say that life is better than ever before. We understand this evaluation to reflect experiences that are richer, more complex, and emotionally meaningful.

According to the theory, restricting the social world to longtime friends and loved ones in later life is adaptive, reflecting careful allocation of resources to the relationships that engender pleasure and meaning. Such a view helps to reconcile the findings that despite a myriad of well-documented losses and overall reductions in social contact, older people, on average, are even more satisfied with their lives than younger people (Diener & Suh, 1997) and, with the exception of the dementias and other organic brain syndromes, display lower prevalence rates of all psychiatric disorders, including depression (Lawton, Kleban, & Dean, 1993).

WHEN TIME IS LIMITED, EMOTIONALLY CLOSE SOCIAL PARTNERS ARE PREFERRED

If changes in social networks involve a proactive pruning process, explicit preferences for close over less close social partners should be evident in people faced with limited time. In a series of studies, we found age-related differences in social preferences and also demonstrated the notable malleability of these age differences as a function of perceived time.

In this series of studies, we presented research participants with three prospective social partners, instructed them to imagine that they had 30 min free and wished to spend it with another person, and asked them to choose a social partner from among the three options. Next, the research subjects were presented with experimental conditions in which future time was hypothetically constrained or expanded and were asked once again to indicate their preferred social partners.

The social partners subjects could choose from represented familiar and unfamiliar social partners who were more and less likely to satisfy different social goals: (a) a member of the immediate family, (b) the author of a book the subject just read, and (c) a recent acquaintance with whom the subject seemed to have much in common. Our previous work had shown that all three options promised enjoyable interactions and represented the conceptual categories we intended them to represent. A

family member, for example, represents to most people an emotionally close social partner; the author represents a good source of new information; the acquaintance offers prospects in the future. We expected that approaching endings would be associated with preferences for the emotionally meaningful partner.

In our first study using this paradigm, we compared social choices of young and old research participants (Fredrickson & Carstensen, 1990). We hypothesized that older people, but not younger people, would display preferences for the familiar social partner. In a second condition, we imposed a hypothetical time constraint by asking subjects to imagine that they would soon be moving across the country (by themselves) but currently had 30 min free. We then had them choose again from among the same set of social partners. As predicted, older people chose the familiar social partner under both experimental conditions. In the open-ended condition, younger people did not display such a preference. In the time-limited condition, however, younger adults displayed the same degree of preference for the familiar social partner as the older subjects.

Recently, we replicated these findings in Hong Kong (Fung, Carstensen, & Lutz, in press), and even in this very different culture, older people, compared with their younger counterparts, showed a relative preference for familiar social partners. In the Hong Kong study, subjects were asked to imagine an impending emigration as the time-limiting condition. The findings replicated our previous ones. In the emigration condition, younger people also displayed a preference for familiar social partners.

In a third study, instead of limiting time, we presented American subjects with a hypothetical scenario that expanded time. Research subjects in that condition were asked to imagine that they had just received a telephone call from their physician telling them about a new medical advance that virtually ensured that they would live 20 years longer than they expected in relatively good health (Fung et al., in press). We also included the time-unspecified condition, which replicated previous findings. Older, but not younger, subjects expressed strong preferences for the familiar social partner. However, in the expanded-time condition, the preference observed among older subjects disappeared: Older and younger subjects' choices were indistinguishable. Thus, when the time constraint associated with age is removed, older individuals' preferences for familiar social partners disappear.

In another line of research, we used an experimental approach based on similarity judgments to examine age differences in the emphasis and use of emotion when forming mental representations of possible social partners. In these studies, research participants sorted descriptions of a variety of social partners according to how similarly they would feel interacting with them. A technique called multidimensional scaling was used to identify the dimensions along which these categorizations were based, and we also computed the weights various subgroups placed on particular dimensions.

In three different studies, we found evidence that place in the life cycle is associated with the salience of emotion in mental representations (Carstensen & Fredrickson, 1998; Fredrickson & Carstensen, 1990). Two of these studies examined age differences in the weights placed on the emotion dimension, and a third study compared how the dimensions were weighted by groups of men who were the same age but varied according to their HIV status. In this way, age was disentangled from place in the life cycle. Findings from all three studies suggest that when individuals are closer to end of their lives, whether because of age or health status, emotion is more salient in their mental representations of other people.

In light of findings suggesting increased salience of emotion among people approaching the end of life, we hypothesized that age differences in memory for emotional versus nonemotional material might be evident as well. That is, if emotional information is more salient, it should be processed more deeply than nonemotional information and therefore remembered better subsequently. To test this hypothesis, we employed an incidental memory paradigm and examined age differences in the type of information recalled (Carstensen & Turk-Charles, 1994). Older and younger adults read a two-page narrative that described a social interaction and contained comparable amounts of neutral and emotionally relevant information. Roughly 45 min later, after completing a series of unrelated tasks, participants were asked to recall all that they could about the passage. Responses were transcribed, and the information in them was classified as either emotional or neutral. The proportion of emotional material correctly recalled from the original text was related to age; the proportion of recalled information that was emotional information was greater for older adults than younger adults. The differences in proportions were driven by a decrease in the amount of neutral information recalled by older adults, and not by an increase in their recall of emotional information. We speculate that the increased salience of emotion may have cognitive costs, in this case a focus on emotional information at the expense of nonemotional information, but these ideas are as yet untested (cf. Isaacowitz, Charles, & Carstensen, in press).

Thus, whether one asks people directly about the types of social partners they prefer, examines the ways in which people mentally represent social partners, or measures the proportion of emotional and informational material people remember, those people approaching the end of life appear to place more value on emotion, choosing social partners along affective lines and processing emotionally salient information more deeply.

THE INTEGRITY OF THE EMOTION SYSTEM IS WELL MAINTAINED IN OLD AGE

Do older adults experience emotions similarly to younger adults, or do age-related biological changes—from facial wrinkles to alterations in the central nervous system—degrade emotional experience? Despite numerous social reasons that could increase the likelihood of negative emotional experiences and biological reasons that might appear to decrease the ability to control them, research findings suggest the opposite.

A biological argument for the reduction of self-reported negative experiences lies in the notion of a reduced capacity to feel emotions. If emotions are not felt as strongly physiologically, they will not be subjectively perceived, and consequently, they will not be reported. However, findings from laboratory studies in which emotions are induced speak against a reduced-capacity argument. In a study measuring subjective experience, spontaneous facial expression, and psychophysiological responding (Levenson, Carstensen, Friesen, & Ekman, 1991), subjective intensity of emotional experience, outward facial expression, and the specific profiles of physiological activation were indistinguishable among older and younger adults. Interestingly, however, the overall level of physiological arousal was significantly reduced among the elderly. Similar reductions in levels of physiological arousal were observed in a study of married couples we describe later (Levenson, Carstensen, & Gottman, 1994).

AGE DIFFERENCES IN EMOTIONAL EXPERIENCE ARE POSITIVE

In addition to the findings concerning intact physiological mechanisms and greater emotional salience, there is evidence pointing to greater overall well-being—that is, less negative emotion and equivalent if not greater levels of positive emotions—among older adults compared with younger adults. Survey studies suggest that levels of positive affect are similar across successively older age cohorts, but a reliable reduction in negative affect is observed, and in studies finding reductions in positive affect, a closer analysis of the findings suggests that a circumscribed reduction in surgency (i.e., excitability) may account for this reduction. Excitement and sensation seeking, for example, are relatively reduced in old age. Other positive emotions, such as happiness and joy, are maintained (Lawton et al., 1993; Lawton, Kleban, Rajagopal, & Dean, 1992).

We recently completed a study in which emotions were sampled in everyday life (Carstensen, Pasupathi, & Mayr, 1998). Research participants spanning the ages 18 to 94 years carried electronic pagers and indicated on a response sheet the degree to which they were experiencing each of 19 positive and negative emotions at random times throughout the days and evenings for a week-long period. Findings revealed no age differences in the intensity of positive or negative experience. However, the frequency of negative emotional experience was lower among older than younger adults.

Data collected in this experience-sampling study also allowed us to explore the postulate that emotional experience is more mixed among older than younger people. In day-to-day life, people can experience multiple emotions in response to an event. Socioemotional selectivity theory predicts that emotional experience becomes more multifaceted with age because awareness of limited time elicits positive emotions and negative emotions, thus changing the very character of the experience. We tested this hypothesis in two ways. First, we computed the simple correlation between positive and negative emotional experience. Although, as expected, the correlation between positive and negative emotions was low, it was positively and significantly associated with age. That is, older adults tended to experience mixed positive and negative emotions more than younger adults. Second, with the use of factor analysis, we computed for each research participant the number of factors

that best characterized his or her responses over the course of the study. More factors were required to account for older people's responses, suggesting that their emotional reactions were more complex or differentiated.

Thus, studies that measure subjective emotional experience, either in the laboratory or as they occur in everyday life, speak against an unqualified reduced-capacity argument. Once elicited, positive and negative emotions are experienced subjectively as intensely among the old as the young. Interestingly, the few studies that have measured autonomic nervous system activity have found that the strength of physiological arousal is reduced in the elderly. Whether the reduction is emotion-specific or due to more global age-related degradation of the autonomic nervous system remains unclear. Either way, to the extent that lessened physiological arousal is associated with less subjective discomfort, it may have serendipitously positive consequences. As P. Baltes (1991) argued cogently, deficits in circumscribed domains can sometimes prompt growth in other domains. Reduced physiological arousal associated with negative emotions may represent a case in point, a matter to which we turn in the next section.

OLDER PEOPLE REGULATE THEIR EMOTIONS BETTER THAN YOUNGER PEOPLE

Socioemotional selectivity theory maintains that an emphasis on emotional goals leads to active efforts on the part of individuals to emphasize and enhance emotional experience. Existing empirical evidence from cross-sectional studies about perceived control over emotions is clear: Compared with younger adults, older adults report greater control over emotions, greater stability of mood, less psychophysiological agitation, and greater faith in their ability to control the internal and external expression of emotions. Remarkably similar age-related patterns have been found across five diverse samples: Catholic nuns; African, European, and Chinese Americans; and Norwegians (Gross et al., 1997).

The consistency of findings across these diverse ethnic, religious, and regional groups reduces concern that the findings reflect stable differences among age groups (viz., cohort effects), as opposed to aging per se. In other words, although cohort effects cannot be ruled out entirely, the reliability of the profile across very different types of samples at least speaks against the alternative that emotional differences are unique to younger and older generations of white Americans.

Findings from three other recent studies also reduce the concern that older people's subjective sense that they have good control over their emotions is limited to their beliefs and fails to reflect age differences in actual control. First, Lawton, Parmelee, Katz, and Nesselroade (1996) examined reported negative affect sampled during the course of a 1-month period in a group of adults. Not only did older adults report relatively low levels of negative affect, but they varied little over time.

Second, in the experience-sampling study described earlier (Carstensen et al., 1998), we examined the probability that negative or positive emotions would occur given their occurrence at the immediately preceding time when subjects reported their emotions. Using the 35 emotion samples collected over a 1-week period for each subject, we examined the duration of positive and negative emotional experience. As did Lawton et al. (1996), we found that the duration of negative emotions was shorter for older than younger adults; interestingly, the natural duration of positive emotional experience was similar for old and young adults (Carstensen et al., 1998). Thus, even when emotions are sampled close to the time they occurred, so that global self-evaluations are avoided, similarly positive profiles of emotional experience are revealed.

Third, we conducted a study involving observations of married couples discussing emotionally charged conflicts in their relationships. Resolution of interpersonal conflict, especially in intimate relationships, provides an opportunity to examine a special case of emotion regulation. Effective resolution of marital conflict requires that spouses deal simultaneously with their own negative emotions and the negative emotions expressed by their partner. In this study, we hypothesized that older couples resolve conflicts better than their middle-aged counterparts. Middle-aged and older couples, all of whom had been married many years, were asked to identify a mutually-agreed-upon conflict area and then to discuss the conflict with one another toward its resolution (Carstensen, Gottman, & Levenson, 1995; Carstensen, Graff, Levenson, & Gottman, 1996; Levenson, Carstensen, & Gottman, 1993; Levenson et al., 1994). Discussions were videotaped and psychophysiological responses were measured throughout the interaction. As predicted, compared with middle-aged couples, older couples displayed lesser overall negative affect, expressing less anger, disgust, belligerence, and whining in their discussions. In addition, older couples were more likely to express affection to their spouses during the exchange, interspersing positive expressions with negative ones. The pattern appears to be highly effective in curbing the negative affect typically associated with emotionally charged discussions.

Thus, older adults are notably effective at managing negative emotions. This finding, in combination with findings that positive emotions are maintained in frequency and duration during old age, paints a picture that is quite positive. The findings are in keeping with socioemotional selectivity theory. In the studies reviewed, older individuals limited negative emotional experiences in day-to-day life more effectively than younger individuals. Similarly, older couples engaged in discussions of personally relevant topics in a way that limited their negativity. If, as the theory suggests, people become increasingly aware of endings toward the end of life, aging individuals are increasingly motivated to optimize the emotional climate of their lives. It is not that negative emotions do not occur or that felt emotions are less intense. Rather, negative emotions are better regulated.

CONCLUSION

The study of emotion in old age is relatively young, yet within a short period of time, empirical findings have suggested a reasonably cohesive profile of emotional experience and emotion regulation in the later years. Efforts on the part of multiple investigative teams have documented the ubiquitousness of emotion in cognitive processing, from mental representations to social preferences; stability in the frequency of positive affect; reductions in negative affect; reduced physiological arousability; and superior regulation of emotion.

Of course, a comprehensive understanding of emotion in later life is only beginning to take shape. Greater emphasis on emotional aspects of life probably entails benefits for some areas of functioning and costs to others. The manner in which emotions change and the conditions associated with such change remain elusive. The role of perceived time in emotional experience, suggested in socioemotional selectivity theory, requires further investigation to identify the precise conditions under which emotions grow mixed, are better regulated, and are less negative as people age. Implications of the reduction in the physiological arousal accompanying emotional experience also demand clarification.

The profile of empirical evidence reviewed here provides a far different picture of old age than the literatures on cognitive aging and physical health. Numerous problems are associated with old age. Health insults, loss of economic and political status, and deaths of friends and loved ones are but a few of the problems associated with old age, yet research on emotion and aging suggests that the emotion domain may be well preserved and perhaps selectively optimized (M. M. Baltes & Carstensen, 1996). The inherent paradox of aging refers to the fact that despite loss and physical decline, adults enjoy good mental health and positive life satisfaction well into old age. We suggest that the uniquely human ability to monitor the passage of time, coupled with the inevitable constraints of mortality, heightens the value placed on emotional aspects of life and deepens the complexity of emotional experience as people age.

Acknowledgments—We thank Ursula Staudinger for her comments about an earlier draft of this article.

Note

1. Address correspondence to Laura Carstensen, Department of Psychology, Bldg. 420, Jordan Hall, Stanford University, Stanford, CA 94305; e-mail: llc@psych.stanford.edu.

Recommended Reading

Carstensen, L. L., & Frederickson, B. L. (1998). (See References)
Carstensen, L. L. Isaacowitz, D. M., & Charles, S. T. (1999). (See References)
Magai, C., & McFadden, S. H. (1996). *Handbook of emotion, adult development and aging.* San Diego: Academic Press.
Schaie, K. W., & Lawton, M. P. (Eds.). (1997). *Annual review of gerontology and geriatrics: Vol. 17. Focus on emotion and adult development.* New York: Springer.

References

Baltes, M. M. (1998). The psychology of the oldest-old: The fourth age. *Current Opinion in Psychiatry, 11,* 411–418.

Baltes, M. M., & Carstensen, L. L. (1996). The process of successful ageing. *Ageing and Society, 16,* 397–422.

Baltes, P. (1991). The many faces of human aging: Toward a psychological culture of old age. *Psychological Medicine, 21,* 837–854.

Carstensen, L. L. (1992). Social and emotional patterns in adulthood: Support for socioemotional selectivity theory. *Psychology and Aging, 7,* 331–338.

Carstensen, L. L. (1993). Motivation for social contact across the life span: A theory of socioemotional selectivity. In J. Jacobs (Ed.), *Nebraska Symposium on Motivation: Vol. 40. Developmental perspectives on motivation* (pp. 209–254). Lincoln: University of Nebraska Press.

Carstensen, L. L. (1995). Evidence for a life-span theory of socioemotional selectivity. *Current Directions in Psychological Science, 4,* 151–156.

Carstensen, L. L. (1998). A life-span approach to social motivation. In J. Heckhausen & C. Dweck (Eds.), *Motivation and self-regulation across the life span* (pp. 341–364). New York: Cambridge University Press.

Carstensen, L. L., & Fredrickson, B. L. (1998). Socioemotional selectivity in healthy older people and younger people living with the Human Immunodeficiency Virus: The centrality of emotion when the future is constrained. *Health Psychology, 17,* 1–10.

Carstensen, L. L. & Gottman, J. M., & Levenson, R. W. (1995). Emotional behavior in long-term marriage. *Psychology and Aging, 10,* 140–149.

Carstensen, L. L., Graff, J., Levenson, R. W., & Gottman, J. M. (1996). Affect in intimate relationships: The developmental course of marriage. In C. Magai & S. H. McFadden (Eds.), *Handbook of emotion, adult development, and aging* (pp. 227–247). San Diego: Academic Press.

Carstensen, L. L., Gross, J., & Fung, H. (1997). The social context of emotion. In K. W. Schaie & M. P. Lawton (Eds.), *Annual review of gerontology and geriatrics: Vol. 17. Focus on emotion and adult development* (pp. 325–352). New York: Springer.

Carstensen, L. L., Isaacowitz, D. M., & Charles, S. T. (1999). Taking time seriously: A life-span theory of social selectivity. *American Psychologist, 54,* 165–181.

Carstensen, L. L. Pasupathi, M., & Mayr, U. (1998). *Emotion experience in the daily lives of older and younger adults.* Manuscript submitted for publication.

Carstensen, L. L., & Turk-Charles, S. (1994). The salience of emotion across the adult life span. *Psychology and Aging, 9,* 259–264.

Diener, E., & Suh, M. E. (1997). Subjective well-being and age: An international analysis. In K. W. Schaie & M. P. Lawton (Eds.), *Annual review of gerontology and geriatrics: Vol. 17. Focus on emotion and adult development* (pp. 304–324). New York: Springer.

Fredrickson, B. F., & Carstensen, L. L. (1990). Choosing social partners: How old age and anticipated endings make us more selective. *Psychology and Aging, 5,* 335–347.

Fung, H. Carstensen, L. L., & Lutz, A. (in press). The influence of time on social preferences: Implications for life-span development. *Psychology and Aging.*

Gross, J. Carstensen, L. L., Pasupathi, M., Tsai, J., Götestam Skorpen, C., & Hsu, A. (1997). Emotion and aging: Experience, expression and control. *Psychology and Aging, 12,* 590–599.

Isaacowitz, D., Charles, S. T., & Carstensen, L. L. (in press). Emotion and cognition. In F. I. M. Craik & T. A. Salthouse (Eds.), *Handbook of aging and cognition* (2nd ed.) Mahwah, NJ: Erlbaum.

Jung, C. G. (1933). The stages of life. In *Modern man in search of a soul* (pp. 109–131). London: Kegan, Paul, Trench & Trubner.

Lang, F., Staudinger, U., & Carstensen, L. L. (1998). Socioemotional selectivity in late life: How personality and social context do (and do not) make a difference. *Journal of Gerontology: Psychological Sciences, 53,* P21–P30.

Lang, F. R., & Carstensen, L. L. (1994). Close emotional relationships in late life: Further support for proactive aging in the social domain. *Psychology and Aging, 9,* 315–324.

Lawton, M. P., Kleban, M. H. & Dean, J. (1993). Affect and age: Cross-sectional comparisons of structure and prevalence. *Psychology and Aging, 8,* 165–175.

Lawton, M. P., Kleban, M. H., Rajagopal, D., & Dean, J. (1992). The dimensions of affective experience in three age groups. *Psychology and Aging, 7,* 171–184.

Lawton, M. P., Parmelee, P. A., Katz, I., & Nesselroade, J. (1996). Affective states in normal and depressed older people. *Journal of Gerontology: Psychological Sciences, 51,* P309–P316.

Levenson, R. W., Carstensen, L. L., Friesen, W. V., & Ekman, P. (1991). Emotion, physiology, and expression in old age. *Psychology and Aging, 6,* 28–35.

Levenson, R. W., Carstensen, L. L., & Gottman, J. M. (1993). Long-term marriage: Age, gender and satisfaction. *Psychology and Aging, 8,* 301–313.

Levenson, R. W., Carstensen, L. L., & Gottman, J. M. (1994). Marital interaction in old and middle-aged long-term marriages: Physiology, affect and their interrelations. *Journal of Personality and Social Psychology, 67,* 56–68.

Smith, J., & Baltes, P. B. (1997). Profiles of psychological functioning in the old and oldest old. *Psychology and Aging, 12,* 458–472.

Our Nation's You-Know-What Detectors

Psychology: A study finds that among professions, the Secret Service is best at distinguishing between lies and truth.

By SUSAN CAMPBELL, *Hartford Courant*

Since his impeachment, President Clinton has been the focus of study after study about detecting truths and untruths in sworn testimony.

But for the professionals who are best at detecting even a well-trained liar, one need look no further than the agency assigned to protect the president, the U.S. Secret Service.

More than sheriffs, small-town police officers, psychologists and even judges, agents of the Secret Service show the greatest capacity to distinguish truth from untruth, says the author of one recent study.

The ability of certain professions to tell truth from lies was examined in "A Few Can Catch a Liar," a study published last month in "Psychological Science," a journal of the American Psychological Society.

One of the authors, Paul Ekman, psychology professor at UC San Francisco, began studying liars nearly 30 years ago, when the psychiatric residents he was teaching at the university asked for guidance.

"Many of them had heard of incidents in which patients would deliberately lie, be released for a weekend pass, and then go out and take their own life," said Ekman, who is in London on leave writing a book about emotions. "I thought that was a very practical question, and it raised basic issues about how well we can conceal our emotions."

Ekman thought it would be helpful to examine jobs, such as law-enforcement agents and psychologists, where the ability to discern the truth is particularly valuable.

Most of the study's participants did about as well as one would do if one just guessed, Ekman said. People in the CIA, and some Los Angeles County sheriffs, scored relatively high, but not as high as Secret Service agents have scored in past studies.

The study of lying has been fascinating in its scope, he said.

"It initially surprised me when I began examining lies that they occur in every arena of life," he said. "Once you begin to look, there's no arena in which lies don't occur."

In the study, 20 men ages 18 to 28 were asked to discuss in an interview a belief that they hold true about random social issues. Some were asked to speak truthfully. Others were asked to lie. In earlier studies researchers feared the results

From the *Los Angeles Times*, June 29, 1999. © 1999 by the Hartford Courant. Reprinted by permission.

were inaccurate because participants had no stake in the outcome of whether they were believed. So this time, researchers sweetened the pot a bit with money.

Truth tellers who convinced their interrogators—male and female—that they were honest got a $10 bonus. Liars who were believed got a $50 bonus. Failed attempts to convince interrogators were not rewarded.

Ekman said upping the ante increases the likelihood of making a lie believable.

Observers were told that at least some of the speakers were lying.

Their decisions were based on actual observation, not mechanical lie detectors of any sort.

Among the groups observed were agents from the CIA, Los Angeles County sheriffs, municipal law enforcement officers, federal judges, and psychologists both clinical and academic. Academic psychologists proved the least effective in telling truth from fiction, surpassed only slightly by clinical psychologists.

In a previous study when Ekman focused on college students, one subject was exceptionally good at detecting lies. When the professor discussed the student's career goal, the answer was "the U.S. Secret Service." James Mackin, a Secret Service special agent based in Washington, says his organization's penchant for discerning the truth is a combination of training and selection.

"We have, unlike other agencies, a dual focus," Mackin said. "We concentrate on criminal activities, like counterfeiting and credit card fraud and cell phone fraud, and we end up doing interviews for that on the criminal side.

"On the other side, we also talk to a wide range of people with a wide range of backgrounds in regard to our protection mission."

As Ekman said, Secret Service agents are "always looking for a needle in a haystack in a crowd, and that would increase their alertness." Certainly, when the stakes are the life of a dignitary, agents are motivated to recognize truth—or the shifty character who might create havoc or harm their charge, he said.

Other authors of the study were Maureen O'Sullivan of the University of San Francisco and Mark G. Frank of Rutgers, the State University of New Jersey.

THE BIOLOGY OF *Joy*

By Jeremiah Creedon

Scientists are unlocking the secrets of pleasure— and discovering what poets already knew

Pleasure, like fire, is a natural force that from the beginning humans have sought to harness and subdue. We've always sensed that pleasure is somehow crucial to life, perhaps the only tangible payoff for its hardships. And yet many have discovered that unbridled pleasure can also be dangerous, even fatal. Since ancient times, philosophers and spiritual leaders have debated its worth and character, often comparing it unfavorably to its more stable sibling, happiness. No one, however, saint or libertine, has ever doubted which of the pair would be the better first date.

Happiness is a gift for making the most of life. Pleasure is born of the reckless impulse to forget life and give yourself to the moment. Happiness is partly an abstract thing, a moral condition, a social construct: The event most often associated with happiness, some researchers say, is seeing one's children grow up to be happy themselves. How nice. Pleasure, pure pleasure, is a biological reflex, a fleeting "reward" so hot and lovely you might sell your children to get it. Witness the lab rat pressing the pleasure bar until it collapses. Or the sad grin of the crack addict as the molecules of mountain shrub trip a burst of primal gratitude deep in a part of the human brain much like a rat's. Both know all too well that pleasure, uncaged, can eat you alive.

Some scientists claim they're close to knowing what pleasure is, biologically speaking. Their intent is to solve the riddle of pleasure much as an earlier generation unleashed the power of the atom. Splitting pleasure down to its very molecules will have many benefits, they say, including new therapies for treating drug abuse and mental illness. Others note that research on the biology of pleasure is part of a wider trend that's exploding old ideas about the human brain, if not the so-called "Western biomedical paradigm" in general, with its outmoded cleaving of body from mind.

The assumption is that somehow our lives will be better once this mystery has been unraveled. Beneath that is the enduring belief that we can conquer pleasure as we've conquered most everything else, that we can turn it into a docile beast and put it to work. That we've never been able to do so before, and yet keep trying, reveals a lot about who we are, as creatures of a particular age—and species.

Of all the animals that humans have sought to tame, pleasure most resembles the falcon in its tendency to revert to the wild. That's why we're often advised to keep it hooded. The Buddha warned that to seek pleasure is to chase a shadow; it only heightens the unavoidable pain of life, which has to be accepted. Nevertheless, most have chosen to discover that for

From *Utne Reader,* November/December 1997, pp. 66-71, 106. © 1997 by Jeremiah Creedon. Reprinted by permission.

themselves. The early Greek hedonists declared pleasure the ultimate good, then immediately began to hedge. Falling in love, for instance, wasn't really a pleasure, given the inevitable pain of falling out of it. The hedonists thought they could be masters of pleasure, not its slaves; yet their culture's literature is a chronicle of impetuous, often unspeakable pleasures to be indulged at any cost.

When the Christians crawled out of the catacombs to make Rome holy, they took revenge on pagan pleasure by sealing it in—then pretended for centuries not to hear its muffled protests. Eclipsed was the Rose Bowl brilliance of the Roman circus, where civic pleasure reached a level of brutal spectacle unmatched until the advent of *Monday Night Football.* Pleasure as a public function seemed to vanish.

The end of the Dark Ages began with the Italian poet Dante, who, for all his obsession with the pains of hell, endures as one of the great, if ambivalent, students of pleasure. His *Inferno* is but a portrait of the enjoyments of his day turned inside out, like a dirty sock. For every kind of illicit bliss possible in the light of the world above, Dante created a diabolically fitting punishment in his theme-park hell below. We can only guess what terrible eternity he has since devised for his countryman, the pleasure-loving Versace, felled in what Dante would have considered the worst of ways—abruptly, without a chance to confess his sins. At the very least he's doomed to wear Armani.

Dante's ability to find a certain glee in the suffering of others—not to mention in the act of writing—goes to the heart of the problem of pleasure. Let's face it: Pleasure has a way of getting twisted. Most people, most of the time, are content with simple pleasures: a walk on the beach, fine wine, roses, cuddling, that sort of thing. But pleasure can also be complicated, jaded, and sick. The darker aspects of pleasure surely lie dormant in many of us, like the Minotaur in the heart of the labyrinth waiting for its yearly meal of pretty flesh. In the words of the Mongol ruler Genghis Khan, "Happiness lies in conquering one's enemies, in driving them in front of oneself, in taking their property, in savoring their despair, in outraging their wives and daughters." He meant pleasure, of course, not happiness—but *you* tell him.

In the Age of Reason, the vain hope that humans could reason with pleasure returned. Thinkers like Jeremy Bentham took up the old Greek idea of devising a "calculus" of pleasure—complex equations for estimating what pleasure really is, in light of the pain often caused by the quest for it. But the would-be moral engineers, rational to a fault, found the masses oddly attached to the older idea of pleasure being a simple sum of parts, usually private parts. As for the foundlings thus multiplied, along with certain wretched venereal ills, well, who would have figured?

The first "scientists of mind" were pretty sure that the secrets of pleasure, and the emotions in general, lay locked beyond their reach, inside our heads. Throughout the 19th century, scientists could only speculate about the human brain and its role as "the organ of consciousness." Even more galling, the era's writers and poets clearly speculated so much better—especially those on drugs.

Two of them, Samuel Taylor Coleridge and Thomas De Quincey, both opium addicts, also may have been early explorers of the brain's inner geography. Images of a giant fountain gushing from a subterranean river in Coleridge's most famous poem—"Kubla Khan; or, A Vision in a Dream" bear an odd resemblance to modern models of brain function, especially brains steeped in mind-altering chemicals. Writing in *The Human Brain* (BasicBooks, 1997), Susan A. Greenfield, professor of pharmacology at Oxford University, describes the "fountainlike" nerve-cell structures that arise in the brain stem and release various chemical messengers into the higher brain areas. As Greenfield notes, and Coleridge perhaps intuited, these geysers of emotion are "often the target of mood-modifying drugs."

De Quincey describes a similar terrain in *Confessions of an English Opium Eater (1821).* He even suggests that the weird world he envisioned while he was on the drug might have been his own fevered brain projected, a notion he fears will seem "ludicrous to a medical man." Not so. Sherwin B. Nuland, National Book Award winner and clinical professor of surgery at Yale, expresses an updated version of that concept in *The Wisdom of the Body* (Knopf, 1997). In Nuland's view, we may possess an "awareness" distinct from rational thought, a kind of knowledge that rises up from our cells to "imprint itself" on how we interpret the world. "It is by this means that our lives . . . and even our culture come to be influenced by, and are the reflection of, the conflict that exists within cells," he writes.

Maybe De Quincey really could see his own brain. Maybe that's what many artists see. Think of Dante's downward-spiraling hell, or the Minotaur in the labyrinth, even the cave paintings at Altamira and Lascaux. The first known labyrinth was built in Egypt nearly 4,000 years ago, a convoluted tomb for both a pharaoh's remains and those of the sacred crocodiles teeming in a nearby lake. It's an odd image to find rising up over and over from the mind's sunless sea, of subterranean passages leading ever deeper to an encounter with . . . the Beast. In an age when high-tech imaging devices can generate actual images of the brain at work, it's intriguing to think that artists ventured to the primordial core of that process long ago. And left us maps.

Today, Paul D. MacLean, National Institute of Mental Health scientist and author of *The Triune Brain in Evolution* (Plenum, 1990), describes a similar geography. He theorizes that the human brain is "three-brains-in-one," reflecting its "ancestral relationship to reptiles, early mammals, and recent mammals." Peter C. Whybrow, director of the Neuropsychiatric Institute at UCLA, uses this model to explain what he calls "the anatomical roots of emotion." Writing in *A Mood Apart* (BasicBooks, 1997), his study of depression and other "afflictions of the self," Whybrow notes: "The behavior of human beings is more complicated than that of other animals . . . but nonetheless we share in common with many creatures such behaviors as sexual courtship, pleasure-seeking, aggression, and the defense of territory. Hence it is safe to conclude that the evolution of human behavior is, in part, reflected in the evolution and hierarchical development of other species."

Sensuous LIKE ME

How I got back in my body through my nose

Some mornings my head is like a little dog panting, whimpering, and straining at his leash. *Let's go, let's go, let's go!* My head gets me up and leads me around all day. Sometimes it's dinnertime before I remember that I have a body.

And the idea that this body can give me pleasure—well, that's a really hard one. I used to think that because I read hip French books about sexual ecstasy I had somehow escaped my Calvinist heritage—the idea that the body is shameful and only a narcissistic lazybones would pay any attention to it. No such luck. My version of Calvinist body-denial was compulsive reading, and the more I read about French people's ecstasies, which are usually pretty cerebral anyway—the more I hid out from my own body. A body that, let's face it, is plumper, paler, and more easily winded than I would prefer.

Falling in love changed things. Intimacy with a woman who was learning to accept and even love her body gave me new eyes to see (and new nerve endings to feel) my own. I started—just started—to think of my body as a means of communication with the world, not a sausage case for Great Thoughts. I wanted to go further.

It was my wife who found Nancy Conger, professor of the five senses. A slender young woman with apparently bottomless reserves of energy and optimism, she lives in an old farmhouse in western Wisconsin, plays the violin, and teaches people how to get out of debt, simplify their lives, and use their senses for entertainment and joy. She even teaches a one-night class called "Sensuous Living." Laurie and I enrolled.

A class in sensuousness. An idea not without irony, amazing that we actually have to study this stuff. Five perfectly sensible-looking adults perched on plastic chairs in a drab little classroom in Minneapolis, with Nancy presiding in a sleeveless black jumpsuit. On two tables toward the front: nasturtiums in a vase, a strip of fur, a piece of sandpaper, a twig, a violin, a seashell.

"Lick your forearm," said Nancy, "and smell yourself."

Lick my forearm and smell myself?

I looked around me. The matronly woman in the purple blouse and matching shoes was licking her forearm. So was the shy, 40ish guy with the salt-and-pepper beard, and the thin, Italian-looking young woman with the big braid. Finally, feeling uncomfortably canine, I licked myself. I sniffed ("Little, short sniffs, like perfumers use," said Nancy). Hmm. A faintly metallic aroma. Sniff, sniff. Beneath it, something breadlike.

Like a wine, I had a bouquet.

Deciphering the code of art into the language of modern science took most of two centuries. One discipline after another tried to define what feelings like pleasure were, and from where they arose, only to fall short. Darwin could sense that emotions were important in his evolutionary scheme of things, but he was limited to describing how animals and humans expressed them on the outside, using their bodies, especially faces. William James, in a famous theory published in 1884, speculated that the brain only translates various sensations originating below the neck into what we think of as, say, joy and fear. Others saw it the other way around—emotions begin in the brain and the bodily reactions follow. Without knowing what pleasure actually is, Freud could see that the inability to feel it is a kind of disease, or at least a symptom, that he traced to (you guessed it) neurotic conflict.

By then, though, many people were fed up with all the talking. The study of mind had reached that point in the movie where the gung-ho types shove aside the hostage negotiator and shout, *We're going in."* And with scalpels drawn, they did. In 1872, Camillo Golgi, a young doctor working at a "home for incurables" in an Italian village, discovered the basic component of brain tissue, the neuron. During the 1920s, German scientist Otto Loewi, working with frog hearts, first identified neurotransmitters: chemical messengers that carry information across the gap between the neurons—the synapse—to receptors on the other side. Meanwhile, the Canadian neurosurgeon Wilder Penfield, operating on conscious patients with severe epilepsy, managed to trigger various emotions and dreamlike memories by electrically stimulating their brains. Such work gave rise to the idea that various mental functions might be "localized" in particular brain areas.

In 1954, psychologists James Olds and Peter Milner made a remarkable breakthrough—by accident. While researching the alerting mechanism in rat brains, they inadvertently placed an electrode in what they soon identified as a rat's pleasure-and-reward center: the so-called limbic system deep inside the brain. When the rats were later wired in a way that let them press a lever and jolt themselves, they did so as many as 5,000 times an hour.

This became the basis for current research on the "biology of reward." Scientists like Kenneth Blum have linked what they call reward deficiency syndrome to various human behavioral disorders: alcoholism, drug abuse, smoking, compulsive eating and gambling. Blum traces these disorders to genetically derived flaws in the neurotransmitters and receptors now associated with pleasure, including the pathways tied to the brain chemicals serotonin and dopamine, and the endorphins. Other researchers aren't so sure.

We all know by now that endorphins are the "body's own natural morphine." The discovery of endorphins in the early '70s marked the start of what some have declared the golden age of modern neuroscience. The impact was clear from the beginning to Candace B. Pert, whose work as a young scientist was crucial to the discovery. A few years earlier, she had helped identify the receptors that the endorphins fit into, as a lock fits a key, thus popping the lid of pleasure. According to

Then Nancy got us out of our chairs to wander around and "smell what doesn't seem to have a smell." I put my nose right up next to a big pad of paper on an easel. Faint wheaty aroma like my school tablets in fifth grade. All the sunshiny, chalk-dusty, gentle boredom of elementary school came back, like a tune.

A brick gave off a mysterious musty tang, charged with the past. A quarter smelled sour, a metal door bitter and somehow sad.

"Smell detours right around your thinking brain, back to the limbic system at the bottom of the brain, where memory is," Nancy told us. She also explained that smell can be hugely improved, made more subtle and precise, if you keep sniffing. "Smell dishes. Smell clothes. Smell everything," she exhorted.

I did want to keep on smelling, but we were on to a trust-and-touch experiment. We paired off (I went with the big-braid woman) and took turns blindfolding and leading each other. I put my partner's hand on a brick, a door, a seashell, a twig.

Then I put on the blindfold (it smelled powdery and lusciously feminine), and she led me. Without any visual clues to tell me what things were supposed to feel like, I met each surface with a small thrill of tactile freshness. A metal door, I discovered, was studded with sharp little grains. A twig was as rough as sandpaper, and the sandpaper itself practically made me jump out of my skin. With most of the objects, I enjoyed a few wonderful seconds of pure sensation before the thinking brain clicked in and gave the thing a name. But click in it did; and that's when the magic ended.

The evening concluded with experiments in sound (Nancy played her violin very near each of us so we could feel the vibration in our bodies) and taste (we passed around a loaf of focaccia), but as we drove home I was still hung up on the smell and touch thing.

My nose, which I had mostly used as a passive receiver of pretty large and often alarming signals (skunk crushed on an Iowa road, underarms needing immediate attention, and so on) felt amazingly discriminating, having actually sniffed the difference between a door and a quarter. My fingers still tingled with the thrill of sandpaper and brick and (blessed relief!) fur.

The part of my head that names, makes distinctions, and is vigilant against stupidities pointed out that five middle-class white folks in a certain demographic had just spent three hours rubbing, if not exactly gazing at, their navels.

The honorable side of my Calvinism (as a kid I lived on Calvin Avenue in Grand Rapids, Michigan, just down the street from Calvin College) bridled at the idea of stroking my nerve endings like some French decadent poet, while an entire society—an entire world—splits along economic fault lines.

A third part of me rejoiced: I had discovered the cleverest answer yet to television. It was the exquisite entertainment technology of a body—my body. Anyone's body. It is—or could be—an immediate rebuke and alternative to the technologies of consumerism, which coarsen, obscure, jack up, deny, extend beyond reason, and in general do numbing violence to the subtle, noble equipment for receiving the joys of life that we were all issued at birth.

Anyone can sniff a leaf or reach out to the rough bark of a tree. Anyone can listen for a little while to the world. And anyone can do it now, at the kitchen table, in the schoolroom, at the racetrack, in the hospital bed. And we can keep doing it until we believe again in the wondrous beauty of our own equipment (absolutely no amplification from Sony required).

—Jon Spayde

Pert, "it didn't matter if you were a lab rat, a First Lady, or a dope addict—everyone had the exact same mechanism in the brain for creating bliss and expanded consciousness." As she recounts in *Molecules of Emotion* (Scribner, 1997), her early success led to a career at the National Institute of Mental Health identifying other such messenger molecules, now known as neuropeptides.

Pert's interest in the natural opiates soon took her into uncharted territory—sexual orgasm. Working with Nancy Ostrowski, a scientist "who had left behind her desire to become a nun and gone on instead to become an expert on the brain mechanisms of animal sex," Pert turned her clinical gaze on the sexual cycle of hamsters. "Nancy would inject the animals with a radioactive opiate before copulation, and then, at various points in the cycle, decapitate them and remove the brains," Pert writes. "We found that blood endorphin levels increased by about 200 percent from the beginning to the end of the sex act." She doesn't say what happened to their own endorphin levels while they watched—but Dante has surely kept a log.

Modern students of pleasure and emotion have their differences. Pert, for instance, having worked so much with neuropeptides, doesn't buy the idea that emotions are localized in certain brain areas. "The hypothalamus, the limbic system, and the amygdala have all been proposed as the center of emotional expression," she writes. "Such traditional formulations view only the brain as important in emotional expressivity, and as such are, from the point of view of my own research, too

limited. From my perspective, the emotions are what link body and mind into bodymind."

This apparent reunion of body and mind is, in one sense, Pert's most radical conjecture. And yet, oddly, it's the one idea that many modern researchers do seem to share, implicitly or otherwise, to varying degrees. Most would agree that the process of creating human consciousness is vastly complex. It is also a "wet" system informed and modulated by dozens of neurochemical messengers, perhaps many more, all moving at incredible speeds. Dare we call it a calculus? Not on your life. Any analogy of the brain that summons up a computer is definitely uncool. For now.

There also seems to be a shared sense, not always stated, that some sort of grand synthesis may be, oh, 20 minutes away. In other words, it's only a matter of time before the knowledge of East and West is melded back into oneness, a theory that reunifies body and mind—and, as long as we're at it, everything else. That may be. But given that a similar impulse seems so prevalent throughout the culture, could it be that what we're really seeing is not purely science, but a case of primal yearning, even wishful thinking? A generation of brilliant scientists, their sensibilities formed in the psychedelic '60s, could now be looking back to the vision of mystical union they experienced, or at least heard about over and over again, in their youth. Perhaps they long to reach such a place, abstract though it is, for the same reason a salmon swims to the placid pool where its life began. We, like all creatures, are driven by the hope of an ultimate reward, a pleasure that has no name, a

THE NEW
Pleasure PRINCIPLE

This just in: Pain is not the route to happiness

Don't worry. Be happy.

The philosophy is simple, but living it is not, especially in our achievement-oriented society. According to Los Angeles-based therapist Stella Resnick, that's because we focus on the pain in our lives—getting through it, around it, or over it. Pleasure, the "visceral, body-felt experience of well-being," is a better path to growth and happiness, she contends in her book *The Pleasure Zone* (Conari Press, 1997). If only we knew how to feel it.

Resnick had to learn, too. Her childhood was unpleasant; her father left when she was 5, and, for 10 years, she endured beatings from her stepfather. She hung out on street corners and dated a gang leader. By age 32, she'd had two brief marriages and was involved in another stormy relationship. Although she'd built a successful San Francisco therapy practice, she was lonely and miserable. Nothing helped: not yoga, nor meditation, nor exercise, nor a vegetarian diet. "I was a very unhappy young woman," she recalls. "I'd had the best therapy from the best therapists, but even with all the work I had done on myself, something was missing."

What was missing, she discovered, was the ability to enjoy herself. At 35, after she lost her mother to cancer, she moved to a small house in the Catskill Mountains, where she lived alone for a year and, for the first time, paid attention to what felt good. At first she cried and felt sorry for herself. But by year's end, she was dancing to Vivaldi and the Temptations, and finding creativity in cooking and chopping wood.

She soon realized that most of her patients shared the same pleasure deprivation. "Our whole society diminishes the value of pleasure," she writes. "We think of it as fun and games, an escape from reality—rarely a worthwhile end in itself. Amazingly, we don't make the connection between vitality—the energy that comes from feeling good—and the willingness to take pleasure in moment-by-moment experience."

Therapy too often concentrates on pain and what the mind thinks; Resnick focused on pleasure and what the body feels. But when she first published her ideas in 1978, epithets were hurled: "narcissist," "hedonist," "icon for the Me Decade." It wasn't until research on the positive effects of pleasure and the negative effects of stress began to accumulate in the '80s that people became more receptive. "This is not about creating a society of me-first people," she says of her work. "There's no joy in hoarding all the goodies for our lonesome."

To help people understand pleasure, Resnick divides it into eight "core" categories: primal (the feeling of floating); pain relief (being touched and soothed); elemental (childlike laughter, play, movement, and voice); mental (the fun of learning); emotional (the feeling of love); sensual (the five senses, plus imagination); sexual (arousal, eroticism, orgasm); and spiritual (empathy, morality, and altruism).

Her prescription is body-based and simple. Listen to a fly buzz. Float on your back. Tell a dream. Her number-one tip for falling and staying in love is . . . breathe. Conscious breathing enhances relationships, she claims, because it allows us to let go in

sweet surrender, rather than fighting or resisting ourselves or each other.

Experiencing pleasure opens the body, releasing enormous energy, says Resnick. Ironically, this flow is what scares us, causing us to tense up and shut down, because we don't know what to do with it. We can miss the healing power of great sex, for example, by wanting to release the energy as soon as we get turned on. She advises allowing the excitement to build and circulate so that "it's something you feel in your heart. And in your big toes."

Repressing one's desire for pleasure was once considered virtuous, a sign of moral superiority. But Resnick questions whether it's good to continue in that vein. "We have poor race relations, poor man-woman relations, whole segments of society that have problems with parents and institutions," she says. "Could we do better if we enjoyed our relationships more, if people knew how to encourage and inspire themselves instead of being motivated by shame, guilt, and other negative emotions?"

Resnick doesn't advocate always succumbing to immediate gratification—there's pleasure in yearning—or fear and anger, which can inform and protect us. But using negative means to pursue positive ends simply doesn't work. "The secret to success in all things—business, creativity, art, relationships, family, spirituality—is to be relaxed during challenging times," she says. "Don't hold yourself in, or brace yourself for what might go wrong." And if you don't get it at first, don't worry. Even Resnick has to remind herself to breathe.

—*Cathy Madison*

pleasure that in fact may not be ours to feel. Thus, we never conquer pleasure; pleasure conquers us. And for its own reasons, both wondrous and brutal.

None of which makes the alleged new paradigm any less real. As the poets of our day, for better or worse, the modern scientists of mind have already shaped our reality with their words and concepts. Who hasn't heard of the endorphin-driven runner's high, or traced a pang of lover's jealousy to their reptilian brain?

On *Star Trek Voyager*, a medical man of the future waves his magic wand over a crewmate emerging from a trance and declares, "His neuropeptides have returned to normal!"

You didn't have to be a Darwin to see that the news gave Captain Janeway a certain . . . pleasure.

Jeremiah Creedon is a senior editor of Utne Reader.

The Moral Development of Children

It is not enough for kids to tell right from wrong. They must develop a commitment to acting on their ideals. Enlightened parenting can help

by William Damon

With unsettling regularity, news reports tell us of children wreaking havoc on their schools and communities: attacking teachers and classmates, murdering parents, persecuting others out of viciousness, avarice or spite. We hear about feral gangs of children running drugs or numbers, about teenage date rape, about youthful vandalism, about epidemics of cheating even in academically elite schools. Not long ago a middle-class gang of youths terrorized an affluent California suburb through menacing threats and extortion, proudly awarding themselves points for each antisocial act. Such stories make *Lord of the Flies* seem eerily prophetic.

What many people forget in the face of this grim news is that most children most of the time do follow the rules of their society, act fairly, treat friends kindly, tell the truth and respect their elders. Many young-

sters do even more. A large portion of young Americans volunteer in community service—according to one survey, between 22 and 45 percent, depending on the location. Young people have also been leaders in social causes. Harvard University psychiatrist Robert Coles has written about children such as Ruby, an African-American girl who broke the color barrier in her school during the 1960s. Ruby's daily walk into the all-white school demonstrated a brave sense of moral purpose. When taunted by classmates, Ruby prayed for their redemption rather than cursing them. "Ruby," Coles observed, "had a will and used it to make an ethical choice; she demonstrated moral stamina; she possessed honor, courage."

All children are born with a running start on the path to moral development. A number of inborn responses predispose them to act in ethical ways. For example, empa-

thy—the capacity to experience another person's pleasure or pain vicariously—is part of our native endowment as humans. Newborns cry when they hear others cry and show signs of pleasure at happy sounds such as cooing and laughter. By the second year of life, children commonly console peers or parents in distress.

Sometimes, of course, they do not quite know what comfort to provide. Psychologist Martin L. Hoffman of New York University once saw a toddler offering his mother his security blanket when he perceived she was upset. Although the emotional disposition to help is present, the means of helping others effectively must be learned and refined through social experience. Moreover, in many people the capacity for empathy stagnates or even diminishes. People can act cruelly to those they refuse to empathize with. A New York police officer once asked a teenage thug how he could have crippled an 83-year-old woman during a mugging. The boy replied, "What do I care? I'm not her."

A scientific account of moral growth must explain both the good and the bad. Why do most children act in reasonably—sometimes exceptionally—moral ways, even when it flies in the face of their immediate self-interest? Why do some children depart from accepted standards, often to the great harm of themselves and others? How does a child acquire mores and develop a life-long commitment to moral behavior, or not?

Psychologists do not have definitive answers to these questions, and often their studies seem merely to confirm parents' observations and intuition. But parents, like all people, can be led astray by subjective biases, incomplete information and media sensationalism. They may blame a relatively trivial event—say, a music concert—for a deep-seated problem such as drug dependency. They may incorrectly attribute their own problems to a strict upbringing and then try to compensate by raising their children in an overly permissive way. In such a hotly contested area as children's moral values, a systematic, scientific approach is the only way to avoid wild swings of emotional reaction that end up repeating the same mistakes.

The Genealogy of Morals

The study of moral development has become a lively growth industry within the social sciences. Journals are full of new findings and competing models. Some theories focus on natural biological forces; others stress social influence and experience; still others, the judgment that results from children's intellectual development. Although each theory has a different emphasis, all recognize that no single cause can account for either moral or immoral behavior. Watching violent videos or

The Six Stages of Moral Judgment

Growing up, children and young adults come to rely less on external discipline and more on deeply held beliefs. They go through as many as six stages (grouped into three levels) of moral reasoning, as first argued by psychologist Lawrence Kohlberg in the late 1950s (*below*). The evidence includes a long-term study of 58 young men interviewed periodically over two decades. Their moral maturity was judged by how they analyzed hypothetical dilemmas, such as whether a husband should steal a drug for his dying wife. Either yes or no was a valid answer; what mattered was how the men justified it. As they grew up, they passed through the stages in succession, albeit at different rates (*bar graph*). The sixth stage remained elusive. Despite the general success of this model for describing intellectual growth, it does not explain people's actual behavior. Two people at the same stage may act differently. —*W.D.*

LEVEL 1: SELF-INTEREST
◻ STAGE 1 PUNISHMENT "I won't do it, because I don't want to get punished."
▦ STAGE 2 REWARD "I won't do it, because I want the reward."

LEVEL 2: SOCIAL APPROVAL
◼ STAGE 3 INTERPERSONAL RELATIONS "I won't do it, because I want people to like me."
▩ STAGE 4 SOCIAL ORDER "I won't do it, because it would break the law."

LEVEL 3: ABSTRACT IDEALS
▨ STAGE 5 SOCIAL CONTRACT "I won't do it, because I'm obliged not to."
▥ STAGE 6 UNIVERSAL RIGHTS "I won't do it, because it's not right, no matter what others say."

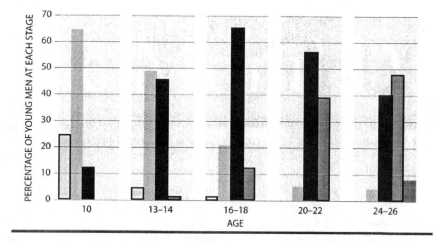

playing shoot-'em-up computer games may push some children over the edge and leave others unaffected. Conventional wisdom dwells on lone silver bullets, but scientific understanding must be built on an appreciation of the complexity and variety of children's lives.

Biologically oriented, or "nativist," theories maintain that human morality springs from emotional dispositions that are hardwired into our species. Hoffman, Colwyn Trevarthen of the University of Edinburgh and Nancy Eisenberg of Arizona State University have established

that babies can feel empathy as soon as they recognize the existence of others—sometimes in the first week after birth. Other moral emotions that make an early appearance include shame, guilt and indignation. As Harvard child psychologist Jerome S. Kagan has described, young children can be outraged by the violation of social expectations, such as a breach in the rules of a favorite game or rearranged buttons on a piece of familiar clothing.

Nearly everybody, in every culture, inherits these dispositions. Mary D. Ainsworth of the University of Virginia reported empathy among Ugandan and American infants; Norma Feshbach of the University of California at Los Angeles conducted a similar comparison of newborns in Europe, Israel and the U.S.; Millard C. Madsen of U.C.L.A. studied sharing by preschool children in nine cultures. As far as psychologists know, children everywhere start life with caring feelings toward those close to them and adverse reactions to inhumane or unjust behavior. Differences in how these reactions are triggered and expressed emerge only later, once children have been exposed to the particular value systems of their cultures.

In contrast, the learning theories concentrate on children's acquisition of behavioral norms and values through observation, imitation and reward. Research in this tradition has concluded that moral behavior is context-bound, varying from situation to situation almost independently of stated beliefs. Landmark studies in the 1920s, still frequently cited, include Hugh Hartshorne and Mark May's survey of how children reacted when given the chance to cheat. The children's behavior depended largely on whether they thought they would be caught. It could be predicted neither from their conduct in previous situations nor from their knowledge of common moral rules, such as the Ten Commandments and the Boy Scout's code.

Later reanalyses of Hartshorne and May's data, performed by Roger Burton of the State University of New York at Buffalo, discovered at least one general trend: younger children were more likely to cheat than adolescents. Perhaps socialization or mental growth can restrain dishonest behavior after all. But the effect was not a large one.

The third basic theory of moral development puts the emphasis on intellectual growth, arguing that virtue and vice are ultimately a matter of conscious choice. The best-known cognitive theories are those of psy-

"Could You Live with Yourself?"

In a distressed neighborhood in Camden, N.J., social psychologist Daniel Hart of Rutgers University interviewed an African-American teenager who was active in community service:

How would you describe yourself?
I am the kind of person who wants to get involved, who believes in getting involved. I just had this complex, I call it, where people think of Camden as being a bad place, which bothered me. Every city has its own bad places, you know. I just want to work with people, work to change that image that people have of Camden. You can't start with adults, because they don't change. But if you can get into the minds of young children, show them what's wrong and let them know that you don't want them to be this way, then it could work, because they're more persuadable.

Is there really one correct solution to moral problems like this one?
Basically, it's like I said before. You're supposed to try to help save a life.

How do you know?
Well, it's just—how could you live with yourself? Say that I could help save this person's life—could I just let that person die? I mean, I couldn't live with myself if that happened. A few years ago my sister was killed, and . . . the night she was killed I was over at her house, earlier that day. Maybe if I had spent the night at her house that day, maybe this wouldn't have happened.

You said that you're not a bad influence on others. Why is that important?
Well, I try not to be a bad role model. All of us have bad qualities, of course; still, you have to be a role model even if you're a person walking down the street. You know, we have a society today where there are criminals and crooks. There are drug users. Kids look to those people. If they see a drug dealer with a lot of money, they want money, too, and then they're going to do drugs. So it's important that you try not to be a bad influence, because that can go a long way. Even if you say, oh, wow, you tell your little sister or brother to be quiet so Mom and Dad won't wake so you won't have to go to school. And they get in the habit of being quiet [laughs], you're not going to school, things like that. So when you're a bad influence, it always travels very far.

Why don't you want that to happen?
Because in today's society there's just really too much crime, too much violence. I mean everywhere. And I've even experienced violence, because my sister was murdered. You know, we need not to have that in future years, so we need to teach our children otherwise.

chologists Jean Piaget and Lawrence Kohlberg. Both described children's early moral beliefs as oriented toward power and authority. For young children, might makes right, literally. Over time they come to understand that social rules are made by people and thus can be renegotiated and that reciprocity in relationships is more fair than unilateral obedience. Kohlberg identified a six-stage sequence in the maturation of moral judgment [see box, "The Six Stages of Moral Judgment]." Several thousand studies have used it as a measure of how advanced a person's moral reasoning is.

Conscience versus Chocolate

Although the main parts of Kohlberg's sequence have been confirmed, notable exceptions stand out. Few if any people reach the sixth and most advanced stage, in which their moral view is based purely on abstract principles. As for the early stages in the sequence, many studies (including ones from my own laboratory) have found that young children have a far richer sense of positive morality than the model indicates. In other words, they do not act simply out of fear of punishment. When a playmate hogs a plate of cookies or refuses to relinquish a swing, the protest "That's not fair!" is common. At the same time, young children realize that they have an obligation to share with others—even when their parents say not to. Preschool children generally believe in an equal distribution of goods and back up their beliefs with reasons such as empathy ("I want my friend to feel nice"), reciprocity ("She shares her toys with me") and egalitarianism ("We should all get the same"). All this they figure out through confrontation with peers at play. Without fairness, they learn, there will be trouble.

In fact, none of the three traditional theories is sufficient to explain children's moral growth and behavior. None captures the most essential dimensions of moral life: character and commitment. Regardless of how children develop their initial system of values, the key question is: What makes them live up to their ideals or not? This issue is the focus of recent scientific thinking.

Like adults, children struggle with temptation. To see how this tug of war plays itself out in the world of small children, my colleagues and I (then at Clark University) devised

How Universal Are Values?

The observed importance of shared values in children's moral development raises some of the most hotly debated questions in philosophy and the social sciences today. Do values vary from place to place, or is there a set of universal values that guides moral development everywhere? Do children growing up in different cultures or at different times acquire fundamentally different mores?

Some light was shed on the cultural issue by Richard A. Shweder of the University of Chicago and his colleagues in a study of Hindu-Brahmin children in India and children from Judeo-Christian backgrounds in the U.S. The study revealed striking contrasts between the two groups. From an early age, the Indian children learned to maintain tradition, to respect defined rules of interpersonal relationships and to help people in need. American children, in comparison, were oriented toward autonomy, liberty and personal rights. The Indian children said that breaches of tradition, such as eating beef or addressing one's father by his first name, were particularly reprehensible. They saw nothing wrong with a man caning his errant son or a husband beating his wife when she went to the movies without his permission. The American children were appalled by all physically punitive behavior but indifferent to infractions such as eating forbidden foods or using improper forms of address.

Moreover, the Indians and Americans moved in opposite directions as they matured. Whereas Indian children restricted value judgments to situations with which they were directly familiar, Indian adults generalized their values to a broad range of social conditions. American children said that moral standards should apply to everyone always; American adults modified values in the face of changing circumstances. In short, the Indians began life as relativists and ended up an universalists, whereas the Americans went precisely the other way.

It would be overstating matters, however, to say that children from different cultures adopt completely different moral codes. In Schweder's study, both groups of children thought that deceitful acts (a father breaking a promise to a child) and uncharitable acts (ignoring a beggar with a sick child) were wrong. They also shared a repugnance toward theft, vandalism and harming innocent victims, although there was some disagreement on what constitutes inno-

cence. Among these judgments may be found a universal moral sense, based on common human aversions. It reflects core values—benevolence, fairness, honesty—that may be necessary for sustaining human relationships in all but the most dysfunctional societies.

A parallel line of research has studied gender differences, arguing that girls learn to emphasize caring, whereas boys incline toward rules and justice. Unlike the predictions made by culture theory, however, these gender claims have not held up. The original research that claimed to find gender differences lacked proper control groups. Well-designed studies of American children—for example, those by Lawrence Walker of the University of British Columbia—rarely detect differences between boys' and girls' ideals. Even for adults, when educational or occupational levels are controlled, the differences disappear. Female lawyers have almost the same moral orientations as their male counterparts; the same can be said for male and female nurses, homemakers, scientists, high school dropouts and so on. As cultural theorists point out, there is far more similarity between male and female moral orientations within any given culture than between male and female orientations across cultures.

Generational differences are also of interest, especially to people who bemoan what they see as declining morality. Such complaints, of course, are nothing new [see "Teenage Attitudes,"by H. H. Remmersand D. H. Radler; SCIENTIFIC AMERICAN, June 1958; and "The Origins of Alienation," by Urie Bronfenbrenner; SCIENTIFIC AMERICAN, August 1974]. Nevertheless, there is some evidence that young people today are more likely to engage in antisocial behavior than those a generation ago were. According to a survey by Thomas M. Achenbach and Catherine T. Howell of the University of Vermont, parents and teachers reported more behavioral problems (lying, cheating) and other threats to healthy development (depression, withdrawal) in 1989 than in 1976 (above). (The researchers are now updating their survey.) But in the long sweep of human history, 13 years is merely an eye blink. The changes could reflect a passing problem, such as overly permissive fashions in child rearing, rather than a permanent trend.

—W.D.

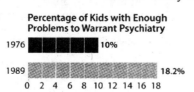

Percentage of Kids with Enough Problems to Warrant Psychiatry

1976	10%
1989	18.2%

0 2 4 6 8 10 12 14 16 18

KIDS THESE DAYS are likelier to need mental health services, judging from parents' reports of behavioral and emotional problems.

EDWARD BELL; SOURCE; THOMAS M. ACHENBACH AND CATHERINE T. HOWELL the following experiment. We brought groups, each of four children, into our lab, gave them string and beads, and asked them to make bracelets and necklaces for us. We then thanked them profusely for their splendid work and rewarded them, as a group, with 10 candy bars. Then the real experiment began: we told each group that it would need to decide the best way to divide up the reward. We left the room and watched through a one-way mirror.

Before the experiment, we had interviewed participants about the concept of fairness. We were curious, of course, to find out whether the prospect of gobbling up real chocolate would overwhelm their abstract sense of right and wrong. To test this thoroughly, we gave one unfortunate control group an almost identical conundrum, using cardboard rectangles rather than real chocolate—a not so subtle way of defusing their self-interest. We observed groups of four-, six-, eight- and 10-year-old children to see whether the relationship between situational and hypothetical morality changed with age.

The children's ideals did make a difference but within limits circumscribed by narrow self-interest. Children given cardboard acted almost three times more generously toward one another than did children given chocolate. Yet moral beliefs still held some sway. For example, children who had earlier expressed a belief in merit-based solutions ("The one who did the best job should get more of the candy") were the ones most likely to advocate for merit in the real situation. But they did so most avidly when they themselves could claim to have done more than their peers. Without such a claim, they were easily persuaded to drop meritocracy for an equal division.

Even so, these children seldom abandoned fairness entirely. They may have switched from one idea of justice to another—say, from merit to equality—but they did not resort to egoistic justifications such as "I should get more because I'm big" or "Boys like candy more than girls, and I'm a boy." Such rationales generally came from children who had declared no belief in either equality or meritocracy. Older children were more likely to believe in fairness and to act accordingly, even when such action favored others. This finding was evidence for the reassuring proposition that ideals can have an increasing influence on conduct as a child matures.

Do the Right Thing

But this process is not automatic. A person must adopt those beliefs as a central part of his or her personal identity. When a person moves from saying "People should be honest" to "I want to be honest," he or she becomes more likely to tell the truth in everyday interactions. A person's use of moral principles to define the self is called the person's moral identity. Moral identity determines not merely what the person considers to be the right course of action but also why he or she would decide: "I myself must take this course." This distinction is crucial to understanding the variety of moral behavior. The same basic ideals are widely shared by even the youngest members of society; the difference is the resolve to act on those ideals.

Most children and adults will express the belief that it is wrong to allow others to suffer, but only a subset of them will conclude that they themselves must do something about, say, ethnic cleansing in Kosovo. Those are the ones who are most likely to donate money or fly to the Balkans to help. Their concerns about human suffering are central to the way they think about themselves and their life goals, and so they feel a responsibility to take action, even at great personal cost.

In a study of moral exemplars—people with long, publicly documented histories of charity and civil-rights work—psychologist Anne Colby of the Carnegie Foundation and I encountered a high level of integration between self-identity and moral concerns. "People who define themselves in terms of their moral goals are likely to see moral problems in everyday events, and they are also likely to see themselves as necessarily implicated in these problems," we wrote. Yet the exemplars showed no signs of more insightful moral reasoning. Their ideals and Kohlberg levels were much the same as everyone else's.

Conversely, many people are equally aware of moral problems, but to them the issues seem remote from their own lives and their senses of self. Kosovo and Rwanda sound far away and insignificant; they are easily put out of mind. Even issues closer to home—say, a maniacal clique of peers who threaten a classmate—may seem like someone else's problem. For people who feel this way, inaction does not strike at their self-conception. Therefore, despite commonplace assumptions to the contrary, their moral knowledge will not be enough to impel moral action.

The development of a moral identity follows a general pattern. It normally takes shape in late childhood, when children acquire the capacity to analyze people—including themselves—in terms of stable character traits. In childhood, self-identifying traits usually consist of action-related skills and interests ("I'm smart" or "I love music"). With age, children start to use moral terms to define themselves. By the onset of puberty, they typically invoke adjectives such as "fairminded," "generous" and "honest."

Some adolescents go so far as to describe themselves primarily in terms of moral goals. They speak of noble purposes, such as caring for others or improving their communities, as missions that give meaning to their lives. Working in Camden, N.J., Daniel Hart and his colleagues at Rutgers University found that a high proportion of so-called care exemplars—teenagers identified by teachers and peers as highly committed to volunteering—had self-identities that were based on moral belief systems. Yet they scored no higher than their peers on the standard psychological tests of moral judgment. The study is noteworthy because it was conducted in an economically deprived urban setting among an adolescent population often stereotyped as high risk and criminally inclined [*see* box, "Could You Live with Yourself?"].

At the other end of the moral spectrum, further evidence indicates that moral identity drives behavior. Social psychologists Hazel Markus of Stanford University and Daphne Oyserman of the University of Michigan have observed that delinquent youths have immature senses of self, especially when talking about their future selves (a critical part of adolescent identity). These troubled teenagers do not imagine themselves as doctors, husbands, voting citizens, church members—any social role that embodies a positive value commitment.

How does a young person acquire, or not acquire, a moral identity? It is an incremental process, occurring gradually in thousands of small ways: feedback from others; observations of actions by others that either inspire or appall; reflections on one's own experience; cultural influences such as family, school, religious institutions and the mass media. The relative importance of these factors varies from child to child.

Teach Your Children Well

For most children, parents are the original source of moral guidance. Psychologists such as Diana Baumrind of the University of California at Berkeley have shown that "authoritative" parenting facilitates children's moral growth more surely than either "permissive" or "authoritarian" parenting. The authoritative mode establishes consistent family rules and firm limits but also en-courages open discussion and clear communication to explain and, when justified, revise the rules. In contrast, the permissive mode avoids rules entirely; the authoritarian mode ir-regularly enforces rules at the parent's whim—the "because I said so" approach.

Although permissive and authoritarian parenting seem like opposites, they actually tend to produce similar patterns of poor self-control and low social responsibility in children. Neither mode presents children with the realistic expectations and structured guidance that challenge them to expand their moral horizons. Both can foster habits—such as feeling that mores come from the outside—that could inhibit the development of a moral identity. In this way, moral or immoral conduct during adulthood often has roots in childhood experience.

As children grow, they are increasingly exposed to influences beyond the family. In most families, however, the parent-child relationship remains primary as long as the child lives at home. A parent's comment on a raunchy music lyric or a blood-drenched video usually will stick with a child long after the media experience has faded. In fact, if salacious or violent media programming opens the door to responsible parental feedback, the benefits can far outweigh the harm.

One of the most influential things parents can do is to encourage the right kinds of peer relations. Interactions with peers can spur moral growth by showing children the conflict between their preconceptions and social reality. During the debates about dividing the chocolate, some of our subjects seemed to pick up new—and more informed—ideas about justice. In a follow-up study, we confirmed that the peer debate had heightened their awareness of the rights of others. Children who participated actively in the debate, both expressing their opinions and listening to the viewpoints of others, were especially likely to benefit.

In adolescence, peer interactions are crucial in forging a self-identity. To be sure, this process often plays out in cliquish social behavior: as a means of defining and shoring up the sense of self, kids will seek out like-minded peers and spurn others who seem foreign. But when kept within reasonable bounds, the in-group clustering generally evolves into a more mature friendship pattern. What can parents do in the meantime to fortify a teenager who is bearing the brunt of isolation or persecution? The most important message they can give is that cruel behavior reveals something about the perpetrator rather than about the victim. If this advice helps the youngster resist taking the treatment personally, the period of persecution will pass without leaving any psychological scars.

Some psychologists, taking a sociological approach, are examining community-level variables, such as whether various moral influences—parents, teachers, mass media and so on—are consistent with one another. In a study of 311 adolescents from 10 American towns and cities, Francis A. J. Ianni of the Columbia University Teachers College noticed high degrees of altruistic behavior and low degrees of antisocial behavior among youngsters from communities where there was consensus in expectations for young people.

Everyone in these places agreed that honesty, for instance, is a fundamental value. Teachers did not tolerate cheating on exams, parents did not let their children lie and get away with it, sports coaches did not encourage teams to bend the rules for the sake of a win, and people of all ages expected openness from their friends. But many communities were divided along such lines. Coaches espoused winning above all else, and parents protested when teachers reprimanded their children for cheating or shoddy schoolwork. Under such circumstances, children learned not to take moral messages seriously.

Ianni named the set of shared standards in harmonious communities a "youth charter." Ethnicity, cultural diversity, socioeconomic status, geographic location and population size had nothing to do with whether a town offered its young people a steady moral compass. The notion of a youth charter is being explored in social interventions that foster communication among children, parents, teachers and other influential adults. Meanwhile other researchers have sought to understand whether the specific values depend on cultural, gender or generational background [see box, "How Universal Are Values?"].

Unfortunately, the concepts embodied in youth charters seem ever rarer in American society. Even when adults spot trouble, they may fail to step in. Parents are busy and often out of touch with the peer life of their children; they give kids more autonomy than ever before, and kids expect it—indeed, demand it. Teachers, for their part, feel that a child's nonacademic life is none of their business and that they could be censured, even sued, if they intervened in a student's personal or moral problem. And neighbors feel the same way: that they have no business interfering with another family's business, even if they see a child headed for trouble.

Everything that psychologists know from the study of children's moral development indicates that moral identity—the key source of moral commitment throughout life—is fostered by multiple social influences that guide a child in the same general direction. Children must hear the message enough for it to stick. The challenge for pluralistic societies will be to find enough common ground to communicate the shared standards that the young need.

The Author

WILLIAM DAMON remembers being in an eighth-grade clique that tormented an unpopular kid. After describing his acts in the school newspaper, he was told by his English teacher, "I give you an A for the writing, but what you're doing is really shameful." That moral feedback has stayed with him. Damon is now director of the Center on Adolescence at Stanford University, an interdisciplinary program that specializes in what he has called "the least understood, the least trusted, the most feared and most neglected period of development." A developmental psychologist, he has studied intellectual and moral growth, educational methods, and peer and cultural influences on children. He is the author of numerous books and the father of three children, the youngest now in high school.

Further Reading

THE MEANING AND MEASUREMENT OF MORAL DEVELOPMENT. Lawrence Kohlberg. Clark University, Heinz Werner Institute, 1981.

THE EMERGENCE OF MORALITY IN YOUNG CHILDREN. Edited by Jerome Kagan and Sharon Lamb. University of Chicago Press, 1987.

THE MORAL CHILD: NURTURING CHILDREN'S NATURAL MORAL GROWTH. William Damon. Free Press, 1990.

ARE AMERICAN CHILDREN'S PROBLEMS GETTING WORSE? A 13-YEAR COMPARISON. Thomas M. Achenbach and Catherine T. Howell in *Journal of the American Academy of Child and Adolescent Psychiatry*, Vol. 32, No. 6, pages 1145–1154; November 1993.

SOME DO CARE: CONTEMPORARY LIVES OF MORAL COMMITMENT. Anne Colby. Free Press, 1994.

THE YOUTH CHARTER: HOW COMMUNITIES CAN WORK TOGETHER TO RAISE STANDARDS FOR ALL OUR CHILDREN. William Damon. Free Press, 1997.

Unit Selections

Key Points to Consider

❖ What are the various milestones or developmental landmarks that mark human development? What purpose do various developmental events serve? Can you give examples of some of these events? Costanza Villalba claims that there are seven stages to development. What are these stages and how are they different for men and women? How are they similar?

❖ Why is embryonic life so important? How do the experiences of the fetus affect the child after it is born? What factors deter the fetus from achieving its full potential?

❖ Do parents matter or do you think that child development is mostly dictated by genes? Do you think that both nature and nurture affect development? Do you think one of these factors is more important than the other? Which one and why? Do you think it is important for both parents to be present during their child's formative years? Do you think fathers and mothers differ in their interactions with their children? How so?

❖ What is puberty? How does puberty differ from sexual attraction? Do you think that puberty and first sexual attraction are, in fact, two different stages of adolescent development? Is adolescence one stage of development or several stages of development?

❖ Why do we age? Can we stay younger longer? What do Americans say is more important—a high quality but shorter life or a poorer quality, longer life? Why do you think they answered the way they did? How would you answer and why?

 **Links**   **www.dushkin.com/online/**

These sites are annotated on pages 4 and 5.

The Garcias and the Szubas are parents of newborns. Both sets of parents wander down to the hospital's neonatal nursery where both babies, Juan Garcia and Kimberly Szuba, are cared for by pediatric nurses when the babies are not in their mothers' rooms. Kimberly is alert, active, and often crying and squirming when her parents watch her. On the other hand, Juan is quiet, often asleep, and less attentive to external stimuli when his parents watch him.

Why are these babies so different? Are the differences gender-related? Will these differences disappear as the children develop or will the differences become exaggerated? What does the future hold for each child? Will Kimberly excel at sports and Juan excel at English? Can Kimberly overcome her parents' poverty and succeed in a professional career? Will Juan become a doctor like his mother or a pharmacist like his father? Will both of these children escape childhood disease, abuse, and the other misfortunes sometimes visited upon children?

Developmental psychologists are concerned with all of the Kimberlys and Juans of our world. Developmental psychologists study age-related changes in language, motor and social skills, cognition, and physical health. They are interested in the common skills shared by all children as well as the differences between children and the events that create these differences.

In general, developmental psychologists are concerned with the forces that guide and direct development. Some developmental theorists argue that the forces that shape a child are found in the environment, in such factors as social class, quality of available stimulation, parenting style. Other theorists insist that genetics and related physiological factors, such as hormones, underlie the development of humans. A third set of psychologists—in fact many—believe that some combination or interaction of both factors, physiology and environment (or nature and nurture), is responsible for development.

In this unit, we are going to look at issues of development in a chronological fashion. The first selection, "The Seven Stages of Man," provides a brief review of the various developmental periods for men. The next article pertains to fetal development, which is crucial to the development of the child after it is born. Various environmental factors can deter development of or even damage

the fetus. Janet Hopson reviews these in "Fetal Psychology."

In "Do Parents Really Matter? Kid Stuff" Annie Murphy Paul asks the critical question, which, when interpreted, speaks to whether nurture or environment really make a difference. After pondering much evidence about nature and nurture, Paul infers that parental nurturance does matter. She concludes that nurture interacts with nature to affect the developing child.

We move next to some information about adolescence. In "Rethinking Puberty: The Development of Sexual Attraction," puberty is differentiated from adolescence. In fact, the author suggests that there is more than one developmental era in adolescence. One is puberty; the other is the first instance of sexual attraction.

The next article is about adulthood and aging. The American Association for Retired People conducted a poll recently to determine whether quality of life or quantity (age) is more important to its members. Most elderly opted for a shorter life with better quality rather than a longer life with poor quality.

The Seven Stages of Man

Men are often portrayed as big boys, differing from their younger selves only in the sums of money they spend on their toys. Indeed, because men can reproduce well into old age, and do not experience cyclical hormonal changes, their health is regarded as fairly static. But medical experts are learning that between the boy and the man stand a variety of genetic, biological and social changes. Understanding these factors may help men prepare for the stages that await them.

CONSTANZA VILLALBA

INFANCY

At the precise moment when a single sperm wiggles its way into an awaiting egg, the sex of the developing baby is defined. If that sperm carries a portly X chromosome, the egg turned embryo will give rise to a baby girl. If that sperm carries a diminutive Y chromosome, the baby will be a boy. With the blueprint for the male architecture, however, come several, often unfortunate genetic predispositions: hemophilia and Duchenne's Muscular Dystrophy afflict boys and men almost exclusively, while boys are more likely than girls to suffer from Fragile-X Syndrome, the nation's leading cause of mental retardation.

But being born a boy also comes with perks. Baby boys are an animated lot who display a marked curiosity about the world. Compared with girls, they are more alert and emotionally interactive with caretakers. They begin suppressing their emotions later in life, suggesting that masculine stoicism is learned, not hard-wired.

BOYHOOD

Once in school, boys tend to excel at mathematics and other tasks controlled by the brain's right side, or hemisphere. These natural aptitudes may be strengthened by the spike of testosterone that infant boys experience before and right after birth. But the biological machinery that gives boys an advantage in math and spatial tasks may predispose them to learning and developmental disorders: that is, in boys the left brain hemisphere, which controls language and facilitates socialization, may be underdeveloped.

On the playground, school-age boys resist playing with girls. They enjoy rough-and-tumble play and have inherent skill at games involving hit-the-target motor and navigational challenges. This time spent among other boys relays lessons—not all of them healthy—about what it means to be male. Chase and target games, for example, may be an evolutionary throwback to when men had to be good hunters.

ADOLESCENCE

Testosterone's effects on boys' development become most obvious during adolescence. As their soprano voices morph into tenors, boys squawk. Muscles begin replacing baby fat. Male hormones are also responsible for teen-age boys' novel interest in sex. Unfortunately, this interest is not always coupled with mature attitudes about safety and promiscuity. Data show that adolescents account for one-quarter of the 12 million cases of sexually transmitted diseases reported each year. The good news is that teen-agers may be getting the message. Gonorrhea among adolescent boys has been decreasing over the last seven years.

Reported cases of gonorrhea, per 100,000, for boys ages 15 to 19.

800
600
400
200
0
'92 '93 '94 '95

But boys' interest in girls is not purely sexual. Compared with previous generations, teen-age boys are more likely to have Platonic relationships with girls and to agree with survey statements like "Boys and girls should both be allowed to express feelings."

The hormones that pique boys' interest in sex goad them toward

risky and aggressive behavior. At the same time, parental and societal expectations about masculinity may prevent them from expressing confusion or fear about the changes befalling them. These factors make teen-age boys 2.5 times more likely than girls to die of an unintentional injury and 5 times more likely to die from a homicide or suicide.

YOUNG ADULTHOOD

Men are physically in their prime. This period is characterized by a drive for achievement and by the realization that the foolhardiness of youth has unavoidable consequences. Fatherhood gives men the opportunity to redefine masculinity in a healthful way for themselves and their children.

Bad habits, like smoking, become less appealing but more difficult to shake; more than 80 percent of adults who ever smoked began doing so before age 18. Still, men are smoking less than they did and the incidence of lung cancer in men is falling. Although the incidence of smoking—28.8 percent for black men, 27.1 percent for white men—is similar, black men are at much higher risk of lung cancer than white men.

H.I.V. infection, the leading cause of death among men between ages 25 and 44, is often contracted during adolescence, when boys are experimenting with sex and are oblivious to the risks of infection. But with advances in drug therapies, the incidence of H.I.V.-related deaths has declined over the last four years.

MIDDLE AGE

Beginning in their early 40's, men experience a decline in testosterone of 1 percent each year. These reductions coincide with increased depressive

symptoms, including anxiety and sexual dissatisfaction. While some doctors consider this stage tantamount to "male menopause," others argue that the hormonal changes are too subtle to account for these symptoms. They note, too, that impotence and other conditions associated with middle age can be caused by ailments that tend to strike men in this age group, like diabetes.

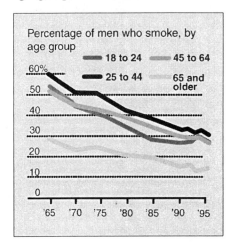

Percentage of men who smoke, by age group
18 to 24   45 to 64
25 to 44   65 and older
60%
50
40
30
20
10
0
'65 '70 '75 '80 '85 '90 '95

The risk of heart disease, hypertension and diabetes is exacerbated by obesity, and middle age is when men are likely to be overweight. They lose 3 percent to 5 percent of their muscle mass for every decade after age 25. Reduced muscle mass and physical activity conspire to decrease men's resting metabolic rate. As men age, then, they burn less energy while resting and can gain weight even without changing their eating habits. And they do gain—2 to 3 pounds for every year over age 30.

Heart disease continues to be the leading cause of death for men in the United States. But the rate of heart disease-related deaths among men has decreased more than 50 percent since 1950; those who die of heart disease are dying later in life.

EARLY OLD AGE

Because men continue to produce testosterone throughout life, they are protected from—though not immune to—conditions like Alzheimer's Disease and osteoporosis. Their larger bone size also helps protect against this bone-weakening illness. Men can further maintain their mental acuity by engaging in intellectual activities. They can strengthen their bones and stem bone loss by undertaking weight-bearing exercise. The continued production of testosterone, however, can also adversely affect men. Testosterone aggravates hair loss and stimulates growth of the prostate gland. Noncancerous enlargement of the prostate occurs in more than half of men in their 60's and up to 90 percent of men in their 70's and 80's. At the same time, 80 percent of all prostate cancer cases occur in men age 65 and over.

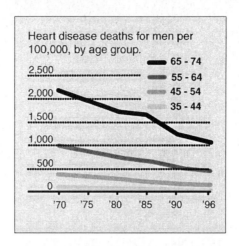

Heart disease deaths for men per 100,000, by age group.

LATER OLD AGE

Studies indicate that men are less likely than women to have difficulty maintaining normal routines, like bathing, dressing and using the toilet, as they age.

Still, the trend among the elderly in general is that they become less active, and so need fewer calories. Their appetites diminish, yet their nutritional needs increase because their bodies have lost the ability to synthesize and absorb important vitamins and nutrients. Their skin, for example, no longer easily synthesizes vitamin D when exposed to the sun. The benefits of avoiding potentially harmful foods, such as those high in cholesterol, lessen with age. Maintaining weight and making sure the right nutrients are present in the diet become more important.

pFsEYTcAHLoLoGY

> **Behaviorally speaking, there's little difference between a newborn baby and a 32-week-old fetus. A new wave of research suggests that the fetus can feel, dream, even enjoy *The Cat in the Hat*. The abortion debate may never be the same.**
>
> **By Janet L. Hopson**

The scene never fails to give goose bumps: the baby, just seconds old and still dewy from the womb, is lifted into the arms of its exhausted but blissful parents. They gaze adoringly as their new child stretches and squirms, scrunches its mouth and opens its eyes. To anyone watching this tender vignette, the message is unmistakable. Birth is the beginning of it all, ground zero, the moment from which the clock starts ticking. Not so, declares Janet DiPietro. Birth may be a grand occasion, says the Johns Hopkins University psychologist, but "it is a trivial event in development. Nothing neurologically interesting happens."

Armed with highly sensitive and sophisticated monitoring gear, DiPietro and other researchers today are discovering that the real action starts weeks earlier. At 32 weeks of gestation—two months before a baby is considered fully prepared for the world, or "at term"—a fetus is behaving almost exactly as a newborn. And it continues to do so for the next 12 weeks.

As if overturning the common conception of infancy weren't enough, scientists are creating a startling new picture of intelligent life in the womb. Among the revelations:

• By nine weeks, a developing fetus can hiccup and react to loud noises. By the end of the second trimester it can hear.

• Just as adults do, the fetus experiences the rapid eye movement (REM) sleep of dreams.

• The fetus savors its mother's meals, first picking up the food tastes of a culture in the womb.

A fetus spends hours in the rapid eye movement sleep of dreams.

• Among other mental feats, the fetus can distinguish between the voice of Mom and that of a stranger, and respond to a familiar story read to it.

• Even a premature baby is aware, feels, responds, and adapts to its environment.

• Just because the fetus is responsive to certain stimuli doesn't mean that it should be the target of efforts to enhance development. Sensory stimulation of the fetus can in fact lead to bizarre patterns of adaptation later on.

The roots of human behavior, researchers now know, begin to develop early—just weeks after conception, in fact. Well before a woman typically knows she is pregnant, her embryo's brain has already begun to bulge. By five weeks, the organ that looks like a lumpy inchworm has already embarked on the most spectacular feat of human development: the creation of the deeply creased and convoluted cerebral cortex, the part of the brain that will eventually allow the growing person to move, think, speak, plan, and create in a human way.

At nine weeks, the embryo's ballooning brain allows it to bend its body, hiccup, and react to loud sounds. At week ten, it moves its arms, "breathes" amniotic fluid in and out, opens its jaw, and stretches. Before the first trimester is over, it yawns, sucks, and swallows as well as feels and smells. By the end of the second trimester, it can hear; toward the end of pregnancy, it can see.

FETAL ALERTNESS

Scientists who follow the fetus' daily life find that it spends most of its time not exercising these new abilities but sleeping. At 32 weeks, it drowses 90 to 95% of the day. Some of these hours are spent in deep sleep, some in REM sleep, and some in an indeterminate state, a product of the fetus' immature brain that is different from sleep in a baby, child, or adult. During REM sleep, the fetus' eyes move back and forth just as an adult's eyes do, and many researchers believe that it is dreaming. DiPietro speculates that fetuses dream about what they know—the sensations they feel in the womb.

Closer to birth, the fetus sleeps 85 to 90% of the time, the same as a newborn. Between its frequent naps, the fetus seems to have "something like an awake alert period," according to developmental psychologist William Fifer, Ph.D., who with his Columbia University colleagues is monitoring these sleep and wakefulness cycles in order to identify patterns of normal and abnormal brain development, including potential predictors of

sudden infant death syndrome. Says Fifer, "We are, in effect, asking the fetus: 'Are you paying attention? Is your nervous system behaving in the appropriate way?' "

FETAL MOVEMENT

Awake or asleep, the human fetus moves 50 times or more each hour, flexing and extending its body, moving its head, face, and limbs and exploring its warm wet compartment by touch. Heidelise Als, Ph.D., a developmental psychologist at Harvard Medical School, is fascinated by the amount of tactile stimulation a fetus gives itself. "It touches a hand to the face, one hand to the other hand, clasps its feet, touches its foot to its leg, its hand to its umbilical cord," she reports.

Als believes there is a mismatch between the environment given to preemies in hospitals and the environment they would have had in the womb. She has been working for years to change the care given to preemies so that they can curl up, bring their knees together, and touch things with their hands as they would have for weeks in the womb.

Along with such common movements, DiPietro has also noted some odder fetal activities, including "licking the uterine wall and literally walking around the womb by pushing off with its feet." Laterborns may have more room in the womb for such maneuvers than first babies. After the initial pregnancy, a woman's uterus is bigger and the umbilical cord longer, allowing more freedom of movement. "Second and subsequent children may develop more motor experience in utero and so may become more active infants," DiPietro speculates.

Fetuses react sharply to their mother's actions. "When we're watching the fetus on ultrasound and the mother starts to laugh, we can see the fetus, floating upside down in the womb, bounce up and down on its head, bum-bum-bum, like it's bouncing on a trampoline," says DiPietro. "When mothers watch this on the screen, they laugh harder, and the fetus goes up and down even faster. We've wondered whether this is why people grow up liking roller coasters."

FETAL TASTE

Why people grow up liking hot chilies or spicy curries may also have something to do with the fetal environment. By 13 to 15 weeks a fetus' taste buds already look like a mature adult's, and doctors know that the amniotic fluid that surrounds it can smell strongly of curry, cumin,

By 15 weeks, a fetus has an adult's taste buds and may be able to savor its mother's meals.

What's the Impact on Abortion?

Though research in fetal psychology focuses on the last trimester, when most abortions are illegal, the thought of a fetus dreaming, listening and responding to its mother's voice is sure to add new complexity to the debate. The new findings undoubtedly will strengthen the convictions of right-to-lifers—and they may shake the certainty of pro-choice proponents who believe that mental life begins at birth.

Many of the scientists engaged in studying the fetus, however, remain detached from the abortion controversy, insisting that their work is completely irrelevant to the debate.

"I don't think that fetal research informs the issue at all," contends psychologist Janet DiPietro of Johns Hopkins University. "The essence of the abortion debate is: When does life begin? Some people believe it begins at conception, the other extreme believes that it begins after the baby is born, and there's a group in the middle that believes it begins at around 24 or 25 weeks, when a fetus can live outside of the womb, though it needs a lot of help to do so.

"Up to about 25 weeks, whether or not it's sucking its thumb or has personality or all that, the fetus cannot survive outside of its mother. So is that life, or not? That is a moral, ethical, and religious question, not one for science. Things can behave and not be alive. Right-to-lifers may say that this research proves that a fetus is alive, but it does not. It cannot."

"Fetal research only changes the abortion debate for people who think that life starts at some magical point," maintains Heidelise Als, a psychologist at Harvard University. "If you believe that life begins at conception, then you don't need the proof of fetal behavior." For others, however, abortion is a very complex issue and involves far more than whether research shows that a fetus hiccups. "Your circumstances and personal beliefs have much more impact on the decision," she observes.

Like DiPietro, Als realizes that "people may use this research as an emotional way to draw people to the pro-life side, but it should not be used by belligerent activists." Instead, she believes, it should be applied to helping mothers have the healthiest pregnancy possible and preparing them to best parent their child. Columbia University psychologist William Fifer, Ph.D., agrees. "The research is much more relevant for issues regarding viable fetuses—preemies."

Simply put, say the three, their work is intended to help the babies that live—not to decide whether fetuses should.—*Camille Chatterjee*

garlic, onion and other essences from a mother's diet. Whether fetuses can taste these flavors isn't yet known, but scientists have found that a 33-week-old preemie will suck harder on a sweetened nipple than on a plain rubber one.

"During the last trimester, the fetus is swallowing up to a liter a day" of amniotic fluid, notes Julie Mennella, Ph.D., a biopsychologist at the Monell Chemical Senses Center in Philadelphia. She thinks the fluid may act as a "flavor bridge" to breast milk, which also carries food flavors from the mother's diet.

FETAL HEARING

Whether or not a fetus can taste, there's little question that it can hear. A very premature baby entering the world at 24 to 25 weeks responds to the sounds around it, observes Als, so its auditory apparatus must already have been functioning in the womb. Many pregnant women report a fetal jerk or sudden kick just after a door slams or a car backfires.

Even without such intrusions, the womb is not a silent place. Researchers who have inserted a hydrophone into the uterus of a pregnant woman have picked up a noise level "akin to the background noise in an apartment," according to DiPietro. Sounds include the whooshing of blood in the mother's vessels, the gurgling and rumbling of her stomach and intestines, as well as the tones of her voice filtered through tissues, bones, and fluid, and the voices of other people coming through the amniotic wall. Fifer has found that fetal heart rate slows when the mother is speaking, suggesting that the fetus not only hears and recognizes the sound, but is calmed by it.

FETAL VISION

Vision is the last sense to develop. A very premature infant can see light and shape; researchers presume that a fetus has the same ability. Just as the womb isn't completely quiet, it isn't utterly dark, either. Says Fifer: "There may be just enough visual stimulation filtered through the mother's tissues that a fetus can respond when the mother is in bright light," such as when she is sunbathing.

Japanese scientists have even reported a distinct fetal reaction to flashes of light shined on the mother's belly. However, other researchers warn that exposing fetuses (or premature infants) to bright light before they are ready can be dangerous. In fact, Harvard's Als believes that retinal damage in premature infants, which has long been ascribed to high concentrations of oxygen, may actually be due to overexposure to light at the wrong time in development.

A six-month fetus, born about 14 weeks too early, has a brain that is neither prepared for nor expecting signals from the eyes to be transmitted into the brain's visual cortex, and from there into the executive-branch frontal lobes, where information is integrated. When the fetus

> ## A fetus prefers hearing Mom's voice over a stranger's—speaking in her native, not a foreign tongue—and being read aloud familiar tales rather than new stories.

is forced to see too much too soon, says Als, the accelerated stimulation may lead to aberrations of brain development.

FETAL LEARNING

Along with the ability to feel, see, and hear comes the capacity to learn and remember. These activities can be rudimentary, automatic, even biochemical. For example, a fetus, after an initial reaction of alarm, eventually stops responding to a repeated loud noise. The fetus displays the same kind of primitive learning, known as habituation, in response to its mother's voice, Fifer has found.

But the fetus has shown itself capable of far more. In the 1980s, psychology professor Anthony James DeCasper, Ph.D., and colleagues at the University of North Carolina at Greensboro, devised a feeding contraption that allows a baby to suck faster to hear one set of sounds through headphones and to suck slower to hear a different set. With this technique, DeCasper discovered that within hours of birth, a baby already prefers its mother's voice to a stranger's, suggesting it must have learned and remembered the voice, albeit not necessarily consciously, from its last months in the womb. More recently, he's found that a newborn prefers a story read to it repeatedly in the womb—in this case, *The Cat in the Hat*—over a new story introduced soon after birth.

DeCasper and others have uncovered more mental feats. Newborns can not only distinguish their mother from a stranger speaking, but would rather hear Mom's voice, especially the way it sounds filtered through amniotic fluid rather than through air. They're xenophobes, too: they prefer to hear Mom speaking in her native language than to hear her or someone else speaking in a foreign tongue.

By monitoring changes in fetal heart rate, psychologist Jean-Pierre Lecanuet, Ph.D., and his colleagues in Paris have found that fetuses can even tell strangers' voices apart. They also seem to like certain stories more than others. The fetal heartbeat will slow down when a familiar French fairy tale such as *"La Poulette"* ("The Chick") or *"Le Petit Crapaud"* ("The Little Toad"), is read near the mother's belly. When the same reader delivers another unfamiliar story, the fetal heartbeat stays steady.

The fetus is likely responding to the cadence of voices and stories, not their actual words, observes Fifer, but the conclusion is the same: the fetus can listen, learn, and remember at some level, and, as with most babies

and children, it likes the comfort and reassurance of the familiar.

FETAL PERSONALITY

It's no secret that babies are born with distinct differences and patterns of activity that suggest individual temperament. Just when and how the behavioral traits originate in the womb is now the subject of intense scrutiny.

In the first formal study of fetal temperament in 1996, DiPietro and her colleagues recorded the heart rate and movements of 31 fetuses six times before birth and compared them to readings taken twice after birth. (They've since extended their study to include 100 more fetuses.) Their findings: fetuses that are very active in the womb tend to be more irritable infants. Those with irregular sleep/wake patterns in the womb sleep more poorly as young infants. And fetuses with high heart rates become unpredictable, inactive babies.

"Behavior doesn't begin at birth," declares DiPietro. "It begins before and develops in predictable ways." One of the most important influences on development is the fetal environment. As Harvard's Als observes, "The fetus gets an enormous amount of 'hormonal bathing' through the mother, so its chronobiological rhythms are influenced by the mother's sleep/wake cycles, her eating patterns, her movements."

The hormones a mother puts out in response to stress also appear critical. DiPietro finds that highly pressured mothers-to-be tend to have more active fetuses—and more irritable infants. "The most stressed are working pregnant women," says DiPietro. "These days, women tend to work up to the day they deliver, even though the implications for pregnancy aren't entirely clear yet. That's our cultural norm, but I think it's insane."

Als agrees that working can be an enormous stress, but emphasizes that pregnancy hormones help to buffer both mother and fetus. Individual reactions to stress also matter. "The pregnant woman who chooses to work is a different woman already from the one who chooses not to work," she explains.

She's also different from the woman who has no choice but to work. DiPietro's studies show that the fetuses of poor women are distinct neurobehaviorally—less active, with a less variable heart rate—from the fetuses of middle-class women. Yet "poor women rate themselves as less stressed than do working middle-class women," she notes. DiPietro suspects that inadequate nutrition and exposure to pollutants may significantly affect the fetuses of poor women.

Stress, diet, and toxins may combine to have a harmful effect on intelligence. A recent study by biostatistician Bernie Devlin, Ph.D., of the University of Pittsburgh, suggests that genes may have less impact on IQ than previously thought and that the environment of the womb may account for much more. "Our old notion of nature influencing the fetus before birth and nurture after birth needs an update," DiPietro insists. "There is an antenatal environment, too, that is provided by the mother."

Parents-to-be who want to further their unborn child's mental development should start by assuring that the antenatal environment is well-nourished, low-stress, drug-free. Various authors and "experts" also have suggested poking the fetus at regular intervals, speaking to it through a paper tube or "pregaphone," piping in classical music, even flashing lights at the mother's abdomen.

Does such stimulation work? More importantly: Is it safe? Some who use these methods swear their children are smarter, more verbally and musically inclined, more physically coordinated and socially adept than average. Scientists, however, are skeptical.

"There has been no defended research anywhere that shows any enduring effect from these stimulations," asserts Fifer. "Since no one can even say for certain when a fetus is awake, poking them or sticking speakers on the mother's abdomen may be changing their natural sleep patterns. No one would consider poking or prodding a newborn baby in her bassinet or putting a speaker next to her ear, so why would you do such a thing with a fetus?"

Als is more emphatic: "My bet is that poking, shaking, or otherwise deliberately stimulating the fetus might alter its developmental sequence, and anything that affects the development of the brain comes at a cost."

Gently talking to the fetus, however, seems to pose little risk. Fifer suggests that this kind of activity may help parents as much as the fetus. "Thinking about your fetus, talking to it, having your spouse talk to it, will all help prepare you for this new creature that's going to jump into your life and turn it upside down," he says— once it finally makes its anti-climactic entrance.

Do Parents Really Matter?

Once, parents were given all the credit—and all the blame—for how their children turned out. Then researchers told us that heredity determines who we are. The latest take: parents can work with their children's innate tendencies to rear happy, healthy kids. It's a message many parents will find reassuring—but it may make others very nervous.

By Annie Murphy Paul

David Reiss, M.D., didn't want to believe it. The George Washington University psychiatrist had worked for more than 12 years on a study of adolescent development—just completed—and its conclusions were a surprise, to say the least. "I'm talking to you seven or eight years after the initial results came out, so I can sound very calm and collected now," says Reiss. "But I was shocked." This, even though other scientists had previously reached similar conclusions in many smaller-scale studies. "We knew about those results, but we didn't believe it," says Reiss, speaking of himself and one of his collaborators, E. Mavis Heatherington, Ph.D. "Now we've done the research ourselves, so . . ." He sighs. "We're not ever going to believe it, but we're going to have to act as if we do."

What Reiss and his colleagues discovered, in one of the longest and most thorough studies of child development ever attempted, was that parents appear to have relatively little effect on how children turn out, once genetic influences are accounted for. "The original objective was to look for environmental differences," says Reiss. "We didn't find many." Instead, it seems that genetic influences are largely responsible for how "adjusted" kids are: how well they do in school, how they get along with their peers, whether they engage in dangerous or delinquent behavior. "If you follow the study's implications through to the end, it's a radical revision of contemporary theories of child development," says Reiss. "I can't even describe what a paradigm shift it is."

The way heredity shapes who we are is less like one-way dictation and more like spirited rounds of call and response.

The only member of the research team who wasn't surprised by the results, Reiss recalls, was Robert Plomin, Ph.D., a researcher at the Institute of Psychiatry in London. Plomin is a behavioral geneticist, and he and others in his field have been saying for years what Reiss has just begun to accept: genes have a much greater influence on our personalities than previously thought, and parenting much less. The work of behavioral geneticists has been the focus of considerable controversy among psychologists, but it has been mostly ignored by parents, despite ample attention from the media. That may be because such coverage has rarely described just how genes are thought to wield their purported influence. Behavioral geneticists don't claim that genes are blueprints that depict every detail of our personality and behavior; rather, they propose that heredity reveals itself through complex interactions with the environment. Their theories are far more subtle, and more persuasive, than the simple idea of heredity as destiny. It is by participating in these very interactions, some scientists now say, that parents exert their own considerable influence—and they can learn to exert even more.

Nature Meets Nurture

As behavioral geneticists understand it, the way heredity shapes who we are is less like one-way dictation and more like spirited rounds of call and response, with each

phrase spoken by heredity summoning an answer from the environment. Scientists' unwieldy name for this exchange is "evocative gene-environment correlations," so called because people's genetic makeup is thought to bring forth particular reactions from others, which in turn influence their personalities. A baby with a sunny disposition will receive more affection than one who is difficult; an attractive child will be smiled at more often than a homely one. And the qualities that prompt such responses from parents are likely to elicit more of the same from others, so that over time a self-image is created and confirmed in others' eyes.

Even as genes are calling forth particular reactions, they're also reaching out for particular kinds of experience. That's because each person's DNA codes for a certain type of nervous system: one that feels alarm at new situations, one that craves strong sensations, or one that is sluggish and slow to react. Given an array of opportunities, some researchers say, children will pick the ones that are most suited to their "genotype," or genetic endowment. As they grow older, they have more chances to choose—friends, interests, jobs, spouses—decisions that both reflect and define personality.

In order for genes and environment to interact in this way, they need to be in constant conversation, back and forth. Since parents usually raise the children to whom they have passed on their genes, that's rarely a problem: they are likely to share and perhaps appreciate the qualities of their offspring. And the environment they provide their children with may further support their natural abilities: highly literate parents might give birth to an equally verbal child, then raise her in a house full of books. Developmental psychologists call this fortunate match "goodness of fit." But problems may arise if nurture and nature aren't on speaking terms—if a child's environment doesn't permit or encourage expression of his natural tendencies. That may happen when children's abilities don't match their parents' expectations; when their genetically-influenced temperament clashes with that of their parents; or when their environment offers them few opportunities to express themselves constructively, as is often the case with children who grow up in severe poverty. Research has shown that a poor person-to-environment match can lead to decreased motivation, diminished mental health, and rebellious or antisocial behavior.

The dialogue between genes and environment becomes more complicated when a sibling adds another voice. Although siblings share an average of 50 percent of their genes, the half that is different—and the kaleidoscopic ways that genes can combine—leads their genotypes to ask different

questions and get different answers from what would seem to be the same environment. In fact, siblings create individual environments of their own by seeking out different experiences and by evoking different responses from parents, friends, and others. Like the proverbial blind men touching the leg, the trunk, or the tail of an elephant, they "see" different parts of the same animal. "Our studies show that parents do indeed treat their children differently, but that they are in large measure responding to differences that are already there," says Robert Plomin. "Family environment does have an effect on personality development, but not in the way we've always thought. It's the experiences that siblings *don't* share that matter, not the ones they do."

Kids In Charge?

One intriguing implication of behavioral genetic research is that children are in many ways driving their own development, through the choices they make, the reactions they elicit, even the friends they pick (see "The Power of Peers"). But parents are crucial collaborators in that process, and that means that their role in shaping their children may actually be larger than it first appears. *How* a parent responds to a child's genetically-influenced characteristics may make all the difference in how those traits are expressed, says David Reiss. In his formulation, the parent-child relationship acts as a sort of translator of genetic influence: the genotype provides the basic plot, but parenting gives it tone and inflection, accent and emphasis. He calls this conception of gene-environment correlation "the relationship code," and says that it returns to parents some of the influence his study would seem to give to genes. "Our data actually give the role of parents a real boost—but it's saying that the story doesn't necessarily start with the parent," says Reiss. "It starts with the kid, and then the parent picks up on it."

To Reiss, parents' role as interpreters of the language of heredity holds out an exciting possibility. "If you could intervene with parents and get them to respond differently to troublesome behavior, you might be able to offset much of the genetic influence" on those traits, he says. In other words, if genes become behavior by way of the environment, then changing the environment might change the expression of the genes. Although such intervention studies are years away from fruition, small-scale research and clinical experience are pointing the way toward working with children's hereditary strengths and weaknesses. Stanley Greenspan, M.D., a pediatric psychiatrist at George Washington Medical School and author of *The Growth*

THE **POWER**
OF **peers**

IT'S A WORLD OUT OF A FANCIFUL children's book: a place where parents and teachers don't matter, where the company of other kids is most meaningful, where nothing much would change if we left children in their homes and schools "but switched all the parents around." That doesn't describe an imagined never-never land, however, but the environment that every one of us grows up in, contends Judith Rich Harris. The maverick writer and theoretician believes that peers, not parents, determine our personalities, and her unorthodox views have made the very real world of psychology sit up and take notice.

Harris, who is unaffiliated with any university or institution, laid out her radical theory in a 1995 *Psychological Review* paper, which was later cited as one of the year's outstanding articles by the American Psychological Association. Like

behavioral geneticists, Harris believes that heredity is a force to be reckoned with. But she sees another powerful force at work: group socialization, or the shaping of one's character by one's peers.

Central to this theory is the idea that behavior is "context-specific": we act in specific ways in specific circumstances. "Children today live in two different worlds: home and the world outside the home," says Harris. "There is little overlap between these two worlds, and the rules for how to behave in them are quite different." Displays of emotion, for example, are often accepted by parents but discouraged by teachers or friends. Rewards and punishments are different too. At home, children may be scolded for their failures and praised for their successes; outside the home, they may be ridiculed when they make a mistake or ignored when they behave appropriately.

As children grow older and peer influence grows stronger, says Harris, they come to prefer the ways of peers over those of their parents. She like to use language as an example: the children of immigrants, she notes, will readily learn to speak the language of the new country without an accent.

They may continue to speak in their parents' tongue when at home, but over time the language of their peers will become their "native" language. Adopting the ways of their contemporaries makes sense, says Harris, because children will live among them, and not among older adults, for the greater part of their lives. "Parents are past, peers are future," she says.

It's evolutionarily adaptive, too. "Humans were designed to live not in nuclear families, but in larger groups," observes Harris. "The individuals who became our ancestors succeeded partly

of the Mind, is actively applying the discoveries of genetics to parenting. "Genes do create certain general tendencies, but parents can work with these by tailoring their actions to the nervous system of the child," says Greenspan. He believes that the responses children "naturally" elicit may not

----

The exact same temperament that might predispose a kid to become a criminal can also make for a hot test pilot.

----

be in their best interests—but that parents can consciously and deliberately give them the ones that are. "You have to pay attention to what you're doing intuitively, and make sure that is what the kids really need," he says.

A baby with a sluggish temperament, for example, won't respond as readily to his parents' advances as a child with a more active nervous system. Disappointed at their offsprings' lack of engagement, parents may respond with dwindling interest and attention. Left to his own devices, the baby may become even more withdrawn, failing to make crucial connections and to master developmental challenges. But if the parents resist their inclinations, and engage the baby with special enthusiasm, Greenspan has found that the child will change his own behavior in response. The same principle of working against the grain of a child's genotype applies to those who are especially active or oversensitive, suggests Greenspan, comparing the process to a right-handed baseball player who practices throwing with his left hand. "It feels funny at first, but gradually you build up strength in an area in which you would naturally be weak," he says.

Of course, honing a right-handed pitch is important, too. Parents can improve on their children's hereditary strengths by encouraging their tendency to seek out experiences in tune with their genes. "Parents should think of themselves as resource providers," says Plomin. "Expose the child to a lot of things, see what they like, what

they're good at, and go with that." By offering opportunities congenial to children's genetic constitutions, parents are in a sense improving their "goodness of fit" with the environment.

WILL YOUR KID GO TO YALE—OR TO JAIL?

For those traits that could easily become either assets or liabilities, parenting may be especially critical to the outcome. "The same temperament that can make for a criminal can also make for a hot test pilot or astronaut," says David Lykken, Ph.D., a behavioral geneticist at the University of Minnesota. "That kind of little boy—aggressive, fearless, impulsive—is hard to handle. It's easy for parents to give up and let him run wild, or turn up the heat and the punishment and thereby alienate him and lose all control. But properly handled, this can be the kid who grows up to break the sound barrier." Lykken believes that especially firm, conscientious, and responsive parents can make the difference—but not all behavioral geneticists agree. David Rowe, Ph.D., a University of Arizona psychologist and author of *The Limits of Family Influence,* claims that "much of the effort of 'superparents' may be wasted, if not because they had the ability to get along with the other members." The group continues to influence us in a number of ways: we identify ourselves with it, and change our behavior to conform to its norms. We define our group by contrasting it with other groups, and seek to distinguish our group by our actions and appearance. Within the group, we compare ourselves to others and jockey for higher status. We may receive labels from our peers, and strive to live up (or down) to them. Finally, we may be most lastingly affected by peers by being rejected by them. People who were rejected as children often report long-term self-esteem problems, poor social skills, and increased rates of psychopathology.

Our personalities become less flexible as we grow older, says Harris, so

that "the language and personality acquired in childhood and adolescent peer groups persist, with little modification, for the remainder of the life span." It's a startling conclusion, but Harris claims that her greatest challenge lies not in persuading people that peers matter, but in convincing them that parents don't. She calls the belief in parents' enduring importance "the nurture assumption," and her forthcoming book by that title will argue that it's simply a myth of modern culture. She doesn't deny that children need the care and protection of parents, and acknowledges that mothers and fathers can influence things like religious affiliation and choice of career. But, she maintains, "parental behaviors have no effect on the psychological characteristics their children will have as adults."

In fact, she says, "probably the most important way that parents can influence their children is by determining who their peers are. The immigrants who move their children to another country have provided them with a completely different set of peers. But a less dramatic shift—simply deciding which neighborhood to live in—can also make a difference." From one area to another, she notes, there are substantial variations in the rates of delinquency, truancy, and teen pregnancy—problems parents can try to avoid by surrounding their offspring with suitable friends. Beyond that, however, children will make their own choices. "It's pretty easy to control the social life of a three-year-old," says Harris. "But once the kids are past age 10 or 12, all bets are off."

—A.M.P.

counter-productive." And as for exposing children to a variety of experiences, Rowe thinks that this can give genetically talented children the chance they need, "but not many children have that much potential. This may not be so in Lake Wobegon [where every child is "above average"], but it is true in the rest of the world."

But with an optimism worthy of Garrison Keillor, advocates of parental influence insist that genes aren't the end of the story "The old idea is that you tried to live up to a potential that was set by genes," says Greenspan. "The new idea is that environment helps create potential." His view is supported by recent research that suggests a baby is born with only basic neural "wir-

ing" in place, wiring whose connections are then elaborated by experience. Both sides will have to await the next chapter of genetic research, which may reveal even more complicated interactions between the worlds within and without. In the long-running debate between genes and the environment, neither one has yet had the last word.

Rethinking Puberty: The Development of Sexual Attraction

Martha K. McClintock and Gilbert Herdt[1]

Department of Psychology, The University of Chicago, Chicago, Illinois

A youth remembers a time when he was sitting in the family room with his parents watching the original "Star Trek" television series. He reports that he was 10 years old and had not yet developed any of the obvious signs of puberty. When "Captain Kirk" suddenly peeled off his shirt, the boy was titillated. At 10 years of age, this was his first experience of sexual attraction, and he knew intuitively that, according to the norms of his parents and society, he should not be feeling this same-gender attraction. The youth relating this memory is a self-identified gay 18-year-old in Chicago. He also reports that at age 5 he had an absence of sexual attractions of any kind, and that even by age 8 he had not experienced overt awareness of sexual attraction. By age 10, however, a profound transformation had begun, and it was already completed by the time he entered puberty; sexual attraction to the same gender was so familiar to him (Herdt & Boxer, 1993) that it defined his selfhood.

Recent findings from three distinct and significant studies have pointed to the age of 10 as the mean age of first sexual attraction—well before puberty, which is typically defined as the age when the capacity to procreate is attained (Timiras, 1972). These findings are at odds with previous developmental and social science models of behavioral sexual development in Western countries, which suggested that *gonadarche* (final maturation of the testes or ovaries) is the biological basis for the child's bud-ding interest in sexual matters. Earlier studies postulated that the profound maturational changes during puberty instigate the transition from preadolescent to adult forms of sexuality that involve sexual attraction, fantasy, and behavior (Money & Ehrhardt, 1972). Thus, adult forms of sexuality were thought to develop only after gonadarche, typically around ages 12 for girls and 14 for boys, with early and late bloomers being regarded as "off time" in development (Boxer, Levinson, & Petersen, 1989). But the new findings, which locate the development of sexual attraction before these ages, are forcing researchers to rethink the role of gonadarche in the development of sexual attraction as well as the conceptualization of puberty as simply the product of complete gonadal maturation.

Many researchers have conflated puberty and gonadarche, thinking that the two are synonymous in development. The new research on sexual orientation has provided data that invalidate the old model of gonadarche as the sole biological cause of adult forms of sexuality. To the extent that sexual attraction is affected by hormones, the new data indicate that there should be another significant hormonal event around age 10. Indeed, there is: the maturation of the adrenal glands during middle childhood, termed *adrenarche*. (The adrenal glands[2] are the biggest nongonadal source of sex steroids.) This biological process, distinctively different from gonadarche, may underlie the development not only of sexual attraction, but of cognition, emotions, motivations, and social behavior as well. This observation, in turn, leads to a redefinition of prepubertal and pubertal development.

GONADARCHE IS NOT A SUFFICIENT EXPLANATION

Previous biopsychological models of sexual development have attributed changes in adolescent behavior to changes in hormone levels accompanied by gonadarche (Boxer et al., 1989), presumably because of a focus on the most dramatic features of gonadal development in each gender: menarche in girls and spermarche in boys. If gonadarche were responsible for first sexual attractions, then the mean age of the development of sexual attractions should be around the age of gonadarche. Moreover, one would expect a sex difference in the age of first attraction, corresponding to the sex difference in age of gonadarche: 12 for girls and 14 for boys. Neither of these predictions, however, has been borne out by recent data.

In three studies attempting to illuminate the sources of sexual orientation, adolescents have been asked to recall their earliest sexual thoughts; their answers are surprising. One study (Herdt & Boxer, 1993) investigated the development of sexual identity and social relations in a group of self-identified gay and lesbian teenagers (ages 14–20, with a mean age of 18) from Chicago. The mean age for first same-sex attraction was around age 10 for both males and females. Moreover, sexual attraction marked

From *Current Directions in Psychological Science*, December 1996, pp. 178-183. © 1996 by the American Psychological Society. Reprinted by permission of Blackwell Publishers.

the first event in a developmental sequence: same-sex attraction, same-sex fantasy, and finally same-sex behavior (see Table 1).

This evidence provides a key for understanding sexuality as a process of development, rather than thinking of it as a discrete event, which emerges suddenly at a single moment in time. Virtually all models of adolescent sexual development, from Anna Freud and Erik Erikson up to the present, have been based on the gonadarche model (Boxer et al., 1989). It conceptualizes the development of sexuality as a precipitous, singular, psychological event, fueled by intrinsic changes in hormone levels. Gonadarche is seen as a "switch," turning on desire and attraction, and hence triggering the developmental sequelae of adult sexuality.

Instead, the new data suggest a longer series of intertwined erotic and gender formations that differentiate beginning in middle childhood. Indeed, the psychological sequence of attraction, fantasy, and behavior may parallel the well-known Tanner stages, which are routinely used by clinicians to quantify the process of physical development during puberty (Timiras, 1972). For example, in girls, onset of sexual attraction may co-occur with Tanner Stage II (development of breast buds); sexual fantasy may co-occur with Tanner Stage III (enlargement of mammary glands); and sexual behavior may co-occur with Tanner Stage IV (full breast development), with each psychosexual stage reflecting a different stage of hormonal development. If so, then we may begin to look for a biological mechanism for psychosexual development in the physiological basis for these early Tanner stages that occur prior to the final gonadal maturation that enables procreation.

The generality of these psychological findings is substantiated by two other recent studies that also reported the age of first sexual attraction to be around 10 (see Fig. 1). Pattatucci and Hamer (1995) and Hamer, Hu, Magnuson, Hu, and Pattatucci (1993) asked similar retrospective questions of two distinctive samples

of gay- and lesbian-identified adults in the United States. Unlike the Chicago study (Herdt & Boxer, 1993), these studies gathered information from subjects throughout the United States and interviewed adults who were mostly in their mid-30s (range from 18 to 55). They also used different surveys and interview methodologies. Nevertheless, all three studies pinpointed 10 to 10.5 as the mean age of first sexual attraction. Admittedly, none of the studies was ideal for assessing early development of sexuality; the age of first recalled sexual attraction may not be the actual age. Nonetheless, this work is an essential part of the systematic investigation of same-gender attractions in children.

The question then arises whether there is a similar developmental pattern among heterosexuals. We know of no reason to assume that heterosexuals and homosexuals would have different mechanisms for the activation of sexual attraction and desire. Fortunately, we could test this hypothesis because both Pattatucci's and Hamer's samples had comparison groups of heterosexuals. Indeed, the reported age of first attraction was the same for heterosexually as for homosexually identified adults (only the attraction was toward the opposite sex). Thus, regardless of sexual orientation or gender, the age of initial sexual attraction hovered just over age 10. In sum, the switch mechanism responsible for "turning on" sexual attraction seems to be operating at the same time both for boys and for girls, and regardless of whether their sexual orientation is toward the same or opposite gender.

Thus, we surmise that the maturation of the gonads cannot explain the data found independently by these three studies in different samples and geographic areas. There is no known mechanism that would enable the gonads to supply sufficient levels of hormones at that age to cause sexual attraction, because they are not fully developed. The mean age of sexual attraction is the same in both genders and in both structural forms of sexual orientation; therefore, the biologi-

cal counterpart in both genders and in both structural forms of sexual orientation of sexual attraction is probably the same. These constraints effectively eliminate gonadarche as a candidate to explain the observed findings.

ADRENARCHE IN MIDDLE CHILDHOOD

In the pediatric literature, it is well recognized that children between the ages of 6 and 11 are experiencing a rise in sex steroids. These hormones come from the maturing adrenal glands. Adrenarche is clinically recognized primarily by the onset of pubic hair, but it also includes a growth spurt, increased oil on the skin, changes in the external genitalia, and the development of body odor (New, Levine, & Pang, 1981; Parker, 1991). Nonetheless, both the psychological literature and the institutions of our culture regard this period of middle childhood as hormonally quiescent. Freud's (1905/1965) classic notion of a "latency" period between ages 4 to 6 and puberty perhaps best distills the cultural prejudices. In contrast, we have hypothesized that the rise in adrenal steroid production is critical for understanding interpersonal and intrapsychic development in middle childhood.

Both male and female infants have adult levels of sex steroids during the first days of life, and their adrenal androgens also approach the adult range (see Fig. 2). After a few months, the sex hormone levels begin to fall to a very low level and then remain low until the maturation of the adrenal glands and gonads. When children are between 6 and 8 years of age, their adrenal glands begin to mature. Specifically, the adrenal cortex begins to secrete low levels of androgens, primarily dehydroepiandrosterone (DHEA; see Fig. 2) (Parker, 1991). The metabolism of DHEA leads to both testosterone and estradiol, the primary sex steroids in men and women.

It is noteworthy that both girls and boys experience a rise in androgens, although androgens are typically misidentified as male hormones. Moreover, there is no sex difference in the age at which these androgens begin to rise or the rate at which they do so. After adrenarche, an individual's level of androgens plateaus until around 12 years of age in girls and 14 years of age in boys, whereupon gonadarche triggers a second hormonal rise into the adult range (Parker, 1991).

In adults, the androgens that are produced by the adrenal cortex and their metabolites are known to have psychological effects in a variety of developmental areas relating to aggression,

Table 1. *Ages (years) at which males and females recall having their first same-sex attraction, fantasy, and activity (from Herdt & Boxer, 1993)*

Developmental event	Males			Females		
	M	SD	n	M	SD	n
First same-sex attraction	9.6	3.6	146	10.1	3.7	55
First same-sex fantasy	11.2	3.5	144	11.9	2.9	54
First same-sex activity	13.1	4.3	136	15.2	3.1	49

cognition, perception, attention, emotions, and sexuality. Although adult levels of DHEA are not reached until after gonadarche, levels of this hormone do increase significantly around age 10 (see Fig. 2; De Peretti & Forest, 1976), when they become 10 times the levels experienced by children between 1 and 4 years or age. It is plausible that this marked increase in androgen levels alters the brain, and thus behavior, either by modifying neural function or by permanently altering cellular structure.

WHAT IS SPECIAL ABOUT THE FOURTH GRADE?

We considered the hypothesis that the age of first sexual attraction is similar for boys and girls, both homosexual and heterosexual, because there is some marked change in environmental stimuli, socialization, or cognitive abilities around the age of 10. If so, then the 10-fold rise in DHEA would be only correlated with the emergence of sexuality and should not be considered its direct cause.

A major weakness of the idea that environmental stimuli lead to the emergence of sexual attraction at age 10 is the fact that, in the United States, there is no marked cultural prompt for sexuality in a 10-year-old. Children this age are typically in fourth grade. To our knowledge, there is no overt change in social expectations between Grades 3 and 4, or between Grades 4 and 5, that might account for the developmental emergence of sexual attraction at age 10. In U.S. culture, the typical ages for the so-called rites of passage are 12 to 13, when the adolescent becomes a "teenager," or around 15 to 16, when the driver's license is issued. Perhaps between Grades 5 and 6 (or, depending on the school system, between Grades 6 and 7), we might identify a critical change during the transition from elementary to middle school. Yet all of these culturally more prominent transitions occur later than age 10. Other subtle changes, such as girls wearing ornate earrings or boys forming preteenage groups, may occur around age 10, but these social factors seem too weak to adequately explain the sudden emergence of sexual attraction before anatomical changes are noteworthy in the child.

We also considered the possibility that although the social environment does not change at age 10, sexual attraction arises at this age because of an increase in the child's cognitive capability to perceive and understand the sexual and social environment. When the child becomes cognitively capable of un-

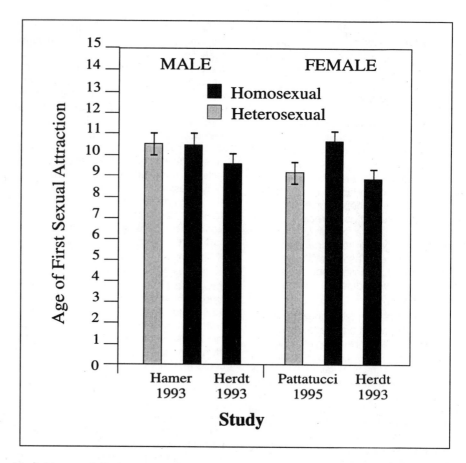

Fig. 1. Mean age (±*SEM*) of first sexual attraction reported by males and females, both homosexual and heterosexual. The data are reported in three studies: Herdt and Boxer (1993), Pattatucci and Hamer (1995), and Hamer, Hu, Magnuson, Hu, and Pattatucci (1993).

derstanding sexual interactions among adults, the child is capable also of imitating and putting into action the behaviors he or she has observed. This may be a plausible explanation for development of an awareness of sexual attraction in heterosexuals, and no doubt plays a role in the development of sexuality (after all, people typically do not develop sexuality in a vacuum). But does the explanation hold for children who are sexually attracted to the same gender?

The simple social-learning hypothesis predicts that as soon as children become aware of a strong cultural taboo on the expression of homosexual feelings, they should inhibit or even extinguish these desires in subsequent sexual development. We would therefore expect to find that homosexuals would reveal same-sex attraction significantly later than the age when heterosexuals reveal opposite-sex attraction. But this is not the case.

If 10-year-old children are simply mimicking the sexual behavior most commonly seen in adults (and the biological ability to actually carry out the behavior will arise only with gonadarche), then, given the predominant culture, all

10-year-old boys should demonstrate sexual attraction toward females, and all 10-year-old girls should show sexual attraction toward males. However, this also is not the case.

Other criticisms of simple learning-theory hypotheses regarding sexual development are well known and need not be repeated here (Abramson & Pinkerton, 1995). However, the Sambia of Papua New Guinea (Herdt, 1981) provide particularly compelling counterevidence to a simple learning theory model. The Sambia provide powerful reinforcement for same-gender relations by institutionalizing the practice of men inseminating boys over a period of many years beginning at age 7 to 10. The goal of the men is to masculinize and "grow" the youths into competent reproductive adult men. This intensive training and reinforcement of sexual relationships between males does not result in exclusive homosexuality in adulthood. Instead, adult Sambia men reveal marked bifurcation of their sexual interest; they generally stop all same-gender relations after marriage and enjoy sexual relations with women.

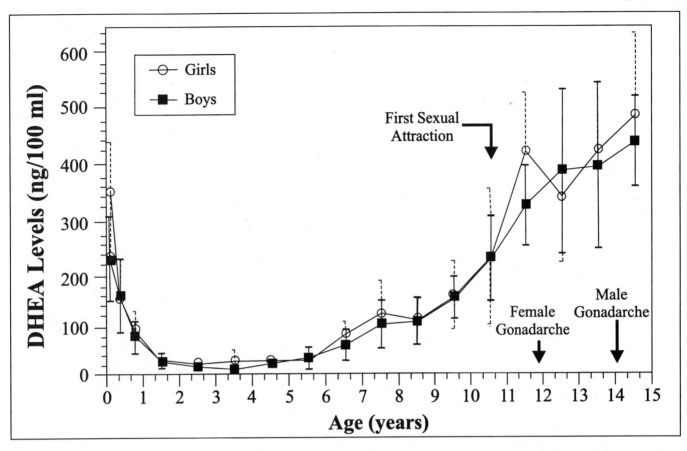

Fig. 2. Mean levels (±*SEM*) of the primary adrenal androgen dehydroepiandrosterone (DHEA) from birth through gonadarche in boys (solid error bars) and girls (dashed error bars). (Data redrawn from De Peretti & Forest, 1976.)

THE RELATIONSHIP BETWEEN ADRENARCHE AND SEXUALITY: CAUSE OR CORRELATION?

Does the inability of the hypotheses of gonadarche and social learning to explain the data imply that adrenarche is the key to the emergence of sexual attraction at age 10? That question cannot yet be answered conclusively. It is entirely possible that the sequential changes in attraction, fantasy, and behavior result from major structural changes in the brain that have their etiology in sources other than sex steroids. However, there has been no documented evidence for such neural structures as of yet. Moreover, if structural changes in the brain do prove to be the cause of the emergence of sexual attraction, modification of all current sexual developmental models and theories will still be needed because they assume that adult desires and behaviors develop from gonadarche.

A change in the nervous system that results from hormones released at adrenarche does look like the most likely developmental mechanism for several

reasons. First, girls and boys experience their first sexual attraction, but not gonadarche, at the same age. Second, DHEA, the primary androgen released by the adrenal, is intimately linked with testosterone and estradiol, the major adult sex hormones. Their dynamic relationship is based on the fact that they share many of the fundamental features of steroid function: metabolic pathways that produce the steroids, binding proteins in the blood that carry them to their target tissue, and receptors that enable the cells in the target tissue, including the brain, to change their function in response to the hormonal information. Third, these androgens are known to affect the sexual fantasies and behavior of adolescents and adults, and it is plausible that the same hormones would have similar effects at an earlier age.

RETHINKING PUBERTY: IMPLICATIONS FOR MANY DOMAINS

Given the strong possibility that the currently popular model of puberty is limited, if not incorrect, researchers need

to rethink puberty and test the new models in a wide range of psychological disciplines. Adrenarche clearly raises androgens to significant levels, and if these hormones are responsible for the effects seen in sexual attraction, then they are likely to affect a wide range of other behaviors: aggression, cognition, perception, attention, arousal, emotions, and, of course, sexual identity, fantasy, and behavior.

Even if it turns out that hormones released from the adrenal glands are not responsible for the onset of sexual attraction, the behavioral data themselves demonstrate that the concept of puberty must be greatly elaborated and its various stages unpacked. Indeed, Freud's idea of a latency period is seriously flawed. The current behavioral work reinforces the well-established clinical understanding that puberty is composed of at least two separate maturational processes: adrenarche and gonadarche. Any psychosocial research that uses puberty as a stage in development needs to break down the relevant developmental and social behaviors into these two different stages. Researchers need to take into account the hormonal fact that the start of puberty in normal individuals is around ages 6 to 8 and the end of puberty is not until around ages 15 to 17.

The idea of sexuality developing in stages is nothing new to social scientists. But the idea that sexuality is a continuous process that begins from the inside, well before gonadarche, and extends into adulthood is a conceptual advance. These new data from sexual orientation research force a reevaluation of the social and health models of sexual development. No longer can the brain at puberty be treated as a black box, which is suddenly able to process sexual stimuli *de novo* at the time of gonadal change.

Although adrenarche may not be the answer to all the riddles of sexual development, the new data from the developmental and social study of sexual identity have triggered a major conceptual advance in the understanding of both puberty and sexual development as psychobiological phenomena.

Acknowledgements—We extend our profound thanks to Colin Davis, who coordinated the data and helped substantially with manuscript preparation; to Ruvance Pietrz, who edited text and figures; and to Amanda Woodward for her insightful and constructive comments. This work was supported by National Institute of Mental Health MERIT Award R37 MH41788 to Martha K. McClintock.

Notes

1. Address correspondence to Martha K. McClintock, 5730 Woodlawn Ave., Chicago, IL 60637; e-mail: mkml@midway.uchicago.edu.
2. The adrenal glands are small, pyramidal glands located above the kidneys. They produce hormones that affect metabolism, salt regulation, response to stress, and reproductive function, in part by binding in the brain and altering neural function.

References

Abramson, P., & Pinkerton, S. (Eds.). (1995). *Sexual nature, sexual culture.* Chicago: University of Chicago Press.

Boxer, A., Levinson, R. A., & Petersen, A. C. (1989). Adolescent sexuality. In J. Worell & F. Danner (Eds.), *The adolescent as decision-maker* (pp. 209–244). San Diego: Academic Press.

De Peretti, E., & Forest, M. G. (1976). Unconjugated dehydroepiandrosterone plasma levels in normal subjects from birth to adolescence in humans: The use of a sensitive radioimmunoassay. *Journal of Clinical Endocrinology and Metabolism, 43,* 982–991.

Freud, S. (1965). *Three essays on the theory of sexuality.* New York: Basic Books. (Original work published 1905)

Hamer, D. H., Hu, S., Magnuson, V. L., Hu, N., Pattatucci, A. M. L. (1993). A linkage between DNA markers on the X chromosome and male sexual orientation. *Science, 261,* 321–327.

Herdt, G. (1981). *Guardians of the flutes.* New York: McGraw-Hill.

Herdt, G., & Boxer, A. (1993). *Children of horizons.* New York: Beacon Press.

Money, J., & Ehrhardt, A. (1972). *Man, woman, boy, girl.* Baltimore: Johns Hopkins University Press.

New, M. I., Levine, L. S., & Pang, S. (1981). Adrenal androgens and growth. In M. Ritzen (Ed.), *The biology of normal human growth: Transactions of the First Karolinska Institute Nobel Conference* (pp. 285–295). New York: Raven Press.

Parker, L. N. (1991). Adrenarche. *Endocrinology and Metabolism Clinics of North America, 20(1),* 71–83.

Pattatucci, A. M. L., & Hamer, D. H. (1995). Development and familiality of sexual orientation in females. *Behavior Genetics, 25,* 407–420.

Timiras, P. S. (1972). *Developmental physiology and aging.* New York: Macmillan.

Recommended Reading

Becker, J. B., Breedlove, S. M., & Crews, D. (Ed.). (1992). *Behavioral endocrinology.* London: MIT Press.

Boxer, A., & Cohler, B. (1989). The life-course of gay and lesbian youth: An immodest proposal for the study of lives. In G. Herdt (Ed.), *Gay and lesbian youth* (pp. 315–335). New York: Harrington Park Press.

Korth-Schütz, S. S. (1989). Precocious adrenarche. In F. G. Maguelone (Ed.), *Pediatric and adolescent endocrinology* (pp. 226–235). New York: Karger.

Rosenfield, R. L. (1994). Normal and almost normal precocious variations in pubertal development: Premature pubarche and premature thelarche revisited. *Hormone Research, 41,* (Suppl. 2), 7–13.

Live to 100? No thanks

Most people opt for quality, not quantity, in later years

BY SUSAN L. CROWLEY

Despite stunning medical advances that can extend life, most Americans do not want to live to be 100. They fear the disabilities, impoverishment and isolation commonly thought to accompany old age.

The finding emerged in a wide-ranging AARP survey on attitudes toward longevity. When asked how long they want to live, 63 percent of the 2,032 respondents opted for fewer than 100 years.

"What this says to me," notes Constance Swank, director of research at AARP, "is that people are more interested in the quality of their lives than the length. They don't want to be encumbered by poor health and financial worries in their older years."

Survey respondents reported they would like to live to an average of about 91 years, but expect to live to 80. According to the U.S. Census Bureau, the life expectancy for a child born in 1997 is 76.5 years. A person turning 65 in 1997 could expect to live another 17.6 years.

The telephone survey, conducted from April 9 to 14 for AARP by Market Facts, Inc. of McLean, Va., also found that a huge majority of people are aware that their behavior and habits can affect how well they age.

This was "the real take-home message for me," says Terrie Wetle, deputy director of the National Institute on Aging. "It was very good news that more than 90 percent recognized that they had some control over how they age."

Harvard neuropsychologist Margery Hutter Silver, who is associate director of the New England Centenarian Study, agrees: "Just the fact of thinking you have control is going to have tremendous impact."

Over eight out of 10 respondents reported doing things to stay healthy. Seventy percent said they exercise, 33 percent watch their diets, 10 percent watch their weight and 10 percent maintain a positive attitude.

Most Americans are also optimistic that life will be better for the typical 80-year-old in 2050 and that medical advances will lead to cures for cancer, heart disease, AIDS and Alzheimer's disease.

Yet, even though they are taking steps to age well and are upbeat about the future, most people are still leery of what might befall them if they live to be 100.

That shouldn't come as a surprise, people of all ages told the Bulletin.

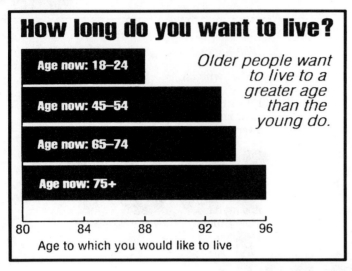

How long do you want to live?

Age now: 18–24

Age now: 45–54

Age now: 65–74

Age now: 75+

Older people want to live to a greater age than the young do.

80   84   88   92   96

Age to which you would like to live

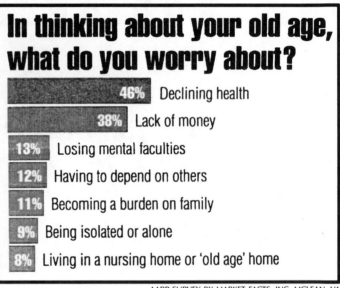

In thinking about your old age, what do you worry about?

46% Declining health

38% Lack of money

13% Losing mental faculties

12% Having to depend on others

11% Becoming a burden on family

9% Being isolated or alone

8% Living in a nursing home or 'old age' home

AARP SURVEY BY MARKET FACTS, INC. MCLEAN, VA.

"Our society bases its economy on young stars and young entrepreneurs," says Lynda Preble, 28, who works for a public relations firm in San Francisco. "I'm sure most people don't understand where they fit in once they are older."

"I was not surprised," says writer and publicist Susan Hartt, 57, of Baltimore. "As the saying goes, 'Old age is not for sissies.'"

Even though disability rates among the old are declining, chronic health problems and poverty are still more likely to appear in advanced age, Wetle says, and "people know that."

"I'm going to hang it up when I'm restricted to bed," say Marion Ballard, 59, a former software company owner in Bethesda, Md.

"A slow mental decline scares me the most," says Lilavati Sinclair, a 32-year-old mother in Bothell, Wash. For Peter Winkert, 47, a sales executive in Cazenovia, N.Y., "running out of income is my biggest concern."

Others express fear of being alone, burdening their families, living in a nursing home or, as one person puts it, "losing my joy and will to keep on living."

How old a person is tends to influence his or her views on age and aging. Among those ages 18 to 24, a person is "old" at 58, according to the survey, while those 65 or older think "old" starts at 75.

"I used to think I would be dead at 30," jokes one woman who just turned 30. "Now that I know I'll be around a while, I want to enjoy life as long as possible."

Not unexpectedly, older people hope and expect to live to greater ages than the young. Survey respondents 75 and older want to live to 96, but for 18- to 24-year-olds, 88 is enough.

Julie Vermillion, 24, who is a public affairs assistant in Washington, D.C., and Erin Laughlin, 23, a dog trainer in Sebastopol, Calif., say that living to 85 is about right.

Yet 85-year-old Lucille Runkel of Cochranton, Pa., is still in good shape and still active. "I wouldn't mind living to be 100 if I'm in good health," she says, "but I don't want to be dependent on my children."

"If I feel well enough," says lawyer Lester Nurick, 84, of Potomac, Md., "I could go on forever. . . .but I would never put a number on it."

"Young people deal with the mythology instead of the reality of aging," says AARP's Swank. "Older people are living it, and many embrace the challenges, the joys. No one wants to be debilitated, but for many, the later years are highly satisfying. So why walk away from it?"

Older people have also witnessed the development of life-saving vaccines, drugs and surgical techniques and are more confident of continuing medical breakthroughs. "What we see here," Swank says, "is the wisdom of age."

Writer Hartt says she wouldn't mind putting up with some infirmities to achieve such wisdom. "So what was adolescence—a day at the beach?"

Lack of information helps fuel the myths of old age. For example, only 28 percent of survey respondents know that the 85-plus age group is the fastest-growing segment of the population.

And many people don't know that most Americans over 65 live independently, with fewer than 5 percent in nursing homes, adds Harvard's Silver.

Other survey highlights:

• On average, people with a college education hope to live longer (to age 92) than those with a high-school education (to 89).

• Fifty-two percent of those with a yearly household income of over $50,000 worry about poor health in old age, compared to 41 percent among those with incomes lower than $50,000.

• Those who say they are doing things to stay healthy and active expect to live to 81, while others expect to live to 76.

Given new findings about centenarians—whose numbers in the United States grew to more than 62,000 by 1998 and by some estimates could reach 1 million by 2050—aiming for the century mark is not unreasonable.

Living to 100 doesn't mean you'll be in poor health, says Silver, who is co-author with Thomas T. Perls, M.D., of "Living to 100" (Basic Books, 1999). To the contrary, centenarians are often healthier than people in their 80s.

But there's a trick, according to their book: "One must stay healthy the vast majority of one's life in order to live to 100."

Some think it's a worthy goal.

"It would be cool to live for over a century, just because of the history involved," says one 30-something. "I can't even guess what will come."

Key Points to Consider

❖ What is the study of personality; what is the definition of personality? What are some of the major tenets of most personality theories? Can you differentiate psychoanalysis from trait theory from humanistic theory?

❖ What do you think contributes most to our unique personalities, biology or environment? If you answered biology, what does this imply about the possibility of personality change? If you answered environment, do you think that biology plays any role in personality?

❖ What are the major tenets of psychoanalysis? Is the theory practiced in different ways around the world? How so? What do you think Freud would say about the practice and interpretation of his theory in today's society?

❖ Is personality stable or ever-changing across a lifetime? What are the advantages of a stable personality? What would be the advantages of an ever-changing personality? How is trait theory different from other personality theories?

❖ What is self-esteem? Do you think self-esteem comes exclusively from appraisals by others? If not, from where else does it originate? How can we raise children with high self-esteem? What are the consequences of low self-esteem?

❖ From where does the trait of shyness originate? What can shy individuals do to overcome their shyness? What other traits do you think would be important to measure besides shyness? Psychologists have now identified five traits that they think describe all individuals fairly well. Do you think shyness is one of these traits? What other traits do you think are included in the Big Five, as they are known?

 **Links** www.dushkin.com/online/

23. **The Personality Project**
    http://fas.psych.nwu.edu/personality.html

These sites are annotated on pages 4 and 5.

Sabrina and Sadie are identical twins. When the girls were young, their parents tried very hard to treat them equally. Whenever Sabrina received a present, Sadie received one. Both girls attended dance school and completed early classes in ballet and tap dance. In elementary school, the twins were both placed in the same class. Their teacher also tried to treat them alike.

In junior high school, Sadie became a tomboy. She loved to play rough-and-tumble sports with the neighborhood boys. On the other hand, Sabrina remained indoors and practiced on her piano. Sabrina was keenly interested in the domestic arts such as sewing and needlepoint. Sadie was more interested in reading science fiction novels, and in watching adventure on television.

As the twins matured, they decided it would be best to attend different colleges. Sabrina went to a small, quiet college in a rural setting, and Sadie matriculated at a large public university. Sabrina majored in English, with a specialty in poetry; Sadie switched majors several times and finally decided on a communications major.

Why, when these twins were exposed to the same early childhood environment, did their interests and paths diverge later? What makes even identical twins so unique, so different from one another?

The study of individual differences is the domain of personality. The psychological study of personality has included two major thrusts. The first has focused on the search for the commonalties of human life and development. Its major question would be: How are humans, especially their personalities, affected by specific events or activities? Personality theories are based on the assumption that a given event, if it is important, will affect almost all people in a similar way, or that the processes by which events affect people are common across events and people. Most psychological research into personality variables has made this assumption. Failures to replicate a research project are often the first clues that differences in individual responses require further investigation.

While some psychologists have focused on personality-related effects that are presumed to be universal among humans, others have devoted their efforts to discovering the bases on which individuals differ in their responses to environmental events. In the beginning, this specialty was called genetic psychology, because most people assumed that individual differences resulted from differences in genetic inheritance. By the 1950s the term genetic psychology had given way to the more current term: the psychology of individual differences.

Does this mean that genetic variables are no longer the key to understanding individual differences? Not at all. For a time, psychologists took up the philosophical debate over whether genetic or environmental factors were more important in determining behaviors. Even today, behavior geneticists compute the heritability coefficients for a number of personality and behavior traits, including intelligence. This is an expression of the degree to which differences in a given trait can be attributed to differences in inherited capacity or ability. Most psychologists, however, accept the principle that both genetic and environmental determinants are important in any area of behavior. These researchers are devoting more of their efforts to discovering how the two sources of influence interact to produce the unique individual. Given the above, the focus of this unit is on personality characteristics and the differences and similarities among individuals.

What is personality? Most researchers in the area define personality as patterns of thoughts, feelings, and behaviors that persist over time and over situations, are characteristic or typical of the individual, and usually distinguish one person from another.

In our first few articles we will delve into some of the major theories of personality. In the first article, "Who Are the Freudians?" Edith Kurzweil examines psychoanalytic theory as practiced in modern times. Psychoanalytic or Freudian theory is one of the oldest theories of personality. Kurzweil concludes that this particular theory today is practiced differently around the world, so much so that Freud himself might not recognize it.

The second article is about another personality theory—trait theory. "The Stability of Personality: Observations and Evaluations" features research on individual differences, the crux of personality. This research examines whether people, despite differences among them, remain the same over a lifetime or whether they change. Robert McCrae and Paul Costa conclude that our personality characteristics remain relatively stable across a life span.

A third theory of personality is humanistic theory. The humanists focus on self-concept, especially self-esteem. They do not fragment the personality into traits or smaller units as do the trait theorists. Similarly, humanistic theorists believe that people know themselves well, which is unlike the assumption in Freudian theory that we are constantly deceived by our unconscious. In "Making Sense of Self-Esteem," Mark Leary redefines self-esteem and offers a conception of it that includes evaluations from others as its antecedent. He continues with the notion that those with low self-esteem are bound to experience psychological disorders. High esteem, then, is important to mental health, as proposed by the humanistic theorists.

Last, we look at a specific aspect of personality. The specific trait is shyness. In "Social Anxiety," the authors explain that shyness is caused by social anxiety. The authors then elaborate upon the causes of and cures for shyness or extreme social anxiety.

Who Are the Freudians?

Edith Kurzweil

To answer this question, I began in the late 1970s to undertake a cross-cultural study of psychoanalysis. I had been aware that neither celebrations nor condemnations, neither revisions nor distortions of Freud's and his disciples' insights had attempted to assess the profusion of clinical studies and theories in relation to their local, taken-for-granted cultural assumptions. By then, I already had written a chapter on the French psychoanalyst Jacques Lacan in my book, *The Age of Structuralism: Lévi-Strauss to Foucault* (1980), and had noted that some Parisian psychoanalysts (and not only Lacanians) were elaborating on the early Freudians' discoveries in entirely different directions than were, for instance, the members of the New York Psychoanalytic Society or of the Sigmund Freud-Institut in Frankfurt. At the time, however, I was not yet fully aware that psychoanalysis had so many offshoots, and offshoots of offshoots.

Although I expanded on, and demonstrated, that my previous observations of cultural differences were major elements in the role that psychoanalysis was being accorded within various societies, I still underestimated the personal preferences and affinities among analysts and proponents who are purported to share a specific theory, a culture, and who either belong to the International Psychoanalytic Association or attend its meetings. The very profusion of theories and practices led me, reluctantly, to limit my book to the so-called classical Freudians alone.

As a result of that research, I maintained that "the fragmentation of psychoanalytic theory proves, among other things, that the Freudians primarily are united by their profession rather than by their ideas." And I predicted that even a victory in court by American psychologists, who in 1985 were suing for membership in the American Psychoanalytic Association (APA) and in the International Psychoanalytic Association (IPA), might not bring the equality of prestige and income they expected, and did not bode well for future cooperation among Freudian therapists.

Still, there now are many local attempts to present a united front, but it is not clear that this has put an end to earlier rivalries.

Since *The Freudians. A Comparative Perspective* was published, in 1989, there have been significant changes not only in the make-up of the psychoanalysts' professional organizations, but in specific culturally induced attitudes towards Freud and psychoanalysis, and in the transliteration of practices from one country to another. After the fall of the Berlin Wall and the demise of the Soviet empire, Sandor Ferenczi's "active" clinical method, that is, his advocacy of closer, personal involvement with an analysand than Freud had approved of, began being introduced and pursued in America. This meant that the detached stance advocated by American ego psychologists was being further relaxed—a change in clinical method that appears to be more suitable to analysands accustomed to today's permissive climate. But this shift also has initiated yet other examinations of the disagreements between Ferenczi and Freud, again has questioned Jones's dismissal of Ferenczi as incompetent at the end of his life, and has led Ferenczi's follower, Clara Thompson who criticized psychoanalytic "scientificity" in the 1940s to be taken more seriously. And Ferenczi's assumptions about child abuse, which is of current concern in America (and elsewhere) where more and more instances are being reported, have been useful to researchers investigating psychic and family dynamics. Both medically and psychologically trained therapists, of every school, are engaged in these endeavors.

The political upheavals in such countries as the former Czechoslovakia, the former East Germany, the former Yugoslavia, and in Russia, have allowed, also, for freedom of expression in general, and for psychoanalytic practices as well. New teaching institutes have been set up in these countries, and psychoanalysts from Western Europe have been traveling there, regularly, to conduct seminars and personal analyses.

In Paris, Lacanian therapy has become less pervasive, while its focus on the use of a psychoanalyst's language has become more pronounced, also, among classical Freudians—a phenomenon clearly observable at international gatherings. In Germany, *Sozioanalyse*—which is meant to penetrate to the unconscious elements that allowed the Germans to sit by or participate in the Holocaust—increasingly has been taking a backseat, while psychoanalytic therapy has become more acceptable. A number of studies in the Frankfurt school tradition continue being pursued. In the United States, classical ego psychology has suffered a decline, as have all other long-term therapies, while short-term interventions, and the use of drug induced psychic changes have moved to the fore. And whereas Parisian intellectuals rarely quote

 From *Society*, May/June 1999, pp. 67-71.

Lacan, some of his ideas, and reverberations of them, have proliferated in many American universities—albeit in non-therapeutic versions of postmodernism.

My predictions, or should I say premonitions, about *psychoanalytic theory*, were based on the dynamic contradictions intrinsic to the following points: 1) clinical approaches grounded in case studies keep evolving and, in turn, reflect personality changes due to cultural pressures; 2) each case study is rooted in the psychic interactions between an analyst and a patient and, therefore, is an objective abstraction from a subjective interpersonal experience; 3) this subjective element is bound to lead every other self-respecting analyst to ponder, or even argue, on how differently he/she might have handled the case; 4) since this holds true for analysts of the same training, the same nationality, the same gender, and the same affiliation as well, the more inclusive of diversity, the more glaring must be the discrepant interpretations; 5) and because psychoanalysts, in the course of their training, must learn to identify fully with their supervisors and analysts, they are bound to have difficulties accepting intrapsychic theories contradicting what, for good reason, have become gut reactions.

My forebodings about the future of *Freud's movement* resulted from my recognition that in the past there were so many dissimilar developments and nationally based interests; 1) all along, to be admitted to membership by the IPA bestowed prestige, but did not add to a psychoanalyst's range or number of patients at home; 2) since "properly" trained psychologists from every country around the world always had been accepted by the IPA, having won the legal right to join was of significance only to Americans, who had restricted admission to medical doctors; 3) although attendance at international meetings, and the possibility of being asked to present a paper, inevitably sparks intellectual activity, American psychologists, who always were free to attend IPA meetings—except for business sessions—would not gain much after becoming members; 4) as in other international organizations, I expected increasing size, diversity of languages, and of cultural assumptions, to lead to more bureaucratization, more internal politicking, and more impersonal contacts, conditions that are anathema to the intimacy on which psychoanalysis thrives.

Still, I had fewer misgivings in relation to *psychoanalytic practice*. For in the course of observing the European scene, I had not noted any major variations in the way clinicians—whatever their formal credentials—were talking about their patients, and about their concerns and practices. Most of them were reiterating the need for rigorous instructional and supervisory standards. This held true for Americans as well: major intellectual disagreements had occurred in-line with specific theoretical stances, with particular details over psychoanalytic formation, and with clinical evaluations of patients. And there had been little contact with therapists of "dubious" training by them all. But, altogether, international ex-

changes always had helped broaden individuals' outlook and tolerance, thereby enriching participants' theoretical and clinical knowledge—while introducing them to new perspectives.

The Continuing Conflicts

Unresolvable conflicts continue to ensue when, at international meetings, psychoanalysts assume that the idiom of their own countries, and their own professional societies, ipso facto applies everywhere else; and when, even within the same cultural milieu, they take for granted that clinicians, historians, and postmodernists share similar concerns, or are based on the same premises. In fact, most Freudian scholars in departments of literature, and most historians of psychoanalysis, are much more involved with numerous, and detailed, textual, biographical and historical questions than with clinical issues. However, the foremost focus of practicing analysts is on what goes on in their own and their patients' minds. This activity cannot be successful unless psychoanalysts listen carefully in order to sort out their patients' fantasies from their lives. Since these patients often introduce the relativistic notions of postmodern attitudes, the analysts easily confuse these with the openness to their patients' problems and are influenced in that direction. Nevertheless, the openness of psychoanalysts and the openness of postmodernists are basically opposed to each other. For, ultimately, psychoanalysts try to sort out fantasies from reality, whereas postmodernists have another set of assumptions of what constitutes reality.

Ever since the first psychoanalytic congress in Salzburg, in 1908, Freud's followers have responded to aspects of local conditions and preoccupations, to public demand and professional opportunities, however unconsciously they may have done so. Furthermore, only after traditions have begun to unravel, and after modernization has begun to take its emotional toll, do societies introduce psychoanalytic and related therapeutic means to alleviate the pressures of modern life. At that point, increasing numbers of people start to enter the profession which, in turn, experiences an upsurge of activities. In America, the peak was reached in the 1950s and 1960s, and we now have a surfeit of therapists. Consequently, therapists of many stripes, from the most classical Freudians to the least trained social workers, are competing for patients, sometimes by offering innovative treatment. This trend, though much less pronounced, already is beginning in France, and to some extent in Germany.

The global reach of Freud's hypotheses, his penetration of so many different domains—challenging professionals and amateurs in them all—and his formulations and reformulations of earlier concepts of psychic functioning, has left a grab bag of ideas. In America, for instance, clinicians continue to debate the viability of narrow conceptions of ego psychology versus narcissism, of self-psychology versus interpersonal and relational approaches, whereas social scientists tend to understand narcissism in terms of Christopher Lasch's comments on the behavior of the 1970s generation. That Erik Erikson noted that little girls tend to build enclosed spaces while boys are more likely to construct towers, started the protracted debate with, and among, feminists that still is going on. Such debates, themselves, in recent years, have turned into scholarly subjects. These general polemics, however, are not of particular interest to psychoanalysts. They tend to focus on the clinical advances based on Freud's conceptions, while conceding that here and there he might have been wrong, and going on to explain their differences in more or less psychoanalytic terms. Culturally inclined critics, on the other hand, search for the contradictions within his *oevre* and in the interactions among the disciples. They speculate on the extent to which his cancer of the jaw, or his patriarchal surroundings, might have influenced his thinking. They tend to resort to conspiracy theories, assuming that Ferenczi's concepts were suppressed to uphold Freud's; that Freud rooted seduction by the little girl's father. in fantasy rather than reality, not because he assumed that though it certainly occurred it could not possibly be so frequent, or because treatment failed, but because he deferred to his friend, Wilhelm Fliess; or that he had an affair with his sister-in-law, Minna, because Jung said so in an obscure interview many years after they already had broken up. This is not to say that classical Freudians are on track when they choose to accept Freud's *History of the Psychoanalytic Movement* (1914) as gospel. Moreover, speculations and historical reevaluations have little bearing on what 'clinicians do in their work with patients. All in all, both Freud's followers and his detractors, his imitators and his adversaries, have been able to explore many interesting avenues of research—in line with clinical findings, with professional affinities, and with the general Zeitgeist.

Freud in the Larger Culture

The familiar disputes, as a rule, tend to arise within a national context, and to address specific concerns—a murder trial, a controversial book, a political scandal. But where psychoanalytic thought already permeates the culture, it usually is applied loosely by the media as well. In other words, after a certain time, psychoanalysis becomes everyone's intellectual property. Practicing psychoanalysts, however, take their cues from colleagues within their immediate professional associations, and to a much lesser extent from the leading psychoanalysts within the national and international associations. Thus they frequently overlook that their immediate concerns, for the most part, are rooted in their own societal context. As a result, they tend to judge cultural events and phenomena from a specific vantage point.

The postponement of the Freud exhibit at the Library of Congress, in the fall of 1995, was an example of how professional and personal biases, and interests, intersect in America today, and how a handful of individuals were able to exert political pressure. This is what happened: A few Freud scholars, who are known for their antagonism to psychoanalysts, maintained that "the show was conceived as a means of mobilizing support for the besieged practice of psychoanalysis . . . and [did not account for] the radically different view of Freud from the one promoted by the psychoanalytic establishment." They collected forty-two signatures from people who had intellectual, professional, or personal disagreements with Freudians, mostly from a few historians who wanted immediate access to the Freud archives, and from psychologists who for so long had been kept out of the APA and the IPA. They chose to ignore that this "establishment" is besieged and dwindling. And they apparently were unaware of the fact that this exposition had been initiated, and partially paid for, by the Austrian government—to celebrate the country's millennium as well as the one hundredth birthday of Freud's inception of psychoanalysis. These detractors wanted to have their views represented, to choose the contents of the exhibition, to criticize Freud rather than praise him.

The resulting brouhaha led the Librarian of Congress, James H. Billington, to postpone the exhibit which, by March 1996, induced 180 well-known figures from around the world—psychoanalysts, writers, philosophers, and cinematographers—to protest the cancellation. They could not accept that "as prestigious an institution as the Library of Congress would allow itself to be manipulated by public opinion and to be impressed by the dictatorship by a few intellectuals turned into inquisitors." Essentially, they asked Billington not give in to this "witch hunt," and to reschedule the event "under conditions that would not succumb to a blackmail of fear, and to open the archives to all researchers, from every country and every tendency."

In response, the Librarian of Congress announced that the event had been postponed and would open in the fall of 1998. The critics were placated by having some of their own put on the organizing committee. Ultimately, the exhibit came off, opened with much fanfare and will travel to Los Angeles, New York, London and Vienna. (It is aimed at the general public, whatever that is, and thus features more applications of Freud's ideas in films and comic strips than of his original, significant manuscripts.) But what is astonishing, is the fact that most of the American psychoanalysts to whom I have spoken know very little of what had been going on, although those who do tend to be angry, or to dismiss this affair as "just politics." Unlike their opponents, who, for the most part, were radical graduate students in the late 1960s and now have tenure in universities, they are either unfamiliar with real political tactics or unwilling to waste time on these activities, which take their minds off their analytic work. But French, German, and Chilean psychoanalysts, for instance, and Freud sympathizers from most other countries, are more politically astute, and are differentially integrated into their societies. No matter what their clinical preferences may be, they consider their American colleagues politically naive, their milieu strange and/or provincial, and in this particular instance repressive of freedom of speech as well.

Whether or not this assessment is correct is a moot point. However, disputes within American culture, the psychoanalysts' need for fundamental integrity, and the discounting of milieu generated differences tend, also, to confuse clinical questions with technical ones, and institutional ones with prestige in the public realm. Inevitably, Freudian analysts and Freudian critics talk past each other. Following are some examples of the sources of these disputes:

1. The combination of addressing a public that, generally, is ignorant of history, and preoccupations with personal careers both among practicing psychoanalysts and among Freud scholars cannot help but encourage tunnel vision and superficiality.

2. Clinicians' focus on Freud's past centers on what made him move away from certain theoretical concepts, and to construct others, in the hope to better understand one or another of their patients. Thus they ignore, for the most part, the evolution of these concepts in terms of their historical context; they are not overly concerned with scandals, and, except in rare instances, don't arouse (or titillate) the current Zeitgeist. But reconstructions of this history are meant for academics.

3. Specific disputes and issues in the public realm no longer question the ubiquity of unconscious forces which have changed how we perceive our entire culture. And the very pervasiveness of the therapeutic mindset encourages the public, also, to go for simplistic explanations of intrapsychic dynamics.

4. Freudian therapy has changed medical practices around the world, and psychoanalysis has spread—however differently—over all of Western Europe, Latin America and beyond. This proliferation lulls psychoanalysts into believing that cultural influences—then and now—either don't matter or are the same everywhere.

5. Within the international psychoanalytic realm, multiple theoretical frames are now accepted. Their proponents as a rule present cases that demonstrate one or more clinical successes. In addition to Freudian structural theory, modern ego psychology, Kleinian-Bionian theory, British object relations theory, self-psychology, American object relations theory and Lacanian theories are being debated, always in terms of their viability in working with patients.

6. The current interest in biography, among other things, is unconnected to questions of therapy. Neither is it relevant to the therapy whether psychoanalysis is an art or a science. However, the clinicians' relative ignorance of the ins and outs of the history of their discipline, of the personal animosities among Freud's followers who were responsible for the early theoretical splits, and their defensive stances, are bound to make them lose when debating historians and critics, as well as philosophers of science.

The public, however, expects its psychoanalysts to be on top of all issues—precisely because they are therapists—and does not realize that working with patients all day long keeps them somewhat isolated from the larger cultural trends which, currently, are dominated by postmodern ideas that no one in a university is able to escape.

While talking about *The Freudians: A Comparative Perspective* in European countries, my listeners reaffirmed the thesis that every country creates the Freud it needs. In fact, the questions I was asked not only reflected the specific cultural context, but allowed me to guess, correctly, whether an interlocutor was a historian, a therapist, or a social critic.

By now, Freud's legacy is claimed by some therapists whose practices he would reject and rejected by some scholars who spend their lives studying his every word. In the meantime, notions of the unconscious are being accepted around the world, Freudian therapies—and their bastard offspring—are introduced in more and more countries, and the city of Vienna, which at first was so unreceptive to psychoanalysis, has proclaimed Freud its most favorite son. As they say, "what goes around comes around," or, to paraphrase Freud, the voice of the intellect moves slowly, but in the end it will win out.

Edith Kurzweil is University Professor of Social Thought at Adelphi University. She is the editor of Partisan Review. *Her writings have appeared in* Society, Commentary, *and other journals in the United States and Europe. She is the author of several books, including* The Freudians: A Comparative Perspective *and* The Age of Structuralism: From Lévi-Strauss to Foucault, *both published by Transaction.*

The Stability of Personality: Observations and Evaluations

**Robert R. McCrae and
Paul T. Costa, Jr**.

Robert R. McCrae is Research Psychologist and **Paul T. Costa, Jr.,** is Chief, Laboratory of Personality and Cognition, both at the Gerontology Research Center, National Institute on Aging, National Institutes of Health. Address correspondence to Robert R. McCrae, Personality, Stress and Coping Section, Gerontology Research Center, 4940 Eastern Ave., Baltimore, MD 21224.

"There is an optical illusion about every person we meet," Ralph Waldo Emerson wrote in his essay on "Experience":

In truth, they are all creatures of given temperament, which will appear in a given character, whose boundaries they will never pass: but we look at them, they seem alive, and we presume there is impulse in them. In the moment it seems impulse; in the year, in the lifetime, it turns out to be a certain uniform tune which the revolving barrel of the music-box must play.[1]

In this brief passage, Emerson anticipated modern findings about the stability of personality and pointed out an illusion to which both laypersons and psychologists are prone. He was also perhaps the first to decry personality stability as the enemy of freedom, creativity, and growth, objecting that "temperament puts all divinity to rout." In this article, we summarize evidence in support of Emerson's observations but offer arguments against his evaluation of them.[2]

EVIDENCE FOR THE STABILITY OF ADULT PERSONALITY

Emerson used the term temperament to refer to the basic tendencies of the individual, dispositions that we call personality traits. It is these traits, measured by such instruments as the Minnesota Multiphasic Personality Inventory and the NEO Personality Inventory, that have been investigated in a score of longitudinal studies over the past 20 years. Despite a wide variety of samples, instruments, and designs, the results of these studies have been remarkably consistent, and they are easily summarized.

1. The mean levels of personality traits change with development, but reach final adult levels at about age 30. Between 20 and 30, both men and women become somewhat less emotional and thrill-seeking and somewhat more cooperative and self-disciplined—changes we might interpret as evidence of increased maturity. After age 30, there are few and subtle changes, of which the most consistent is a small decline in activity level with advancing age. Except among individuals with dementia, stereotypes that depict older people as being withdrawn, depressed, or rigid are unfounded.

2. Individual differences in personality traits, which show at least some continuity from early childhood on, are also essentially fixed by age 30.

Stability coefficients (test-retest correlations over substantial time intervals) are typically in the range of .60 to .80, even over intervals of as long as 30 years, although there is some decline in magnitude with increasing retest interval. Given that most personality scales have short-term retest reliabilities in the range from .70 to .90, it is clear that by far the greatest part of the reliable variance (i.e., variance not due to measurement error) in personality traits is stable.

3. Stability appears to characterize all five of the major domains of personality—neuroticism, extraversion, openness to experience, agreeableness, and conscientiousness. This finding suggests that an adult's personality profile as a whole will change little over time, and studies of the stability of configural measures of personality support that view.

4. Generalizations about stability apply to virtually everyone. Men and women, healthy and sick people, blacks and whites all show the same pattern. When asked, most adults will say that their personality has not changed much in adulthood, but even those who claim to have had major changes show little objective evidence of change on repeated administrations of personality questionnaires. Important exceptions to this generalization include people suffering from dementia and certain

From *Current Directions in Psychological Science*, December 1994, pp. 173–175. Reprinted by permission of Cambridge University Press.

categories of psychiatric patients who respond to therapy, but no moderators of stability among healthy adults have yet been identified.[3]

When researchers first began to publish these conclusions, they were greeted with considerable skepticism—"I distrust the facts and the inferences" Emerson had written—and many studies were designed to test alternative hypotheses. For example, some researchers contended that consistent responses to personality questionnaires were due to memory of past responses, but retrospective studies showed that people could not accurately recall how they had previously responded even when instructed to do so. Other researchers argued that temporal consistency in self-reports merely meant that individuals had a fixed idea of themselves, a crystallized self-concept that failed to keep pace with real changes in personality. But studies using spouse and peer raters showed equally high levels of stability.[4]

The general conclusion that personality traits are stable is now widely accepted. Some researchers continue to look for change in special circumstances and populations; some attempt to account for stability by examining genetic and environmental influences on personality. Finally, others take the view that there is much more to personality than traits, and seek to trace the adult developmental course of personality perceptions or identity formation or life narratives.

These latter studies are worthwhile, because people undoubtedly do change across the life span. Marriages end in divorce, professional careers are started in mid-life, fashions and attitudes change with the times. Yet often the same traits can be seen in new guises: Intellectual curiosity merely shifts from one field to another, avid gardening replaces avid tennis, one abusive relationship is followed by another. Many of these changes are best regarded as variations on the "uniform tune" played by individuals' enduring dispositions.

ILLUSORY ATTRIBUTIONS IN TEMPORAL PERSPECTIVE

Social and personality psychologists have debated for some time the accuracy of attributions of the causes of behavior to persons or situations. The "optical illusion" in person perception that Emerson pointed to was somewhat different. He felt that people attribute behavior to the live and spontaneous person who freely creates responses to the

situation, when in fact behavior reveals only the mechanical operation of lifeless and static temperament. We may (and we will!) take exception to this disparaging, if common, view of traits, but we must first concur with the basic observation that personality processes often appear different when viewed in longitudinal perspective: "The years teach much which the days never know."

Consider happiness. If one asks individuals why they are happy or unhappy, they are almost certain to point to environmental circumstances of the moment: a rewarding job, a difficult relationship, a threat to health, a new car. It would seem that levels of happiness ought to mirror quality of life, and that changes in circumstances would result in changes in subjective well-being. It would be easy to demonstrate this pattern in a controlled laboratory experiment: Give subjects $1,000 each and ask how they feel!

But survey researchers who have measured the objective quality of life by such indicators as wealth, education, and health find precious little association with subjective well-being, and longitudinal researchers have found surprising stability in individual differences in happiness, even among people whose life circumstances have changed markedly. The explanation is simple: People adapt to their circumstances rapidly, getting used to the bad and taking for granted the good. In the long run, happiness is largely a matter of enduring personality traits.[5] "Temper prevails over everything of time, place, and condition, and . . . fix[es] the measure of activity and of enjoyment."

A few years ago, William Swann and Craig Hill provided an ingenious demonstration of the errors to which too narrow a temporal perspective can lead. A number of experiments had shown that it was relatively easy to induce changes in the self-concept by providing self-discrepant feedback. Introverts told that they were really extraverts rated themselves higher in extraversion than they had before. Such studies supported the view that the self-concept is highly malleable, a mirror of the evaluation of the immediate environment.

Swann and Hill replicated this finding, but extended it by inviting subjects back a few days later. By that time, the effects of the manipulation had disappeared, and subjects had returned to their initial self-concepts. The implication is that any one-shot experiment may give a seriously misleading view of personality processes.[6]

The relations between coping and adaptation provide a final example. Cross-sectional studies show that individuals who use such coping mechanisms as

self-blame, wishful thinking, and hostile reactions toward other people score lower on measures of well-being than people who do not use these mechanisms. It would be easy to infer that these coping mechanisms detract from adaptation, and in fact the very people who use them admit that they are ineffective. But the correlations vanish when the effects of prior neuroticism scores are removed; an alternative interpretation of the data is thus that individuals who score high on this personality factor use poor coping strategies and also have low well-being: The association between coping and well-being may be entirely attributable to this third variable.[7]

Psychologists have long been aware of the problems of inferring causes from correlational data, but they have not recognized the pervasiveness of the bias that Emerson warned about. People tend to understand behavior and experience as the result of the immediate context, whether intrapsychic or environmental. Only by looking over time can one see the persistent effects of personality traits.

THE EVALUATION OF STABILITY

If few findings in psychology are more robust than the stability of personality, even fewer are more unpopular. Gerontologists often see stability as an affront to their commitment to continuing adult development; psychotherapists sometimes view it as an alarming challenge to their ability to help patients;[8] humanistic psychologists and transcendental philosophers think it degrades human nature. A popular account in *The Idaho Statesman* ran under the disheartening headline "Your Personality—You're Stuck With It."

In our view, these evaluations are based on misunderstandings: At worst, stability is a mixed blessing. Those individuals who are anxious, quarrelsome, and lazy might be understandably distressed to think that they are likely to stay that way, but surely those who are imaginative, affectionate, and carefree at age 30 should be glad to hear that they will probably be imaginative, affectionate, and carefree at age 90.

Because personality is stable, life is to some extent predictable. People can make vocational and retirement choices with some confidence that their current interests and enthusiasms will not desert them. They can choose friends and mates with whom they are likely to remain compatible. They can vote on the basis of candidates' records, with some assurance that future policies will resemble past ones. They can learn which coworkers they can depend on, and which they cannot. The personal and social utility of personality stability is enormous.

But it is precisely this predictability that so offends many critics. ("I had fancied that the value of life lay in its inscrutable possibilities," Emerson complained.) These critics view traits as mechanical and static habits and believe that the stability of personality traits dooms human beings to lifeless monotony as puppets controlled by inexorable forces. This is a misunderstanding on several levels.

First, personality traits are not repetitive habits, but inherently dynamic dispositions that interact with the opportunities and challenges of the moment.[9] Antagonistic people do not yell at everyone; some people they flatter, some they scorn, some they threaten. Just as the same intelligence is applied to a lifetime of changing problems, so the same personality traits can be expressed in an infinite variety of ways, each suited to the situation.

Second, there are such things as spontaneity and impulse in human life, but they are stable traits. Individuals who are open to experience actively seek out new places to go, provocative ideas to ponder, and exotic sights, sounds, and tastes to experience. Extraverts show a different kind of spontaneity, making friends, seeking thrills, and jumping at every chance to have a good time. People who are introverted and closed to experience have more measured and monotonous lives, but this is the kind of life they choose.

Finally, personality traits are not inexorable forces that control our fate, nor are they, in psychodynamic language, ego alien. Our traits characterize us; they are our very selves;[10] we act most freely when we express our enduring dispositions. Individuals sometimes fight against their own tendencies, trying perhaps to overcome shyness or curb a bad temper. But most people acknowledge even these failings as their own, and it is well that they do. A person's recognition of the inevitability of his or her one and only personality is a large part of what Erik Erikson called ego integrity, the culminating wisdom of a lifetime.

Notes

1. All quotations are from "Experience," in *Essays: First and Second Series,* R.W. Emerson (Vintage, New York, 1990) (original work published 1844).

2. For recent and sometimes divergent treatments of this topic, see R.R. McCrae and P.T. Costa, Jr., *Personality in Adulthood* (Guilford, New York, 1990); D. C. Funder, R.D. Parke, C. Tomlinson-Keasey and K. Widaman, Eds., *Studying Lives Through Time: Personality and Development* (American Psychological Association, Washington, DC, 1993); T. Heatherton and J. Weinberger, *Can Personality Change?* (American Psychological Association, Washington, DC, 1994).

3. L.C. Siegler, K.A. Welsh, D.V. Dawson, G.G. Fillenbaum, N.L. Earl, E.B. Kaplan, and C.M. Clark, Ratings of personality change in patients being evaluated for memory disorders, *Alzheimer Disease and Associated Disorders, 5,* 240–250 (1991); R.M.A. Hirschfeld, G.L. Klerman, P. Clayton, M.B. Keller, P. McDonald-Scott, and B. Larkin, Assessing personality: Effects of depressive state on trait measurement, *American Journal of Psychiatry, 140,* 695–699 (1983); R.R. McCrae, Moderated analyses of longitudinal personality stability, *Journal of Personality and Social Psychology, 65,* 577–585 (1993).

4. D. Woodruff, The role of memory in personality continuity: A 25 year follow-up, *Experimental Aging Research, 9,* 31–34 (1983); P.T. Costa, Jr., and R.R. McCrae, Trait psychology comes of age, in *Nebraska Symposium on Motivation: Psychology and Aging,* T.B. Sonderegger, Ed. (University of Nebraska Press, Lincoln, 1992).

5. P.T. Costa, Jr., and R.R. McCrae, Influence of extraversion and neuroticism on subjective well-being: Happy and unhappy people, *Journal of Personality and Social Psychology, 38,* 668–678 (1980).

6. The study is summarized in W.B. Swann, Jr., and C.A. Hill, When our identities are mistaken: Reaffirming self-conceptions through social interactions, *Journal of Personality and Social Psychology, 43,* 59–66 (1982). Dangers of single-occasion research are also discussed in J.R. Council, Context effects in personality research, *Current Directions in Psychological Science, 2,* 31–34 (1993).

7. R.R. McCrae and P.T. Costa, Jr., Personality, coping, and coping effectiveness in an adult sample, *Journal of Personality, 54,* 385–405 (1986).

8. Observations in nonpatient samples show what happens over time under typical life circumstances; they do not rule out the possibility that psychotherapeutic interventions can change personality. Whether or not such change is possible, in practice much of psychotherapy consists of helping people learn to live with their limitations, and this may be a more realistic goal than "cure" for many patients. See P.T. Costa, Jr., and R.R. McCrae, Personality stability and its implications for clinical psychology, *Clinical Psychology Review, 6,* 407–423 (1986).

9. A. Tellegen, Personality traits: Issues of definition, evidence and assessment, in *Thinking Clearly About Psychology: Essays in Honor of Paul E. Meehl,* Vol. 2, W. Grove and D. Cicchetti, Eds. (University of Minnesota Press, Minneapolis, 1991).

10. R.R. McCrae and P.T. Costa, Jr., Age, personality, and the spontaneous self-concept, *Journals of Gerontology: Social Sciences, 43,* S177–S185 (1988).

Making Sense of Self-Esteem

Mark R. Leary[1]

Department of Psychology, Wake Forest University, Winston-Salem, North Carolina

Abstract

Sociometer theory proposes that the self-esteem system evolved as a monitor of social acceptance, and that the so-called self-esteem motive functions not to maintain self-esteem per se but rather to avoid social devaluation and rejection. Cues indicating that the individual is not adequately valued and accepted by other people lower self-esteem and motivate behaviors that enhance relational evaluation. Empirical evidence regarding the self-esteem motive, the antecedents of self-esteem, the relation between low self-esteem and psychological problems, and the consequences of enhancing self-esteem is consistent with the theory.

Keywords

self-esteem; self; self-regard; rejection

Self-esteem has been regarded as an important construct since the earliest days of psychology. In the first psychology textbook, William James (1890) suggested that the tendency to strive to feel good about oneself is a fundamental aspect of human nature, thereby fueling a fascination—some observers would say obsession—with self-esteem that has spanned more than a century. During that time, developmental psychologists have studied the antecedents of self-esteem and its role in human development, social psychologists have devoted attention to behaviors that appear intended to maintain self-esteem, personality psychologists have examined individual differences in the trait of self-esteem, and theorists of a variety of orientations have discussed the importance of self-regard to psychological adjustment. In the past couple of decades, practicing psychologists and social engineers have suggested that high self-esteem is a remedy for many psychological and social problems.

Yet, despite more than 100 years of attention and thousands of published studies, fundamental issues regarding self-esteem remain poorly understood. Why is self-esteem important? Do people really have a need for self-esteem? Why is self-esteem so strongly determined by how people believe they are evaluated by others? Is low self-esteem associated with psychological difficulties and, if so, why? Do efforts to enhance self-esteem reduce personal and social problems as proponents of the self-esteem movement claim?

PERSPECTIVES ON THE FUNCTION OF SELF-ESTEEM

Many writers have assumed that people seek to maintain their self-esteem because they possess an inherent "need" to feel good about themselves. However, given the apparent importance of self-esteem to psychological functioning, we must ask why self-esteem is so important and what function it might serve. Humanistic psychologists have traced high self-esteem to a congruency between a person's real and ideal selves and suggested that self-esteem signals people as to when they are behaving in self-determined, autonomous ways. Other writers have proposed that people seek high self-esteem because it facilitates goal achievement. For example, Bednar, Wells, and Peterson (1989) proposed that self-esteem is subjective feedback about the adequacy of the self. This feedback—self-esteem—is positive when the individual copes well with circumstances but negative when he or she avoids threats. In turn, self-esteem affects subsequent goal achievement; high self-esteem increases coping, and low self-esteem leads to further avoidance.

The ethological perspective (Barkow, 1980) suggests that self-esteem is an adaptation that evolved in the service of maintaining dominance in social relationships. According to this theory, human beings evolved mechanisms for monitoring dominance because dominance facilitated the acquisition of mates and other reproduction-enhancing resources. Because attention and favorable reactions from others were associated with being dominant, feelings of self-esteem became tied to social approval and deference. From this perspective, the motive to evaluate oneself positively reduces, in evolutionary terms, to the motive to enhance one's relative dominance.

One of the more controversial explanations of self-esteem is provided by terror management theory, which suggests that the function of self-esteem is to buffer people against the existential terror they experience at the prospect of their own death and annihilation (Solomon, Greenberg, & Pyszczynski, 1991). Several experiments have supported aspects of the theory, but not the strong argument that the function of the self-esteem system is to provide an emotional buffer specifically against death-related anxiety.

All of these perspectives offer insights into the nature of self-esteem, but each has conceptual and empirical difficulties (for critiques, see Leary, 1999; Leary & Baumeister, in press). In the past few years, a novel perspective—sociometer theory—has cast self-esteem in a somewhat different light as it attempts to address lingering questions about the nature of self-esteem.

SOCIOMETER THEORY

According to sociometer theory, self-esteem is essentially a psychological meter, or gauge, that monitors the quality of people's relationships with others (Leary, 1999; Leary & Baumeister, in

From *Current Directions in Psychological Science*, February 1999, pp. 32–35. © 1999 by the American Psychological Society. Reprinted by permission of Blackwell Publishers.

press; Leary & Downs, 1995). The theory is based on the assumption that human beings possess a pervasive drive to maintain significant interpersonal relationships, a drive that evolved because early human beings who belonged to social groups were more likely to survive and reproduce than those who did not (Baumeister & Leary, 1995). Given the disastrous implications of being ostracized in the ancestral environment in which human evolution occurred, early human beings may have developed a mechanism for monitoring the degree to which other people valued and accepted them. This psychological mechanism—the *sociometer*—continuously monitors the social environment for cues regarding the degree to which the individual is being accepted versus rejected by other people.

The sociometer appears to be particularly sensitive to changes in relational evaluation—the degree to which others regard their relationship with the individual as valuable, important, or close. When evidence of low relational evaluation (particularly, a decrement in relational evaluation) is detected, the sociometer attracts the person's conscious attention to the potential threat to social acceptance and motivates him or her to deal with it. The affectively laden self-appraisals that constitute the "output" of the sociometer are what we typically call self-esteem.

Self-esteem researchers distinguish between *state self-esteem*—momentary fluctuations in a person's feelings about him- or herself—and *trait self-esteem*—the person's general appraisal of his or her value; both are aspects of the sociometer. Feelings of state self-esteem fluctuate as a function of the degree to which the person perceives others currently value their relationships with him or her. Cues that connote high relational evaluation raise state self-esteem, whereas cues that connote low relational evaluation lower state self-esteem. Trait self-esteem, in contrast, reflects the person's general sense that he or she is the sort of person who is valued and accepted by other people. Trait self-esteem may be regarded as the resting state of the sociometer in the absence of incoming information relevant to relational evaluation.

SELF-ESTEEM AND ITS RELATIONSHIP TO BEHAVIOR

Sociometer theory provides a parsimonious explanation for much of what we know about self-esteem. Here I examine how sociometer theory answers four fundamental questions about self-esteem raised earlier.

The Self-Esteem Motive

As noted, many psychologists have assumed that people possess a motive or need to maintain self-esteem. According to sociometer theory, the so-called self-esteem motive does not function to maintain self-esteem but rather to minimize the likelihood of rejection (or, more precisely, relational devaluation). When people behave in ways that protect or enhance their self-esteem, they are typically acting in ways that they believe will increase their relational value in others' eyes and, thus, improve their chances of social acceptance.

The sociometer perspective explains why events that are known (or potentially known) by other people have much greater effects on self-esteem than events that are known only by the individual him- or herself. If self-esteem involved only private self-judgments, as many psychologists have assumed, public events should have no greater impact on self-esteem than private ones.

Antecedents of Self-Esteem

Previous writers have puzzled over the fact that self-esteem is so strongly tied to people's beliefs about how they are evaluated by others. If self-esteem is a *self*-evaluation, why do people judge themselves by *other* people's standards? Sociometer theory easily explains why the primary determinants of self-esteem involve the perceived reactions of other people, as well as self-judgments on dimensions that the person thinks are important to significant others. As a monitor of relational evaluation, the self-esteem system is inherently sensitive to real and potential reactions of other people.

Evidence shows that state self-esteem is strongly affected by events that have implications for the degree to which one is valued and accepted by other people (Leary, Haupt, Strausser, & Chokel, 1998; Leary, Tambor, Terdal, & Downs, 1995). The events that affect self-esteem are precisely the kinds of things that, if known by other people, would affect their evaluation and acceptance of the person (Leary, Tambor, et al., 1995). Most often, self-esteem is lowered by failure, criticism, rejection, and other events that have negative implications for relational evaluation; self-esteem rises when a person succeeds, is praised, or experiences another's love—events that are associated with relational appreciation. Even the mere possibility of rejection can lower self-esteem, a finding that

makes sense if the function of the self-esteem system is to warn the person of possible relational devaluation in time to take corrective action.

The attributes on which people's self-esteem is based are precisely the characteristics that determine the degree to which people are valued and accepted by others (Baumeister & Leary, 1995). Specifically, high trait self-esteem is associated with believing that one possesses socially desirable attributes such as competence, personal likability, and physical attractiveness. Furthermore, self-esteem is related most strongly to one's standing on attributes that one believes are valued by significant others, a finding that is also consistent with sociometer theory.

In linking self-esteem to social acceptance, sociometer theory runs counter to the humanistic assumption that self-esteem based on approval from others is false or unhealthy. On the contrary, if the function of self-esteem is to avoid social devaluation and rejection, then the system must be responsive to others' reactions. This system may lead people to do things that are not always beneficial, but it does so to protect their interpersonal relationships rather than their inner integrity.

Low Self-Esteem and Psychological Problems

Research has shown that low self-esteem is related to a variety of psychological difficulties and personal problems, including depression, loneliness, substance abuse, teenage pregnancy, academic failure, and criminal behavior. The evidence in support of the link between low self-esteem and psychological problems has often been overstated; the relationships are weaker and more scattered than typically assumed (Mecca, Smelser, & Vasconcellos, 1989). Moreover, high self-esteem also has notable drawbacks. Even so, low self-esteem tends to be more strongly associated with psychological difficulties than high self-esteem.

From the standpoint of sociometer theory, these problems are caused not by low self-esteem but rather by a history of low relational evaluation, if not outright rejection. As a subjective gauge of relational evaluation, self-esteem may parallel these problems, but it is a coeffect rather than a cause. (In fact, contrary to the popular view that low self-esteem causes these problems, no direct evidence exists to document that self-esteem has any causal role in thought, emotion, or behavior.) Much research shows that interpersonal rejection results in emotional problems, difficulties relating with others, and maladaptive efforts to be accepted (e.g., excessive dependency, membership in deviant groups), precisely the concomitants of low self-esteem (Leary, Schreindorfer, & Haupt, 1995). In addition, many personal problems lower self-esteem because they lead other people to devalue or reject the individual.

Consequences of Enhancing Self-Esteem

The claim that self-esteem does not cause psychological outcomes may appear to fly in the face of evidence showing that interventions that enhance self-esteem do, in fact, lead to positive psychological changes. The explanation for the beneficial effects of programs that enhance self-esteem is that these interventions change people's perceptions of the degree to which they are socially valued individuals. Self-esteem programs always include features that would be expected to increase real or perceived social acceptance; for example, these programs include components aimed at enhancing social skills and interpersonal problem solving, improving physical appearance, and increasing self-control (Leary, 1999).

CONCLUSIONS

Sociometer theory suggests that the emphasis psychologists and the lay public have placed on self-esteem has been somewhat misplaced. Self-esteem is certainly involved in many psychological phenomena, but its role is different than has been supposed. Subjective feelings of self-esteem provide ongoing feedback regarding one's relational value vis-à-vis other people. By focusing on the monitor rather than on what the monitor measures, we have been distracted from the underlying interpersonal processes and the importance of social acceptance to human well-being.

Recommended Reading

Baumeister, R. F. (Ed.). (1993). *Self-esteem: The puzzle of low self-regard.* New York: Plenum Press.
Colvin, C. R., & Block, J. (1994). Do positive illusions foster mental health? An examination of the Taylor and Brown formulation. *Psychological Bulletin, 116,* 3–20.
Leary, M. R. (1999). (See References)
Leary, M. R., & Downs, D. L. (1995). (See References)
Mecca, A. M., Smelser, N. J., & Vasconcellos, J. (Eds.). (1989). (See References)

Note

1. Address correspondence to Mark Leary, Department of Psychology, Wake Forest University, Winston-Salem, NC 27109; e-mail: leary@wfu.edu.

References

Barkow, J. (1980). Prestige and self-esteem: A biosocial interpretation. In D. R. Omark, F. F. Strayer, & D. G. Freedman (Eds.), *Dominance relations: An ethological view of human conflict and social interaction* (pp. 319–332). New York: Garland STPM Press.
Baumeister, R. F., & Leary, M. R. (1995). The need to belong: Desire for interpersonal attachments as a fundamental human motivation. *Psychological Bulletin, 117,* 497–529.
Bednar, R. L., Wells, M. G., & Peterson, S. R. (1989). *Self-esteem: Paradoxes and innovations in clinical theory and practice.* Washington, DC: American Psychological Association.
James, W. (1890). *The principles of psychology* (Vol. 1). New York: Henry Holt.
Leary, M. R. (1999). The social and psychological importance of self-esteem. In R. M. Kowalski & M. R. Leary (Eds.), *The social psychology of emotional and behavioral problems: Interfaces of social and clinical psychology* (pp. 197–221). Washington, DC: American Psychological Association.
Leary, M. R., & Baumeister, R. F. (in press). The nature and function of self-esteem: Sociometer theory. *Advances in Experimental Social Psychology.*
Leary, M. R., & Downs, D. L. (1995). Interpersonal functions of the self-esteem motive: The self-esteem system as a sociometer. In M. H. Kernis (Ed.), *Efficacy, agency, and self-esteem* (pp. 123–144). New York: Plenum Press.
Leary, M. R., Haupt, A. L., Strausser, K. S., & Chokel, J. L. (1998). Calibrating the sociometer: The relationship between interpersonal appraisals and state self-esteem. *Journal of Personality and Social Psychology, 74,* 1290–1299.
Leary, M. R., Schreindorfer, L. S., & Haupt, A. L. (1995). The role of self-esteem in emotional and behavioral problems: Why is low self-esteem dysfunctional? *Journal of Social and Clinical Psychology, 14,* 297–314.
Leary, M. R., Tambor, E. S., Terdal, S. J., & Downs, D. L. (1995). Self-esteem as an interpersonal monitor. The sociometer hypothesis. *Journal of Personality and Social Psychology, 68,* 518–530.
Mecca, A. M., Smelser, N. J., & Vasconcellos, J. (Eds.). (1989). *The social importance of self-esteem.* Berkeley: University of California Press.
Solomon, S., Greenberg, J., & Pyszczynski, T. (1991). A terror management theory of social behavior: The psychological functions of self-esteem and cultural worldviews. *Advances in Experimental Social Psychology, 24,* 93–159.

Social Anxiety

For millions of Americans, every day is a struggle with debilitating shyness

BY JOANNIE M. SCHROF AND STACEY SCHULTZ

It is something of a miracle that Grace Dailey is sitting in a restaurant in a coastal New Jersey town having an ordinary lunch, at ease with her world. Her careful, tiny bites of a tuna sandwich may seem unremarkable, but they are in fact a milestone. Back in her grade school cafeteria, she could only sip a bit to drink each day, unable to eat while she imagined her classmates' eyes boring into her. (Her high school teachers mistook her anxiety about eating for anorexia.) Only in her 20s, when panic attacks began to hit, did Dailey learn about the condition called social anxiety disorder, also known as "social phobia." But despite some success with behavioral therapy and anxiety-reducing medication, the 32-year-old still struggles. "I would be a different person in a different place if I didn't have to deal with this on a daily basis," she says, frustration apparent in her furrowed brow.

Shyness is a nearly universal human trait. Most everyone has bouts of it, and half of those surveyed describe themselves as shy. Perhaps because it's so widespread, and because it suggests vulnerability, shyness is often an endearing trait: Princess Diana, for example, won millions of admirers with her "Shy Di" manner. The human species might not even exist if not for an instinctive wariness of other creatures. In fact, the ability to sense a threat and a desire to flee are lodged in the most primitive regions of the brain.

But at some life juncture, roughly 1 out of every 8 people becomes so timid that encounters with others turn into a source of overwhelming dread. The heart races, palms sweat, mouth goes dry, words vanish, thoughts become cluttered, and an urge to escape takes over.

This is the face of social phobia, the third most common mental disorder in the United States, behind depression and alcoholism. Like Woody Allen in the film *Annie Hall,* some social phobics can barely utter a sentence without obsessing over the impression they are making. Others refuse to use public restrooms or talk on the telephone. Sometimes they go mute in front of the boss or a member of the opposite sex. At the extreme, they build a hermitic life, avoiding contact with others (think of young Laura in Tennessee Williams's *Glass Menagerie* or the ghostly Boo in *To Kill a Mockingbird*).

Though social anxiety's symptoms have been noted since the time of Hip-

SUCCESS STORY. In high school, cheerleaders made a sport of saying "hello" to Steve Fox just to watch him blush. Now he is married to one of the girls who used to tease him.

From *U.S. News & World Report,* June 21, 1999, pp. 45-51. © 1999 by U.S. News & World Report. Reprinted by permission.

Coming to you direct

Public service ads—or just a sales pitch?

BY BRENDAN I. KOERNER

Pasted on bus shelters nationwide, the posters ask passersby to imagine being allergic to people. The picture is of a handsome young man, despondently staring at a coffee cup as an apparently happy couple sits at the other end of his table. "Over 10 million Americans suffer from social anxiety disorder," the text reads. "The good news is that this disorder is treatable." A toll-free number and a Web site are listed.

The ads bear the seals of three nonprofit advocacy groups: the American Psychiatric Association, the Anxiety Disorders Association of America, and Freedom From Fear, a trio that together make up the Social Anxiety Disorder Coalition. But funding for their public awareness campaign comes from a far less visible partner: SmithKline Beecham, the pharmaceutical giant whose flagship antidepressant, Paxil, was recently approved by the Food and Drug Administration for the treatment of debilitating shyness, formally known as social anxiety disorder.

Top of the pack. The move made Paxil the first selective serotonin reuptake inhibitor (SSRI) to win that designation. In the crowded SSRI marketplace, which rang up sales of near $7 billion last year, companies are constantly on the lookout for new ways in which their brands can be used—for social phobia, panic disorder, obsessive-compulsive disorder, bulimia. "You really need to keep your brand on the top of the pack," says Sergio Traversa of Mehta Partners, which does investment research on pharmaceutical companies. When you have multiple users, then "it's a relatively cheap alternative to developing new drugs. . . . On one side, it's cheaper, and it also helps keep the brand popular." Not surprisingly, some critics see profit, rather than altruism, as the motive behind SmithKline's financial backing of the "Imagine being allergic to people" campaign, and they question whether the statistics put forward in such advertising are accurate.

Blurring the line between public service and marketing is common practice in the industry. Back in 1996, when Paxil was cleared for the treatment of panic disorder, SmithKline sponsored the "Paxil Report on Panic," in which one third of those surveyed said either they or someone they knew had suffered from a panic attack—a sudden rush of terror or extreme fear. Bristol-Myers Squibb, which sells the antidepressants Serzone and Desyrel, sponsors the popular Depression.com Web site, which includes an "Are You Depressed?" quiz. And Eli Lilly, the maker of Prozac, the top-selling SSRI, launched an "educational television campaign" last month, featuring a 30-minute program chronicling the tales of 10 depression sufferers—all recovered, thanks to its brand.

SmithKline insists that helping the afflicted, not boosting sales, is the goal of the poster blitz. "We find that less than 5 percent of patients are really treated today," says Barry Brand, product director for Paxil. "There's tremendous need out there." The company, he adds, is adamant about deterring frivolous use. "We don't want this to be a pill that you take for shyness," continues Brand. "We don't want you to think, 'Oh, I'll take a Paxil and I'll feel good.'"

Market forces. Hollow words, says Elliot Valenstein, professor of psychology and neuroscience at the University of Michigan and author of *Blaming the Brain.* "[Drug companies] can anticipate criticism very well. But at the same time, their marketing will assume there are many more people out there" whom they will attract. Indeed, the track records of other "lifestyle drugs" show that many are used to achieve modest goals such as shedding a few pounds or becoming more productive at work. "When Prozac came on the market, it was just approved for severe depression," says Sidney Wolfe, director of the Health Research Group of Public Citizen, a consumer advocacy group. "But it was used for all kinds of depression," Just as Prozac became a $3 billion-a-year seller thanks in part to those users, Paxil will bolster its sales by targeting the merely meek, predicts Valenstein. "Shyness can't be marketed because most people recognize it as a normal variation on personality," he says. "But 'social phobia' sounds like a disease. I'm sure a lot of thought was given to pushing that particular terminology."

The coalition's brochure is careful to highlight the tag line "It's not just shyness," and the campaign's literature never directly mentions Paxil. But some of the symptoms described are familiar to virtually anyone who has faced pressure: blushing, sweating, dry mouth, pounding heart. And SSRIs are praised as vital to the recovery process. In the campaign's video, a sufferer gives testimony to the healing role of her medication: "I wouldn't have been able to concentrate on therapy and the coping skills" without the drug's ability to "take the edge off." Valenstein says that since Paxil is the only FDA-approved SSRI for the disorder, it will become the prescription of choice for general practitioners, who prescribe the majority of antidepressants.

Alec Pollard, director of the anxiety disorders center at the St. Louis Behavioral Medicine Institute, says the cynicism surrounding Paxil clouds its positive effects, which can be remarkable. "I can't say to you that people won't be given Paxil that don't need it," says Pollard. "But we wouldn't want to judge a treatment based on the fact that sometimes it will be inappropriately applied. That's inevitable. That's why particularly primary-care physicians need to be educated on proper use."

But Wolfe is concerned that the direct-to-consumer marketing approach will drive some patients to demand the medication without proper evaluation. "People are going to ask for it, and they're going to get it," he says. In the realms of managed care, doctors may be only too willing to acquiesce to those demands. "It is possible to give people careful diagnosis," says Erik Parens, an associate at the Hastings Center, a bioethics think tank. "But diagnosis takes time, and it costs money. Therefore, it is cheaper to give people the drug they ask for."

pocrates, the disorder was a nameless affliction until the late 1960s and didn't make its way into psychiatry manuals until 1980. As it became better known, patients previously thought to suffer panic disorder were recognized as being anxious only in social settings. A decade ago, 40 percent of people said they were shy, but in today's "nation of strangers"—in which computers and ATMs make face-to-face relations less and less common—that number is nearing 50 percent. Some psychologists are convinced that the Internet culture, often favored by those who fear human interaction, greases the slope from shyness down to social anxiety. "If people were slightly shy to begin with, they can now interact less and less," says Lynne Henderson, a Stanford University researcher and director of the Shyness Clinic in Menlo Park, Calif. "And that will make the shyness much worse."

Much worse—and, for drug companies, far more lucrative: Recently, Smith Kline Beecham won FDA approval to market the antidepressant Paxil for social phobia, leading to a raft of "public education campaigns"—on top of those already put out by the National Institute of Mental Health and the Anxiety Disorders Association of America. This media blitz has raised concerns that normally shy people will conclude they're social phobics and seek medications for what is a complex, emotional problem, or opt for such drugs merely as "lifestyle" aids to win friends and influence people (story, "Coming to You Direct").

Hard-hitting. Social phobia hit Steve Fox so hard in high school that girls made a sport of saying "hello" just to watch him turn beet red. He refused to speak in class and never dated; even walking in front of other people left him with sweaty palms and gasping for air. By the time Fox was 19, his father was concerned enough to find a doctor, and a combination of medication and therapy has helped him recover. Fox, now

UNABLE TO DRIVE. Roland Bardon had to rely on his mother to chauffeur him when he was overwhelmed by anxiety about what others thought of his driving.

23, recently gave a speech in front of 1,700 people, and he is married to one of the cheerleaders who used to tease him. Normal shyness and serious social phobia are clearly different, but they are related. Emanuel Maidenberg, associate director of UCLA's Social Phobia and Performance Anxiety Clinic, says that shyness is to social phobia what a fair complexion is to skin cancer. "It's a predisposing factor but will only translate into disease under certain circumstances," he says. "For pale people, that might be 10,000 hours in the sun. For shy people, it might be a string of embarrassing events." Even though some people are born with a tendency toward extreme shyness, biology is by no means destiny. Harvard researcher Jerome Kagan has shown that by 8 weeks of age, babies display innate shyness or boldness. Roughly 1 in 5 will consistently be frightened of and avoid anything or anyone new, while the others welcome the unknown, reaching out to touch strangers or to grab new objects. Yet, many shy babies become gregarious 10-year-olds, and some outgoing babies become shy, even socially phobic, adults.

Life experiences can mold the brain to become more or less shy over time. Through a process psychologists call "contextual conditioning," the brain attaches a fear "marker" to the details of a situation that causes trauma (place, time of day, background music). So when a child gets a disparaging tongue-lashing from a teacher, the student will feel at least a bit nervous the next few times he or she steps into that class-

room. But sometimes the brain is too good at making those associations, says Maidenberg, and the anxiety grows like a cancer, attaching itself to the act of entering any classroom or talking to any teacher.

The classic behavior of a child who does not know how to handle these "daggers to the heart," says University of Pennsylvania psychiatrist Moira Rynn, is to avoid any attention at all. In fact, social phobia used to be known as avoidant personality disorder. First, avoidant kids may stop inviting friends over. Some will only speak to certain people, usually their parents, a condition known as "selective mutism" (box, "Suffering in Silence"). Others develop "school refusal." By avoiding the very situations they need to learn the social skills of adulthood, these children end up diminishing their ability to cope. Not only can a parent who is highly critical train a child to cower, but even the gentlest parent can raise a fearful child. "If parents avoid social situations or worry excessively about what the neighbors think of them," says Richard Heimberg, director of the Adult Anxiety Clinic at Temple University in Philadelphia, "the message to a child is that the world is full of danger, humiliation, and embarrassment."

Social phobia affects about half of its victims by age 8, and many others during adolescence, when social fears are more pronounced. Others live with an undetected problem that surfaces when facing a new public arena (college, a new job) that overwhelms them. Grace Dailey, who had managed to suffer qui-

A spectrum of shyness

A touch of timidity is human, but too much shyness can be debilitating

NORMAL SHYNESS

■ **You are jittery beginning a public speech, but afterward you are glad you did it.**

■ **Your mind goes blank on a first date, but eventually you relax and find things to talk about.**

■ **Your palms sweat in a job interview, but you ask and answer thoughtful questions.**

EXTREME SHYNESS

■ **You clam up and your heart races when you know people are looking at you.**

■ **You tremble when speaking up at a meeting, even if it is only to say your name.**

etly through high school, was seized with sudden panic attacks in her college classes. The episodes were so distressing that she would race out of lecture halls, and she considered dropping out. She did graduate, with the help of thoughtful professors who let her take tests by herself and who kept classroom doors open so that she didn't feel so trapped.

More women than men are thought to suffer social anxiety, but because shyness and demureness are smiled upon in females and less acceptable in males, more men turn to professionals for help. Roland Bardon, 27, knew he needed to see a psychologist after becoming too anxious to drive a car. "I worry about making other drivers mad," he says. "When people honk, that kind of criticism drives me crazy." He still avoids taking the wheel whenever he can.

Talking to strangers. It's Friday night at the Shyness Clinic in Menlo Park, Calif., time for this week's social phobia information session. But in the tiny room decorated haphazardly with fake flowers, only one man has shown up. The very nature of their disorder often causes social phobics to hide, and revealing themselves to a stranger is the last thing they want to do. Tonight's newcomer put off coming for two months. Clinic patients attend group meetings once a week, but some cannot even bring themselves to show up at all.

When the socially anxious do make it into clinics, they usually start with a few months of cognitive behavioral therapy. The cognitive element fights what psychiatrist Isaac Tylim of the Maimonides Medical Center in Brooklyn calls the intellectual core of social phobia: the belief that others will pass negative judgments on you and that unbearable humiliation will result. "I turn down invitations to go to lunch with people I really admire, even though I desperately want to go," says a Kentucky housewife and mother of two girls who exhibit a similar timidity. "I assume that as soon

as we get together, they'll regret having asked and want to get away from me as soon as possible." These distortions cause an emotional reaction that sends social phobics running away from even the most promising friendships. Through cognitive restructuring—a fancy term for replacing faulty thoughts with realistic ones—many social phobics learn to question the insidious fears that, no matter how irrational, paralyze them in their everyday lives.

Perhaps the most salient feature of social anxiety is what is known as flooding: the sensation of being so overwhelmed that panic sets in. Almost everyone feels mild flooding at the podium during the first minute or so of an important speech, but for most people the discomfort soon subsides. A social phobic can suffer such agony for more than an hour. But even in social phobics, flooding will eventually subside, if only because of sheer exhaustion. That is why behavioral therapists coach social phobics to remain in terrifying situations until the symptoms abate and it becomes clear that nothing bad is going to happen.

The first place that Melinda Stanley, professor of behavioral sciences at the University of Texas-Houston Health Sci-

in front of Stanley and an audience of graduate-student volunteers. Other therapists take social phobics through practice runs of embarrassing situations, like walking through a hotel lobby with toilet paper on their shoes or spilling a drink. It's not unlike physical training, says Henderson. "Just as our gym workouts get easier as time goes by, to stay socially fit we must push ourselves to engage with others until it is second nature."

When a case is so severe that patients cannot even ride an elevator with a therapist, drugs can enable the social phobic to endure behavioral therapy. The perfect medication has yet to be found. Antidepressants known as monoamine oxidase inhibitors (MAOs) have been used for over a decade, but they can cause side effects such as fainting spells, heart palpitations, and blurred vision, and users must follow strict diets excluding everything from coffee to cheese to red wine. Researchers have experimented with Xanax, Valium, and other tranquilizers but have had mixed success, not least because those drugs can cause physical dependence. Some sufferers try beta blockers, which are helpful for surviving a speech or a party but use less as a long-term therapeutic tool.

IN HIDING. Mark Goomishian dropped out of high school and has spent decades in virtual seclusion.

ence Center, takes many patients is the elevator. Riding up and down, the patient practices greeting and making small talk with fellow passengers. "Sometimes it takes 10 or 15 rides, and sometimes it takes all day," says Stanley, "but the phobic's heart will eventually stop racing for fear of what the newcomer might think of him or her." Eventually, the patients progress to giving speeches

Most popular now are the antidepressants known as selective serotonin reuptake inhibitors (SSRIs), which have fewer side effects than the old anxiety drugs. "[Patients treated for depression] were spontaneously reporting that they were losing their social anxiety," explains Murray Stein, director of the anxiety clinic at the University of California-San Diego. Studies of the SSRIs Paxil and

SOCIAL ANXIETY				**SEVERE SOCIAL ANXIETY**		
■ You avoid starting conversations for fear of saying something awkward.	■ You will do anything, even skip work, to avoid being introduced to new people.	■ You have trouble swallowing in public, making it hard to dine out or go to parties.	■ You feel you never make a good impression and that you are a social failure.	■ You are free of nervousness only when alone and you can barely leave the house.	■ You constantly worry about being embarrassed or humiliated by others.	■ You have panic attacks and often leave the room rather than hold a conversation.

THE SHY CHILD
Suffering in silence

Samantha Williams seems like a typical 11-year-old, enchanted with the prospect of teenage life as she begins to lose interest in childish activities. But at the end-of-the-year cookout she's planning for the girls in her fifth-grade class, Samantha will stand out in one particular way: Most of Samantha's friends have never heard the sound of her voice. Since kindergarten, she has never spoken to any of her teachers or uttered a single word in class, and until very recently, she hasn't made so much as a peep on the playground.

Samantha has a form of childhood social anxiety known as selective mutism. She can comprehend spoken language and she is able to speak, but because she is very shy and anxious around even familiar people, she is unable to talk in public. About 1 percent of kids are like Samantha and have extreme trouble talking to strangers. These children almost always converse easily with their parents—one or both of whom are likely to suffer themselves from some form of social phobia.

Selective mutism has been mistakenly associated in the past with childhood abuse or trauma, charges that researchers say are not supported by scientific evidence. Until recently, it was called "elective mutism," but doctors changed the name because it implied a willful stubbornness of the child that "we've found is really not the case," says Anne Marie Albano, director of the anxiety disorders program at the New York University Child Study Center.

A child's inability to speak in public is not only frustrating for parents, it can also be frightening. When Samantha missed the bus home from school one day, she was unable to tell school officials that she needed to call home for a ride. Instead, she began the 2½-mile trek home, until her mother, in a frantic search of the neighborhood, spotted her. "I worry about her safety," her mother says. "I especially worry that she won't be able to ask for help if she needs it."

Fortunately, behavioral therapy can be effective. Parents, teachers, and friends can play a role, too, says NYU's Albano. "Everyone must maintain the expectation that the child will speak," she says. "We offer rewards and privileges when kids do talk, and we let them experience the consequences when they don't speak," such as earning a poor grade if they miss an oral report in class.

For some children, medication such as Prozac is helpful, but it can take months before the drugs take effect. "One third of the kids we treat get a great deal of benefit from the medica-

WITHOUT A SOUND. Samantha Williams, 11, has not spoken in school since kindergarten. She is being treated for "selective mutism."

tion," says Bruce Black, assistant professor of psychiatry at Tufts University School of Medicine. Another third see some benefit, and the rest don't respond at all, he says. Samantha Williams has been taking Paxil, a drug similar to Prozac, for a few months. Her parents hope she will respond as well as 10-year-old Jenna, a selective mute from Maine. After six months of Prozac, Jenna silently decided one day last November that she would talk in school. When she did, her classmates cheered—and her teachers cried. —S.S.

Luvox show great improvement in about half of social phobics, and studies now under way of other new antidepressants, like Effexor and Serzone, are also showing promise. But Henderson urges caution amid the current hoopla over drugs, which she worries are too often used as temporary crutches. "People tend to relapse as soon as they get off the medication," she warns, adding that research indicates that over the long run, therapy might keep a person in better stead. Just as troubling, says Tylim, is the message that only a drug can save them. "These are people whose very problem is a feeling of inadequacy, and the use of drugs can exacerbate that."

Because some social phobics have been out of the habit of talking with others for so long, therapists often have to help patients brush up on the most basic of social skills. For example, it never dawns on many of the most shy that they should introduce themselves to the person standing in front of them. And they often are stuck in the conversation-killing habit of answering questions with one-word answers. "I had to learn that if someone doesn't seem interested in the first sentence out of my mouth, I should not just turn and walk away cold," says Rick Robbins, a 31-year-old who was voted most shy of his Indiana high school class and whose social anxiety led him to drop out of college.

Perhaps the most common thing social phobics have to learn for the first time is to listen. "All kinds of alarm bells and sirens are distracting to social phobics," says Maidenberg. "So it is nearly impossible to hear what a person standing 4 inches away is saying." In fact, it is sometimes difficult for an extremely shy person to even feign interest in a companion's words. "Social pho-bics don't realize that most people in a room are not taking much notice of them," says Tylim, who says that social phobics in some ways crave the spotlight but fear that humiliation will come from it.

That's why Bernardo Carducci, author of *Shyness* and director of the Shyness Research Institute at Indiana University Southeast, is convinced that shifting the focus away from the self is the most therapeutic thing a shy person can do. "They desperately want to connect with others," he says; otherwise, they would merely be contented introverts or recluses who simply prefer their own company. Carducci sends patients to soup kitchens, hospitals, and nursing homes as a way of escaping the tyranny of self-centeredness. "It works because you get out there and start to see how shy other people can be," says Rick Robbins. "And then you don't feel so all alone, so different from every one else." At first, he tried to pry himself out of his problem with alcohol, what therapists dub "liquid extroversion." Then he forced himself to go to social occasions, where he would sit—miserable, silent, and sick to his stomach. If anything, these kinds of efforts at beating shyness will only aggravate the condition, because they are negative experiences that reinforce the fear.

Learning to cope. And because shyness is at least partially genetic, researchers unanimously agree that it is a mistake to try to become "unshy." Rather, the goal is to take steps to function despite the pounding heart and sweaty palms. Some do advance work for the tough moments. "Before I go out, I come up with four or five topics I would like to talk about," says Robbins. "Usually by the third one I bring up, I find something in common and forget about my nerves." Mark Goomishian, who has trouble even signing a check in public, looks for social arenas where he can be more himself, such as the local coffee shop, where he meets others for regular games of chess. "Because you don't have to talk during the game," he says, "it's a socially anxious person's sport."

In fact, many therapists say that if the socially phobic could rein in their anxiety enough to function, they would help make the world a better place. Many beloved figures in history have suffered shyness, including Eleanor Roosevelt, Robert Frost, and Albert Einstein. Shyness in its milder forms is associated with traits such as greater empathy, more acute perceptiveness, canny intuition, and beneficent sensitivity. All qualities that are nothing to be shy about.

With Brendan I. Koerner and Danielle Svetcov in Menlo Park, Calif.

PANIC ON THE PODIUM
Why everyone gets stage fright

From behind the counter of his Louisville, Ky., smoke shop, Gayle Sallee says he could chat forever with customers who wander through. But when the cigar boom hit in the early 1990s, and requests poured in

TERRORS OF FAME. The cigar craze shoved smoke shop owner Gayle Sallee into the spotlight, where he was forced to overcome his dread of public speaking.

for him to give lectures, seminars, and radio and TV interviews, Sallee says he was petrified: "Even if I was only asked to speak to 10 old slobs who like to smoke, I would get sick just thinking about it."

The fear of public speaking is by far the most prevalent social anxiety, affecting many people who are not the least bit shy in other settings. That makes perfect sense to researchers, who say that stage fright is the same ancient anxiety that hits all creatures when they are in full view of potential predators. But many of us freeze up even before a group of trusted friends. *Shyness* author Bernardo Carducci says this is because of the psychological rule of "salient objects." It is human nature, according to this principle, to scrutinize the most noticeable person in a

room (i.e., the professor, the workshop leader, the soloist, the only African-American, the only woman) far more critically than those who blend into the background. And standing in front of a crowd makes us the "salient object," so that we become only too conscious of each gesture and phrase.

Hang in there. Speech coaches say that the self-consciousness fades if nervous speakers don't give up too soon. Many speakers mistakenly assume their cottony mouths and shaking hands means they are failing miserably. "Those sensations are merely signals that you are trying to do something meaningful and important," says Brooklyn psychiatrist Isaac Tylim. That knowledge was small comfort to Sallee as he struggled through months of stammering and stuttering on the cigar circuit. "None of the stuff about picturing people in their underwear worked at all," he recalls. But after six months of weekly presentations, Sallee suddenly realized halfway through a radio interview one Saturday morning that he was relaxed. "Once the fear died down, the fun began," he says. "Now it's to the point where when I'm in an audience, I really wish it was me up there on the stage."

—*J.M.S.*

Unit Selections

Key Points to Consider

❖ What are friends? How do friendships differ from other relationships? What do friends "give" us that we wouldn't have without them? To what kinds of friends are we most attracted? How may adult friendships be different from childhood friendships? Why do you think friendships end? How are romantic relationships different from friendships?

❖ What is emotional intelligence? What makes people with emotional intelligence different from or better than individuals without it? Why do people with high emotional intelligence make good leaders? Do you know any individuals, well-known or otherwise, who have high emotional intelligence?

❖ What is prejudice? Is there any such thing as old-fashioned prejudice and modern prejudice? Can you provide an example of each? Are most biased thoughts processed automatically? Can we overcome our prejudices if they are fairly automatic? How so? Or should we give up and let prejudice exist?

❖ Do you think we live in a violent society? From where does the violence originate? Does the mass media play a role in promoting violent behavior? How so? Which media are most responsible for promoting violence? Are video games different compared to other media? Why? Would you ban violent media in the United States?

 **Links**   **www.dushkin.com/online/**

24. **National Clearinghouse for Alcohol and Drug Information**
   http://www.health.org

These sites are annotated on pages 4 and 5.

Everywhere we look there are groups of people. Your general psychology class is a group. It is what social psychologists would call a secondary group, a group that comes together for a particular, somewhat contractual reason and then disbands after its goals have been met. Other secondary groups include athletic teams, church associations, juries, and committees.

There are other types of groups, too. One other type is a primary group. A primary group has much face-to-face contact, and there is often a sense of "we-ness" (cohesiveness, as social psychologists would call it) in the group. Examples of primary groups include families, suite mates, sororities, and fraternities.

Collectives are loosely knit, large groups of people. A bleacher full of football fans would be a collective. A line of people waiting to get into a rock concert would also be a collective. As you might guess, collectives behave differently from primary and secondary groups.

Mainstream American society and any other large group that shares common rules and norms is also a group, albeit an extremely large group. While we might not always think about our society and how it shapes our behavior and our attitudes, society and culture nonetheless have a measureless influence on us. Psychologists, anthropologists, and sociologists alike are all interested in studying the effects of a culture on its members.

In this unit we will look at both positive and negative forms of social interaction. The first two articles are about generally acceptable social behaviors, friendship and leadership. In general, both involve getting along well with others.

In "Friendship and Adaptation across the Life Span," the purpose of friendships is examined. Friends provide us with a sense of well-being. The authors caution that adults and children may well define friendship differently.

The second article, about leadership, is really about a concept named emotional intelligence. Daniel Goleman, in a landmark book on that topic, claims that successful people have exceptionally good social skills. They are liked by others because of their social competence. Such competent individuals have an acute sense of self and often make popular leaders.

The next two articles investigate the darker side of social relationships. One lingering social problem in the United States is prejudice. Hate groups and white supremacy groups are active in many communities. Two prominent psychologists in the field of prejudice and stigma differentiate various forms of prejudice as well as suggest means for reducing prejudice and intergroup bias.

In the final article of this unit on social behavior, we explore yet another disturbing social issue–violence. Most psychologists link some or all of our societal violence to the mass media. H. J. Cummins links video games to violence. The main problem with such games, aside from the fact that they promote violence, is that they do not teach us when violence is not appropriate and when or how to stop the violence.

Social Process

Friendships and Adaptation Across the Life Span

Willard W. Hartup[1] and Nan Stevens

Institute of Child Development, University of Minnesota, Minneapolis, Minnesota (W.W.H.),
and Department of Psychogerontology, University of Nijmegen, Nijmegen, The Netherlands (N.S.)

Abstract

Friends foster self-esteem and a sense of well-being, socialize one another, and support one another in coping with developmental transitions and life stress. Friends engage in different activities with one another across the life span, but friendship is conceived similarly by children and adults. Friends and friendships, however, are not all alike. The developmental significance of having friends depends on the characteristics of the friends, especially whether the friends are antisocial or socially withdrawn. Outcomes also depend on whether friendships are supportive and intimate or fractious and unstable. Among both children and adults, friendships have clear-cut developmental benefits at times but are mixed blessings at other times.

Keywords

friendships; life-span development; relationships

Friendships are important to the well-being of both children and adults. Parents worry if their children do not have friends; adolescents are anxious and upset when they lose their friends; and older adults go to considerable lengths to maintain old friendships and establish new ones. People who have friends generally feel better about themselves and others than do people who do not have friends. Recent studies, however, show that over the life span, the dynamics of friendship are complicated. These relationships sometimes contain a "dark side," and in these instances, developmental benefits are mixed.

In this report, we begin by showing that understanding friendships across the life span requires thinking about these relationships from two perspectives: It is necessary to consider, first, what friendships mean to both children and adults and, second, what distinctive patterns of social interaction characterize friendships. We then suggest that, in order to appreciate the significance of friends over the life span, one must take into account (a) whether a person does or does not have friends, (b) characteristics of the person's friends, and (c) the quality of these relationships.

HOW TO THINK ABOUT FRIENDSHIPS IN LIFE-SPAN PERSPECTIVE

The significance of friendship across the life span can be established only by examining what children and adults believe to be the social meaning (essence) of these relationships, as well as the social exchanges they actually have with their friends. When researchers examine what people believe friendships to be, or what elements constitute a friendship, reciprocity is always involved. Friends may or may not share likes and dislikes, but there is always the sense that one supports and sustains one's friends and receives support in return. Most people do not describe the relation between friends narrowly as a *quid pro quo,* but rather describe the relationship broadly as *mutuality*—that is, friendship involves social giving and taking, and returning in kind or degree. Children, adolescents, newlyweds, middle-aged adults, and soon-to-be retirees differ relatively little from one another in their emphasis on these reciprocities when asked to describe an ideal friend (Weiss & Lowenthal, 1975). Older people describe their friendships more elaborately and with greater subtlety than children do, but then older people generally describe other persons in more complex terms than younger persons do. Consequently, we can assert that the meaning structure specifying friendships changes relatively little from the preschool years through old age; social reciprocities are emphasized throughout the life span (Hartup & Stevens, 1997).

The actual exchanges that occur between friends change greatly with age. Social reciprocities between toddlers are reflected in the time they spend together and the connectedness of their interaction; reciprocities between kindergartners are more elaborated but remain basically concrete ("We play"). Among adolescents, friends engage in common activities (mainly socializing) and social disclosure; among young adults, friendships become "fused" or "blended" with work and parenting. Among older persons, friendships are separated from work once again and centered on support and companionship. The behavioral structures associated with friendship thus change greatly across the life span, generally in accordance with the distinctive tasks or challenges that confront persons at different ages.

HAVING FRIENDS

Occurrence

As early as age 3 or 4, children show preferences for interacting with particular children, and the word "friend" enters their vocabularies. About 75% of preschool-aged children are involved in mutual friendships as identified by mothers or nursery school teachers or measured in terms of the time the children spend together. Mutual friends among school-aged children and older persons are usually identified by asking individuals to name their "best friends," "good friends," or "casual friends," categories differentiated in terms of time spent together and intimacy. Among teenagers, 80% to 90% report having mutual friends, usually including one or two best friends and several good friends. The proportion of people who have friends remains high through adulthood, then declines in old age. More older persons, however, have friends than do not. Small numbers of individuals, about 7%, have no friends in adulthood; after age 65, this friendless group increases to 12% for women and 24% for men.

Friendship networks vary in size according to age and sex. During the nursery school years, boys have an average of two friends, whereas girls have one; during the school years, the number of best friends varies from three to five. Girls' networks are usually smaller and more exclusive than boys' during childhood; this situation reverses, however, in adolescence. Number of friends remains fairly constant through adolescence and early adulthood. Newlyweds have the largest numbers of friends, with fewer friendships being maintained during middle age. Friendship networks increase again before retirement, but a decline occurs following retirement, owing primarily to the loss of casual friends. Close friendships, however, are frequently retained into old, old age (Hartup & Stevens, 1997).

The amount of time spent with friends is greatest during middle childhood and adolescence; in fact, teenagers spend almost a third of their waking time in the company of friends. The percentage of time spent with friends declines until middle age, when adults spend less than 10% of their time with friends. A slight increase occurs at retirement, although it is not as great as one might expect (Larson, Zuzanek, & Mannell, 1985).

Behavior With Friends and Nonfriends

More positive engagement (i.e., more talk, smiling, and laughter) is observed among friends than among nonfriends in childhood and adolescence. Friends also have more effective conflict management and a more mutual orientation when working together (Newcomb & Bagwell, 1995). Differences in behavior between friends and mere acquaintances are similar in adulthood: Self-disclosure occurs more frequently and involves more depth of disclosure among friends than nonfriends; friends are more directive and authoritative with one another than nonfriends.

Companionship and talk continue to distinguish interactions between friends in middle and old age. Sharing, exchange of resources, and emotional support remain salient, especially during crises, such as divorce. Problem solving involves more symmetrical interaction between friends than between nonfriends; conflicts are more effectively managed. Adults' conflicts with friends center on differences in values and beliefs, as well as lifestyles. Conflicts between older friends mainly concern expectations related to age and resource inequities.

Developmental Significance

From early childhood through old age, people with friends have a greater sense of well-being than people without friends. Friendlessness is more common among people who seek clinical assistance for emotional and behavioral problems than among better adjusted persons (Rutter & Garmezy, 1983). But these results mean relatively little: They do not clarify whether friends contribute to well-being or whether people who feel good about themselves have an easier time making friends than those who do not.

Longitudinal studies show that children entering first grade have better school attitudes if they already have friends and are successful both in keeping old ones and making new ones (Ladd, 1990). Similarly, among adolescents, psychological disturbances are fewer when school changes (e.g., from grade to grade or from primary school to middle school) occur in the company of friends than when they do not (Berndt & Keefe, 1992). Once again, the direction of influence is not clear: Does merely having friends support successful coping with these transitions, or are those people who are better able to cope with these transitions also able to make friends more easily?

Despite these difficulties in interpretation, well-controlled longer term studies extending from childhood into adulthood show similar patterns, thereby strengthening the conclusion that friendships are in some way responsible for the outcome. Self-esteem is greater among young adults who had friends while they were children than among those who did not, when differences in childhood self-esteem are controlled for statistically. Social adjustment in adulthood, however, is more closely related to having been generally liked or disliked by classmates than to having had mutual friends (Bagwell, Newcomb, & Bukowski, 1998).

CHARACTERISTICS OF ONE'S FRIENDS

Although friends may support positive developmental outcomes through companionship and social support, these outcomes depend on who one's friends are. Friendships with socially well-adjusted persons are like money in the bank, "social capital" that can be drawn upon to meet challenges and crises arising every day. In contrast, poorly adjusted friends may be a drain on resources, increasing one's risk of poor developmental outcomes.

Children of divorce illustrate these dynamics: Preadolescents, adolescents, and young adults whose parents have divorced are at roughly three times the risk for psychosocial problems as their peers whose parents are not divorced. Preadolescents who have positive relationships with both custodial and noncustodial parents have a significantly reduced risk if the parents are well-adjusted; friends do not provide the same protection. In contrast, resilience among adolescents whose parents are divorced is influenced by friends as well as family. Specifically, adolescent children of divorce are more resilient (better adapted) if they have both family and friends who have few behavior problems and who are socially mature. Friends continue to promote resilience among the offspring of divorce during early adulthood, but again friends provide this benefit only if they are well-adjusted themselves (Hetherington, in press). Two conclusions can be drawn: First, social capital does not reside merely in having friends, but rather resides in having socially competent friends; and second, whether friends are a protective factor in social development depends on one's age.

Research indicates that the role of friendships as a risk factor also depends on one's age. Friendship risks are especially evident among antisocial children and adolescents. First, antisocial children are more likely to have antisocial friends than other children. Second, antisocial behavior increases as a consequence of associating with antisocial friends. Antisocial children have poor social skills and thus are not good models. Relationships between antisocial children are also problematic: Interactions are more contentious and conflict-ridden, more marked by talk about deviance and talk that is deviant in its social context (e.g., swearing), and more lacking in intimacy than exchanges between nonaggressive children (Dishion, Andrews, & Crosby, 1995). Other studies show that behavior problems increase across the transition from childhood to adolescence when children have stable relationships with friends who have behavior problems themselves (Berndt, Hawkins, & Jiao, in press).

FRIENDSHIP QUALITY

Friendships are not all alike. Some are marked by intimacy and social support, others by conflict and contention. Some friends engage in many different activities, others share narrower interests. Some friendships are relatively stable, others are not. These features of friendships differentiate relationships among both children and adolescents, and define some of the ways that relationships differ from one another among adults.

Friendship quality is related to the psychological well-being of children and adolescents and to the manner in which they manage stressful life events. During the transition from elementary to secondary school, for example, sociability and leadership increase among adolescents who have stable, supportive, and intimate friendships, but decline or do not change among other adolescents. Similarly, social withdrawal increases among students with unstable, poor-quality friendships, but not among students who have supportive and intimate friendships (Berndt et al., in press).

Friendship quality contributes to antisocial behavior and its development. Conflict-ridden and contentious relationships are associated with increases in delinquent behavior during adolescence, especially among young people with histories

of troublesome behavior; increases in delinquent behavior are smaller for youngsters who have supportive and intimate friends (Poulin, Dishion, & Haas, in press). Friendship quality is also important to the adaptation of young women from divorced families: Those who have supportive and intimate friendships tend to be resilient, but those who have nonsupportive friendships tend not to be resilient (Hetherington, in press).

Among older adults, support from friends also compensates for missing relationships (e.g., partners). Emotional support and receiving assistance from friends are among the most important protections against loneliness for persons without partners (Dykstra, 1995). There may be two sides to this coin, however: Older widows with "problematic" social ties (e.g., widows with friends who break promises, invade their privacy, and take advantage of them) have lower psychological well-being than widows whose social ties are not problematic (Rook, 1984). In other words, the absence of problematic qualities in these relationships may be as important as the presence of positive qualities.

CONCLUSION

Friendships are developmentally significant across the life span. The meaning assigned to these relationships changes relatively little with age, although the behavioral exchanges between friends reflect the ages of the individuals involved. Whether friendships are developmental assets or liabilities depends on several conditions, especially the characteristics of one's friends and the quality of one's relationships with them.

Recommended Reading

Blieszner, R., & Adams, R. G. (1992). *Adult friendship*. Newbury Park, CA: SAGE.
Bukowski, W. M., Newcomb, A. F., & Hartup, W. W. (Eds.). (1996). *The company they keep: Friendship in childhood and adolescence*. New York: Cambridge University Press.
Hartup, W. W., & Stevens, N. (1997). (See References)
Matthews, S. H. (1986). *Friendships through the life course*. Beverly Hills, CA: SAGE.

Note

1. Address correspondence to Willard W. Hartup, Institute of Child Development, University of Minnesota, 51 E. River Rd., Minneapolis, MN 55455.

References

Bagwell, C. L., Newcomb, A. F., & Bukowski, W. M. (1998). Preadolescent friendship and peer rejection as predictors of adult adjustment. *Child Development, 69*, 140–153.

Berndt, T. J., Hawkins, J. A., & Jiao, Z. (in press). Influences of friends and friendships on adjustment to junior high school. *Merrill-Palmer Quarterly*.

Berndt, T. J., & Keefe, K. (1992). Friends' influence on adolescents' perceptions of themselves in school. In D. H. Schunk & J. L. Meece (Eds.), *Students' perceptions in the classroom* (pp. 51–73). Hillsdale, NJ: Erlbaum.

Dishion, T. J., Andrews, D. W., & Crosby, L. (1995). Anti-social boys and their friends in early adolescence: Relationship characteristics, quality, and interactional process. *Child Development, 66*, 139–151.

Dykstra, P. (1995). Loneliness among the never and formerly married: The importance of supportive friendships and a desire for independence. *Journals of Gerontology: Psychological Sciences and Social Sciences, 50B*, S321–S329.

Hartup, W. W., & Stevens, N. (1997). Friendships and adaptation in the life course. *Psychological Bulletin, 121*, 355–370.

Hetherington, E. M. (in press). Social capital and the development of youth from non-divorced, divorced, and remarried families. In W. A. Collins & B. Laursen (Eds.), *Minnesota Symposia on Child Psychology: Vol. 30. Relationships as developmental contexts*. Hillsdale, NJ: Erlbaum.

Ladd, G. W. (1990). Having friends, keeping friends, making friends, and being liked by peers in the classroom: Predictors of children's early school adjustment? *Child Development, 61*, 1081–1100.

Larson, R., Zuzanek, J., & Mannell, R. (1985). Being alone versus being with people: Disengagement in the daily experience of older adults. *Journal of Gerontology, 40*, 375–381.

Newcomb, A. F., & Bagwell, C. (1995). Children's friendship relations: A meta-analytic review. *Psychological Bulletin, 117*, 306–347.

Poulin, F., Dishion, T. J., & Haas, E. (in press). The peer paradox: Relationship quality and deviancy training within male adolescent friendships. *Merrill-Palmer Quarterly*.

Rook, K. S. (1984). The negative side of social interaction: Impact on psychological well-being. *Journal of Personality and Social Psychology, 46*, 1156–1166.

Rutter, M., & Garmezy, N. (1983). Developmental psychopathology. In P. H. Mussen (Series Ed.) & E. M. Hetherington (Vol. Ed.), *Handbook of child psychology: Vol. 4. Socialization, personality, and social development* (4th ed., pp. 775–911). New York: Wiley.

Weiss, L., & Lowenthal, M. F. (1975). Life-course perspectives on friendship. In M. F. Lowenthal, M. Thurnher, & D. Chiriboga (Eds.), *Four stages of life: A comparative study of women and men facing transitions* (pp. 48–61). San Francisco: Jossey-Bass.

IQ and technical skills are important, but emotional intelligence is the sine qua non of leadership.

What Makes a Leader?

BY DANIEL GOLEMAN

Every businessperson knows a story about a highly intelligent, highly skilled executive who was promoted into a leadership position only to fail at the job. And they also know a story about someone with solid—but not extraordinary—intellectual abilities and technical skills who was promoted into a similar position and then soared.

Such anecdotes support the widespread belief that identifying individuals with the "right stuff" to be leaders is more art than science. After all, the personal styles of superb leaders vary: some leaders are subdued and analytical; others shout their manifestos from the mountaintops. And just as important, different situations call for different types of leadership. Most mergers need a sensitive negotiator at the helm, whereas many turnarounds require a more forceful authority.

I have found, however, that the most effective leaders are alike in one crucial way: they all have a high degree of what has come to be known as *emotional intelligence*. It's not that IQ and technical skills are irrelevant. They do matter, but mainly as "threshold capabilities"; that is, they are the entry-level requirements for executive positions. But my research, along with other recent studies, clearly shows that

Daniel Goleman is the author of Emotional Intelligence *(Bantam, 1995) and* Working with Emotional Intelligence *(Bantam, 1998). He is cochairman of the Consortium for Research on Emotional Intelligence in Organizations, which is based at Rutgers University's Graduate School of Applied and Professional Psychology in Piscataway, New Jersey. He can be reached at Goleman@javanet.com.*

emotional intelligence is the sine qua non of leadership. Without it, a person can have the best training in the world, an incisive, analytical mind, and an endless supply of smart ideas, but he still won't make a great leader.

Effective leaders are alike in one crucial way: they all have a high degree of emotional intelligence.

In the course of the past year, my colleagues and I have focused on how emotional intelligence operates at work. We have examined the relationship between emotional intelligence and effective performance, especially in leaders. And we have observed how emotional intelligence shows itself on the job. How can you tell if someone has high emotional intelligence, for example, and how can you recognize it in yourself? In the following pages, we'll explore these questions, taking each of the components of emotional intelligence—self-awareness, self-regulation, motivation, empathy, and social skill—in turn.

Evaluating Emotional Intelligence

Most large companies today have employed trained psychologists to develop what are known as "competency models" to aid them in identifying, training, and promoting likely stars in the leadership firmament. The psychologists have also developed such models for lower-level positions. And in recent years, I have analyzed competency models from 188 companies, most of which were large and global and included the likes of Lucent Technologies, British Airways, and Credit Suisse.

In carrying out this work, my objective was to determine which personal capabilities drove outstanding performance within these organizations, and to what degree they did so. I grouped capabilities into three categories: purely technical skills like accounting and business planning; cognitive abilities like analytical reasoning; and competencies demonstrating emotional intelligence such as the ability to work with others and effectiveness in leading change.

To create some of the competency models, psychologists asked senior managers at the companies to identify the capabilities that typified the organization's most outstanding leaders. To create other models, the psychologists used objective criteria such as a division's profitability to differentiate the star performers at senior levels within their organizations from the average ones. Those

individuals were then extensively interviewed and tested, and their capabilities were compared. This process resulted in the creation of lists of ingredients for highly effective leaders. The lists ranged in length from 7 to 15 items and included such ingredients as initiative and strategic vision.

When I analyzed all this data, I found dramatic results. To be sure, intellect was a driver of outstanding performance. Cognitive skills such as big-picture thinking and long-term vision were particularly important. But when I calculated the ratio of technical skills, IQ, and emotional intelligence as ingredients of excellent performance, emotional intelligence proved to be twice as important as the others for jobs at all levels.

Moreover, my analysis showed that emotional intelligence played an increasingly important role at the highest levels of the company, where differences in technical skills are of negligible importance. In other words, the higher the rank of a person considered to be a star performer, the more emotional intelligence capabilities showed up as the reason for his or her effectiveness. When I compared star performers with average ones in senior leadership positions, nearly 90% of the difference in their profiles was attributable to emotional intelligence factors rather than cognitive abilities.

Other researchers have confirmed that emotional intelligence not only distinguishes outstanding leaders but can also be linked to strong performance. The findings of the late David McClelland, the renowned researcher in human and organizational behavior, are a good example. In a 1996 study of a global food and beverage company, McClelland found that when senior managers had a critical mass of emotional intelligence capabilities, their divisions outperformed yearly earnings goals by 20%. Meanwhile, division leaders without that critical mass underperformed by almost the same amount. McClelland's findings, interestingly, held as true in the company's U.S. divisions as in its divisions in Asia and Europe.

In short, the numbers are beginning to tell us a persuasive story about the link between a company's success and the emotional intelligence of its leaders. And just as important, research is also demonstrating that people can, if they take the right approach, develop their emotional intelligence. (See "Can Emotional Intelligence Be Learned?")

Self-Awareness

Self-awareness is the first component of emotional intelligence—which makes sense when one con-

The Five Components of Emotional Intelligence at Work

	Definition	Hallmarks
Self-Awareness	the ability to recognize and understand your moods, emotions, and drives, as well as their effect on others	self-confidence realistic self-assessment self-deprecating sense of humor
Self-Regulation	the ability to control or redirect disruptive impulses and moods the propensity to suspend judgment—to think before acting	trustworthiness and integrity comfort with ambiguity openness to change
Motivation	a passion to work for reasons that go beyond money or status a propensity to pursue goals with energy and persistence	strong drive to achieve optimism, even in the face of failure organizational commitment
Empathy	the ability to understand the emotional makeup of other people skill in treating people according to their emotional reactions	expertise in building and retaining talent cross-cultural sensitivity service to clients and customers
Social Skill	proficiency in managing relationships and building networks an ability to find common ground and build rapport	effectiveness in leading change persuasiveness expertise in building and leading teams

siders that the Delphic oracle gave the advice to "know thyself" thousands of years ago. Self-awareness means having a deep understanding of one's emotions, strengths, weaknesses, needs, and drives. People with strong self-awareness are neither overly critical nor unrealistically hopeful. Rather, they are honest—with themselves and with others.

People who have a high degree of self-awareness recognize how their feelings affect them, other people, and their job performance. Thus a self-aware person who knows that tight deadlines bring out the worst in him plans his time carefully and gets his work done well in advance. Another person with high self-awareness will be able to work with a demanding client. She will understand the client's impact on her moods and the deeper reasons for her frustration. "Their trivial demands take us away from the real work that needs to be done," she might explain. And she

will go one step further and turn her anger into something constructive.

Self-awareness extends to a person's understanding of his or her values and goals. Someone who is highly self-aware knows where he is headed and why; so, for example, he will be able to be firm in turning down a job offer that is tempting financially but does not fit with his principles or long-term goals. A person who lacks self-awareness is apt to make decisions that bring on inner turmoil by treading on buried values. "The money looked good so I signed on," someone might say two years into a job, "but the work means so little to me that I'm constantly bored." The decisions of self-aware people mesh with their values; consequently, they often find work to be energizing.

How can one recognize self-awareness? First and foremost, it shows itself as candor and an ability to assess oneself realistically. People with high self-awareness are able to speak accurately and openly—although not necessarily effusively or confessionally—about their emotions and the impact they have on their work. For instance, one manager I know of was skeptical about a new personal-shopper service that her company, a major department-store chain, was about to introduce. Without prompting from her team or her boss, she offered them an explanation: "It's hard for me to get behind the rollout of this service," she admitted, "because I really wanted to run the project, but I wasn't selected. Bear with me while I deal with that." The manager did indeed examine her feelings; a week later, she was supporting the project fully.

Self-aware job candidates will be frank in admitting to failure—and will often tell their tales with a smile.

Such self-knowledge often shows itself in the hiring process. Ask a candidate to describe a time he got carried away by his feelings and did something he later regretted. Self-aware candidates will be frank in admitting to failure—and will often tell their tales with a smile. One of the hallmarks of self-awareness is a self-deprecating sense of humor.

Self-awareness can also be identified during performance reviews. Self-aware people know—and are comfortable talking about—their limitations and strengths, and they often demonstrate a thirst for constructive criticism. By contrast, people with low self-awareness interpret the message that they need to improve as a threat or a sign of failure.

People who have mastered their emotions are able to roll with the changes. They don't panic.

Self-aware people can also be recognized by their self-confidence. They have a firm grasp of their capabilities and are less likely to set themselves up to fail by, for example, overstretching on assignments. They know, too, when to ask for help. And the risks they take on the job are

calculated. They won't ask for a challenge that they know they can't handle alone. They'll play to their strengths.

Consider the actions of a mid-level employee who was invited to sit in on a strategy meeting with her company's top executives. Although she was the most junior person in the room, she did not sit there quietly, listening in awestruck or fearful silence. She knew she had a head for clear logic and the skill to present ideas persuasively, and she offered cogent suggestions about the company's strategy. At the same time, her self-awareness stopped her from wandering into territory where she knew she was weak.

Despite the value of having self-aware people in the workplace, my research indicates that senior executives don't often give self-awareness the credit it deserves when they look for potential leaders. Many executives mistake candor about feelings for "wimpiness" and fail to give due respect to employees who openly acknowledge their shortcomings. Such people are too readily dismissed as "not tough enough" to lead others.

In fact, the opposite is true. In the first place, people generally admire and respect candor. Further, leaders are constantly required to make judgment calls that require a candid assessment of capabilities—their own and those of others. Do we have the management expertise to acquire a competitor? Can we launch a new product within six months? People who assess themselves honestly—that is, self-aware people—are well suited to do the same for the organizations they run.

Self-Regulation

Biological impulses drive our emotions. We cannot do away with them—but we can do much to manage them. Self-regulation, which is like an ongoing inner conversation, is the component of emotional intelligence that frees us from being prisoners of our feelings. People engaged in such a conversation feel bad moods and emotional impulses just as everyone else does, but they find ways to control them and even to channel them in useful ways.

Imagine an executive who has just watched a team of his employees present a botched analysis to the company's board of directors. In the gloom that follows, the executive might find himself tempted to pound on the table in anger or kick over a chair. He could leap up

Can Emotional Intelligence Be Learned?

For ages, people have debated if leaders are born or made. So too goes the debate about emotional intelligence. Are people born with certain levels of empathy, for example, or do they acquire empathy as a result of life's experiences? The answer is both. Scientific inquiry strongly suggests that there is a genetic component to emotional intelligence. Psychological and developmental research indicates that nurture plays a role as well. How much of each perhaps will never be known, but research and practice clearly demonstrate that emotional intelligence can be learned.

One thing is certain: emotional intelligence increases with age. There is an old-fashioned word for the phenomenon: maturity. Yet even with maturity, some people still need training to enhance their emotional intelligence. Unfortunately, far too many training programs that intend to build leadership skills—including emotional intelligence—are a waste of time and money. The problem is simple: they focus on the wrong part of the brain.

Emotional intelligence is born largely in the neurotransmitters of the brain's limbic system, which governs feelings, impulses, and drives. Research indicates that the limbic system learns best through motivation, extended practice, and feedback. Compare this with the kind of learning that goes on in the neocortex, which governs analytical and technical ability. The neocortex grasps concepts and logic. It is the part of the brain that figures out how to use a computer or make a sales call by reading a book. Not surprisingly—but mistakenly—it is also the part of the brain targeted by most training programs aimed at enhancing emotional intelligence. When such programs take, in effect, a neocortical approach, my research with the Consortium for Research on Emotional Intelligence in Organizations has shown they can even have a *negative* impact on people's job performance.

To enhance emotional intelligence, organizations must refocus their training to include the limbic system. They must help people break old behavioral habits and establish new ones. That not only takes much more time than conventional training programs, it also requires an individualized approach.

Imagine an executive who is thought to be low on empathy by her colleagues. Part of that deficit shows itself as an inability to listen; she interrupts people and doesn't pay close attention to what they're saying. To fix the problem, the executive needs to be motivated to change, and then she needs practice and feedback from others in the company. A colleague or coach could be tapped to let the executive know when she has been observed failing to listen. She would then have to replay the incident and give a better response; that is, demonstrate her ability to absorb what others are saying. And the executive could be directed to observe certain executives who listen well and to mimic their behavior.

With persistence and practice, such a process can lead to lasting results. I know one Wall Street executive who sought to improve his empathy—specifically his ability to read people's reactions and see their perspectives. Before beginning his quest, the executive's subordinates were terrified of working with him. People even went so far as to hide bad news from him. Naturally, he was shocked when finally confronted with these facts. He went home and told his family—but they only confirmed what he had heard at work. When their opinions on any given subject did not mesh with his, they, too, were frightened of him.

Enlisting the help of a coach, the executive went to work to heighten his empathy through practice and feedback. His first step was to take a vacation to a foreign country where he did not speak the language. While there, he monitored his reactions to the unfamiliar and his openness to people who were different from him. When he returned home, humbled by his week abroad, the executive asked his coach to shadow him for parts of the day, several times a week, in order to critique how he treated people with new or different perspectives. At the same time, he consciously used on-the-job interactions as opportunities to practice "hearing" ideas that differed from his. Finally, the executive had himself videotaped in meetings and asked those who worked for and with him to critique his ability to acknowledge and understand the feelings of others. It took several months, but the executive's emotional intelligence did ultimately rise, and the improvement was reflected in his overall performance on the job.

It's important to emphasize that building one's emotional intelligence cannot—will not—happen without sincere desire and concerted effort. A brief seminar won't help; nor can one buy a how-to manual. It is much harder to learn to empathize—to internalize empathy as a natural response to people—than it is to become adept at regression analysis. But it can be done. "Nothing great was ever achieved without enthusiasm," wrote Ralph Waldo Emerson. If your goal is to become a real leader, these words can serve as a guidepost in your efforts to develop high emotional intelligence.

and scream at the group. Or he might maintain a grim silence, glaring at everyone before stalking off.

But if he had a gift for self-regulation, he would choose a different approach. He would pick his words carefully, acknowledging the team's poor performance without rushing to any hasty judgment. He would then step back to consider the reasons for the failure. Are they personal—a lack of effort? Are there any mitigating factors? What was his role in the debacle? After considering these questions, he would call the team together, lay out the incident's consequences, and offer his feelings about it. He would then present his analysis of the problem and a well-considered solution.

Why does self-regulation matter so much for leaders? First of all, people who are in control of their feelings and impulses—that is, people who are reasonable—are able to create an environment of trust and fairness. In such an environment, politics and infighting are sharply reduced and productivity is high. Talented people flock to the organization and aren't tempted to leave. And self-regulation has a trickle-down effect. No one wants to be known as a hothead when the boss is known for her calm approach.

Fewer bad moods at the top mean fewer throughout the organization.

Second, self-regulation is important for competitive reasons. Everyone knows that business today is rife with ambiguity and change. Companies merge and break apart regularly. Technology transforms work at a dizzying pace. People who have mastered their emotions are able to roll with the changes. When a new change program is announced, they don't panic; instead, they are able to suspend judgment, seek out information, and listen to executives explain the new program. As the initiative moves forward, they are able to move with it.

Sometimes they even lead the way. Consider the case of a manager at a large manufacturing company. Like her colleagues, she had used a certain software program for five years. The program drove how she collected and reported data and how she thought about the company's strategy. One day, senior executives announced that a new program was to be installed that would radically change how information was gathered and assessed within the organization. While many people in the company complained bitterly about how disruptive the change would be, the manager mulled over the reasons for the new program and was convinced of its potential to improve performance. She eagerly attended training sessions—some of her colleagues refused to do so—and was eventually promoted to run several divisions, in part because she used the new technology so effectively.

I want to push the importance of self-regulation to leadership even further and make the case that it enhances integrity, which is not only a personal virtue but also an organizational strength. Many of the bad things that happen in companies are a function of impulsive behavior. People rarely plan to exaggerate profits, pad expense accounts, dip into the till, or abuse power for selfish ends. Instead, an opportunity presents itself, and people with low impulse control just say yes.

By contrast, consider the behavior of the senior executive at a large food company. The executive was scrupulously honest in his negotiations with local distributors. He would routinely lay out his cost structure in detail, thereby giving the distributors a realistic understanding of the company's pricing. This approach meant the executive couldn't always drive a hard bargain. Now, on occasion, he felt the urge to increase profits by withholding information about the company's costs. But he challenged that impulse—he saw that it made more sense in the long run to counteract it. His emotional self-regulation paid off in strong, lasting relationships with distributors that benefited the company more than any short-term financial gains would have.

The signs of emotional self-regulation, therefore, are not hard to miss: a propensity for reflection and thoughtfulness; comfort with ambiguity and change; and integrity—an ability to say no to impulsive urges.

Like self-awareness, self-regulation often does not get its due. People who can master their emotions are sometimes seen as cold fish—their considered responses are taken as a lack of passion. People with fiery temperaments are frequently thought of as "classic" leaders—their outbursts are considered hallmarks of charisma and power. But when such people make it to the top, their impulsiveness often works against them. In my research, extreme displays of negative emotion have never emerged as a driver of good leadership.

Motivation

If there is one trait that virtually all effective leaders have, it is motivation. They are driven to achieve beyond expectations—their own and everyone else's. The key word here is *achieve*. Plenty of people are motivated by external factors such as a big salary or the status that comes from having an impressive title or being part of a prestigious company. By contrast, those with leadership potential are motivated by a deeply embedded desire to achieve for the sake of achievement.

If you are looking for leaders, how can you identify people who are motivated by the drive to achieve rather than by external rewards? The first sign is a passion for the work itself—such people seek out creative challenges, love to learn, and take great pride in a job well done. They also display an unflagging energy to do things better. People with such energy often seem restless with the status quo. They are persistent with their questions about why things are done one way rather than another; they are eager to explore new approaches to their work.

A cosmetics company manager, for example, was frustrated that he had to wait two weeks to get sales results from people in the field. He finally tracked down an automated phone system that would beep each of his salespeople at 5 p.m. every day. An automated message then prompted them to punch in their numbers—how many calls and sales they had made that day. The system shortened the feedback time on sales results from weeks to hours.

That story illustrates two other common traits of people who are driven to achieve. They are forever raising the performance bar, and they like to keep score. Take the performance bar first.

During performance reviews, people with high levels of motivation might ask to be "stretched" by their superiors. Of course, an employee who combines self-awareness with internal motivation will recognize her limits—but she won't settle for objectives that seem too easy to fulfill.

And it follows naturally that people who are driven to do better also want a way of tracking progress—their own, their team's, and their company's. Whereas people with low achievement motivation are often fuzzy about results, those with high achievement motivation often keep score by tracking such hard measures as profitability or market share. I know of a money manager who starts and ends his day on the Internet, gauging the performance of his stock fund against four industry-set benchmarks.

Interestingly, people with high motivation remain optimistic even when the score is against them. In such cases, self-regulation combines with achievement motivation to overcome the frustration and depression that come after a setback or failure. Take the case of another portfolio manager at a large investment company. After several successful years, her fund tumbled for three consecutive quarters, leading three large institutional clients to shift their business elsewhere.

Some executives would have blamed the nosedive on circumstances outside their control; others might have seen the setback as evidence of personal failure. This portfolio manager, however, saw an opportunity to prove she could lead a turnaround. Two years later, when she was promoted to a very senior level in the company, she described the experience as "the best thing that ever happened to me; I learned so much from it."

Executives trying to recognize high levels of achievement motivation in their people can look for one last piece of evidence: commitment to the organization. When people love their job for the work itself, they often feel committed to the organizations that make that work possible. Committed employees are likely to stay with an organization even when they are pursued by headhunters waving money.

It's not difficult to understand how and why a motivation to achieve translates into strong leadership. If you set the performance bar high for yourself, you will do the same for the organization when you are in a position to do so. Likewise, a drive to surpass goals and an interest in keeping score can be contagious. Leaders with these traits can often build a team of managers around them with the same traits. And of course, optimism and organizational commitment are

The very word *empathy* seems unbusinesslike, out of place amid the tough realities of the marketplace.

fundamental to leadership—just try to imagine running a company without them.

Empathy

Of all the dimensions of emotional intelligence, empathy is the most easily recognized. We have all felt the empathy of a sensitive teacher or friend; we have all been struck by its absence in an unfeeling coach or boss. But when it comes to business, we rarely hear people praised, let alone rewarded, for their empathy. The very word seems unbusinesslike, out of place amid the tough realities of the marketplace.

But empathy doesn't mean a kind of "I'm okay, you're okay" mushiness. For a leader, that is, it doesn't mean adopting other people's emotions as one's own and trying to please everybody. That would be a nightmare—it would make action impossible. Rather, empathy means thoughtfully considering employees' feelings—along with other factors—in the process of making intelligent decisions.

For an example of empathy in action, consider what happened when two giant brokerage companies merged, creating redundant jobs in all their divisions. One division manager called his people together and gave a gloomy speech that emphasized the number of people who would soon be fired. The manager of another division gave his people a different kind of speech. He was upfront about his own worry and confusion, and he promised to keep people informed and to treat everyone fairly.

The difference between these two managers was empathy. The first manager was too worried about his own fate to consider the feelings of his anxiety-stricken colleagues. The second knew intuitively what his people were feeling, and he acknowledged their fears with his words. Is it any surprise that the first manager saw his division sink as many demoralized people, especially the most talented, departed? By contrast, the second manager continued to be a strong leader, his best people stayed, and his division remained as productive as ever.

Empathy is particularly important today as a component of leadership for at least three reasons:

the increasing use of teams; the rapid pace of globalization; and the growing need to retain talent.

Consider the challenge of leading a team. As anyone who has ever been a part of one can attest, teams are cauldrons of bubbling emotions. They are often charged with reaching a consensus—hard enough with two people and much more difficult as the numbers increase. Even in groups with as few as four or five members, alliances form and clashing agendas get set. A team's leader must be able to sense and understand the viewpoints of everyone around the table.

Social skill is friendliness with a purpose: moving people in the direction you desire.

That's exactly what a marketing manager at a large information technology company was able to do when she was appointed to lead a troubled team. The group was in turmoil, overloaded by work and missing deadlines. Tensions were high among the members. Tinkering with procedures was not enough to bring the group together and make it an effective part of the company.

So the manager took several steps. In a series of one-on-one sessions, she took the time to listen to everyone in the group—what was frustrating them, how they rated their colleagues, whether they felt they had been ignored. And then she directed the team in a way that brought it together: she encouraged people to speak more openly about their frustrations, and she helped people raise constructive complaints during meetings. In short, her empathy allowed her to understand her team's emotional makeup. The result was not just heightened collaboration among members but also added business, as the team was called on for help by a wider range of internal clients.

Globalization is another reason for the rising importance of empathy for business leaders. Cross-cultural dialogue can easily lead to miscues and misunderstandings. Empathy is an antidote. People who have it are attuned to subtleties in body language; they can hear the message beneath the words being spoken. Beyond that, they have a deep understanding of the existence and importance of cultural and ethnic differences.

Consider the case of an American consultant whose team had just pitched a project to a potential Japanese client. In its dealings with Americans, the team was accustomed to being bombarded with questions after such a proposal,

but this time it was greeted with a long silence. Other members of the team, taking the silence as disapproval, were ready to pack and leave. The lead consultant gestured them to stop. Although he was not particularly familiar with Japanese culture, he read the client's face and posture and sensed not rejection but interest—even deep consideration. He was right: when the client finally spoke, it was to give the consulting firm the job.

Finally, empathy plays a key role in the retention of talent, particularly in today's information economy. Leaders have always needed empathy to develop and keep good people, but today the stakes are higher. When good people leave, they take the company's knowledge with them.

That's where coaching and mentoring come in. It has repeatedly been shown that coaching and mentoring pay off not just in better performance but also in increased job satisfaction and decreased turnover. But what makes coaching and mentoring work best is the nature of the relationship. Outstanding coaches and mentors get inside the heads of the people they are helping. They sense how to give effective feedback. They know when to push for better performance and when to hold back. In the way they motivate their protégés, they demonstrate empathy in action.

In what is probably sounding like a refrain, let me repeat that empathy doesn't get much respect in business. People wonder how leaders can make hard decisions if they are "feeling" for all the people who will be affected. But leaders with empathy do more than sympathize with people around them: they use their knowledge to improve their companies in subtle but important ways.

Social Skill

The first three components of emotional intelligence are all self-management skills. The last two, empathy and social skill, concern a person's ability to manage relationships with others. As a component of emotional intelligence, social skill is not as simple as it sounds. It's not just a matter of friendliness, although people with high levels of social skill are rarely mean-spirited. Social skill, rather, is friendliness with a purpose: moving people in the direction you desire, whether that's agreement on a new marketing strategy or enthusiasm about a new product.

Socially skilled people tend to have a wide circle of acquaintances, and they have a knack for finding common ground with people of all kinds—a knack for building rapport. That doesn't mean they socialize continually; it means they work according to the assumption that nothing important gets done alone. Such people have a network in place when the time for action comes.

Social skill is the culmination of the other dimensions of emotional intelligence. People tend to be very effective at managing relationships when they can understand and control their own emotions and can empathize with the feelings of others. Even motivation contributes to social skill. Remember that people who are driven to achieve tend to be optimistic, even in the face of setbacks or failure. When people are upbeat, their "glow" is cast upon conversations and other social encounters. They are popular, and for good reason.

Because it is the outcome of the other dimensions of emotional intelligence, social skill is recognizable on the job in many ways that will by now sound familiar. Socially skilled people, for instance, are adept at managing teams—that's their empathy at work. Likewise, they are expert persuaders—a manifestation of self-awareness, self-regulation, and empathy combined. Given those skills, good persuaders know when to make an emotional plea, for instance, and when an appeal to reason will work better. And motivation, when publicly visible, makes such people excellent collaborators; their passion for the work spreads to others, and they are driven to find solutions.

But sometimes social skill shows itself in ways the other emotional intelligence components do not. For instance, socially skilled people may at times appear not to be working while at work. They seem to be idly schmoozing—chatting in the hallways with colleagues or joking around with people who are not even connected to their "real" jobs. Socially skilled people, however, don't think it makes sense to arbitrarily limit the scope of their relationships. They build bonds widely because they know that in these fluid times, they may need help someday from people they are just getting to know today.

For example, consider the case of an executive in the strategy department of a global computer manufacturer. By 1993, he was convinced that the company's future lay with the Internet. Over the course of the next year, he found kindred spirits and used his social skill to stitch together a virtual community that cut across levels, divisions, and nations. He then used this de facto team to put up a corporate Web site, among the first by a major company. And, on his own initiative, with no budget or formal status, he signed up the company to participate in an annual Internet industry convention. Calling on his allies and persuading various divisions to donate funds, he recruited more than 50 people from a dozen different units to represent the company at the convention.

Emotional intelligence can be learned. The process is not easy. It takes time and commitment.

Management took notice: within a year of the conference, the executive's team formed the basis for the company's first Internet division, and he was formally put in charge of it. To get there, the executive had ignored conventional boundaries, forging and maintaining connections with people in every corner of the organization.

Is social skill considered a key leadership capability in most companies? The answer is yes, especially when compared with the other components of emotional intelligence. People seem to know intuitively that leaders need to manage relationships effectively; no leader is an island. After all, the leader's task is to get work done through other people, and social skill makes that possible. A leader who cannot express her empathy may as well not have it at all. And a leader's motivation will be useless if he cannot communicate his passion to the organization. Social skill allows leaders to put their emotional intelligence to work.

It would be foolish to assert that good-old-fashioned IQ and technical ability are not important ingredients in strong leadership. But the recipe would not be complete without emotional intelligence. It was once thought that the components of emotional intelligence were "nice to have" in business leaders. But now we know that, for the sake of performance, these are ingredients that leaders "need to have."

It is fortunate, then, that emotional intelligence can be learned. The process is not easy. It takes time and, most of all, commitment. But the benefits that come from having a well-developed emotional intelligence, both for the individual and for the organization, make it worth the effort.

Reducing Prejudice: Combating Intergroup Biases

John F. Dovidio[1] and Samuel L. Gaertner

Department of Psychology, Colgate University, Hamilton, New York (J.F.D.), and Department of Psychology, University of Delaware, Newark, Delaware (S.L.G.)

Abstract

Strategies for reducing prejudice may be directed at the traditional, intentional form of prejudice or at more subtle and perhaps less conscious contemporary forms. Whereas the traditional form of prejudice may be reduced by direct educational and attitude-change techniques, contemporary forms may require alternative strategies oriented toward the individual or involving intergroup contact. Individual-oriented techniques can involve leading people who possess contemporary prejudices to discover inconsistencies among their self-images, values, and behaviors such inconsistencies can arouse negative emotional states (e.g., guilt), which motivate the development of more favorable attitudes. Intergroup strategies can involve structuring intergroup contact to produce more individualized perceptions of the members of the other group, foster personalized interactions between members of the different groups, or redefine group boundaries to create more inclusive, superordinate representations of the groups. Understanding the nature and bases of prejudice can thus guide, theoretically and pragmatically, interventions that can effectively reduce both traditional and contemporary forms of prejudice.

Keywords

attitude change; intergroup contact; prejudice; racism; social categorization

Prejudice is commonly defined as an unfair negative attitude toward a social group or a member of that group. Stereotypes, which are overgeneralizations about a group or its members that are factually incorrect and inordinately rigid, are a set of beliefs that can accompany the negative feelings associated with prejudice. Traditional approaches consider prejudice, like other attitudes, to be acquired through socialization and supported by the beliefs, attitudes, and values of friends and peer groups (see Jones, 1997). We consider the nature of traditional and contemporary forms of prejudice, particularly racial prejudice, and review a range of techniques that have been demonstrated empirically to reduce prejudice and other forms of intergroup bias. Bias can occur in many forms, and thus it has been assessed by a range of measures. These measures include standardized tests of prejudice toward another social group, stereotypes, evaluations of and feelings about the group in general, support for policies and individual actions benefiting the other group, and interaction and friendship patterns.

In part because of changing norms and the Civil Rights Act and other legislative interventions that made discrimination not simply immoral but also illegal, overt expressions of prejudice have declined significantly over the past 35 years. Contemporary forms of prejudice, however, continue to exist and affect the lives of people in subtle but significant ways (Dovidio & Gaertner, 1998; Gaertner & Dovidio, 1986). The negative feelings and beliefs that underlie contemporary forms of prejudice may be rooted in either individual processes (such as cognitive and motivational biases and socialization) or intergroup processes (such as realistic group conflict or biases associated with the mere categorization of people into in-groups and out-groups). These negative biases may occur spontaneously, automatically, and without full awareness.

Many contemporary approaches to prejudice based on race, ethnicity, or sex acknowledge the persistence of overt, intentional forms of prejudice but also consider the role of these automatic or unconscious processes[2] and the consequent indirect expressions of bias. With respect to the racial prejudice of white Americans toward blacks, for example, in contrast to "old-fashioned" racism, which is blatant, aversive racism represents a subtle, often unintentional, form of bias that characterizes many white Americans who possess strong egalitarian values and who believe that they are nonprejudiced. Aversive racists also possess negative racial feelings and beliefs (which develop through normal socialization or reflect social-categorization biases) that they are unaware of or that they try to dissociate from their nonprejudiced self-images. Because aversive racists consciously endorse egalitarian values, they will not discriminate directly and openly in ways that can be attributed to racism; however, because of their negative feelings, they will discriminate, often unintentionally, when their behavior can be justified on the basis of some factor other than race (e.g., questionable qualifications for a position). Thus, aversive racists may regularly engage in discrimination while they maintain self-images of being nonprejudiced. According to symbolic racism theory, a related perspective

From *Current Directions in Psychological Science*, August 1999, pp. 101-105. © 1999 by the American Psychological Society. Reprinted by permission of Blackwell Publishers.

that has emphasized the role of politically conservative rather than liberal ideology (Sears, 1988), negative feelings toward blacks that whites acquire early in life persist into adulthood but are expressed indirectly and symbolically, in terms of opposition to busing or resistance to preferential treatment, rather than directly or overtly, as in support for segregation.

Contemporary expressions of bias may also reflect a dissociation between cultural stereotypes, which develop through common socialization experiences and because of repeated exposure generally become automatically activated, and individual differences in prejudicial motivations. Although whites both high and low in prejudice may be equally aware of cultural stereotypes and show similar levels of automatic activation, only those low in prejudice make a conscious attempt to prevent those negative stereotypes from influencing their behavior (Devine & Monteith, 1993).

INDIVIDUAL PROCESSES AND PREJUDICE REDUCTION

Attempts to reduce the direct, traditional form of racial prejudice typically involve educational strategies to enhance knowledge and appreciation of other groups (e.g., multicultural education programs), emphasize norms that prejudice is wrong, and involve direct persuasive strategies (e.g., mass media appeals) or indirect attitude-change techniques that make people aware of inconsistencies in their attitudes and behaviors (Stephan & Stephan, 1984). Other techniques are aimed at changing or diluting stereotypes by presenting counter-stereotypic or nonstereotypic information about group members. Providing stereotype-disconfirming information is more effective when the information concerns a broad range of group members who are otherwise typical of their group rather than when the information concerns a single person who is not a prototypical representative of the group. In the latter case, people are likely to maintain their overall stereotype of the group while subtyping, with another stereotype, group members who disconfirm the general group stereotype (e.g., black athletes; Hewstone, 1996). The effectiveness of multicultural education programs is supported by the results of controlled intervention programs in the real world; evidence of the effectiveness of attitude- and stereotype-change approaches, and the hypothesized underlying processes, comes largely (but not exclusively) from experimental laboratory research.

Approaches for dealing with the traditional form of prejudice are generally less effective for combating the contemporary forms. With respect to contemporary racism, for example, whites already consciously endorse egalitarian, nonprejudiced views and disavow traditional stereotypes. Instead, indirect strategies that benefit from people's genuine motivation to be nonprejudiced may be more effective for reducing contemporary forms of prejudice. For example, techniques that lead people who possess contemporary prejudices to discover inconsistencies among their self-images, values, and behaviors may arouse feelings of guilt, tension about the inconsistencies, or other negative emotional states that can motivate the development of more favorable racial attitudes and produce more favorable intergroup behaviors (even nonverbal behaviors) several months later. Also, people who consciously endorse nonprejudiced attitudes, but whose behaviors may reflect racial bias, commonly experience feelings of guilt and compunction when they become aware of discrepancies between their potential behavior toward minorities (i.e., what they *would* do) and their personal standards (i.e., what they *should* do) during laboratory interventions. These emotional reactions, in turn, can motivate people to control subsequent spontaneous stereotypical responses and behave more favorably in the future (Devine & Monteith, 1993). People's conscious efforts to suppress stereotypically biased reactions can inhibit even the immediate activation of normally automatic associations, and with sufficient practice, these efforts can eliminate automatic stereotype activation over the long term.

Approaches oriented toward the individual, however, are not the only way to combat contemporary forms of prejudice. Strategies that emphasize intergroup processes, such as intergroup contact and social categorization and identity, are alternative, complementary approaches.

INTERGROUP CONTACT

Real-world interventions, laboratory studies, and survey studies have demonstrated that intergroup contact under specified conditions (including equal status between the groups, cooperative intergroup interactions, opportunities for personal acquaintance, and supportive egalitarian norms) is a powerful technique for reducing intergroup bias and conflict (Pettigrew, 1998). Drawing on these principles, cooperative learning and "jigsaw" classroom interventions (Aronson & Patnoe, 1997) are designed

to increase interdependence between members of different groups working on a designated problem-solving task and to enhance appreciation for the resources they bring to the task. Cooperation is effective for reducing subsequent intergroup bias when the task is completed successfully, group contributions to solving the problem are seen as different or complementary, and the interaction among participants during the task is friendly, personal, and supportive.

Recent research has attempted to elucidate how the different factors of intergroup contact (e.g., cooperation, personal interaction) operate to reduce bias. Engaging in activities to achieve common, superordinate goals, for instance, changes the functional relations between groups from actual or symbolic competition to cooperation. Through psychological processes to restore cognitive balance or reduce inconsistency between actions and attitudes, attitudes toward members of the other group and toward the group as a whole may improve to be consistent with the positive nature of the interaction. Also, the rewarding properties of achieving success may become associated with members of other groups, thereby increasing attraction.

SOCIAL CATEGORIZATION AND IDENTITY

Factors of intergroup contact, such as cooperation, may also reduce bias through reducing the salience of the intergroup boundaries, that is, through *decategorization*. According to this perspective, interaction during intergroup contact can individuate members of the out-group by revealing variability in their opinions (Wilder, 1986) or can produce interactions in which people are seen as unique individuals (personalization), with the exchange of intimate information (Brewer & Miller, 1984). Alternatively, intergroup contact may be structured to maintain but alter the nature of group boundaries, that is, to produce *recategorization*. One recategorization approach involves either creating or increasing the salience of cross cutting group memberships. Making interactants aware that members of another group are also members of one's own group when groups are defined by a different dimension can improve intergroup attitudes (Urban & Miller, 1998). Another recategorization strategy, represented by our own work on the Common In-Group Identity Model, involves interventions to change people's conceptions of groups, so that they think of membership not in terms of several different groups, but in terms of one, more inclusive group

Conditions of Contact	Representational Mediators	Consequences
Intergroup Interdependence (e.g., cooperation)	*One Group* Recategorization ("We")	Cognitive Effects (e.g., stereotyping)
Group Differentiation (e.g., similarity)	*Two Subgroups in One Group* Recategorization ("Us+Them=We")	Affective Consequences (e.g., empathy)
Environmental Context (e.g., egalitarian norms)	*Two Groups* Categorization ("We/They")	
Pre-Contact Experience (e.g., affective priming)	*Separate Individuals* Decategorization ("Me/You")	Behavioral Effects (e.g., helping)

FIG. 1. The Common In-Group Identity Model. In this model, elements of an intergroup contact situation (e.g., intergroup interdependence) influence cognitive representations of the groups as one superordinate group (recategorization), as two subgroups in one group (recategorization involving a dual identity), as two groups (categorization), or as separate individuals (decategorization). Recategorization and decategorization, in turn, can both reduce cognitive, affective, and behavioral biases, but in different ways. Recategorization reduces bias by extending the benefits of in-group favoritism to former out-group members. Attitudes and behavior toward these former out-group members thus become more favorable, approaching attitudes and behaviors toward in-group members. Decategorization, in contrast, reduces favoritism toward original in-group members as they become perceived as separate individuals rather than members of one's own group.

(Gaertner, Dovidio, Anastasio, Bachman, & Rust, 1993).

The Common In-Group Identity Model recognizes the central role of social categorization in reducing as well as in creating intergroup bias (Tajfel & Turner, 1979). Specifically, if members of different groups are induced to conceive of themselves more as members of a single, superordinate group rather than as members of two separate groups, attitudes toward former out-group members will become more positive through processes involving pro-in-group bias. Thus, changing the basis of categorization from race to an alternative dimension can alter who is a "we" and who is a "they," undermining a contributing force to contemporary forms of racism, such as aversive racism. The development of a superordinate identity does not always require people to abandon their previous group identities; they may possess dual identities, conceiving of themselves as belonging both to the superordinate group and to one of the original two groups included within the new, larger group. The model also recognizes that decategorization (seeing people as separate individuals) can also reduce bias. In contrast, perceptions of the groups as

different entities (we/they) maintains and reinforces bias. The Common In-Group Identity Model is presented schematically in Figure 1.

In experiments in the laboratory and in the field, and in surveys in natural settings (a multi-ethnic high school, banking mergers, and blended families), we have found evidence consistent with the Common In-Group Identity Model and the hypothesis that intergroup contact can reduce prejudice. Specifically, we have found that key aspects of intergroup contact, such as cooperation, decrease intergroup bias in part through changing cognitive representations of the groups. The development of a common ingroup identity also facilitates helping behaviors and self-disclosing interactions that can produce reciprocally positive responses and that can further reduce intergroup prejudices through other mechanisms such as personalization.

Moreover, the development of a common in-group identity does not necessarily require groups to forsake their original identities. Threats to important personal identities or the "positive distinctiveness" of one's group can, in fact, exacerbate intergroup prejudices. The development of a dual identity (two sub-

groups in one group; see Fig. 1), in which original and superordinate group memberships are simultaneously salient, is explicitly considered in the model. Even when racial or ethnic identity is strong, perceptions of a superordinate connection enhance interracial trust and acceptance. Indeed, the development of a dual identity, in terms of a bicultural or multicultural identity, not only is possible but can contribute to the social adjustment, psychological adaptation, and overall well-being of minority-group members (LaFromboise, Coleman, & Gerton, 1993). Recognizing both different and common group membership, a more complex form of a common in-group identity, may also increase the generalizability of the benefits of intergroup contact for prejudice reduction. The development of a common in-group identity contributes to more positive attitudes toward members of other groups present in the contact situation, whereas recognition of the separate group memberships provides the associative link by which these more positive attitudes may generalize to other members of the groups not directly involved in the contact situation.

CONCLUSION

Prejudice can occur in its blatant, traditional form, or it may be rooted in unconscious and automatic negative feelings and beliefs that characterize contemporary forms. Whereas the traditional form of prejudice may be combated by using direct techniques involving attitude change and education, addressing contemporary forms requires alternative strategies. Individual-level strategies engage the genuine motivations of people to be nonprejudiced. Intergroup approaches focus on realistic group conflict or the psychological effects of categorizing people into in-groups and out-groups. The benefits of intergroup contact can occur through many routes, such as producing more individualated perceptions of out-group members and more personalized relationships. Intergroup contact can also produce more inclusive, superordinate representations of the groups, which can harness the psychological forces that contribute to intergroup bias and redirect them to improve attitudes toward people who would otherwise be recognized only as out-group members. Understanding the processes involved in the nature and development of prejudice can thus guide, both theoretically and pragmatically, interventions that can effectively reduce both traditional and contemporary forms of prejudice.

Recommended Reading

Brewer, M. B., & Miller, N. (1996). *Intergroup relations.* Pacific Grove, CA: Brooks/Cole.

Brown, R. J. (1995). *Prejudice.* Cambridge, MA: Blackwell.

Hawley, W. D., & Jackson, A. W. (Eds.). (1995). *Toward a common destiny: Improving race and ethnic relations in America.* San Francisco: Jossey-Bass.

Landis, D., & Bhagat, R. S. (Eds.). (1996). *Handbook of intercultural training.* Thousand Oaks, CA: Sage.

Stephan, W. G., & Stephan, C. W. (1996). *Intergroup relations.* Boulder, CO: Westview Press.

Acknowledgments—Preparation of this article was facilitated by National Institute of Mental Health Grant MH 48721.

Notes

1. Address correspondence to John F. Dovidio, Department of Psychology, Colgate University, Hamilton, NY 13346; e-mail: jdovidio@mail.colgate.edu.

2. For further information and a demonstration in which you can test the automaticity of your own racial attitudes using the Implicit Association Test, see Anthony Greenwald's World Wide Web site: http://weber.u.washington.edu/~agg/ (e-mail: agg@u.washington.edu).

References

Aronson, E., & Patnoe, S. (1997). *The jigsaw classroom.* New York: Longman.

Brewer, M. B., & Miller, N. (1984). Beyond the contact hypothesis: Theoretical perspectives on desegregation. In N. Miller & M. B. Brewer (Eds.), *Groups in contact: The psychology of desegregation* (pp. 281–302). Orlando, FL: Academic Press.

Devine, P. G., & Monteith, M. J. (1993). The role of discrepancy-associated affect in prejudice reduction. In D. M. Mackie & D. L. Hamilton (Eds.), *Affect, cognition, and stereotyping: Interactive processes in intergroup perception* (pp. 317–344). Orlando, FL: Academic Press.

Dovidio, J. F., & Gaertner, S. L. (1998). On the nature of contemporary prejudice: The causes, consequences, and challenges of aversive racism. In J. Eberhardt & S. T. Fiske (Eds.), *Confronting racism: The problem and the response* (pp. 3–32). Newbury Park, CA: Sage.

Gaertner, S. L., & Dovidio, J. F. (1986). The aversive form of racism. In J. F. Dovidio & S. L. Gaertner (Eds.), *Prejudice, discrimination, and racism* (pp. 61–89). Orlando, FL: Academic Press.

Gaertner, S. L., Dovidio, J. F., Anastasio, P. A., Bachman, B. A., & Rust, M. C. (1993). The Common Ingroup Identity Model: Recategorization and the reduction of intergroup bias. In W. Stroebe & M. Hewstone (Eds.), *European review of social psychology* (Vol. 4, pp. 1–26). London: Wiley.

Hewstone, M. (1996). Contact and categorization: Social psychological interventions to change intergroup relations. In N. Macrae, M. Hewstone, & C. Stangor (Eds.), *Foundations of stereotypes and stereotyping* (pp. 323–368). New York: Guilford Press.

Jones, J. M. (1997). *Prejudice and racism* (2nd ed.). New York: McGraw-Hill.

LaFromboise, T., Coleman, H. L. K., & Gerton, J. (1993). Psychological impact of biculturalism: Evidence and theory. *Psychological Bulletin, 114,* 395–412.

Pettigrew, T. F. (1998). Intergroup Contact Theory. *Annual Review of Psychology, 49,* 65–85.

Sears, D. O. (1988). Symbolic racism. In P. A. Katz & D. A. Taylor (Eds.), *Eliminating racism: Profiles in controversy* (pp. 53–84). New York: Plenum Press.

Stephan, W. G., & Stephan, C. W. (1984). The role of ignorance in intergroup relations. In N. Miller & M. B. Brewer (Eds.), *Groups in contact: The psychology of desegregation* (pp. 229–257). Orlando, FL: Academic Press.

Tajfel, H., & Turner, J. C. (1979). An integrative theory of intergroup conflict. In W. G. Austin & S. Worchel (Eds.), *The social psychology of intergroup relations* (pp. 33–48). Monterey, CA: Brooks/Cole.

Urban, L. M., & Miller, N. (1998). A theoretical analysis of crossed categorization effects: A meta-analysis. *Journal of Personality and Social Psychology, 74,* 894–908.

Wilder, D. A. (1986). Social categorization: Implications for creation and reduction of intergroup bias. In L. Berkowitz (Ed.), *Advances in experimental social psychology* (Vol. 19, pp. 291–355). Orlando, FL: Academic Press.

Psychologist links video games, violence

H. J. Cummins

It was his career turn from soldier to psychologist that helped David Grossman assemble his answer to the mystery of murderous children.

Like most Americans, Mr. Grossman has been tracking the homicide headlines: In Burlington, Wis., five students' plans for a killing spree were foiled; in Springfield, Ore., the 26 victims of Kip Kinkel weren't so lucky; and in a Jonesboro, Ark., schoolyard, two boys started sniping during a fake fire drill, killing five and wounding 10.

Mr. Grossman lives in Jonesboro.

Suddenly, it seemed so clear: This is happening because we are training our children to kill, he concluded. The training device extraordinaire, in his view, is none other than video games, the kind found on home computers and in mall arcades all across the country.

Mr. Grossman's background brings new meaning to the idea of "war games." His theory is startling, and there are plenty who disagree. But Mr. Grossman believes that every video game that rewards children for shooting characters on their video screens—shooting more quickly than they can think—is no different from the kind of reflex training that armies across the world use to improve their "kill" rates.

"Military training is a powerful thing," he says, "and that's exactly what kids are getting when they play the point-and-shoot games."

Mr. Grossman retired from the Army last February as a lieutenant colonel. He teaches psychology at Arkansas State University and directs his Killology Research Group in Jonesboro.

He describes "killology" as the scholarly study of killing, including how people can be trained to kill or trained not to kill. It's a subject he has explored in magazine articles and his book "On Killing: The Psychological Cost of Learning to Kill in War and Society," published by Little, Brown and Co. in 1996.

These are his basic points:

Throughout military history, the difficulty with soldiers has not been teaching them how to use a weapon; it has been persuading them to use it. That's because people, like most animals, resist killing their own kind.

After the Civil War Battle of Gettysburg, 90 percent of the 27,000 muskets taken from the dead and dying were loaded—most with multiple charges. That's evidence that the soldiers would load their weapons but would not shoot.

The U.S. Army did some organized research during World War II and discovered a "kill" rate of only 15 percent among its battle soldiers. That means that for every 100 soldiers who got a clear shot at the enemy, only 15 actually fired.

"From the military perspective, a 15 percent firing rate among riflemen is like a 15 percent literacy rate among librarians," Mr. Grossman says.

Modern militaries concluded they had to find some way to overcome this human impulse against killing. They turned to something called "operant conditioning," a process of stimulus-response-stimulus-response-stimulus-response that, through hundreds of repetitions, conditions a person to do just as the trainer wants without thinking, simply as a reflex.

In the military, the operant conditioning took the form of sophisticated target practice: first with bull's-eye targets, then human silhouettes, then pop-up human forms and finally with video simulations of combat.

Mr. Grossman says that all helped raise U.S. military kill rates to 55 percent by the Korean War and 90 percent by the war in Vietnam.

What does this have to do with video games?

Some of them are no different from the military simulators, he says. Quarter after quarter, game after game, the play is the same stimulus- response process that conditions soldiers to shoot people.

In some ways, Mr. Grossman says, video games are worse.

"At least the military puts up some important safeguards," he says. "The Army also teaches soldiers when not to shoot. When you pick up a gun, you only fire when the guy in the tower tells you to fire and only in the direction he tells you. Otherwise, those drill sergeants are all over you.

"But with video games, you never put a quarter in that machine and then not shoot."

There's plenty of research on the effects of media violence generally, but it comes down to a story of dueling data.

One question is how often youngsters play the most violent video games. A video industry group, the Interactive Digital Software Association, says a big audience for videos is not youngsters, it's adults: In three-fourths of the households it surveyed, the person who spent the most time playing video games was older than 18.

But in a survey of 900 fourth-through eighth-graders often cited in medical journals, almost half the youngsters said their favorite games involved human violence or "fantasy" violence.

Another question is how much violence in any media can turn youngsters violent. Research published in the Journal of the American Medical Association shows that children generally become more aggressive after viewing violent material.

But the software association's president, Doug Lowenstein, cautions against certain assumptions based on that. "There is a profound difference between running around your house and pretending you're killing aliens and going into a schoolyard and killing students," he says.

He also argues that there are other, clearer causes for violence in youngsters. And, in fact, national studies have linked youth violence most directly to access to guns, drug and alcohol use, and recent suicides within the family.

At the National Crime Prevention Council in Washington, Executive Deputy Director James Copple says the current evidence is basically backward. In other words, research shows that youngsters who have committed violent acts have on average watched more television and played more video games, Mr. Copple says. But there's no definitive research going forward in time—that is, demonstrating that exposure to violence turns average youngsters violent.

The correlation is significant and warrants more research, he says, "but from a scientific perspective, you're hard-pressed at this point to make claims of a direct connection."

Key Points to Consider

❖ Do you believe that everyone has the potential for developing a mental disorder? What circumstances lead an individual to mental illness? Do you think that mental disorders are biologically or psychologically induced? If we discover that most mental disorders are caused by something physiological, do you think mental disorders will remain the purview of psychology? Why? If they are biological, do you think they might somehow be contagious?

❖ What is anxiety? How is an anxiety disorder different from everyday anxiety? What happens to individuals who suffer from massive doses of anxiety? What are the causes of anxiety disorder? What are some possible treatments for anxiety disorders? How can we tame normal anxiety? What means do we have to control intense anxiety?

❖ How pervasive is stress in Americans' lives? What are the physical and psychological consequences of stress? What concrete techniques can we utilize to minimize or manage stress? What role can social support from others play in helping us cope with stress? What do psychologists mean by resiliency? How do resilient individuals differ in their responses to stress compared to other individuals?

❖ What is dysthymia? Does it differ from depression? If so, how? What treatments are available for individuals who suffer from dysthymia?

❖ Why do individuals commit suicide? Is suicide a pervasive problem in the United States? Who is most likely to commit suicide? When is suicide contagious? What is a media-inspired suicide? How does it differ from a point-cluster suicide?

❖ What is obsessive-compulsive disorder? Do you have any obsessions; why and about what do you obsess? Do you think this is normal? What are the treatments for obsessive-compulsive disorder?

 **Links**   **www.dushkin.com/online/**

These sites are annotated on pages 4 and 5.

Jay and Harry were two brothers who owned a service station. They were the middle children of four. The other two children were sisters, the oldest of whom had married and moved out of the family home. The service station was once owned by their father who retired and turned the business over to his sons.

Harry and Jay had a good working relationship. Harry was the "up-front" man. Taking customer orders, accepting payments, and working with parts distributors, Harry was the individual who dealt most directly with the customers and others. Jay worked behind the scenes. While Harry made the mechanical diagnoses, Jay was the one who did the corrective work. Some of his friends thought Jay was a mechanical genius.

Preferring to spend time by himself, Jay had always been a little odd and a bit of a loner. His emotions had been more inappropriate and intense than other people's. Harry was the stalwart in the family. He was the acknowledged leader and decision maker when it came to family finances.

One day Jay did not show up for work on time. When he did, he was dressed in the most garish outfit and was laughing hysterically and talking to himself. Harry at first suspected that his brother had taken some illegal drugs. However, Jay's condition persisted. Out of concern, his family took him to the their physician who immediately sent Jay and his family to a psychiatrist. The diagnosis—schizophrenia. Jay's uncle had also been schizophrenic. The family grimly left the psychiatrist's office. After several other appointments with the psychiatrist, they traveled to the local pharmacy to fill a prescription for antipsychotic medications that Jay would probably have to take for the rest of his life.

What caused Jay's drastic and rather sudden change in mental health? Was Jay destined to be schizophrenic because of his family genes? Did competitiveness with his brother and the feeling that he was a less-revered family member than Harry cause Jay's descent into mental disorder? How can psychiatrists and clinical psychologists make accurate diagnoses? Once a diagnosis of mental disorder is made, can the individual ever completely recover?

These and other questions are the emphasis in this unit. Mental disorder has fascinated and, on the other hand, terrified us for centuries. At various times in our history, those who suffered from these disorders were persecuted as witches, tortured to drive out possessing spirits, punished as sinners, jailed as a danger to society, confined to insane asylums, or, at best, hospitalized for simply being too ill to care for themselves.

Today, psychologists propose that the view of mental disorders as "illnesses" has outlived its usefulness. We should think of mental disorders as either biochemical disturbances or disorders of learning in which the person develops a maladaptive pattern of behavior that is then maintained by an inappropriate environment. At the same time, we need to recognize that these reactions to stressors in the environment or to the inappropriate learning situations may be genetically preordained; some people may more easily develop the disorders than others. Serious disorders are serious problems and not just for the individual who is the patient or client. The impact of mental disorders on the family (just as for Jay's family) and friends deserves our full attention, too. Diagnosis, treatment, and the implications of the disorders are covered in some of the articles in this section. Unit 11 will further explore the treatment of mental disorders.

The first two articles in this unit offer a general introduction to the concept of mental disorder and its causes. The first article is about chronic anxiety. Anxiety seems to underlie much emotional disturbance. Anxiety disorders can be compounded by depression. How to recognize and treat anxiety disorders is the focus of this article. In the second article, Jerry Adler discusses stress. Stress plagues many Americans in their daily lives. With each decade life seems to become more stressful. Stress, along with anxiety, adds to the potential for emotional disorder. Once again, the author helps us understand how to overcome or manage stress.

We turn next to some specific problems of mental health. The first is dysthymia, a chronic form of mild depression. This article from the *Harvard Health Letter* helps differentiate dysthymia from other disorders. It discusses various treatments for individuals suffering from the disorder.

Depression in its severe form can sometimes lead to suicide. Psychologists recently have been interested in whether suicide is contagious. Thomas Joiner provides an answer to this question in an interesting literature review on the subject. What Joiner finds is that, yes, some forms of suicide do seem to be contagious; other forms, however, are not.

The final articles in this series, "Obsessive-Compulsive Disorder–Parts I and II," discuss this peculiar disorder that plagues some Americans. These individuals are obsessed with thoughts that compel them to repeat certain related behaviors. The article also reveals treatments for this disorder.

Psychological Disorders

Chronic Anxiety:

How to Stop Living on the Edge

Feeling nervous is a normal response to stressful situations. Sweaty palms, a racing heart, and butterflies in the stomach are felt by everyone from seasoned performers stepping into the spotlight to the person addressing a group for the first time. These sensations are caused by a rush of stress hormones, such as norepinephrine and cortisol, which prepare the body and mind to rise to a challenge.

Chronic anxiety, however, is very different from the healthy feelings of nervousness that make a speaker effective or enable a sprinter to win a race. Indeed, anxiety disorders are, by definition, psychiatric illnesses that are not useful for normal functioning. Instead of calling a person to action, chronic anxiety can damage relationships, reduce productivity, and make someone terrified of everyday experiences.

Anxiety illnesses are among the most common disorders, affecting more than 23 million Americans (about 1 in 9). Fortunately, sufferers often get substantial relief from various forms of talk therapy, medication, or both. But the majority of people with anxiety disorders do not seek help because they may not recognize their symptoms as a psychiatric problem or may fear being stigmatized with a "mental illness."

There is strong evidence that anxiety conditions run in families. And recent findings suggest that a genetic predisposition to anxiety, when triggered by certain life experiences (such as early losses or trauma), may alter a person's brain chemistry, causing an illness to surface.

Although anxiety disorders are common, many people do not seek help because they don't realize that treatments are available.

The most common of these conditions and, surprisingly, the least understood is *generalized anxiety disorder* (GAD). Believed to affect about 10 million Americans, it is characterized by unrelenting, exaggerated worry and tension; it can keep people from socializing, traveling, getting a better job, or pursuing a sport or avocation. GAD affects people of both sexes and all ages but is diagnosed more often in adult women, possibly because of hormonal differences or because women seek mental health treatment more frequently than men, whose rate of anxiety may be underestimated. Some mental health experts believe that men manifest anxiety (as well as depression) differently from women: they drink more alcohol, smoke more, and are more prone to aggressive behavior.

The psychiatric diagnosis of GAD is chronic, exaggerated worry and tension that has lasted for more than 6 months, although most people with the disorder can trace it back to childhood or adolescence. They may worry excessively about health, money, family, or work, even when there is no sign of difficulty. And they have trouble relaxing and often have insomnia. Many live from day to day with distressing physical symptoms such as trembling, sweating, muscle tension, or headaches, which tend to worsen when they face even mild stress.

Excerpted from *The Harvard Health Letter,* July 1998, pp. 1-3. © 1998 by the President and Fellows of Harvard College.
Reprinted by permission.

GAD frequently coexists with depression, and certain antidepressants seem to work quite well for people with GAD. Many of these medications regulate levels of brain chemicals such as serotonin and norepinephrine, but scientists do not have a complete understanding of the biology of anxiety or depression or why they often go hand in hand.

A March 1998 symposium in Boston, cosponsored by the National Institute of Mental Health and the Anxiety Disorders Association of America, was among the first dedicated to the interplay between fear and anxiety and the workings of the brain. Some scientists are focusing on a brain structure called the *amygdala*, which regulates fear, memory, and emotion. When a person is exposed to a fearful event, the amygdala coordinates the brain's physical responses, such as increased heart rate and blood pressure. And preliminary research suggests that the release of the stress hormones norepinephrine and cortisol may act in a way that greatly increases memory of the fearful or traumatic event, allowing it to remain vivid for years. (For more on stress hormones, see *Harvard Health Letter*, April 1998.)

Because basic research has uncovered chemical and hormonal differences in how males and females respond to fear and anxiety, investigators are studying the role that estrogen and cyclical hormonal changes may play in women with anxiety disorders.

Late-life anxiety

Although studies indicate that the prevalence of major depression and certain anxiety disorders declines in the over-65 population, depression affects about 1 in 7 in this group. But there are no hard data on how many of them are troubled by chronic anxiety. Researchers, however, believe that GAD is the most common form of anxiety in older people. They estimate that up to two thirds of older individuals with depression have GAD, and the same amount with GAD have depression. (For more on late-life depression, see *Harvard Health Letter*, March 1995.)

Doctors may have difficulty diagnosing anxiety disorders in older people because some of the characteristics of anxiety, such as blood pressure elevations or a racing heart, may be attributable to a physical illness. Indeed, anxiety may be overlooked when a potentially serious medical condition captures a doctor's attention.

Getting well

There are two main roads to treating GAD: talk therapy and medication. Some mental health professionals place great value on *cognitive-behavioral therapy* (CBT); instead of focusing on deep-seated childhood feelings, the therapist helps the patient look realistically at the exaggerated or pessimistic beliefs that flood the mind. Eventually, the

Finding Help

The following national organizations can provide referrals for mental health professionals and/or support groups in your area.

American Psychiatric Association
Phone: (202) 682-6220
Internet: http://www.psych.org

American Psychological Association
Phone: (202) 336-5800
Internet: http://www.helping.apa.org

Anxiety Disorders Association of America
Phone: (301) 231-9350
Internet: http://www.adaa.org

National Alliance for the Mentally Ill
Phone: (800) 950-NAMI
Internet: http://www.nami.org

person learns to think rationally about his or her fears, and anxiety is reduced.

However, other mental health experts say that although CBT may have an excellent short-term effect, it is not necessarily a lifetime one. Many psychotherapists believe that the only way to help someone reduce chronic anxiety for good is to work with the patient over time so he or she can talk about and process traumatic or fearful events, which may have occurred years earlier. Indeed, many people experience a substantial reduction in anxious thoughts when they explore childhood fears or secrets with a supportive and knowledgeable psychiatrist, psychologist, or social worker.

Useful medications

Some types of drugs, such as *benzodiazepines* (mild tranquilizers) are taken every day or on an as-needed basis when stress or worry becomes overwhelming; others, such as antidepressants, must be taken daily, sometimes indefinitely. It is best to combine some form of talk therapy with medication, but many people do not feel the need or they lack the financial resources to do both.

Historically, anxiety has been treated with benzodiazepines. These include diazepam (Valium), alprazolam (Xanax), and lorazepam (Ativan). Although many people who consider taking one of these medications or who are currently on one worry that they are addictive, this is usually not the case, particularly if the person has never abused drugs or alcohol in the past. Some individuals may develop a physical dependence on them, which means that they should reduce their dose slowly when going off the medication. Doctors rarely prescribe benzodiazepines for people with addictive tendencies.

Although the medications are generally well tolerated by people who do not abuse them, they can be a problem in older people, because early side effects include drowsiness, impaired reflexes and motor skills, and confusion. Older individuals are more prone to falls and car accidents during the first few weeks of taking a benzodiazepine.

Antidepressants are being used more frequently to treat GAD. They do not generally have the side effects of benzodiazepines and are considered safer and more effective for long-term use. Numerous investigations have shown that the *selective-serotonin reuptake inhibitors* (SSRIs), sold as Prozac, Paxil, and Zoloft, newer antidepressants such as nefazodone (Serzone), and the older tricyclic antidepressants (imipramine, for example) can

significantly reduce symptoms of GAD. A drug called buspirone (BuSpar), which is not an antidepressant but is designed specifically for anxiety, is useful for some people.

The first step in getting help is to see your primary care physician, who can refer you to a mental health professional if you want to explore talk therapy. Another way to find a good counselor is to ask friends or family who have worked with one they liked.

Either your primary care doctor or a psychiatrist can prescribe medication. However, primary care physicians generally do not have time to engage in lengthy or ongoing discussions, so you may prefer to see a mental health professional. Whether you've lived with chronic anxiety for 6 months or 60 years, GAD can be treated. You can get the help you need by asking for it.

How Stress Attacks You

Stress isn't just a catchall complaint; it's being linked to heart disease, immune deficiency and memory loss. We're learning that men and women process stress differently and that childhood stress can lead to adult health problems. The worse part is, we inflict it on ourselves. By Jerry Adler

IT WAS VITAL TO SURVIVAL ONCE— an innate response to danger, inherited directly from the primeval veld down to our own lifetimes, where it causes nothing but trouble. Some people make a virtue of stress, under the mantra "that which does not kill me makes me stronger." But science shows this to be a lie. A whole new body of research shows the damage stress wreaks on the body: not just heart disease and ulcers, but loss of memory, diminished immune function and even a particular type of obesity. That which doesn't kill you, it turns out, really does kill you in the end, but first it makes you fat.

Zen masters, of course, have known this for a long time, and techniques such as yoga are still useful prescriptions for stress. But orthodox Western medicine long resisted the notion that a purely mental condition could have measurable effects in the empirical realm of arteries and organs. "When I started studying stress 30 years ago, I was told I was jeopardizing my medical career," says Dr. Herbert Benson, who founded the Mind/Body Medical Institute at Harvard. It was only in the past few years that researchers came up with a quantifiable measure of stress, based on the concentration of certain hormones in saliva, and began tracing the complex neurological and chemical events that lead from a traffic jam on the Santa Monica Freeway to cardiac intensive care at Cedars-Sinai. Research has revealed that men's and women's bodies process stress differently, and provided disturbing evidence about how stress affects child development from the earliest weeks of life. And it has spawned a whole new discipline, psychoneuroimmunology—which, according to Bruce Rabin of the University of Pittsburgh, has reached the point where research on smoking and cancer was back in the 1960s. "You knew there was a link because of the epidemiology, but you didn't know the mechanism. Now there's enough epidemiology to establish the association [between stress and illness]. We're still working out the mechanisms."

The very concept of stress was formulated only in the 1930s, by the pioneering endocrinologist Hans Selye. It was Selye's insight that organisms show a common biological response to a wide range of unpleasant sensory or psychological experiences. These are called "stressors." Stressors are, in shorthand, whatever you're trying to avoid: an electric shock, if you're a lab rat; the sight of a predator, if you're a prey animal; a 500-point drop in the Dow, if you're a Yuppie. Those are acute stress events; everyone recognizes the adrenaline rush (pounding heart, dry mouth, butterflies in the stomach) that marks their onset. Human beings are equipped to deal with it, if it doesn't happen too often. But when it happens again and again, the effects multiply and cascade, invisibly, compounding over a lifetime.

The classic study linking stress to immune dysfunction was done just in 1991, when Carnegie Mellon psychologist Sheldon Cohen and his colleagues showed that peo-

---

STRESS

In the short term it's vital, but over time it turns destructive. New research shows how chronic stress breaks down the body and makes way for disease.

❶ Immediate

In response to a perceived threat, the body channels resources for strength and speed.

Brain Stress protectively dulls the body's sense of pain. Thinking and memory improve.

Eyes The pupils dilate for better vision

Lungs The lungs take in more oxgyen

Liver Sugar stored as glycogen is converted to glucose

Heart The bloodstream brings extra oxygen and glucose—fuel—for power. Heart rate and blood pressure rise.

Adrenal glands The medulla secretes flight-or-flight hormone epinephrine (adrenaline)

Spleen Extra red blood cells flow out, allowing the blood to carry more oxygen to muscles

Intestines Digestion halts, allowing the body to dedicate energy to the muscles

Hair Body hairs become erect—puffed-up hair makes animals look bigger and more dangerous

❷ Delayed

A few minutes after the fight-or-flight response, the body makes other changes to stabilize and replenish itself.

Brain The hippocampus, a center of memory and learning, gets activated to process the stress

Immune system Infection-fighting is diminished, perhaps increasing available energy

Liver Fat—stored energy—is converted into usable fuel

Adrenal glands The cortex secretes cortisol, which regulates metabolism and immunity. Over time, though, it can be toxic.

❸ Chronic

If activated too often, the stress response may harm the immune system, brain and heart.

Brain Cortisol becomes toxic to brain cells, potentially damaging cognitive ability. Fatigue, anger and depression increase.

Immune system Repeated suppression of disease-fighting cells ultimately weakens resistance to infection

Intestines Decreases in blood flow leave mucous lining vulnerable to ulcers

Circulatory system Elevated blood pressure and heart rate damage elasticity of blood vessels

---

From *Newsweek*, June 14, 1999, pp. 58-63. © 1999 by Newsweek, Inc. All rights reserved. Reprinted by permission.

ple who ranked high on a psychological test of perceived stress were more likely to develop colds when intentionally infected with a respiratory virus. He repeated the study last year and this time refined his results: although a single, large, stressful event in the preceding year did not affect the subjects' chances of getting sick, chronic stress—ongoing conflicts with co-workers or family members, for example—increased the odds by as much as three to five times. Looking at another measure of immune function, response to a standard influenza vaccine, immunologist Ronald Glaser of Ohio State found diminished antibody production (compared with a control group matched for age) among people caring for a spouse with dementia. "The human body," says Dr. Pamela Peeke of the University of Maryland, "was never meant to deal with prolonged chronic stress. We weren't meant to drag around bad memories, anxieties and frustrations."

Other studies (chart) have found an association between long-term stress and heart problems. That's also true of macaque monkeys, favored subjects of stress researchers because they share with humans a hierarchical structure and a susceptibility to coronary-artery disease. Wake Forest University anthropologist Jay Kaplan studied both high- and low-status male macaques in captivity and found, as expected, that the subordinate ones showed more atherosclerosis. But when he artificially shook up the social hierarchy, by introducing new animals into the troop, it was the high-ranking males, forced to fight again and again to establish their dominance, who showed the most signs of coronary disease.

Yet the stress reaction obviously serves an evolutionary purpose. It is, essentially, a response to danger, in two distinct phases. The first of these, involving the "sympathetic-adreno-medullary axis" (SAM), is the familiar flight-or-fight response. Your brain perceives a threat—a lion crouched in the brush is the classic illustration—and sends a message down the spinal cord to the medulla, or core, of the adrenal glands (chart), signaling it to pump out adrenaline. In a matter of seconds, the body is transformed. To prepare for exertion, blood pressure and heart rate skyrocket; the liver pours out glucose and calls up fat reserves to be processed into triglycerides for energy; the circulatory system diverts blood from nonessential functions, such as digestion, to the brain and muscles. This is precisely what you need if your goal is to survive the next 10 minutes.

Civilization, by contrast, gives you the opportunity to experience an adrenaline rush at every traffic light. And—since all you're doing is sitting in your car—the elaborate preparations your body makes are wasted. Worse than wasted: every heartbeat at elevated blood pressure takes its toll on the arteries. The excess fats and glucose don't get metabolized right away, so they stay in the

bloodstream. The fats contribute to the plaques that form inside blood vessels, which can lead to heart disease or strokes; high levels of glucose are a step in the direction of diabetes. "If you mobilize in the first place for a nonsense psychological stressor," says Robert Sapolsky of Stanford, a leading authority on stress, "by definition your defense becomes more damaging than the imaginary challenge."

The second phase to the stress reaction kicks in five to 10 minutes later. This "hypothalamic-pituitary-adrenocortical axis" (HPA) seems more closely associated with emotional and intellectual stress. Researchers have many clever ways of producing intellectual stress, such as asking subjects to name the color of ink a word is written in (blue) when the word itself spells out the name of a different color (red). The HPA axis originates in the hypothalamus, in the middle of the base of the brain. The hypothalamus signals the pituitary to produce a substance called ACTH, which stimulates the adrenal cortex to produce a set of hormones known as glucocorticoids: cortisone, cortisol and corticosterone.

The action of these is complex, because hormones almost always work as part of a loop of positive and negative feedbacks. Glucocorticoids seem to stimulate the hippocampus, a part of the brain vital to memory and learning. But an excess of these hormones can actually be toxic to the hippocampus. People with above-average glucocorticoid levels—including those with depression and post-traumatic-stress syndrome—tend to have impaired memory and cognition. Their hippocampi may actually appear shrunken in an MRI scan. Glucocorticoids also suppress parts of the immune system. Researchers still don't understand why the body should suppress immunity during times of stress—if anything, the opposite would seem to make sense. But the negative effects are clear: chronic stress leaves one more vulnerable to infections.

And, amazingly enough, stress can even change the shape of your body. Since the stress reaction involves mobilizing the body's fat reserves for energy, Peeke says, it makes sense to store that fat near the liver, which processes it so it can be metabolized in the muscles. Sure enough, fat cells in the abdomen appear to be especially sensitive to glucocorticoids, and people with a high concentration of those hormones tend to accumulate fat around their middles—a potbelly—even if the rest of their bodies are thin. Researchers think that waist-hip ratio, the relative circumference of those two body parts, could be a useful way to identify people at risk for stress-related disease.

But not everyone gets all of these diseases, or even any of them. People respond differently to the same objective stressors. Individuals' cortisol levels vary (in general, the older you are, the higher the concentration), and they go up by varying amounts in reaction to stress. But, surprisingly, that effect doesn't seem to follow a normal bell-shaped curve, like most physiological variables. Instead, some studies suggest, people fall into categories of "hot" or "cool" responders. A 1995 study subjected 20 men to five grueling days of mental arithmetic performed before an audience. Starting from about the same baseline—a cortisol concentration in saliva of seven to eight nanomoles per liter—one group, comprising seven men, shot up to an average of 29 in the first day; the rest went only to around 19. The first group, researchers reported, "view themselves as being less attractive than others, having less self-esteem, and being more often in a depressed mood." Not surprisingly, they also reported more health problems.

CATHERINE STONEY OF OHIO State has also found significant differences between men and women. Women's blood pressure goes up less than men's in reaction to stress

The Toll Stress Takes on the Body

Immune response
People who care for spouses with dementia didn't respond to a flu vaccine as well as a control group.

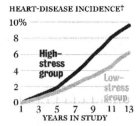

PEOPLE WITH FULL RESPONSE*

Coronary disease
Men who said they were highly stressed were more likely to have heart attacks and strokes.

HEART-DISEASE INCIDENCE†

Viral infection
The chances of catching a cold increase the longer people experience work or interpersonal stress.

RELATIVE RISK OF A COLD

*PERCENT WITH A FOURFOLD ANTIBODY RESISTANCE. †CUMULATIVE ANNUAL INCIDENCE. SOURCES: "CHRONIC STRESS ALTERS THE IMMUNE RESPONSE TO INFLUENZA VIRUS VACCINE IN OLDER ADULTS," "SELF-PERCEIVED PSYCHOLOGICAL STRESS AND INCIDENCE OF CORONARY ARTERY DISEASE IN MIDDLE-AGED MEN," "TYPES OF STRESSORS THAT INCREASE SUSCEPTIBILITY TO THE COMMON COLD IN HEALTHY ADULTS"

STRESS AND GENDER Though a man's blood pressure rises more sharply in response to stress, women react to a wider range of stressors and say they feel stress more often, perhaps because they take a holistic view of everyday life.

(although their response increases noticeably after menopause or hysterectomy, suggesting a buffering effect from estrogen). But women tend to react to a wider range of outside stressors than men, according to Ronald Kessler of Harvard, who asked 166 married couples to keep a daily stress diary for six weeks. Women feel stress more often, says Kessler, because they take a holistic view of everyday life. A man may worry if someone in his immediate family is sick; his wife takes on the burdens of the whole neighborhood.

"Men take care of one thing [at a time]," he says. "Women put the pieces together again."

Apart from gender, early childhood experiences seem to have a powerful influence on how people deal with stress. Children raised in orphanages or in neglectful homes

Stress-Busters: What Works

Some of us are naturally resistant to stress, but anyone can use these proven strategies to calm body and mind

BY GEOFFREY COWLEY

GRANTED, STRESS CAN BE deadly and none of us escapes it. But that doesn't mean we're all doomed. As Stanford psychiatrist David Spiegel puts it, "Living a stress-free life is not a reasonable goal. The goal is to deal with it actively and effectively." Though that's easier for some people than others, studies suggest that anyone can learn to cope better.

One approach is to emulate people who are naturally resistant to stress. Some people weather devastating experiences—captivity, torture, illness, loss—with uncanny serenity. By studying them, researchers have found that they share distinctive habits of mind. They tend to focus on immediate issues (a dying child's comfort) rather than global ones (the prospect of death). And they find ways to rationalize—many interpreting their ordeal as a special assignment from God. As Stanford stress researcher Robert Sapolsky observes in his book "Why Zebras Don't Get Ulcers," "If you can view cancer and Alzheimer's disease, the Holocaust and ethnic cleansing . . . in the context of a loving plan, that must constitute the greatest source of support imaginable."

Stress-resistant people also tend to share what experts call an optimistic "explanatory style." According to University of Pennsylvania psychologist Martin Seligman, they assume their troubles are temporary ("I'm tired today") rather than permanent ("I'm washed up"), and specific ("I have a bad habit") rather than universal ("I'm a bad person"). In addition, they credit themselves when things go right, while externalizing their failures ("That was a tough audience," not "I gave a wretched speech"). Once you start monitoring your explanatory style, you can catch yourself leaping to awful conclusions —and consider the alternatives.

Even a pessimist can learn to modulate the stress response. At the University of Massachusetts' Center for Mindfulness in Medicine, Health Care and Society, specialists have spent two decades teaching people to manage stress through meditation and other relaxation exercises. During their weekly sessions, participants in the center's stress program concentrate on breathing to quell the mind's restless forays into the past and future. Then they lie down and "scan" their bodies, relaxing one muscle at a time. Studies suggest that this type of exercise can stem the flow of stress hormones, helping to lower both heart rate and blood pressure. "It's not a magic potion," says

Mark Gorden, a 43-year-old grocery wholesaler who joined the U Mass program last winter after an undiagnosed illness that lingered for months. "But it helps you deal with everyday stressors."

Massage is another proven antidote to stress. No one knows precisely how the kneading of flesh quells the stress response, but the effects can be dramatic. Over the past 23 years psychologist Tiffany Field of the University of Miami's Touch Research Institute has published studies suggesting it can hasten weight gain in premature infants, improve lung function in asthmatics and bolster immune function in men with HIV. Healthy people may benefit too. In a 1996 study, medical workers who got 10 biweekly rubdowns outscored their unrubbed colleagues on timed math tests.

If massage and meditation are too tame for your tastes, exercise may be your medicine. Researchers have found that after a half hour on a treadmill, young men score 25 percent lower on anxiety tests and exhibit favorable changes in brain activity (less action in the stress-sensitive amygdala and more in the more self-possessed left prefrontal cortex). No one is sure just how these changes come about, but exercise is known to increase the

body's production of morphinelike endorphins, while improving the brain's oxygen supply and releasing tension from the muscles.

There are many other options, from yoga to biofeedback to music therapy, and none of them excludes the others. So do what works for you. And whether you go to confession, join a support group or start a diary, find a way to talk about your feelings. Studies suggest that group support can extend the lives of people with skin or breast cancer. And researchers showed recently that people with asthma or rheumatoid arthritis could ease their symptoms by writing about the most stressful events in their lives. How can such different exercises have such similar benefits? The key, experts agree, is that they combat feelings of helplessness. Anything that fosters a sense of control—putting a traumatic memory into words, calming a racing heart through breathing exercises, even planning your own imminent funeral—lets you stop feeling like a victim. And when that happens, your body stops treating itself like one.

With ANNE UNDERWOOD *and* CLAUDIA KALB

The Science of Serenity

Whether you suffer from bad skin or high blood pressure, these stress-busting techniques have real medical benefits:

Meditation Psoriasis sufferers who combined conventional therapy with guided meditation cut healing time from 95 days to 46

Massage Premature infants, massaged regularly for 10 days, gained 47 percent more weight than other preemies—and left the hospital six days earlier

Exercise Men reported less anxiety after 30 minutes on a treadmill, and EEG tests showed favorable brain-activity changes

Social support Melanoma patients who received six weeks of structured group support suffered only half as many recurrences as their peers

STRESS AND KIDS

Children who were neglected by their parents or raised in orphanages tend to have higher levels of stress hormones and may be 'hot reactors' later in life. As adults, they may feel empty or bored when not on edge.

could be mistaken for medical problems and often are." Parents are frequently wrong about the sources of stress in their children's lives, according to surveys by Georgia Witkin of Mount Sinai Medical School; they think children worry most about friendships and popularity, but they're actually fretting about the grown-ups. "The biggest concern," she says, "was that the parents are going to be sick, or angry, or they're going to divorce." And "often and somewhat surprisingly," says Giedd, "children have very global worries"—wars, environmental issues and crime, the same things adults worry about.

Which raises the question no researcher dares answer: is increasing stress an inevitable hazard of modern life? In many of the ways that count, Kessler muses, life was more stressful 200 years ago, when children routinely died before reaching adulthood. But life was simpler then, too, he thinks, before "anxiety became a core theme in our lives." People knew their place in society and lived with the support of extended families, tribes and villages. What is certain is that people came into the world then, as they do now, prepared by millions of years of evolution for dangers long gone from our lives. The challenge we face is to master not the threats themselves, but our all too-human responses to them.

With CLAUDIA KALB *and* ADAM ROGERS

may have elevated levels of glucocorticoids and "hot" responses to stress later in life. "We're finding," says Frank Treiber of the Medical College of Georgia, "that if you come from a family that's somewhat chaotic, unstable, not cohesive, harboring grudges, very early on, it's associated later with greater blood-pressure reactivity to various types of stress." The brains of children up to around the age of 8 are still developing in response to the environment; cells literally live or die as experiences impinge on it. "The early brain can become hard-wired to deal with high fear states," says Dr. Jay Giedd of the National Institutes of Health. "Its normal state will be to have a lot of adrenaline flowing. When these children become adults they'll feel empty or bored if they're not on edge." Contrariwise, children raised in secure, loving homes learn to modulate the stress reaction, according to Megan Gunnar of the University of Minnesota. Newborns typically show a cortisol spike under the stress of circumcision. But as early as three months, well-cared-for babies can suffer discomfort without evoking a stress response; they'll cry when they get a physical exam, but their stress hormones don't go up commensurately. "Children who are in secure, emotionally supportive relationships are buffered to everyday stressors," she says.

Many authorities think childhood stress is on the rise. Dr. Barbara Howard, a pediatrician at Johns Hopkins, says a quarter of her patients are there for stress-related problems, and the proportion has been rising. 'They'll come in with abdominal pain, urinary frequency, headaches . . . a whole variety of complaints which

STRESSED OUT?

Researchers use this widely respected test to gauge stress levels. Questions apply to the last month only. Put your answers in the boxes and add them up. There's a key below, for scoring.

1 How often have you been upset because of something that happened unexpectedly?

[ ] 0=never 2=sometimes
1=almost 3=fairly often
never 4=very often

2 How often have you felt that you were unable to control the important things in your life?

[ ] 0=never 2=sometimes
1=almost 3=fairly often
never 4=very often

3 How often have you felt nervous and "stressed"?

[ ] 0=never 2=sometimes
1=almost 3=fairly often
never 4=very often

4 How often have you felt confident about your ability to handle your personal problems?

[ ] 4=never 2=sometimes
3=almost 1=fairly often
never 0=very often

5 How often have you felt that things were going your way?

[ ] 4=never 2=sometimes
3=almost 1=fairly often
never 0=very often

6 How often have you been able to control irritations in your life?

[ ] 4=never 2=sometimes
3=almost 1=fairly often
never 0=very often

7 How often have you found that you could not cope with all the things that you had to do?

[ ] 0=never 2=sometimes
1=almost 3=fairly often
never 4=very often

8 How often have you felt that you were on top of things?

[ ] 4=never 2=sometimes
3=almost 1=fairly often
never 0=very often

9 How often have you been angered because of things that were outside your control?

[ ] 0=never 2=sometimes
1=almost 3=fairly often
never 4=very often

10 How often have you felt difficulties were piling up so high that you could not overcome them?

[ ] 0=never 2=sometimes
1=almost 3=fairly often
never 4=very often

How You Measure Up
Stress levels vary among individuals—compare your total score to the averages below:

AGE	GENDER
18-29 ....14.2	Men 12.1
30-44 ....13.0	Women ..13.7
45-54 ....12.6	
55-64 ....11.9	
65 & over..12.0	

MARITAL STATUS
Widowed 12.6
Married or living with 12.4
Single or never wed 14.1
Divorced 14.7
Separated 16.6

SHELDON COHEN

Dysthymia
Treating Mild Depression's Major Effects

Mild, chronic depression has probably existed as long as the human condition, but it was not until 1980 that the medical profession gave it a name and, in essence, gave it its due. That year the disorder, known as *dysthymia*—which literally means ill-humored—was added to the *Diagnostic and Statistical Manual of Mental Disorders (DSM)*, the bible of the mental health professions.

It had long been thought that low-level depression was a stable feature of a person's character or temperament. It was thus assumed that the condition was resistant to antidepressant medications, which are generally used for major depression, a so-called affective or mood disorder that results, at least in part, from chemical imbalances in the brain.

But recent studies have shown that antidepressant medication is indeed effective in treating dysthymia. Though there is not a great deal of research on the condition, a growing body of evidence indicates that antidepressant drugs of all classes help relieve symptoms of dysthymic depression in both young and older adults. This is very good news, because even though the condition is known as "mild" depression, it can make life a constant struggle, and it may make some people prone to major depressive episodes.

According to criteria in the *DSM-IV,* dysthymia in adults is a chronic state of depression characterized by a depressed mood on most days for at least two years. The sufferer must not have gone for more than two months without experiencing two or more of the following symptoms: poor appetite or overeating: difficulty falling or staying asleep, or sleeping too much; low energy or fatigue; low self-esteem; poor concentration or difficulty making decisions; and feelings of hopelessness.

> **A growing body of evidence suggests that chronic, low-level depression can be alleviated with antidepressant medication.**

In order to further meet the criteria, a person will have had no major depressive episodes during the first two years of the illness, and the symptoms should not be due to alcohol or drug abuse or a general medical condition. The symptoms must be serious enough to have caused significant distress or impairment in functioning at work and in social or other settings; indeed, many of those with dysthymia are socially withdrawn and unproductive. People with the condition may also experience *anhedonia*, an inability to derive pleasure from formerly pleasurable activities.

The symptoms of major depression are not dissimilar of those of mild depression, but they are generally more debilitating and acute. People in the throes of major depression often have recurrent thoughts of death or suicide, which makes treatment of this form of the illness a particularly pressing matter. Other symptoms of major depression include feelings of sadness, an inability to experience pleasure, early morning awakenings, multiple awakenings throughout the night, decreased or increased appetite, an inability to concentrate, indecisiveness, feelings of worthlessness or excessive guilt, decreased energy, and motor disturbances. A person who suffers from some or all of these symptoms every day for more than two weeks should

Excerpted from *The Harvard Health Letter*, March 1999, pp. 4-5. © 1999 by the President and Fellows of Harvard College. Reprinted by permission.

seek help from a primary care doctor or mental health professional.

It's important to keep in mind that older depressed people may not always display the classic signs of major depression but instead may show signs of dementia, complain of aches and pains, or feel agitated, anxious, or irritable. Because these symptoms are often chalked up to other ailments or ignored altogether in older people, getting an assessment by an interested and empathetic doctor is essential.

Depressive illnesses affect about 10% of U.S. adults in any given year; of those, about 2.5% suffer from dysthymia. Like major depression, it is most common in young and middle-aged adults, but again, like major depression, dysthymia is under-diagnosed in older people, whose depressive symptoms tend to mistakenly be seen as an inevitable part of aging.

Most people with dysthymia say they first developed a mild, persistent depression in childhood or adolescence, but a small percentage develop it after age 50, usually following a medical illness, particularly heart disease. Depression and cardiovascular disease are known to go hand in hand; scientists are not sure if depression predisposes someone to heart problems or if depression is a reaction to a preexisting cardiovascular condition. (See "Taking Emotions to Heart," *Harvard Health Letter*, October 1996.)

As in those with major depression, people with dysthymia tend to have relatives with higher rates of major depression and bipolar disorder (manic-depressive illness) than the general population. Many experts believe that dysthymia is triggered by a stressful event in people with a genetic or biological predisposition to mood disorders. Regardless of how it starts, scientists know that depression limits the body's availability of certain brain chemicals, such as serotonin, and that antidepressant drugs seem to restore the normal balance of these substances.

Because dysthymic depression is chronic, some experts believe that people with the condition may need to remain on medication indefinitely, but there are no studies to support this. Not surprisingly, people with dysthymia are prone to episodes of major depression, which is referred to as "double depression." There is evidence that cognitive-behavioral therapy, which helps people change negative thought patterns, is useful in treating chronic, low-level depression but it is not clear if it prevents bouts of major depression.

However, a recent study by researchers from the University of Pittsburgh Medical Center sheds new light on the issues of recurrent depression and combined drug and talk therapy for older adults with major depression. Given that dysthymia is treatable with antidepressants, it is possible that the results of the study may also apply to people with low-level depression, but clinical trials are needed to confirm this.

The investigation, which was published in the January 6, 1999, issue of the *Journal of the American Medical Association*, indicated that a combination of drug and talk therapy was superior to either treatment used alone in a group of 107 patients whose average age was 67.

The study, which was funded by the National Institute of Mental Health, is important for two reasons. It is one of the first clinical trials to compare various treatments against a placebo for depression in the elderly, a group whose depression has not been well studied. And it had a relatively long follow-up period: it looked at monthly "maintenance" therapy over three years to determine which treatments prevent recurrent bouts of depression.

Initially, all of the study participants received nortriptyline (Pamelor) and weekly psychotherapy sessions until they achieved a remission of depressive symptoms. In the next, or maintenance, phase of the study, participants received various treatment combinations. At the end of three years, 80% of people who continued with both the drug and psychotherapy staved off further bouts of depression compared to 57% of those who got medication alone and 36% of those who received psychotherapy and a placebo pill. The researchers are currently studying paroxetine (Paxil) in a similar trial.

Historically, one of the distinctions between dysthymia and major depression has been that the former is a chronic disorder and the latter is episodic. This view, however, has shifted somewhat. Studies indicate that about 80% of people who experience a major depressive episode will have at least one more such event during their lifetime, and about 12% of people with major depression will suffer from it chronically. Although it is not clear whether chronic major depression ends up looking more like dysthymia, doctors do know this: both low-level and major depression appear to be lifelong conditions

Getting Help

For literature on depression, support groups, or referrals, contact:

National Institute of Mental Health, 1-800-421-4211

National Alliance for the Mentally Ill, 1-800-950-NAMI

National Mental Health Association, 1-800-969-NMHA

American Association for Geriatric Psychiatry, (301) 654-7850, ext. 100

with a biochemical component, and maintenance therapy seems to be necessary to keep them both at bay.

This is both good and bad news. The bad news, of course, is that no one wants to learn he or she has a chronic condition. The good news, however, is that both depression and dysthymia can be managed, and people can live full, happy lives when the problems are treated. The development of antidepressants that target ever more specific brain chemicals and have fewer side effects than older drugs means more people are considering medication as an option, either for short- or long-term use. And the latest study, which indicates that mainte-nance talk therapy is instrumental in keeping depression at bay, is another tidbit of good news (although many mental health professionals would say this is hardly news).

Over the past several years, insurance companies have severely limited their reimbursement for talk therapy, but this could change if more studies indicate that drugs are not the sole answer to managing depression.

If you are living with mild or major depression, talk to your primary care doctor or a mental health profes-sional. It doesn't matter how old you are—life can feel like it's worth living again. You may just need a little help to see that.

The Clustering and Contagion of Suicide

Thomas E. Joiner, Jr.[1]

Department of Psychology, Florida State University, Tallahassee, Florida

Abstract

Two general types of suicide cluster have been discussed in the literature; roughly, these can be classified as mass clusters and point clusters. Mass clusters are media related, and the evidence for them is equivocal; point clusters are local phenomena, and these do appear to occur. Contagion has not been conceptually well developed nor empirically well supported as an explanation for suicide clusters. An alternative explanation for why suicides sometimes cluster is articulated: People who are vulnerable to suicide may cluster well before the occurrence of any overt suicidal stimulus, and when they experience severe negative events, including but not limited to the suicidal behavior of one member of the cluster, all members of the cluster are at increased risk for suicidality (a risk that may be offset by good social support).

Keywords

suicide clusters; suicide contagion

The phenomena of attempted and completed suicide are troubling and mysterious enough in themselves; the possibility that suicide is socially contagious, even more so. This article considers whether suicide clusters exist, and if so, whether "contagion" processes can account for them.

There is a potentially important distinction between the terms suicide cluster and suicide contagion. A cluster refers to the factual occurrence of two or more completed or attempted suicides that are nonrandomly "bunched" in space or time (e.g., a series of suicide attempts in the same high school or a series of com-

pleted suicides in response to the suicide of a celebrity). The term cluster implies nothing about *why* the cluster came to be, only *that* it came to be. By contrast, contagion refers to a possible explanation (as I argue later, a fairly vague explanation) of *why* a cluster developed. Clusters (of a sort) appear to occur, but the status of contagion as the reason for such occurrences is more equivocal.

CLUSTERS—OF A SORT— APPEAR TO OCCUR

Given that attempted and completed suicides are relatively rare, and given that they tend to be more or less evenly distributed in space and time (e.g., suicides occur at roughly the same rate in various regions of the United States and occur at roughly the same rate regardless of the day of the week or the month), it is statistically unlikely that suicides would cluster by chance alone. Yet cluster they do, at least under some circumstances. (Such clustering is often termed the "Werther effect," after a fictional character of Goethe's whose suicide purportedly inspired actual suicides in 18th-century Europe.) Two general types of suicide cluster have been discussed in the literature: mass clusters and point clusters. Mass clusters are media related; point clusters, local.

Point Clusters

Point clusters occur locally, involving victims who are relatively contiguous in both space and time. The prototypical setting is institutional (i.e., a school or a hospital). Probably the best documented example was reported by Brent and his

colleagues (Brent, Kerr, Goldstein, & Bozigar, 1989). In a high school of approximately 1,500 students, 2 students committed suicide within 4 days. During an 18-day span that included the 2 completed suicides, 7 other students attempted suicide and an additional 23 reported having suicidal thoughts. It is important to note, though, that Brent and his colleagues found that 75% of the members of the cluster had at least one major psychiatric disorder, which had existed before the students' exposure to the suicides (i.e., they were vulnerable to begin with). Also, victims' close friends appeared to develop suicidal symptoms more readily than students who were less close to victims. In other words, social contiguity was an important factor.

Haw (1994) described a point cluster of 14 suicides within a 1-year period among patients of a London psychiatric unit. Thirteen of the 14 patients suffered from severe, chronic mental illness (e.g., schizophrenia), and most had ongoing therapeutic contact with the psychiatric unit. The author reported that the point cluster's occurrence may have stemmed from patients' valid perceptions that the future of the hospital was uncertain and that their access to medical staff was decreasing and ultimately threatened. Several other point clusters have also been described (see, e.g., Gould, Wallenstein, & Davidson, 1989).

When Point Clusters Do Not Occur

Given that suicidality runs in families, and that the suicide of a family member is an enormously traumatic event, one might imagine that point clusters would be particularly likely within a given family (e.g., the suicide of one family member

From *Current Directions in Psychological Science*, June 1999, pp. 89-92. © 1999 by the American Psychological Society. Reprinted by permission of Blackwell Publishers.

might be followed closely by the suicide of another family member). However, within-family point clusters appear to be very rare. (Although certainly at least one has occurred, I could find no documented case in the literature. It is possible, however, that they are underreported or underpublicized.) Point clusters also appear not to occur within groupings beyond the institutional (e.g., at the level of a large community; cf. Chiu, 1988)—except, that is, in the (possible) case of mass clusters.

Mass Clusters

Unlike point cluster, mass clusters are media-related phenomena. They are grouped more in time than in space, and are purportedly in response to the publicizing of actual or fictional suicides. Phillips and his colleagues have examined the possible relation of suicide-related media events and the rate of subsequent suicides (see, e.g., Phillips & Carstensen, 1986, 1988). These researchers have argued that the suicide rate in the population increases in the days after descriptions of suicides appear in televised news reports and in newspapers. Indeed, in many of these studies, the suicide rate did appear to rise after a publicized suicide, although the effect did not always occur, and it appeared to be primarily applicable to adolescent suicide. Interestingly, these researchers also found that accidents, such as motor vehicle fatalities, may increase in the days following a publicized suicide, apparently because many such accidents are actually intentional suicides.

However, a study by Kessler, Downey, Milavsky, and Stipp (1988) cast doubt on the conclusion that mass clusters exist. Examining adolescent suicides from 1973 to 1984, the authors found no reliable relation between suicide-related newscasts and the subsequent adolescent suicide rate. Similarly, these researchers obtained no evidence that the number of teenagers viewing the newscasts (as determined by Neilsen ratings) was correlated with the number of adolescent suicides.

In the case of fictional portrayals of suicide (e.g., a television movie in which a character commits suicide), the evidence indicates, at most, a weak effect. Schmidtke and Haefner (1988) studied responses to a serial, broadcast twice in Germany, showing the railway suicide of a young man. After each broadcast, according to these researchers, railway suicides among young men (but not among other groups) increased sharply. However, several other researchers have conducted similar studies and concluded

that there was no relation between fictionalized accounts of suicide and the subsequent suicide rate, for adolescents in particular (Phillips & Paight, 1987; Simkin, Hawton, Whitehead, & Fagg, 1995), as well as for people in general (Berman, 1988).

CLUSTERING DOES NOT CONTAGION MAKE

If suicide clusters exist (and it appears that point clusters do, although mass clusters may not), contagion—the social, or interpersonal, transmission of suicidality from one victim to another—may or may not be involved. With regard to an array of unfortunate events (e.g., disasters, accidents, even illnesses), it is easy to imagine that there would be point clusters of victims without contagion of any sort. For example, the victims of the Chernobyl nuclear disaster were point-clustered, not because of any type of contagion between victims, but because of victims' simultaneous exposure to radiation. Even cases of mass suicide, the victims of which are point-clustered, are best viewed as instances of mass delusion (e.g., Heaven's Gate) or of a combination of delusion and coercion (e.g., Jonestown), rather than of contagion. In cases such as Chernobyl and even Jonestown, the point clustering of victims may be seen as due to the simultaneous effects of some pernicious, external influence, such as radiation, on a preexisting, socially contiguous group of people, such as those working at or living near the Chernobyl plant.

In disease, the agent of contagion (e.g., some microbial pathogen) is specified, and its mechanism of action delineated. By contrast, no persuasive agent or mechanism of suicide contagion has been articulated. Indeed, with one exception, the very definition of suicide contagion has been so vague as to defy analysis. The one exception is behavioral imitation, which, although clearly defined, lacks explanatory power (e.g., in a school, what determines who, among all the students, imitates a suicide?).

A SPECULATION REGARDING POINT-CLUSTERED SUICIDES

I suggest that the concepts of imitation or contagion may not be needed to explain point-clustered suicides. Rather, four sets of findings, taken together, indicate an alternative view. First, severe negative life events are risk factors for suicidality (and the suicidal behavior of a friend or peer qualifies as one of a large array of severe negative life events).

Second, good social support (e.g., healthy family functioning) buffers people against developing suicidal symptoms. Third, there exists an array of person-based risk factors for suicidality (e.g., personality disorder or other psychiatric disorder). Fourth, people form relationships assortatively—that is, people who possess similar qualities or problems, including suicide risk factors, may be more likely to form relationships with one another. Therefore, it is possible that people who are vulnerable to suicide may cluster well before the occurrence of any overt suicidal stimulus (i.e., suicide point clusters may be, in a sense, prearranged), and when they experience severe negative events, including but not limited to the suicidal behavior of one member of the cluster, all members of the cluster are at increased risk for suicidality (a risk that may be offset by good social support).

Consider, the example, the point cluster described by Haw (1994), in which victims were assortatively related on the basis of, at least in part, shared suicide risk factors (e.g., the chronic mental illness that brought them all to the same psychiatric unit). Vulnerable people were brought together (through contact with the agency), were exposed to severe stress (potential for dissolution of the agency; lack of access to important caregivers; for some, suicides of peers), and may not have been well buffered by good social support (the chronically mentally ill often have low social support; a main source of support may have been the agency, which was threatened).

Or consider the example of point clusters within high schools. In this case, the assortative relationships—the prearrangement of clusters—may occur in one or both of two ways. First, because they have mutual interests, compatible qualities, or similar problems (including vulnerability to and experience of psychopathology), vulnerable adolescents may gravitate toward one another. A point cluster reported by Robbins and Conroy (1983) demonstrates this possibility. In this cluster, two adolescent suicides were followed by five attempts (all five teenagers were subsequently admitted to the hospital) and one hospital admission for having suicidal thoughts. Of the six hospitalized teens, all had regularly socialized with each other, and all visited each other during their hospitalizations. Second, having social contact (for whatever reason, assortative or not) with an adolescent who completes or attempts suicide appears to lower the threshold at which a teen becomes suicidal (Brent et al., 1989). The mere occurrence, then, of suicidality in one adolescent may automatically arrange a potential cluster.

Although the empirical facts on point clusters are limited, they appear to be consistent with my speculation that severe negative life events, person-based risk, social contiguity (perhaps as a function of assortative relationships), and lack of buffering by social support, taken together, explain the phenomenon. In an effort to provide further empirical support for this view, I conducted an analogue study among college roommates. College roommates provide an interesting "natural laboratory" for studying issues involving assortative relationships, because in many large universities, a sizable proportion of roommates are randomly assigned to each other (by the university housing agency) and the rest assortatively choose to room with each other. I predicted that suicidality levels would be more similar among roommates who chose to room together than among those randomly paired together. Moreover, I predicted that suicidality levels would be particularly consonant among pairs who both chose one another and, by their own reports, had been experiencing negative life events that affected both of them. Results supported the view that prearranged point clusters (in this case, arranged by people choosing to live together) would share suicide-related features (in this case, symptoms), and that clustered suicidality was particularly likely in those prearranged clusters that had been affected by negative life events. It must be emphasized that this study was an analogue study, and that, in general, students' levels of suicidality were quite low, making the generalization to attempted or completed suicide questionable. The results, however, converge with those from reports on actual point clusters to make the explanation offered here, at the least, a candidate for further study.

ADDRESSING POTENTIAL CRITICISMS OF THIS EXPLANATION

Why Don't Point Clusters Happen All the Time?

According to my speculation about why point clusters develop, at least two concepts are key to understanding why they are relatively rare. First, my explanation involves the joint operation of several phenomena that themselves are infrequent in occurrence. Severe negative events, high person-based risk, suicidality itself, and low social support—all jointly operating ingredients of

my explanation—are relatively rare; their confluence is even more so. Second, even given the confluence of these factors, attempted or completed suicides represent an extreme and severe psychopathology, the threshold for which is presumably quite high. Thus, even when life events are severely negative, person-based risk is high, and social support is low, the threshold may not be reached.

Why Don't Point Clusters Occur Within Families?

Because suicidality and suicide risk run in families, because the suicide of a family member is arguably the most severe of negative events, and because family members are socially contiguous, families would appear to be likely sources for point-clustered suicides. Apparently, however, they are not. This may be because of the protective action of social support. Social support is, in general, pervasive (indeed, the need to belong has been proposed as a fundamental human motive; Baumeister & Leary, 1995), and it is intensified for families in mourning. Increased social support thus may offset families' risk for additional suicides among family members.

CONCLUSIONS

The evidence for mass clusters is weak or equivocal, whereas point clusters appear to occur. But clustering does not contagion make. By implication at least, suicide clusters often have been explained as analogous to miniepidemics of contagious illness. I have suggested, however, that a more apt analogy is disasters or industrial accidents, in which simultaneous exposure to some external, pernicious agent (e.g., radiation) is the mechanism of action, a mechanism that is particularly harmful to already vulnerable people. Point-clustered suicides may occur similarly: Contiguous people, if exposed to noxious stimuli (e.g., a severe negative life event, such as the suicide of a peer), and if vulnerable but unprotected (by social support), may simultaneously develop suicidal symptoms.

Recommended Reading

Brent, D. A., Kerr, M. M., Goldstein, C., & Bozigar, J. (1989). (See References)
Gould, M. S., Wallenstein, S., & Davidson, L. (1989). (See References)

Kessler, R. C., Downey, G., Milavsky, J. R., & Stipp, H. (1988). (See References)

Note

1. Address correspondence to Thomas Joiner, Department of Psychology, Florida State University, Tallahassee, FL 32306-1270; e-mail: joiner@psy.fsu.edu.

References

Baumeister, R. F., & Leary, M. R. (1995). The need to belong: Desire for interpersonal attachments as a fundamental human motivation. *Psychological Bulletin, 117,* 497–529.

Berman, A. L. (1988). Fictional depiction of suicide in television films and imitation effects. *American Journal of Psychiatry, 145,* 982–986.

Brent, D. A., Kerr, M. M., Goldstein, C., & Bozigar, J. (1989). An outbreak of suicide and suicidal behavior in a high school. *Journal of the American Academy of Child & Adolescent Psychiatry, 28,* 918–924.

Chiu, L. P. (1988). Do weather, day of the week, and address affect the rate of attempted suicide in Hong Kong? *Social Psychiatry & Psychiatric Epidemiology, 23,* 229–235.

Gould, M. S., Wallenstein, S., & Davidson, L. (1989). Suicide clusters: A critical review. *Suicide & Life-Threatening Behavior, 19,* 17–29.

Haw, C. M. (1994). A cluster of suicides at a London psychiatric unit. *Suicide & Life-Threatening Behavior, 24,* 256–266.

Kessler, R. C., Downey, G., Milavsky, J. R., & Stipp, H. (1988). Clustering of teenage suicides after television news stories about suicides: A reconsideration. *American Journal of Psychiatry, 145,* 1379–1383.

Phillips, D. P., & Carstensen, L. L. (1986). Clustering of teenage suicides after television news stories about suicide. *New England Journal of Medicine, 315,* 685–689.

Phillips, D. P., & Carstensen, L. L. (1988). The effect of suicide stories on various demographic groups, 1968–1985. *Suicide & Life-Threatening Behavior, 18,* 100–114.

Phillips, D. P., & Paight, D. J. (1987). The impact of televised movies about suicide: A replicative study. *New England Journal of Medicine, 317,* 809–811.

Robbins, D., & Conroy, R. C. (1983). A cluster of adolescent suicide attempts: Is suicide contagious? *Journal of Adolescent Health Care, 3,* 253–255.

Schmidtke, A., & Haefner, H. (1988). The Werther effect after television films: New evidence for an old hypothesis. *Psychological Medicine, 18,* 665–676.

Simkin, S., Hawton, K., Whitehead, L., & Fagg, J. (1995). Media influence on parasuicide: A study of the effects of a television drama portrayal of paracetamol self-poisoning. *British Journal of Psychiatry, 167,* 754–759.

Obsessive-Compulsive Disorder—Part I

A woman spends hours in the shower washing her body in a sequence that has to be the same each time. She will use a towel only if it is handed to her directly from a dryer and has not touched anything else.

A single mother of three living on welfare throws out $50 a week worth of groceries because of "contamination."

An aunt will not baby-sit for her nieces because she is afraid she will stab them with a knife as they sleep.

A man will not take the subway to work because he fears he will accidentally push someone off the platform into the path of a train.

A man avoids public places because he fears he will not be able to check his sexual impulses and may falsely accuse a stranger of committing a crime.

A woman plugs and unplugs electrical appliances 20 times or more, counts her change 10 times, and rereads addresses on envelopes for minutes to make sure they are correct.

A man has a persistent urge to shout an obscenity or blasphemy in public. He can suppress it only by repeatedly counting slowly backward from 100 to 1.

A man covers everything with a paper towel before touching it. If anything is touched by his clothes, he has to wash it. He can barely use his left hand because he is reluctant to let it touch anything.

For five years, a woman has been washing her arms up to the elbow 50 times a day until they are raw and scabbed because she is worried that her germs will infect the family.

A woman confines herself to the family living room for four years, lets no one else in, and urinates and defecates in tin cans to avoid bathrooms.

A college freshman has stopped showering and dressing normally because the process takes several hours a day. He hisses and coughs when he eats and repeatedly wipes his feet and looks backward when he walks. He stays in his room most of the time, eating only a few carefully selected foods and constantly checking to see that furniture and wastebaskets are in exactly the "right" places.

Most people are taught to be careful, clean, and ethical, and many have worries or routines that we know make little sense. In patients with obsessive-compulsive disorder (OCD), concerns of this kind have become all-consuming and self-destructive. These ruminations and rituals may take hours a day, make sufferers miserable, and disable them for much of the business of everyday life.

Obsessions are persistent repetitious thoughts, images, and urges that are usually experienced as intrusions to be neutralized or suppressed: obscene and blasphemous thoughts, repugnant sexual and violent images, perfectionist scruples. The most common obsessional theme is cleanliness (dirt and germs), followed by aggression and sex, safety, and order or symmetry. Obsessions may take the form of doubts (has something happened to my child?); fears (something might happen to the child); images (I see the child drowning); or impulses (I fear that I am going to harm the child).

Compulsive rituals temporarily restore the comfort destroyed by obsessions. They consist of overt actions (checking, cleaning, ordering, and so on) or countervailing words and thoughts (mental rehearsal, silent prayer or counting, repeated demands for reassurance, repetition of phrases or meaningless sounds). Almost any everyday action can be transformed into a compulsive ritual. People with OCD may repeatedly pass in and out of doorways or sit down and rise from chairs. They read and reread instructions, repeatedly check to see that

Excerpted from *The Harvard Mental Health Letter*, October 1998, pp. 1-4. © 1998 by the President and Fellows of Harvard College. Reprinted by permission.

doors and windows are locked and lights turned off, insist on certain details of dress, conduct lengthy bedtime rituals, adopt peculiar patterns of walking and breathing. Most perform several compulsive actions in different circumstances, and the rituals may change with time. In most cases, yielding to the compulsion relieves mounting anxiety or tension. Some people are eventually unconscious of the tension because their rituals have become routine. Occasionally obsessions seem to serve compulsions by giving a meaning to bizarre behavior.

Compulsions and obsessions are time-consuming and disruptive not only in themselves but also because of efforts to avoid situations that provoke them. OCD can make normal work and family life difficult, if not impossible. In one recent survey of patients at an OCD clinic, many had lost years of work to their symptoms. Some 75% said the disorder interfered with their family lives, and 13% had attempted suicide.

The prevalence of OCD

Until recently, most people with OCD did not see mental health professionals. They might talk to a doctor, religious counselor, or family member, or they might treat the disorder as a shameful secret and confine their rituals to their homes as much as possible. Recent research suggests that OCD is more common than anyone had suspected. According to the Epidemiologic Catchment Area (ECA) survey, 2.5% of Americans have had the symptoms at some time in their lives. A similar survey revealed similar rates in Canada, Puerto Rico, Germany, Korea, and New Zealand.

But there are signs that this may be an overestimate. In the ECA survey, nearly two out of three people with OCD were women, although women generally seek treatment more than men for psychiatric disorders and only 50% of OCD patients are female. Only a small proportion of people in the survey said they had both obsessional thoughts and compulsive rituals, although patients seeking treatment almost always complain of both. Apparently people do not always know what makes a thought or impulse obsessional, and they may not understand an interviewer's questions about the subject without examples to compare with their own experience.

One-third of adult cases of OCD begin in childhood, but unlike the average adult, a child may not realize that compulsions are excessive and obsessions irrational. Very young children have compulsive rituals without any obsessional thoughts that they can articulate. Two-thirds of children with OCD are boys, and they often have attention deficit disorder or developmental disorders as well.

OCD runs in families and has a genetic basis. The concordance (matching) between identical twins is 60%. Among parents, children, brothers, and sisters of patients with OCD, the rate is 10% and 15%, and another 10% may have some of the symptoms in milder forms. Family studies suggest that childhood OCD is under stronger genetic influence than the adult version.

Making a diagnosis

OCD can usually be distinguished from related symptoms that occur in depression and generalized anxiety (rumination, worries), phobias (avoidance of people, places, and activities because of pathological fears), developmental disorders (autistic rituals, stereotyped behavior), eating disorders (obsession with food intake and body size), and hypochondriasis (the belief that one has a serious illness). The worries of generalized anxiety are not regarded as alien intrusions. Depressive brooding is exclusively guilty and sad or directed at personal deficiencies. The source of obsessional fears is one's own thoughts and impulses, not, as in phobias, an external object. In fact, OCD is not classified as an anxiety disorder in the European system of psychiatric diagnosis.

The stereotyped behavior of autistic children is generally less well organized and complex than compulsive rituals, and there is no apparent inner resistance to it. Hypochondriacs too lack resistance to their obsessions, and they usually do not have compulsive rituals. The obsessions and compulsions of people with eating disorders are confined to the subject of food.

Nor is OCD identical to what is sometimes called obsessive-compulsive personality. In fact, the two conditions may not even be related. The symptoms of OCD are not character traits. Apart from their idiosyncratic obsessions and rituals, people with the disorder are not necessarily preoccupied with rules and schedules, excessively conscientious, orderly, morally rigid, fussy about details, indecisive, or perfectionist in a self-defeating way—the standard description of obsessive-compulsive personality. But the distinction is difficult to see in a person with many obsessions and rituals, and what seems to be a personality disorder often disappears when OCD is treated.

Bizarre as they seem, obsessions are rarely delusional, but they can take on such a powerful aura of conviction that they are described as overvalued ideas. Since an overvalued idea may turn into a full-scale delusion if the inner voice repeating it becomes attached to a distinct personality, obsessional and compulsive symptoms are also associated with psychosis. In the ECA survey, 12% of patients with OCD were also schizophrenic, and 40% had developed the symptoms before the onset of psychotic delusions. Others had schizoid and schizotypal personality disorders, which may be mild forms of schizophrenia. In fact, OCD is rarely a person's only psychiatric disorder. In one survey, two thirds had had episodes of major depression and 26% had had panic attacks. In the ECA survey, OCD was also associated with phobias and alcoholism.

The obsessive-compulsive spectrum

Other psychiatric disorders—body dysmorphic disorder, trichotillomania, and Tourette's syndrome—are often described as part of an obsessive-compulsive spectrum, because they respond to some of the same treatments as OCD or may have a similar biological basis. Body dysmorphic disorder (BDD) is an irrational obsession with imagined ugliness, usually involving the hair, skin, or nose. People with BDD constantly check their appearance in mirrors or alter it with hats, unusual haircuts, heavy make-up, and plastic surgery. They may spend hours a day grooming or picking at supposed blemishes. Many believe that people are staring at them or making fun of them because of their looks, and they repeatedly ask for reassurance. They are often severely depressed, and they have a high rate of alcoholism and suicide attempts. Although limited to this one subject, their obsession and compulsive actions respond to some of the same drugs and behavioral techniques that are used in treating OCD.

Genuine cosmetic problems are created by another single-symptom disorder—trichotillomania, or pathological hair pulling, which occurs mostly in women. Some victims will not leave their homes without makeup or wigs to disguise bald patches. To stop themselves, they may tie their hands together or wear a ski mask to bed. No definite obsession is necessarily involved. Some say that pulling out their hair merely relieves tension, but for others it is routine and almost automatic or even gives pleasure. Like BDD, trichotillomania runs in the same families as OCD, has overlapping symptoms, and sometimes responds to the same drugs and behavioral therapies.

The symptoms of Tourette's syndrome are blinking, twitching, touching, squats, jumps, head jerking, throat clearing, grunts, squeals, repeated words and obscene gestures. Unlike compulsive rituals, these tics do not usually resemble deliberate actions, and they are provoked more by physical sensations than by thoughts and images. But tics can be exacerbated by stress and suppressed (for a while) by an exercise of will, and some of them are so elaborate and complex that they could pass for actions—doing deep knee bends while walking, spewing obscenities, imitating the movements of others

or echoing their words. Tics can also be transformed into purposeful movements: an arm jerk directed to brush hair away from the face, apparently pointless side-to-side swinging of the head attributed to a need for symmetry. The symptoms are sometimes accompanied by vague obsessional thoughts, such as a feeling that things must be "just right." Many people with Tourette's syndrome also have more typical compulsive rituals, such as counting and washing, and the two disorders may run in the same families. There may be a range of compulsions running from the "physical" to the "mental", with simple motor tics and cognitive rituals (counting, repetition of words) at the extremes, complex tics and action rituals in the middle.

These symptoms lie on the border between reflexes and actions or between the voluntary and the involuntary. The category of obsessive-compulsive spectrum disorders is sometimes extended to include other conditions in which this distinction is unclear—addictions and disorders of impulse control, including pathological gambling, kleptomania, and binge eating. Obsessional thoughts are analogous to cravings, and impulsive behavior to compulsive behavior. The distinction may depend mainly on how harmful the behavior is, what kind of relief or satisfaction it brings, how senseless it seems, and how intensely the urge is resisted. But it is doubtful how much these disorders have in common. The brain mechanisms involved are probably distinct in each case, although they may be related.

FOR FURTHER READING

Jonathan S. Abramowitz. Effectiveness of psychological and pharmacological treatments for obsessive-compulsive disorder: A quantitative review. *Journal of Consulting and Clinical Psychology 65: 44–52 (1997).*

John S. March, Allen Frances, Daniel Carpenter, and David A. Kahn, eds. The expert consensus guideline: Treatment of obsessive-compulsive disorder. *Journal of Clinical Psychiatry 58, Suppl. 4 (1997).*

Judith L. Rapoport and Alan Fiske. The new biology of obsessive-compulsive disorder: Implications for evolutionary psychology. *Perspectives in Biology and Medicine 41: 159–175 (Winter 1998).*

Michele T. Payto and Gail Steketee, eds. Obsessive-compulsive disorder across the life cycle. *In Leah J. Dickstein, Michelle B. Riba, and John M. Oldham, eds.* Review of Psychiatry, *Vol. 16. Washington, D.C.: American Psychiatric Press, 1997.*

Obsessive-Compulsive Disorder—Part II

In part I* we described the symptoms of obsessive-compulsive disorder and the related disorders of the obsessive-compulsive spectrum. In this part we discuss the brain mechanisms that underlie these symptoms and the most effective treatments.

Underlying causes of OCD

An increasing amount is known about the underlying brain malfunction in OCD. It occurs in a circuit that connects the frontal lobes of the cerebral cortex, a seat of judgment and planning, with the basal ganglia, a region that regulates the execution of movements by filtering messages before passing them to the thalamus and back to the cortex. Injuries and diseases that disrupt the functioning of the basal ganglia (such as Huntington's disease) often cause obsessive and compulsive symptoms. Damage to the frontal lobes, in contrast, tends to weaken the sense of responsibility and need for correctness that accompany obsessions. Symptoms that include obsessional thinking and compulsive rituals, tics, and choreiform (spasmodic) movements may develop in children who are infected with bacteria called group A beta-

hemolytic streptococci. In one form, these symptoms have been known for hundreds of years under the name of St. Vitus's dance or Sydenham's chorea. They are apparently the result of a misdirected attack on the basal ganglia by immune cells responding to the bacteria. The modern general term is PANDAS (pediatric autoimmune neurological disorders associated with streptococcal infection). Children genetically vulnerable to PANDAS may also be susceptible to OCD and Tourette's disorder. PET (positron emission tomography) scans provide more direct evidence for the involvement of the frontal cortex and basal ganglia in OCD. When the brain of a patient with the disorder is scanned while the symptoms are showing (for example, while someone with a germ obsession holds a dirty towel), the most active regions are the orbitofrontal cortex and anterior cingulate cortex, which lie behind the forehead, and the caudate nuclei, which are part of the basal ganglia. The same regions light up when patients with Tourette's syndrome try to suppress their tics. According to one study, when obsessive and compulsive symptoms are effectively treated (with drugs or behavior therapy), the abnormal frontal and caudate activity disappears. These regions may be overactive because the basal ganglia are not supplying the feedback that the frontal lobes need to avoid making a decision to act. The ritual begins when overworked frontal lobes can no longer prevent an obsessional thought from being translated into action.

Evolutionists have pointed out that the checking, cleaning, ordering, and avoidance abnormally displayed in

---

*See *previous article.*

Excerpted from *The Harvard Mental Health Letter,* November 1998, pp. 1-4. © 1998 by the President and Fellows of Harvard College. Reprinted by permission.

compulsive rituals—and the associated fear, doubt, or disgust—are sometimes adaptive or even automatic responses when life, health, or social acceptance is threatened. They suggest that in OCD, the brain circuit that generates these necessary actions is functioning improperly and continues to reverberate, creating the urge to perform them over and over when the need is absent. Compulsive rituals may also be related to genetically based complex fixed action patterns, such as elaborate courtship dances, which are released in animals by certain environmental stimuli. One of these patterns is grooming, which resembles much of the compulsive behavior that occurs in obsessive-compulsive spectrum disorders. Some breeds of dogs develop a condition known as canine acral lick in which they lick away the fur and skin on their legs. It is treated with the same drugs used for OCD, and both disorders may involve the same cortical-basal ganglia circuit.

Exposure and response prevention

People with OCD may not seek treatment because of shame that makes them secretive, obsessional doubt that makes them indecisive, or caution that makes them fearful. This reluctance is unfortunate, because treatment based on behavioral principles is often effective. Behavior therapists assume that some people, who may be genetically vulnerable, have been conditioned (have learned) to regard certain thoughts and impulses as disgusting, immoral, or dangerous, and these thoughts have become sources of anxiety. Compulsive rituals temporarily relieve tension but interrupt the process of habituation that would eliminate the obsessions permanently. The standard behavioral treatment, known for a century and in wide use since the 1960s, is exposure and response prevention (ERP). Patients are exposed to the objects and situations that provoke their obsessions and prevented from performing the usual compulsive rituals. The thoughts and impulses lose their compelling quality as patients become used to them. They realize that there is nothing to fear and they have no need for the rituals. In behavioral terms, the association is weakened and the compulsive response is extinguished.

The process can become complicated, because the patient usually has several obsessional thoughts and compulsive rituals that fluctuate in intensity and change from time to time. Even learning what they are may be difficult because of embarrassment. Once the symptoms are defined, the therapist and patient rank thoughts and situations by the degree of anxiety or discomfort they arouse, and exposure proceeds upward on the scale. Therapy sessions are usually held once a week for three or four months, while the patient practices daily and records the results for review. Occasional visits may be needed thereafter for six months to a year. Some patients do not need a therapist because they can work alone with a manual or self-help book.

In a treatment for cleaning compulsions, the patient might be asked to touch a dirty object and instructed not to wash or clean up for hours afterward. The therapist may have to demonstrate the action first by holding the dirty towel or touching the floor to prove that it can be done without disastrous consequences. Sometimes a helper is needed, especially if the ritual is normally solitary. For example, a man who constantly retraces his path to be sure he hasn't run over someone while driving is encouraged to carry a passenger past pedestrians on bumpy roads while resisting the urge to turn the car around. Parents of a child who will not reuse a bar of soap may be asked to wash their own hands and then sit by the sink while the child uses the same soap.

Habit reversal

A variant of ERP is habit reversal, the cultivation of responses that preclude the ritual. It can be especially useful for arranging and touching compulsions, hair-pulling, and skin-picking. The patient charts the compulsive urges and associated actions and tries to substitute other actions such as deep breathing, muscle relaxation, or fist-clenching. Anxiety management, relaxation training, and assertiveness training are sometimes added.

Techniques that resemble response prevention can also be used when there is no action to forestall because the patient has only obsessional thoughts or only cognitive rituals like silent counting. The patient may be asked to think the obsessional thought and avoid reciting the tension-relieving formula. Another method is thought-stopping. When an obsessional thought intrudes, the patient says, "Stop" (at first aloud, later silently) and snaps a rubber band or delivers a mild electrical shock to the wrist. The opposite approach is saturation—concentrating so hard on the thought that it becomes meaningless and loses its compelling quality. In one variant of saturation, patients record their mental rituals on audiotapes and repeatedly listen to them in a continuous loop.

Cognitive therapy helps people learn to question the importance of their obsessions and the belief that rituals can protect them. It also works to change associations; for example, if a patient regards anything touched by another person as contaminated, the therapist and patient can investigate the origins of this association and find ways to weaken it. Cognitive therapy may be especially useful for pathological doubts and violent obsessional urges. It sometimes encourages patients to continue ERP when they would otherwise quit in frustration.

Primary obsessional slowness

A rare form of OCD is known as primary obsessional slowness. In this condition, every action is performed with great deliberation and attention to detail, patients may take hours to bathe, dress, and eat. The behavioral treatment consists of modeling, prompting, and shaping. The therapist demonstrates the action (models), tells the patient to perform it within an agreed time while the therapist counts aloud (prompts), and praises the patient for approaching the time limit (shapes).

The rate of improvement in behavior therapy is 50% to 80% and is usually maintained for several years, but relapse is common, and a second or third round of treatment may be needed. Group and individual therapies are equally effective. There is no evidence that other symptoms are substituted for compulsive rituals, but precisely what makes a behavioral treatment effective is still unclear. In two controlled studies, ERP was found to be more effective than progressive muscle relaxation. But other researchers have found that cognitive approaches, including thought-stopping, are equally effective. No studies have found a reliable difference between ERP and exposure alone. A meta-analysis (combined analysis) of 52 experiments indicated that success in behavior therapy was correlated mainly with the amount of time spent by patient and therapist in assisted exposure.

Some patients cannot practice behavioral techniques effectively because of severe depression, personality disorders, family problems, or overvalued ideas that are near-delusions. Insight-oriented therapy may help them complete the behavioral treatment, live more easily with their remaining symptoms, and fill the time no longer consumed by obsessions and rituals. Mutual aid groups are also increasingly popular, especially because they allow people with OCD to help themselves by helping others.

Families are often enlisted to encourage and supervise the treatment, especially when children are involved. Surveys show that family members are most disturbed by ruminations, unemployment, rituals, and social withdrawal, in that order. They may have to be taught how to cope with the symptoms; for example, they must avoid reassurance, which perpetuates obsessional doubts and fears. Support groups or family counseling may be useful, especially if the family has been resentful about participating in the rituals or completing acts not finished by the patient.

Pharmacological therapies

All of the drugs used in treating OCD are antidepressants as well, and they all enhance the activity of the neurotransmitter serotonin. Clomipramine (Anafranil) is probably the most effective by a small margin, but it has many side effects, including dry mouth, constipation, weight gain, and sometimes heart rhythm disturbances. Today the first choice is usually a selective serotonin reuptake inhibitor (SSRI): fluoxetine (Prozac), fluvoxamine (Luvox), sertraline (Zoloft), or paroxetine (Paxil). Their chief side effects are overstimulation, insomnia, nausea, and loss of sexual desire or the capacity for orgasm.

On average, OCD requires higher doses than depression, and the drugs take longer to begin working—three months in OCD, one month in depression.

More than two-thirds of patients eventually get some relief from their obsessions and compulsions, but almost all of them relapse within a month unless they either continue drug treatment indefinitely or agree to behavior therapy. In fact, one important function of the drugs is to reduce patients' fears enough so they can begin ERP. For people who are afraid to take a drug, the promise of a more lasting solution through behavior therapy may overcome their reluctance. Although most experts believe that SSRIs and behavioral or cognitive therapies are equally effective, no direct comparisons have been published. In several studies, the combination of drug treatment and behavior therapy has been found more effective than drugs alone, which rarely eliminate the symptoms completely.

The use of SSRIs has not helped much in elucidating the causes of OCD. Serotonin is known to be one of the chemical messengers in the pathway between the basal ganglia and frontal cortex, but the rest of the picture is unclear. SSRIs cause levels of serotonin to rise immediately but take months to affect the symptoms of OCD. If the drugs are used for a long time, receptors for serotonin become less sensitive. Drugs that directly increase the output of serotonin do not relieve the symptoms of OCD, and drugs that suppress its effects do not necessarily make the symptoms worse. To complicate matters, there are more than a dozen kinds of serotonin nerve receptors, and their functions are not completely understood. Tourette's disorder is treated not with serotonin-enhancing drugs but with drugs that block the activity of another transmitter, dopamine, at certain nerve receptors in the caudate nucleus. Changing the activity of serotonin or dopamine is probably an indirect way of compensating for other brain abnormalities.

Surgery, a last resort

Although the introduction of SSRIs and the wider use of behavior therapy have shortened the course of OCD, it is still a chronic condition. According to one estimate, 10% of patients recover completely, 50% improve, 30% remain the same, and 10% deteriorate. Brain surgery, usually performed with special instruments through a small opening in the skull, is a last resort in cases where nothing else works and the symptoms are incapacitating—the patient is spending hours each day on rituals, never leaves his room, or has repeatedly attempted suicide. All the surgical procedures serve to interrupt and eventually alter the routing of neural transmission in the circuit that runs through the frontal cortex and basal ganglia. The names—cingulotomy, capsulotomy, subcaudate tractotomy—depend on where the cut is made. About half the patients get at least some relief. They often take months to respond, which suggests that the brain is substituting new connections or the balance of neurotransmitter activity has slowly changed.

The best source of information and referrals on OCD is the Obsessive-Compulsive Foundation, P.O. Box 70, Milford, CT 06460-0070; tel. 203-878-5669; 203-874-3843 (for recorded information). On the Web, visit: *http://pages. prodigy.com/alwillen/ocf.html.*

FOR FURTHER READING

Jonathan S. Abramowitz. Effectiveness of psychological and pharmacological treatments for obsessive-compulsive disorder: A quantitative review. *Journal of Consulting and Clinical Psychology 65: 44–52 (1997).*

John S. March, Allen Frances, Daniel Carpenter, and David A. Kahn, eds. The expert consensus guideline: Treatment of obsessive-compulsive disorder. *Journal of Clinical Psychiatry 58, Suppl. 4 (1997).*

Michele T. Payto and Gail Steketee, eds. Obsessive-compulsive disorder across the life cycle. *In: Leah J. Dickstein, Michelle B. Riba, and John M. Oldham, eds.* Review of Psychiatry, *Vol. 16. Washington, D.C.: American Psychiatric Press, 1997.*

Judith L. Rapoport and Alan Fiske. The new biology of obsessive-compulsive disorder: Implications for evolutionary psychology. *Perspectives in Biology and Medicine 41: 159–175 (Winter 1998).*

Unit Selections

Key Points to Consider

❖ What varieties of psychotherapy are available? Does psychotherapy work? Are laypersons effective therapists? Is professional assistance for psychological problems always necessary? Can people successfully change themselves? When is professional help needed? What can be changed successfully? What problems seem immune to change?

❖ How can you "think like a shrink?" What rules of thumb do psychologists use for determining clients' mental health status? How can you utilize these rules? Can you think of other rules that are not included in the article "Think Like a Shrink"?

❖ How does clinical depression differ from the everyday blues we sometimes experience? What are some of the treatments for severe depression? What is Prozac? How does Prozac work? What are some of its side effects and disadvantages? If you were a psychiatrist, would your first line of treatment for depression be Prozac? Why?

❖ What is schizophrenia? Why is schizophrenia hard to treat? Is schizophrenia a brain disorder as some claim? What are some of the newer treatments for schizophrenia?

 **Links** | **www.dushkin.com/online/**

These sites are annotated on pages 4 and 5.

Have you ever had the nightmare that you are trapped in a dark, dismal place? No one will let you out. Your pleas for freedom go unanswered and, in fact, are suppressed or ignored by domineering authority figures around you. You keep begging for mercy but to no avail. What a nightmare! You are fortunate to awake to your normal bedroom and to the realities of your daily life. For the mentally ill, the nightmare of institutionalization, where individuals can be held against their will in what are sometimes terribly dreary, restrictive surroundings, is a reality. Have you ever wondered what would happen if we took perfectly normal individuals and institutionalized them? In one well-known and remarkable study, that is exactly what happened.

In 1973, eight people, including a pediatrician, a psychiatrist, and some psychologists, presented themselves to psychiatric hospitals. Each claimed that he or she was hearing voices. The voices, they reported, seemed unclear but appeared to be saying "empty" or "thud." Each of these individuals was admitted to a mental hospital, and most were diagnosed as being schizophrenic. Upon admission, the fake patients gave truthful information and thereafter acted like their usual, normal selves.

Their hospital stays lasted anywhere from 7 to 52 days. The nurses, doctors, psychologists, and other staff members treated them as if they really were schizophrenic and never saw through their trickery. Some of the real patients in the hospital did recognize, however, that the pseudopatients were perfectly normal. Upon discharge almost all of the pseudopatients received the diagnosis of "schizophrenic in remission," meaning that they were still clearly construed as schizophrenic; they just weren't exhibiting any of the symptoms at the time.

What does this study demonstrate about mental illness? Is true mental illness readily detectable? If we can't always detect mental disorders, the more professionally accepted term for mental illness, how can we treat them? What treatments are available

and which work better for various diagnoses? The treatment of mental disorders is a challenge. The array of available treatments is ever-increasing and can be downright bewildering—and not just to the patient or client! In order to demystify and simplify your understanding of various treatments, we will look at them in this unit.

We commence with two general articles on treatment. In the first, renowned psychologist Martin Seligman discusses what we can hope to accomplish if we attempt reform. Some individuals have successfully shed weight, overcome anxiety and phobias, or quit smoking either by themselves or with professional assistance. Seligman takes a realistic look at what can and cannot be successfully changed in "What You Can Change and What You Cannot Change."

In the next article, "Think Like a Shrink," Emanuel Rosen reviews the criteria that psychologists utilize to determine the mental health status of an individual. The main point is that we, too, can use these same guidelines to determine the mental health standing of others and ourselves. Rosen also reveals how psychotherapy seems to function, by reducing defensiveness.

Depression afflicts many of us. Some individuals suffer from chronic and intense depression, known as clinical depression. The fourth article, "The Quest for a Cure," not only details the symptoms of depression, but also provides a good discussion of the possible treatments for severe depression. In particular, the revolutionary drug, Prozac, is showcased.

The final article of this unit and of the book investigates treatments for schizophrenia. Schizophrenia is a psychosis and therefore causes more profound disturbance than the disorders discussed previously. In this final article, new and old treatments for schizophrenia are described. Because we now believe that schizophrenia is the result of a neurochemical problem, many of the new treatments affect brain chemistry.

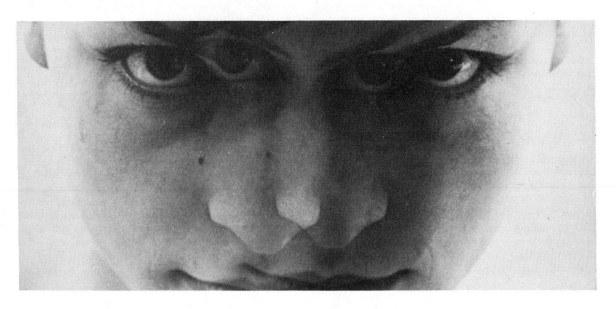

What You Can Change & What You Cannot Change

There are things we can change about ourselves and things we cannot. Concentrate your energy on what is possible—too much time has been wasted.

Martin E. P. Seligman, Ph.D.

This is the age of psychotherapy and the age of self-improvement. Millions are struggling to change: We diet, we jog, we meditate. We adopt new modes of thought to counteract our depressions. We practice relaxation to curtail stress. We exercise to expand our memory and to quadruple our reading speed. We adopt draconian regimens to give up smoking. We raise our little boys and girls to androgyny. We come out of the closet and we try to become heterosexual. We seek to lose our taste for alcohol. We seek more meaning in life. We try to extend our life span.

Sometimes it works. But distressingly often, self-improvement and psychotherapy fail. The cost is enormous. We think we are worthless. We feel guilty and ashamed. We believe we have no willpower and that we are failures. We give up trying to change.

On the other hand, this is not only the age of self-improvement and therapy, but also the age of biological psychiatry. The human genome will be nearly mapped before the millennium is over. The brain systems underlying sex, hearing, memory, left-handedness, and sadness are now known. Psychoactive drugs quiet our fears, relieve our blues, bring us bliss, dampen our mania, and dissolve our delusions more effectively than we can on our own.

Our very personality—our intelligence and musical talent, even our religiousness, our conscience (or its absence), our politics, and our exuberance—turns out to be more the product of our genes than almost anyone would have believed a decade ago. The underlying message of the age of biological psychiatry is that our biology frequently makes changing, in spite of all our efforts, impossible.

But the view that all is genetic and biochemical and therefore unchangeable is also very often wrong. Many people surpass their IQs, fail to "respond" to drugs, make sweeping changes in their lives, live on when their cancer is "terminal," or defy the hormones and brain circuitry that "dictate" lust, femininity, or memory loss.

The ideologies of biological psychiatry and self-improvement are obviously colliding. Nevertheless, a resolution is apparent. There are some things about ourselves that can be changed, others that cannot, and some that can be changed only with extreme difficulty.

What can we succeed in changing about ourselves? What can we not? When can we overcome our biology? And when is our biology our destiny?

I want to provide an understanding of what you can and what you can't change about yourself so that you can concentrate your limited time and energy on what is possible. So much time has been wasted. So much needless frustration has been endured. So much of therapy, so much of child rearing, so much of self-improving, and even some of the great social movements in our century have come to nothing because they tried to change the unchangeable. Too often we have wrongly thought we were weak-willed failures, when the changes we wanted to make in ourselves

From *Psychology Today*, May/June 1994, pp. 34–41, 70, 72–74, 84. Excerpted from *What You Can Change and What You Can't* by Martin E. P. Seligman. © 1993 by Martin E. P. Seligman. Reprinted by permission of Alfred A. Knopf, Inc.

So much child rearing, therapy, and self-improvement have come to nothing.

were just not possible. But all this effort was necessary: Because there have been so many failures, we are now able to see the boundaries of the unchangeable; this in turn allows us to see clearly for the first time the boundaries of what *is* changeable.

With this knowledge, we can use our precious time to make the many rewarding changes that are possible. We can live with less self-reproach and less remorse. We can live with greater confidence. This knowledge is a new understanding of who we are and where we are going.

CATASTROPHIC THINKING: PANIC

S. J. Rachman, one of the world's leading clinical researchers and one of the founders of behavior therapy, was on the phone. He was proposing that I be the "discussant" at a conference about panic disorder sponsored by the National Institute of Mental Health (NIMH).

"Why even bother, Jack?" I responded. "Everyone knows that panic is biological and that the only thing that works is drugs."

"Don't refuse so quickly, Marty. There is a breakthrough you haven't yet heard about."

Breakthrough was a word I had never heard Jack use before.

"What's the breakthrough?" I asked.

"If you come, you can find out."

So I went.

I had known about and seen panic patients for many years, and had read the literature with mounting excitement during the 1980s. I knew that panic disorder is a frightening condition that consists of recurrent attacks, each much worse than anything experienced before. Without prior warning, you feel as if you are going to die. Here is a typical case history:

The first time Celia had a panic attack, she was working at McDonald's. It was two days before her 20th birthday. As she was handing a customer a Big Mac, she had the worst experience of her life. The earth seemed to open up beneath her. Her heart began to pound, she felt she was smothering, and she was sure she was going to have a heart attack and die. After about 20 minutes of terror, the panic subsided. Trembling, she got in her car, raced home and barely left the house for the next three months.

Since then, Celia has had about three attacks a month. She does not know when they are coming. She always thinks she is going to die.

Panic attacks are not subtle, and you need no quiz to find out if you or someone you love has them. As many as five percent of American adults probably do. The defining feature of the disorder is simple: recurrent awful attacks of panic that come out of the blue, last for a few minutes, and then subside. The attacks consist of chest pains, sweating, nausea, dizziness, choking, smothering, or trembling. They are accompanied by feelings of overwhelming dread and thoughts that you are having a heart attack, that you are losing control, or that you are going crazy.

THE BIOLOGY OF PANIC

There are four questions that bear on whether a mental problem is primarily "biological" as opposed to "psychological":

- Can it be induced biologically?
- Is it genetically heritable?
- Are specific brain functions involved?
- Does a drug relieve it?

Inducing panic. Panic attacks can be created by a biological agent. For example, patients who have a history of panic attacks are hooked up to an intravenous line. Sodium lactate, a chemical that normally produces rapid, shallow breathing and heart palpitations, is slowly infused into their bloodstream. Within a few minutes, about 60 to 90 percent of these patients have a panic attack. Normal controls—subjects with no history of panic—rarely have attacks when infused with lactate.

Genetics of panic. There may be some heritability of panic. If one of two identical twins has panic attacks, 31 percent of the cotwins also have them. But if one of two fraternal twins has panic attacks, none of the cotwins are so afflicted.

Panic and the brain. The brains of people with panic disorders look somewhat unusual upon close scrutiny. Their neurochemistry shows abnormalities in the system that turns on, then dampens, fear. In addition, the PET scan (positron-emission tomography), a technique that looks at how much blood and oxygen different parts of the brain use, shows that patients who panic from the infusion of lactate have

We are now able to see the boundaries of the unchangeable.

What Can We Change?

When we survey all the problems, personality types, patterns of behavior, and the weak influence of childhood on adult life, we see a puzzling array of how much change occurs. From the things that are easiest to those that are the most difficult, this rough array emerges:

Panic	Curable
Specific Phobias	Almost Curable
Sexual Dysfunctions	Marked Relief
Social Phobia	Moderate Relief
Agoraphobia	Moderate Relief
Depression	Moderate Relief
Sex Role Change	Moderate Relief
Obsessive-Compulsive Disorder	Moderate Mild Relief
Sexual Preferences	Moderate Mild Change
Anger	Mild Moderate Relief
Everyday Anxiety	Mild Moderate Relief
Alcoholism	Mild Relief
Overweight	Temporary Change
Posttraumatic Stress Disorder (PTSD)	Marginal Relief
Sexual Orientation	Probably Unchangeable
Sexual Identity	Unchangeable

higher blood flow and oxygen use in relevant parts of their brain than patients who don't panic.

Drugs. Two kinds of drugs relieve panic: tricyclic antidepressants and the anti-anxiety drug Xanax, and both work better than placebos. Panic attacks are dampened, and sometimes even eliminated. General anxiety and depression also decrease.

Since these four questions had already been answered "yes" when Jack Rachman called, I thought the issue had already been settled. Panic disorder was simply a biological illness, a disease of the body that could be relieved only by drugs.

A few months later I was in Bethesda, Maryland, listening once again to the same four lines of biological evidence. An inconspicuous figure in a brown suit sat hunched over the table. At the first break, Jack introduced me to him—David Clark, a young psychologist from Oxford. Soon after, Clark began his address.

"Consider, if you will, an alternative theory, a cognitive theory." He reminded all of us that almost all panickers believe that they are going to die during an attack. Most commonly, they believe that they are having heart attacks. Perhaps, Clark suggested, this is more than just a mere symptom. Perhaps it is the root cause. Panic may simply be the *catastrophic misinterpretation of bodily sensations.*

For example, when you panic, your heart starts to race. You notice this, and you see it as a possible heart attack. This makes you very anxious, which means that your heart pounds more. You now notice that your heart is *really* pounding. You are now *sure* it's a heart attack. This terrifies you, and you break into a sweat, feel nauseated, short of breath—all symptoms of terror, but for you, they're confirmation of a heart attack. A full-blown panic attack is under way, and at the root of it is your misinterpretation of the symptoms of anxiety as symptoms of impending death.

I was listening closely now as Clark argued that an obvious sign of a disorder, easily dismissed as a symptom, is the disorder itself. If he was right, this was a historic occasion. All Clark had done so far, however, was to show that the four lines of evidence for a biological view of panic could fit equally well with a misinterpretation view. But Clark soon told us about a series of experiments he and his colleague Paul Salkovskis had done at Oxford.

First, they compared panic patients with patients who had other anxiety disorders and with normals. All the subjects read the following sentences aloud, but the last word was presented blurred. For example:

dying
If I had palpitations, I could be
excited

choking
If I were breathless, I could be
unfit

When the sentences were about bodily sensations, the panic patients, but no one else, saw the catastrophic endings fastest. This showed that panic patients possess the habit of thinking Clark had postulated.

Next, Clark and his colleagues asked if activating this habit with words would induce panic. All the subjects read a series of word pairs aloud. When panic patients

---

Self-Analysis Questionnaire

Is your life dominated by anxiety? Read each statement and then mark the appropriate number to indicate how you generally feel. There are no right or wrong answers.

1. I am a steady person.

Almost never	Sometimes	Often	Almost always
4	3	2	1

2. I am satisfied with myself.

Almost never	Sometimes	Often	Almost always
4	3	2	1

3. I feel nervous and restless.

Almost never	Sometimes	Often	Almost always
1	2	3	4

4. I wish I could be as happy as others seem to be.

Almost never	Sometimes	Often	Almost always
1	2	3	4

5. I feel like a failure.

Almost never	Sometimes	Often	Almost always
1	2	3	4

6. I get in a state of tension and turmoil as I think over my recent concerns and interests.

Almost never	Sometimes	Often	Almost always
1	2	3	4

7. I feel secure.

Almost never	Sometimes	Often	Almost always
4	3	2	1

8. I have self-confidence.

Almost never	Sometimes	Often	Almost always
4	3	2	1

9. I feel inadequate.

Almost never	Sometimes	Often	Almost always
1	2	3	4

10. I worry too much over something that does not matter.

Almost never	Sometimes	Often	Almost always
1	2	3	4

To score, simply add up the numbers under your answers. Notice that some of the rows of numbers go up and others go down. The higher your total, the more the trait of anxiety dominates your life. If your score was:

10–11, you are in the lowest 10 percent of anxiety.

13–14, you are in the lowest quarter.

16–17, your anxiety level is about average.

19–20, your anxiety level is around the 75th percentile.

22–24 (and you are male) your anxiety level is around the 90th percentile.

24–26 (and you are female) your anxiety level is around the 90th percentile.

25 (and you are male) your anxiety level is at the 95th percentile.

27 (and you are female) your anxiety level is at the 95th percentile.

Should you try to change your anxiety level? Here are my rules of thumb:

- If your score is at the 90th percentile or above, you can probably improve the quality of your life by lowering your general anxiety level—regardless of paralysis and irrationality.
- If your score is at the 75th percentile or above, and you feel that anxiety is either paralyzing you or that it is unfounded, you should probably try to lower your general anxiety level.
- If your score is 18 or above, and you feel that anxiety is unfounded and paralyzing, you should probably try to lower your general anxiety level.

got to "breathlessness-suffocation" and "palpitations-dying," 75 percent suffered a full-blown panic attack right there in the laboratory. No normal people had panic attacks, no recovered panic patients (I'll tell you more in a moment about how they got better) had attacks, and only 17 percent of other anxious patients had attacks.

The final thing Clark told us was the "breakthrough" that Rachman had promised.

Issues of the soul can barely be changed by psychotherapy or drugs.

"We have developed and tested a rather novel therapy for panic," Clark continued in his understated, disarming way. He explained that if catastrophic misinterpretations of bodily sensation are the cause of a panic attack, then changing the tendency to misinterpret should cure the disorder. His new therapy was straightforward and brief:

Patients are told that panic results when they mistake normal symptoms of mounting anxiety for symptoms of heart attack, going crazy, or dying. Anxiety itself, they are informed, produces shortness of breath, chest pain, and sweating. Once they misinterpret these normal bodily sensations as an imminent heart attack, their symptoms become even more pronounced because the misinterpretation changes their anxiety into terror. A vicious circle culminates in a full-blown panic attack.

Patients are taught to reinterpret the symptoms realistically as mere anxiety symptoms. Then they are given practice right in the office, breathing rapidly into a paper bag. This causes a buildup of carbon dioxide and shortness of breath, mimicking the sensations that provoke a panic attack. The therapist points out that the symptoms the patient is experiencing—shortness of breath and heart racing—are harmless, simply the result of overbreathing, not a sign of a heart attack. The patient learns to interpret the symptoms correctly.

"This simple therapy appears to be a cure," Clark told us. "Ninety to 100 percent of the patients are panic free at the end of therapy. One year later, only one person had another panic attack."

This, indeed, was a breakthrough: a simple, brief psychotherapy with no side effects showing a 90-percent cure rate of a disorder that a decade ago was thought to be incurable. In a controlled study of 64 patients comparing cognitive therapy to drugs to relaxation to no treatment, Clark and his colleagues found that cognitive therapy is markedly better than drugs or relaxation, both of which are better than nothing. Such a high cure rate is unprecedented.

How does cognitive therapy for panic compare with drugs? It is more effective and less dangerous. Both the antidepressants and Xanax produce marked reduction in panic in most patients, but drugs must be taken forever; once the drug is stopped, panic rebounds to where it was before therapy began for perhaps half the patients. The drugs also sometimes have severe side effects, including drowsiness, lethargy, pregnancy complications, and addictions.

After this bombshell, my own "discussion" was an anticlimax. I did make one point that Clark took to heart. "Creating a cognitive therapy that works, even one that works as well as this apparently does, is not enough to show that the *cause* of panic is cognitive." I was niggling. "The biological theory doesn't deny that some other therapy might work well on panic. It merely claims that panic is caused at the bottom by some biochemical problem."

Anxiety scans your life for imperfections. When it finds one, it won't let go.

Two years later, Clark carried out a crucial experiment that tested the biological theory against the cognitive theory. He gave the usual lactate infusion to 10 panic patients, and nine of them panicked. He did the same thing with another 10 patients, but added special instructions to allay the misinterpretation of the sensations. He simply told them: "Lactate is a natural bodily substance that produces sensations similar to exercise or alcohol. It is normal to experience intense sensations during infusion, but these do not indicate an adverse reaction." Only three out of the 10 panicked. This confirmed the theory crucially.

The therapy works very well, as it did for Celia, whose story has a happy ending. She first tried Xanax, which reduced the intensity and the frequency of her panic attacks. But she was too drowsy to work and she was still having about one attack every six weeks. She was then referred to Audrey, a cognitive therapist who explained that Celia was misinterpreting her heart racing and shortness of breath as symptoms of a heart attack, that they were actually just symptoms of mounting anxiety, nothing more harmful. Audrey taught Celia progressive relaxation, and then she demonstrated the harmlessness of Celia's symptoms of overbreathing. Celia then relaxed in the presence of the symptoms and found that they gradually subsided. After several more practice sessions, therapy terminated. Celia has gone two years without another panic attack.

EVERYDAY ANXIETY

Attend to your tongue—right now. What is it doing? Mine is swishing around near my lower right molars. It has just found a minute fragment of last night's popcorn (debris from *Terminator 2*). Like a dog at a bone, it is worrying the firmly wedged flake.

Attend to your hand—right now. What's it up to? My left hand is boring in on an itch it discovered under my earlobe.

Your tongue and your hands have, for the most part, a life of their own. You can bring them under voluntary control by consciously calling them out of their "default" mode to carry out your commands: "Pick up the phone" or "Stop picking that pimple." But most of the time they are on their own. They are seeking out small imperfections. They scan your entire mouth and skin surface, probing for anything going wrong. They are marvelous, nonstop grooming devices. They, not the more fashionable immune system, are your first line of defense against invaders.

Anxiety is your mental tongue. Its default mode is to search for what may be about to go wrong. It continually, and without your conscious consent, scans your life—yes, even when you are asleep, in dreams and nightmares. It reviews your work, your love, your play—until it finds an imperfection. When it finds one, it worries it. It tries to pull it out from its hiding place, where it is wedged inconspicuously under some rock. It will not let go. If the imperfection is threatening enough, anxiety calls your attention to it by making you uncomfortable. If you do not act, it yells more insistently—disturbing your sleep and your appetite.

You can reduce daily, mild anxiety. You can numb it with alcohol, Valium, or marijuana. You can take the edge off with meditation or progressive relaxation. You can beat it down by becoming more conscious of the automatic thoughts of danger that trigger anxiety and then disputing them effectively.

But do not overlook what your anxiety is trying to do for you. In return for the pain it brings, it prevents larger ordeals by making you aware of their possibility and goading you into planning for and forestalling them. It may even help you avoid them altogether. Think of your anxiety as the "low oil" light flashing on the dashboard of your car. Disconnect it and you will be less distracted and more comfortable for a while. But this may cost you a burned-up engine. Our *dysphoria,* or bad feeling, should, some of the time, be tolerated, attended to, even cherished.

GUIDELINES FOR WHEN TO TRY TO CHANGE ANXIETY

Some of our everyday anxiety, depression, and anger go beyond their useful function. Most adaptive traits fall along a normal spectrum of distribution, and the capacity for internal bad weather for everyone some of the time means that some of us may have terrible weather all of the time. In general, when the hurt is pointless and recurrent—when, for example, anxiety insists we formulate a plan but no plan will work—it is time to take action to relieve the hurt. There are three hallmarks indicating that anxiety has become a burden that wants relieving:

First, is it *irrational?*

We must calibrate our bad weather inside against the real weather outside. Is what you are anxious about out of proportion to the reality of the danger? Here are some examples that may help you answer this question. All of the following are not irrational:

- A fire fighter trying to smother a raging oil well burning in Kuwait repeatedly wakes up at four in the morning because of flaming terror dreams.
- A mother of three smells perfume on her husband's shirts and, consumed by jealousy, broods about his infidelity, reviewing the list of possible women over and over.
- A student who had failed two of his midterm exams finds, as finals approach, that he can't get to sleep for worrying. He has diarrhea most of the time.

The only good thing that can be said about such fears is that they are well-founded.

In contrast, all of the following are irrational, out of proportion to the danger:

- An elderly man, having been in a fender bender, broods about travel and will no longer take cars, trains, or airplanes.
- An eight-year-old child, his parents having been through an ugly divorce, wets his bed at night. He is haunted with visions of his bedroom ceiling collapsing on him.
- A housewife who has an MBA and who accumulated a decade of experience as a financial vice president before her twins were born is sure her job search

will be fruitless. She delays preparing her résumés for a month.

The second hallmark of anxiety out of control is *paralysis.* Anxiety intends action: Plan, rehearse, look into shadows for lurking dangers, change your life. When anxiety becomes strong, it is unproductive; no problem-solving occurs. And when anxiety is extreme, it paralyzes you. Has your anxiety crossed this line? Some examples:

- A woman finds herself housebound because she fears that if she goes out, she will be bitten by a cat.
- A salesman broods about the next customer hanging up on him and makes no more cold calls.
- A writer, afraid of the next rejection slip, stops writing.

'Dieting below your natural weight is a necessary condition for bulimia. Returning to your natural weight will cure it.'

The final hallmark is *intensity.* Is your life dominated by anxiety? Dr. Charles Spielberger, one of the world's foremost testers of emotion, has developed well-validated scales for calibrating how severe anxiety is. To find out how anxious *you* are, use the self-analysis questionnaire.

LOWERING YOUR EVERYDAY ANXIETY

Everyday anxiety level is not a category to which psychologists have devoted a great deal of attention. Enough research has been done, however, for me to recommend two techniques that quite reliably lower everyday anxiety levels. Both techniques are cumulative, rather than one-shot fixes. They require 20 to 40 minutes a day of your valuable time.

The first is *progressive relaxation,* done once or, better, twice a day for at least 10 minutes. In this technique, you tighten and then turn off each of the major muscle groups of your body until you are wholly flaccid. It is not easy to be highly anxious when your body feels like Jell-O. More formally, relaxation engages a response system that competes with anxious arousal.

The second technique is regular *meditation.* Transcendental meditation ™ is one

useful, widely available version of this. You can ignore the cosmology in which it is packaged if you wish, and treat it simply as the beneficial technique it is. Twice a day for 20 minutes, in a quiet setting, you close your eyes and repeat a *mantra* (a syllable whose "sonic properties are known") to yourself. Meditation works by blocking thoughts that produce anxiety. It complements relaxation, which blocks the motor components of anxiety but leaves the anxious thoughts untouched.

Done regularly, meditation usually induces a peaceful state of mind. Anxiety at other times of the day wanes, and hyperarousal from bad events is dampened. Done religiously, TM probably works better than relaxation alone.

There's also a quick fix. The minor tranquilizers—Valium, Dalmane, Librium, and their cousins—relieve everyday anxiety. So does alcohol. The advantage of all these is that they work within minutes and require no discipline to use. Their disadvantages outweigh their advantages, however. The minor tranquilizers make you fuzzy and somewhat uncoordinated as they work (a not uncommon side effect is an automobile accident). Tranquilizers soon lose their effect when taken regularly, and they are habit-forming—probably addictive. Alcohol, in addition, produces gross cognitive and motor disability in lockstep with its anxiety relief. Taken regularly over long periods, deadly damage to liver and brain ensue.

If you crave quick and temporary relief from acute anxiety, either alcohol or minor tranquilizers, taken in small amounts and only occasionally, will do the job. They are, however, a distant second-best to progressive relaxation and meditation, which are each worth trying before you seek out psychotherapy or in conjunction with therapy. Unlike tranquilizers and alcohol, neither of these techniques is likely to do you any harm.

Weigh your everyday anxiety. If it is not intense, or if it is moderate and not irrational or paralyzing, act now to reduce it. In spite of its deep evolutionary roots, intense everyday anxiety is often changeable. Meditation and progressive relaxation practiced regularly can change it forever.

DIETING: A WAIST IS A TERRIBLE THING TO MIND

I have been watching my weight and restricting my intake—except for an occasional binge like this—since I was 20. I weighed about 175 pounds then, maybe 15 pounds over my official "ideal" weight. I weigh 199 pounds now, 30 years later, about 25 pounds over the ideal. I have tried about a dozen regimes—fasting, the Beverly Hills Diet, no carbohydrates, Metrecal for lunch, 1,200 calories a day, low fat, no lunch, no starches, skipping every other dinner. I lost 10 or 15 pounds on each in about a month. The pounds always came back, though, and I have gained a net of about a pound a year—inexorably.

This is the most consistent failure in my life. It's also a failure I can't just put out of mind. I have spent the last few years reading the scientific literature, not the parade of best-selling diet books or the flood of women's magazine articles on the latest way to slim down. The scientific findings look clear to me, but there is not yet a consensus. I am going to go out on a limb, because I see so many signs all pointing in one direction. What I have concluded will, I believe, soon be the consensus of the scientists. The conclusions surprise me. They will probably surprise you, too, and they may change your life.

Here is what the picture looks like to me:

- Dieting doesn't work.
- Dieting may make overweight worse, not better.
- Dieting may be bad for health.
- Dieting may cause eating disorders— including bulimia and anorexia.

ARE YOU OVERWEIGHT?

Are you above the ideal weight for your sex, height, and age? If so, you are "overweight." What does this really mean? Ideal weight is arrived at simply. Four million people, now dead, who were insured by the major American life-insurance companies, were once weighed and had their height measured. At what weight on average do people of a given height turn out to live longest? That weight is called ideal. Anything wrong with that?

You bet. The real use of a weight table, and the reason your doctor takes it seriously, is that an ideal weight implies that, on average, if you slim down to yours, you will live longer. This is the crucial claim. Lighter people indeed live longer, on average, than heavier people, but how much longer is hotly debated.

But the crucial claim is unsound because weight (at any given height) has a normal distribution, *normal* both in a statistical sense and in the biological sense. In the biological sense, couch potatoes who overeat and never exercise can legitimately be called overweight, but the buxom, "heavy-boned" slow people deemed overweight by the ideal table are at their natural and healthiest weight. If you are a 155-pound woman and 64 inches in height, for example, you are "overweight" by around 15 pounds. This means nothing more than that the average 140-pound, 64-inch-tall woman lives somewhat longer than the average 155-pound woman of your height. It

does not follow that if you slim down to 125 pounds, *you* will stand any better chance of living longer.

In spite of the insouciance with which dieting advice is dispensed, no one has properly investigated the question of whether slimming down to "ideal" weight produces longer life. The proper study would compare the longevity of people who are at their ideal weight without dieting to people who achieve their ideal weight by dieting. Without this study the common medical advice to diet down to your ideal weight is simply unfounded.

This is not a quibble; there is evidence that dieting damages your health and that this damage may shorten your life.

MYTHS OF OVERWEIGHT

The advice to diet down to your ideal weight to live longer is one myth of overweight. Here are some others:

- *Overweight people overeat.* Wrong. Nineteen out of 20 studies show that obese people consume no more calories each day than nonobese people. Telling a fat person that if she would change her eating habits and eat "normally" she would lose weight is a lie. To lose weight and stay there, she will need to eat excruciatingly less than a normal person, probably for the rest of her life.
- *Overweight people have an overweight personality.* Wrong. Extensive research on personality and fatness has proved little. Obese people do not differ in any major personality style from nonobese people.
- *Physical inactivity is a major cause of obesity.* Probably not. Fat people are indeed less active than thin people, but the inactivity is probably caused more by the fatness than the other way around.
- *Overweight shows a lack of willpower.* This is the granddaddy of all the myths. Fatness is seen as shameful because we hold people responsible for their weight. Being overweight equates with being a weak-willed slob. We believe this primarily because we have seen people decide to lose weight and do so in a matter of weeks.

But almost everyone returns to the old weight after shedding pounds. Your body has a natural weight that it defends vigorously against dieting. The more diets tried, the harder the body works to defeat the next diet. Weight is in large part genetic. All this gives the lie to the "weak-willed" interpretations of overweight. More accurately, dieting is the conscious will of the

individual against a more vigilant opponent: the species' biological defense against starvation. The body can't tell the difference between self-imposed starvation and actual famine, so it defends its weight by refusing to release fat, by lowering its metabolism, and by demanding food. The harder the creature tries not to eat, the more vigorous the defenses become.

BULIMIA AND NATURAL WEIGHT

A concept that makes sense of your body's vigorous defense against weight loss is *natural weight*. When your body screams "I'm hungry," makes you lethargic, stores fat, craves sweets and renders them more delicious than ever, and makes you obsessed with food, what it is defending is your natural weight. It is signaling that you have dropped into a range it will not accept. Natural weight prevents you from gaining too much weight or losing too much. When you eat too much for too long, the opposite defenses are activated and make long-term weight gain difficult.

There is also a strong genetic contribution to your natural weight. Identical twins reared apart weigh almost the same throughout their lives. When identical twins are overfed, they gain weight and add fat in lockstep and in the same places. The fatness or thinness of adopted children resembles their biological parents—particularly their mother—very closely but does not at all resemble their adoptive parents. This suggests that you have a genetically given natural weight that your body wants to maintain.

The idea of natural weight may help cure the new disorder that is sweeping young America. Hundreds of thousands of young women have contracted it. It consists of bouts of binge eating and purging alternating with days of undereating. These young women are usually normal in weight or a bit on the thin side, but they are terrified of becoming fat. So they diet. They exercise. They take laxatives by the cup. They gorge. Then they vomit and take more laxatives. This malady is called *bulimia nervosa* (bulimia, for short).

Therapists are puzzled by bulimia, its causes, and treatment. Debate rages about whether it is an equivalent of depression, or an expression of a thwarted desire for control, or a symbolic rejection of the feminine role. Almost every psychotherapy has been tried. Antidepressants and other drugs have been administered with some effect but little success has been reported.

I don't think that bulimia is mysterious, and I think that it will be curable. I believe that bulimia is caused by dieting. The bulimic goes on a diet, and her body attempts to defend its natural weight. With repeated dieting, this defense becomes more vigorous. Her body is in massive revolt—insistently demanding food, storing fat, craving sweets, and lowering metabolism. Periodically, these biological defenses will overcome her extraordinary willpower (and extraordinary it must be to even approach an ideal weight, say, 20 pounds lighter than her natural weight). She will then binge. Horrified by what this will do to her figure, she vomits and takes laxatives to purge calories. Thus, bulimia is a natural consequence of self-starvation to lose weight in the midst of abundant food.

The therapist's task is to get the patient to stop dieting and become comfortable with her natural weight. He should first convince the patient that her binge eating is caused by her body's reaction to her diet. Then he must confront her with a question: Which is more important, staying thin or getting rid of bulimia? By stopping the diet, he will tell her, she can get rid of the uncontrollable binge-purge cycle. Her body will now settle at her natural weight, and she need not worry that she will balloon beyond that point. For some patients, therapy will end there because they would rather be bulimic than "loathsomely fat." For these patients, the central issue—ideal weight versus natural weight—can now at least become the focus of therapy. For others, defying the social and sexual pressure to be thin will be possible, dieting will be abandoned, weight will be gained, and bulimia should end quickly.

These are the central moves of the cognitive-behavioral treatment of bulimia. There are more than a dozen outcome studies of this approach, and the results are good. There is about 60 percent reduction in binging and purging (about the same as with antidepressant drugs). But unlike drugs, there is little relapse after treatment. Attitudes toward weight and shape relax, and dieting withers.

Of course, the dieting theory cannot fully explain bulimia. Many people who diet don't become bulimic; some can avoid it because their natural weight is close to their ideal weight, and therefore the diet they adopt does not starve them. In addition, bulimics are often depressed, since binging-purging leads to self-loathing. Depression may worsen bulimia by making it easier to give in to temptation. Further, dieting may just be another symptom of bulimia, not a cause. Other factors aside, I can speculate that dieting below your natural weight is a necessary condition for bulimia, and that returning to your natural weight and accepting that weight will cure bulimia.

OVERWEIGHT VS. DIETING: THE HEALTH DAMAGE

Being heavy carries some health risk. There is no definite answer to how much,

because there is a swamp of inconsistent findings. But even if you could just wish pounds away, never to return, it is not certain you should. Being somewhat above your "ideal" weight may actually be your healthiest natural condition, best for your particular constitution and your particular metabolism. Of course you can diet, but the odds are overwhelming that most of the weight will return, and that you will have to diet again and again. From a health and mortality perspective, should you? *There is, probably, a serious health risk from losing weight and regaining it.*

In one study, more than five thousand men and women from Framingham, Massachusetts, were observed for 32 years. People whose weight fluctuated over the years had 30 to 100 percent greater risk of death from heart disease than people whose weight was stable. When corrected for smoking, exercise, cholesterol level, and blood pressure, the findings became more convincing, suggesting that weight fluctuation (the primary cause of which is presumably dieting) may itself increase the risk of heart disease.

If this result is replicated, and if dieting is shown to be the primary cause of weight cycling, it will convince me that you should not diet to reduce your risk of heart disease.

DEPRESSION AND DIETING

Depression is yet another cost of dieting, because two root causes of depression are failure and helplessness. Dieting sets you up for failure. Because the goal of slimming down to your ideal weight pits your fallible willpower against untiring biological defenses, you will often fail. At first you will lose weight and feel pretty good about it. Any depression you had about your figure will disappear. Ultimately, however, you will probably not reach your goal; and then you will be dismayed as the pounds return. Every time you look in the mirror or vacillate over a white chocolate mousse, you will be reminded of your failure, which in turn brings depression.

On the other hand, if you are one of the fortunate few who can keep the weight from coming back, you will probably have to stay on an unsatisfying low-calorie diet for the rest of your life. A side effect of prolonged malnutrition is depression. Either way you are more vulnerable to it.

If you scan the list of cultures that have a thin ideal for women, you will be struck by something fascinating. All thin-ideal cultures also have eating disorders. They also have roughly twice as much depression in women as in men. (Women diet twice as much as men. The best estimate is that 13 percent of adult men and 25 percent of adult women are now on a diet.) The cultures without the thin ideal have no eating disor-

ders, and the amount of depression in women and men in these cultures is the same. This suggests that around the world, the thin ideal and dieting not only cause eating disorders, but they may also cause women to be more depressed than men.

THE BOTTOM LINE

I have been dieting off and on for 30 years because I want to be more attractive, healthier, and more in control. How do these goals stack up against the facts?

Attractiveness. If your attractiveness is a high-enough priority to convince you to diet, keep three drawbacks in mind. First, the attractiveness you gain will be temporary. All the weight you lose and maybe more will likely come back in a few years. This will depress you. Then you will have to lose it again and it will be harder the second time. Or you will have to resign yourself to being less attractive. Second, when women choose the silhouette figure they want to achieve, it turns out to be thinner than the silhouette that men label most attractive. Third, you may well become bulimic particularly if your natural weight is substantially more than your ideal weight. On balance, if short-term attractiveness is your overriding goal, diet. But be prepared for the costs.

Health. No one has ever shown that losing weight will increase my longevity. On balance, the health goal does not warrant dieting.

Control. For many people, getting to an ideal weight and staying there is just as biologically impossible as going with much less sleep. This fact tells me not to diet, and defuses my feeling of shame. My bottom line is clear: I am not going to diet anymore.

DEPTH AND CHANGE: THE THEORY

Clearly, we have not yet developed drugs or psychotherapies that can change all the problems, personality types, and patterns of behavior in adult life. But I believe that success and failure stems from something other than inadequate treatment. Rather, it stems from the depth of the problem.

We all have experience of psychological states of different depths. For example, if you ask someone, out of the blue, to answer quickly, "Who are you?" they will usually tell you—roughly in this order—their name, their sex, their profession, whether they have children, and their religion or race. Underlying this is a continuum of depth from surface to soul—with all manner of psychic material in between.

I believe that issues of the soul can barely be changed by psychotherapy or by drugs. Problems and behavior patterns somewhere between soul and surface can be changed somewhat. Surface problems can be changed easily, even cured. What is changeable, by therapy or drugs, I speculate, varies with the depth of the problem.

My theory says that it does not matter *when* problems, habits, and personality are acquired; their depth derives only from their biology, their evidence, and their power. Some childhood traits, for example, are deep and unchangeable but not because they were learned early and therefore have a privileged place.

Rather, those traits that resist change do so either because they are evolutionarily prepared or because they acquire great power by virtue of becoming the framework around which later learning crystallizes. In this way, the theory of depth carries the optimistic message that we are not prisoners of our past.

When you have understood this message, you will never look at your life in the same way again. Right now there are a number of things that you do not like about yourself and that you want to change: your short fuse, your waistline, your shyness, your drinking, your glumness. You have decided to change, but you do not know what you should work on first. Formerly you would have probably selected the one that hurts the most. Now you will also ask yourself which attempt is most likely to repay your efforts and which is most likely to lead to further frustration. Now you know your shyness and your anger are much more likely to change than your drinking, which you now know is more likely to change than your waistline.

Some of what does change is under your control, and some is not. You can best prepare yourself to change by learning as much as you can about what you can change and how to make those changes. Like all true education, learning about change is not easy; harder yet is surrendering some of our hopes. It is certainly not my purpose to destroy your optimism about change. But it is also not my purpose to assure everybody they can change in every way. My purpose is to instill a new, warranted optimism about the parts of your life you can change and so help you focus your limited time, money, and effort on making actual what is truly within your reach.

Life is a long period of change. What you have been able to change and what has resisted your highest resolve might seem chaotic to you: for some of what you are never changes no matter how hard you try, and other aspects change readily. My hope is that this essay has been the beginning of wisdom about the difference.

Yes, you too can see through the defenses people hide behind. To guide you, just consult the handy primer below. Put together by psychiatrist Emanuel H. Rosen, it distills years of Freudian analytical training into a few simple principles that make sense of our psyches.

THINK LIKE A
SHRINK

I have always thought it horribly unfortunate that there is such a tremendous gap between psychiatry and popular culture. Psychiatrists are regularly vilified in entertainment, media, and common thought, and our patients are regularly stigmatized. Indeed, I've yet to see a single movie that accurately portrays what we do. From *Silence of the Lambs* to *The Prince of Tides,* we shrinks have a reputation as crazy unbalanced people who can read people's minds. Even the hit comedy *The Santa Clause* made us out to be bimbos.

To some degree, we've gotten just what we deserve. We've allowed ourselves to become, in the public mind at least, mere pill-pushers and to have our uncommon sense dismissed as having zero significance when, in fact, it applies to every moment of every person's life. It is our failure to educate our patients and the general public about the deeper principles of human functioning that have left us so isolated from our communities.

Most patients come to psychiatrists because they recognize that, to some degree, their perceptions contain some distortions. These are usually defensive. For example, a 40-year-old woman may begin her first session with a psychiatrist complaining of a "biological depression" and demanding Prozac. By the end of the hour, however, she may acknowledge that her husband's 10-year refusal to have sex may have as much to do with her unhappy mood.

In my practice, I've engaged in a kind of educational psychotherapy, explaining simply to patients what they are doing and why they are doing it. The result has been not only remarkably effective but catalytic in speeding up the process of psychotherapy The same approach can help the general pub-

> **W**e all play to a hidden audience—Mom and Dad—inside our heads. Especially to Mom, whose nurturing is vital to our self-esteem—though it's not politically correct to say so.

lic delve beneath social images and better understand the deeper struggles of the people around them, and of themselves as well.

Ideas and principles can be introduced directly without the jargon psychiatrists normally hide behind in professional discussions. Doing this in a compassionate and empathic way could lead to a broadening of the vocabulary of the general public and bring about a wider acceptance of certain basic psychological truths.

The core of what we do as psychotherapists is strip away people's protective strategies. If you understand these defensive strategies and the core issues people tend to defend themselves against, you can see through people and, to a lesser extent, yourself.

Here, then, are some general principles to help you think like a shrink. Master them and you will—in some cases dramatically—increase your understanding of the world around you. You *can* see through people. *You* can read their minds.

1.

If you want to know how emotionally healthy someone is, look only at their intimate relationships.

Good-looking, athletic, charismatic, confident, rich, or intelligent people are not always emotionally healthy. For example, chronologically they may be adults, but emotionally, they may be two-year-olds. You will not really be able to make any kind of accurate, in-depth assessment of people until you learn to distinguish their superficial physical qualities from meaningful emotional ones. There are at least three key things you want to know:

• Most importantly how long-lived and committed are their current intimate relationships?

• Secondly, how much negative conflict do they experience in their work environments and how long have they held their current jobs?

• Finally what was their childhood experience like in their family of origin? Or, in plain English, did they get along with their family?

2.

How you feel about yourself (your self-esteem) is significantly determined by how nurturing your mother, father, and siblings were to you when you were growing up—especially your mother, though it is not politically correct to say so.

It is not that mothers are to blame for all of a patient's problems. It is simply that stable healthy mothering is a strong buffer against a tremendous amount of pathology.

3.

How you relate to intimate people is always based on how you related to your family when you were growing up.

Basically, we all keep our families with us forever. We keep them in our heads. For the rest of our lives, we will have tendencies to either take on the roles of our childhood selves or those of our parents. Examine carefully your relationships with your family. It will tell you a lot about who you are.

4.

We all play to a hidden audience—Mom and Dad—inside our heads.

You often see people do strange things in their interpersonal interactions. "Where did *that* come from," you often ask. It came from a hidden screenplay that was written in that person's head.

Ostensibly he's reacting to you, but in his head, he's reacting to his mother. In fact, the less he remembers of his childhood, the more he is going to act out with you. This leads nicely to. . . .

5.

People who say they "don't remember" their childhood are usually emotionally troubled.

Physically healthy individuals who can't recall their youth have frequently endured some painful experiences that their minds are blocking out. As a result, they really don't know who they are. They have what we psychiatrists call a diminished sense of identity.

6.

Victims like to be aggressors sometimes, and aggressors are often reconstituted victims.

People actually may become more actively aggressive when they feel forced into a passive position.

7.

Yes, Virginia, there is an "unconscious" or "non-conscious" mind, and it basically determines your life, everything from what job you choose to whom you marry.

All the feelings that you had about yourself, your parents, and family are buried in this "unconscious mind." Also buried here are some very deep fears which will be touched on below

The more aware you are of your unconscious mind, the more freedom you will have.

8.

Sex is critical, no matter what anyone says.

Sex has become passé as an important explanatory factor of human behavior. Nowadays, it is more politically correct to emphasize the role of feelings, thoughts, and emotions than the role of sex. Nonetheless, sexual functioning and sexual history *do* tell you a tremendous amount about what people are really like.

9.

Whenever you have two men, or two women, in a room, you have homosexual tension.

It is a core truth that all people have both heterosexual and homosexual drives. What varies is how you deal with those drives. Just because you have a homosexual impulse or idea has absolutely nothing to do with your sexual orientation. You are defined by your sexual *behavior*, not your sexual *impulses*.

The people in our society who are most against homosexuality are the people who are most uncomfortable with their own homosexual impulses. These impulses are banished from their conscious awareness.

10.

Yes, children do want to be sexual with the opposite sex parent at some point in their young lives, often between the ages of four and six.

Just about everyone is grossed out at the thought of their parents having sex. This is because there is a significant resistance against one's own memory of sexual feelings towards one's parents.

It does not mean, however, that you have to remember your sexual impulses towards a parent to be emotionally healthy. In fact, one of the most common issues an adult has to deal with is the incomplete repression of this core conflict.

11.

There is indeed such a thing as castration anxiety.

In fact, it's the most frightening core fear that people have. It's probably not only evolutionary adaptive, but emotionally important.

12.

Women do not have nearly as much penis envy as men do.

Men are all deep down very preoccupied with their penis. Concerns usually revolve around how big it is, how long, how thick, and how deep it goes.

This is an important issue that will likely never be researched because it makes everyone way too uncomfortable to talk about. There is more mythology on this subject than the Greeks ever wrote.

13.

The Oedipus complex is what keeps psychiatrists in business.

Though lay people tend to think only of the complex's sexual aspects, it really boils down to competition. It's commonly about being bigger, richer, more powerful, a winner or a loser. The feelings surrounding it are universal—and intense.

Getting through the various stages of psychological development—oral, anal, and Oedipal—can be summarized as teach-

> **M**en have much more penis envy than do women. They're all very preoccupied with their penis—how big it is, how long, how thick, and how deep it goes.

ing you three key things:

• To feel stable and secure, to depend on people reasonably

• To feel in control

• To feel able to compete successfully and to feel like a man or a woman.

14.

People are basically the same underneath it all; that is, they all want to satisfy similar deeper needs and quell identical underlying fears.

In general, people all seem to want money, power, and admiration. They want sexual gratification. They want to, as the Bible notes of Judah and Israel, "sit under their vine and fig tree and have none make them afraid." They want to feel secure. They want to feel loved.

Related to this principle: money and intelligence do not protect you. It is only emotional health that keeps you on an even keel; your feelings about yourself and your intimate stable relationships are the only ballast that matters in life.

> Our best defense is a good offense. When people act in an egotistical fashion, their underlying feeling is that they are "dick-less" or impotent.

15.

People often act exactly the opposite of the way they feel, especially when they are unhealthy.

Or: the best defense is a good offense. When people act egotistical, their underlying feeling is that they are "dick-less" or impotent.

16.

More on defenses . . .

Here is human nature in a nutshell. My favorite line from the movie *The Big Chill* is voiced by the character played by Jeff Goldblum. "Where would you be, where would any of us be, without a good rationalization? Try to live without a rationalization; I bet you couldn't do it."

We distort reality both outside and in our minds in order to survive. Distortions of our inner world are common. *Regression*, one of the most intriguing defenses, can be particularly illuminating to acknowledge; it means acting like a kid to avoid the real world.

"Outside" distortions can get us in very serious trouble.

Denial can be fatal whether it involves alcohol abuse or a herd of charging elephants.

Devaluing, or, in simple terms, throwing the baby out with the bath water, comes in handy when we want to insult somebody. But it can be detrimental—for example, causing us to miss a lecturer's important points because we consider the teacher to be a "total jerk."

Idealizing, or putting people on a pedestal, can be hurtful—say when you realize your ex-Navy Seal stockbroker has been churning your brokerage account.

Projecting feelings onto others is a common defensive distortion. Guilt is a painful feeling, so sometimes we may see other people as angry at us rather than feel guilty ourselves. "I know that you are angry that I forgot your birthday" you say. "Don't deny it."

Finally *splitting* our view of the world into good guys and bad guys is a distortion, even if it makes for a great western.

17.

To be successful in the highly competitive American business marketplace requires a personality ethos that will destroy your intimate relationships.

At this point, you are probably experiencing some confusion. After all, I've been saying that it is unhealthy to be striving continuously to compensate for feelings of inferiority or impotency Yet most people know that it is in fact the strivers who achieve enormous power and success in the world around them.

In order to be emotionally healthy, however, it is necessary for these "winners" to leave their work personalities at the door of their homes and become their natural selves once they cross the threshold. It is absolutely essential that the driven, rushed, acquisitive capitalist ethos not enter into the realm of intimate relationships.

CEOs of corporations and doctors are particularly at risk for this type of contamination of their family life. People who have the best of both worlds—career and relationships—are those who realize that success in the workplace does not make up for lack of success at home.

18.

How well people deal with death is usually identical to how well they have dealt with life.

19.

How people relate to you in everyday life can tell you a lot about their deeper issues, even in a very short time.

You can tell a tremendous amount about somebody's emotional stability and character by the way they say goodbye to you. People who cling or drag out good-byes often have deep-seated issues with separation. Of course, we all have issues with separation; it's a matter of degree. Those of us from loving stable backgrounds carry around a warm fuzzy teddy bear of sorts that helps us cope with saying good-bye and being alone. Without this security blanket of loving memories, being alone or saying good-bye can be hell.

A stranger who tells you his entire life's story on the first interview even if you are a psychiatrist, is also probably emotionally unhealthy because there is no boundary between that person and you—and there should be. After all, you are a stranger to that person.

20.

Listen with your third ear.

One of my mentors at Duke University Medical Center once defined the "third ear" as follows: "While you're listening to what a patient is saying, with your third ear listen to why they are saying it." Psychiatrists listen in a unique way. A family practitioner examines your ears with an otoscope. A psychiatrist examines your feelings with himself as the tool.

When you are interacting with another person, if you notice yourself feeling a certain way the odds are that your companion is somehow intending you to feel that way. You have to be emotionally stable to accurately use yourself as the examining tool.

When you become adept at identifying what you are feeling, the next step is to

> Strangers who blurt out their entire life story at a first meeting, even if it's with a psychiatrist, are likely to be troubled. They have no "boundary"— and they should

determine why. There are usually two reasons. Number one, it may be because you are resonating with what the person is feeling. A second possibility is that you are being subtly provoked to play a complementary emotional role in a scene that has an often hidden script.

The process of using one's own heart as a "scope" is hard work. The fancy term for this process is "counter-transference."

21.

Behind every fear, there is a wish.

Wishes that are often consciously unacceptable can be expressed more easily as "fears." Related to this principle is the maxim: "Beware unsolicited denials." A common example is the seemingly spontaneous statement, "1 don't really care at all about money!" Hold on to your wallet.

THE QUEST FOR A CURE

BY MARK NICHOLS

Every few weeks, several teenage girls arrive at Halifax's Queen Elizabeth II Health Sciences Centre to take part in a study that may someday ease the crippling misery of depression. For two nights, the girls, a different group each time, bunk down in a sleep laboratory with tiny electrodes attached to their heads. Through the night, electronic equipment monitors their brain activity as they pass through the various stages of sleep, including the periods of rapid eye movement (REM) when dreaming occurs. Half of the roughly 80 girls who will take part in the study have no family history of depression. The others do—their mothers have had major depression and researchers know that these girls have a 30 percent chance of being victims,

introduced a product called Prozac almost 10 years ago. The first of a new class of drugs that can alleviate depression without the same nasty side effects of many older antidepressants, it profoundly improved the quality of life for millions of people. Thanks to Prozac and drugs like it, says Dr. Sid Kennedy, head of the mood disorders program at Toronto's Clarke Institute of Psychiatry, "depressed people are able to live normal, productive lives in a way that wouldn't have been possible 10 years ago."

Now, drugs that are potentially even better are undergoing tests, while researchers study the intricate universe of the brain in search of clues that could someday banish depression entirely. "Things are really moving quickly,"

New drugs and therapies join the battle against depression

too. Dr. Stan Kutcher, a Dalhousie University psychiatrist who is involved in the study, wants to see whether a feature of sleep in depressed adults—they reach the REM stage faster than others—shows up in the kids. If it does, doctors for the first time would have a way of predicting depression and starting treatment early. Kutcher has been working with troubled youngsters most of his life. "It's a tremendous feeling to be able to help kids get better," he says. "It's a privilege to be let into their lives."

A pioneer in studying and treating adolescent depression, Kutcher is part of an army of medical researchers whose efforts are bringing new drugs, new therapies and new ways of thinking to bear in the war on the debilitating disorder. One of the biggest breakthroughs came in capsule form when Indianapolis's Eli Lilly and Co.

says Dr. Trevor Young, a neuroscientist at McMaster University in Hamilton. "They're really getting close to understanding the biochemical changes that occur in depressed brains."

And doctors are coming closer to the time when they may be able to start treatment, in some cases, even before depression takes hold. After the Dalhousie researchers finish their current series of tests early next year, they will keep track of their young subjects for five years to see whether their REM sleep patterns pinpoint which of them will become depressed. If they do, then doctors in the future may be able to test children from families with a history of depression, and identify potential victims. One possibility, says Kutcher, would be to begin treating those children with antidepressants even before the first bout of depression occurred—in the hope that it never will.

Underpinning the new wave of research is a quiet revolution that has transformed thinking about depression over the past two decades. As recently as in the 1960s, when Sigmund Freud's psychoanalytic philosophy was still pervasive, depression and most other forms of mental illness were regarded as the consequences of emotional turmoil in childhood. Now, scientists have clear evidence that inherited flaws in the brain's biochemistry are to blame for many mental problems, including manic-depressive illness—with its violent swings between depressive lows and manic highs—and, according to some experts, recurring severe depression. Beyond that, many experts think that damaging events in childhood-sexual or physical abuse, poisoned parental relationships and other blows to the child's psyche—may cause depression later by disrupting development of crucial chemical pathways in the brain. "Losses early in life," says Dr. Jane Garland, director of the mood and anxiety clinic at the British Columbia Children's Hospital in Vancouver, "can raise the brain's level of stress hormones that are associated with depression."

When the dark curtain of depression descends, today's victims have access to quick and effective treatment. Short-term "talk therapies" now in use can help haul a patient out of depression in as little as four months—as opposed to years on a psychoanalyst's couch. The purpose of such therapy, says Dr. Marie Corral, a psychiatrist at the British Columbia Women's Hospital in Vancouver, is "to deal with the skewed thinking that develops when a person has been depressed for a long time." The most widely used methods: interpersonal therapy, which focuses on specific people-related problems, and cognitive therapy, which tries to counter the feelings of worthlessness and hopelessness that plague depressed people. "We try to show the patient that much of this thinking may be unfounded," says Zindel Segal, a Toronto psychologist.

But along with the new approaches to dealing with depression, a treatment introduced nearly 60 years ago that has earned a grim public image—electroconvulsive therapy (ECT)—is still a mainstay. Popularly known as shock treatment, it remains "one of our most potent forms of therapy" for severely depressed patients who do not respond to other treatment, says Dr. David Goldbloom, chief of staff at Toronto's Clarke Institute. ECT is routinely used every year on thousands of depressed Canadians, including older patients who cannot tolerate some of the side-effects of drug therapies.

ECT's bad reputation owes much to the 1975 movie *One Flew over the Cuckoo's Nest*, in which staff members of a mental institution punish a rebellious patient, played by Jack Nicholson, with repeated ECT sessions. Patients *did* endure painful ordeals in the early days of ECT when larger electrical shocks were used to induce a limb-shaking seizure in unanesthetized patients. Electroconvulsive

treatment is gentler now. Doctors administer a muscle relaxant and a general anesthetic before subjecting the patient's brain to the amount of current needed to light a 60-watt bulb for one second.

ECT's aftereffects can include painful headaches lasting half an hour or so, and some memory loss. ECT does its job, they add, by altering the brain's electrical and chemical activity. The therapy has some bitter opponents, who claim that it can cause lasting memory loss and impair other brain functions, such as concentration. "ECT damages people's brains—that's really the whole point of it," says Wendy Funk, a 41-year-old Cranbrook, B.C., housewife. Funk says that after receiving electroconvulsive therapy for depression in 1989 and 1990, she lost virtually all memory—she could not recall even her own name or that she was married and had two children.

Meanwhile, for the approximately 70 per cent of patients who respond to them, Prozac and the family of drugs it spawned—Paxil, Zoloft, Luvox and Serzone—are making life far more bearable. Collectively, the drugs are known as SSRIs (for selective serotonin reuptake inhibitors) because they increase the brain's supply of the chemical messenger serotonin. The SSRIs have foes: the Internet bristles with accusations that the drugs can cause panic attacks, aggressive behavior and suicidal tendencies. But most doctors have nothing but praise for the drugs. It's not that they are better than their predecessors at relieving depression—most physicians say they are not.

But SSRIs are easier to live with than some older antidepressants, which often caused dry mouth, daytime sleepiness, constipation, vision problems and other unpleasant side effects. "The SSRIs are better tolerated," says Dr. Russell Joffe, dean of health sciences at McMaster University, "and it is much harder to overdose on them than the older drugs"—a vital consideration in treating people who may be at risk from suicide. The SSRIs can have side effects of their own, including insomnia and a diminished interest in sex that sometimes persuade patients to stop taking them. "You just don't get sexually aroused," says Giselle, a 41-year-old Manitoba resident who requested anonymity. "There's just nothing there."

Another problem with the SSRIs is that patients usually have to take them for three weeks or more before they start to work. The reason: when an SSRI increases the flow of serotonin in the brain, the thermostat-like mechanism that normally controls the flow of the chemical shuts down—and then takes three to six weeks to adapt and allow serotonin to flow again. "If you have a severely depressed patient who may be thinking about suicide," says Dr. Pierre Blier, a professor of psychiatry at Montreal's McGill University, "telling him he may have to wait that long for relief isn't good enough."

After studying the problem exhaustively, Blier and another McGill psychiatrist, Dr. Claude deMontigny, proposed in 1993 that the SSRIs would probably take effect more rapidly if used in conjunction with another drug that could block the brain mechanism causing the delay. Such a drug, a hypertension medication called Pindolol, existed. And the following year, a Spanish physician tried the combination—and found that it worked. Since then, studies have shown that the Pindolol-SSRI combination can cut the waiting time for SSRIs to take effect to about 10 days. Working with that knowledge, several major drug companies now are trying to develop a new generation of fast-acting SSRIs.

Meanwhile, efforts to lay bare the roots of depression are being pursued by a number of Canadian research teams:

• While most antidepressants concentrate on two of the brain's chemical messengers—serotonin and noradrenaline—a research team at the University of Alberta in Edmonton headed by neurochemist Glen Baker is studying a substance called GABA. Another of the brain's neurotransmitters, GABA appears to play a role in quelling the panic attacks that often accompany depression. GABA (for gamma-aminobutyric acid) seems to work in the brain by preventing selected nerve cells from sending signals down the line. To find out more, Baker's team is

tify which defective chemical pathways make that happen. "Once we know more about these things," says Young, "we may be able to correct the problems with drugs."

• In Toronto, a Clarke Institute team co-headed by psychiatrists Sid Kennedy and Franco Vaccarino is using high-tech imaging equipment to look at brain functioning before and after treatment with antidepressants. Images produced by a PET scan machine show that, in depressed people, some parts of the brain's pre-frontal region—an area associated with emotion—are less active than normal. Surprisingly, when antidepressant drugs start acting on the brain, those areas be come even *less* active. Kennedy thinks that may be because in depression, the brain deliberately dampens down pre-frontal activity to cope with high levels of stress, and antidepressants may help the process by reducing activity even further. Kennedy hopes next to study brains in people who had remained well on antidepressants for at least a year, and thinks "we may find that by then activity in the pre-frontal areas has returned to something normal"—meaning that the brain's overstressed condition has been corrected.

Most doctors praise the Prozac-like drugs

studying the action of two older antidepressants that are used to treat panic, imipramine and phenelzine. They want to find out whether the drugs work by increasing GABA activity in the brain. A possible payoff: a new class of drugs that could some day stem panic by boosting the flow of GABA in the brain.

• At McMaster, Young's team is focusing on manic-depressive illness in an effort to discover which brain chemicals are involved. One approach to the puzzle involves dosing rats—which have many of the same genes as humans—with antidepressants or mood stabilizers and examining tissue samples to see which genes are activated. Eventually, Young hopes to learn more about the signalling process inside the brain that can go awry and lead to depression or mania. He also wants to iden-

The best antidepressants can banish depression—but they do not necessarily protect patients from relapses. Susan Boning, who organizes volunteer services for the Society for Depression and Manic Depression of Manitoba at its Winnipeg headquarters, had been taking Prozac for two years when she felt her mood "dipping" last March. Her condition worsened to the point where she made what she calls "a suicidal gesture" by drinking half a bottle of rum and passing out on her living-room floor. Boning, 37, has stopped taking Prozac and has turned to three other drugs, including Serzone. Boning's experience, like countless others, shows that while medical science is making rapid progress in treating depression, for many in the remorseless grip of the disease it is still not fast enough.

New Treatments for Schizophrenia—Part I

The first major revolution in the treatment of schizophrenia occurred in the 1950s, when effective antipsychotic drugs were introduced. By relieving hallucinations and delusions and suppressing bizarre behavior, they allowed most schizophrenic patients to leave mental hospitals. But the drugs had many limitations and side effects, and most people with schizophrenia remained severely disabled. Along with the opportunities for psychological and social rehabilitation created by the emptying of mental hospitals came many serious problems, including homelessness, suicide, and substance abuse. In the last ten years, pharmacologists and psychiatrists have introduced new antipsychotic drugs that work in different ways and seem to be more effective than the older medications. At the same time, 40 years of experience are giving people with schizophrenia and the people who care for them a better sense of how to seize the opportunities and solve the problems created by community living.

Older drug treatments
Drugs of the first generation suppressed so-called positive symptoms (hallucinations, delusions, disordered thinking) but had less effect on the more persistent negative symptoms—lack of initiative, limited speech, social withdrawal, and emotional unresponsiveness. Even when they took their drugs faithfully, schizophrenic patients had difficulty caring for themselves, finding and keeping work, and maintaining a social life. The drugs themselves had many side effects, including drowsiness, constipation, dry mouth, blurred vision and dizziness from postural hypotension (a rush of the blood to the feet on standing). By raising levels of the hormone prolactin, the drugs could cause overproduction of breast milk, menstrual irregularities, and possibly infertility in women. They could also interfere with sexual functioning in both sexes.

An even more serious problem was abnormal involuntary body movements. Some of these movements, known as extrapyramidal symptoms (a reference to the

brain system involved), occur early in the course of treatment: acute dystonia (muscle spasms or cramps); akathisia ("restless legs," pacing or fidgeting), and parkinsonism (tremors, slow and stiff movements, rigid facial expression, abnormal posture and shuffling gait resembling Parkinson's disease). These symptoms, especially akathisia, make many patients so uncomfortable that they refuse to take the drugs. Relief is provided by lowering the dose or by adding antiparkinsonian medications, but these unfortunately have side effects of their own. Controlling the abnormal body movements can be difficult.

Extrapyramidal symptoms often fade after a few months, but they may be succeeded by tardive ("belated") dyskinesia, a more persistent and disabling condition that includes facial tics, tongue rolling, and spasmodic and writhing motions of the arms, legs, and neck. About a third of patients treated for long periods with conventional drugs develop some signs of tardive dyskinesia. Usually the symptoms are minor, but they can be difficult and sometimes seemingly impossible to treat. In a small proportion of patients, they are disfiguring or socially incapacitating.

New drugs
The new drugs, already in widespread use, are still sometimes called "atypical," a term that may soon become obsolete. In general, they have fewer neurological side effects than the older drugs and are probably more helpful for negative symptoms and negative deficiencies. They may also be more effective in reducing depression and preventing relapse. Their higher present cost, research suggests, is probably made up by savings from lower rates of hospitalization and fewer visits to emergency rooms and doctors' offices. Some of these drugs will be still more valuable when they become available in depot ("deposit") form for slow absorption by intramuscular injection once a month—a technique that can be helpful when patients will not consistently take a daily dose on their own.

Clozapine (Clozaril) is the first substantial qualitative advance in the drug treatment of schizophrenia since the 1950s. It has proved moderately but distinctly superior to conventional drugs in 14 controlled studies; some patients do so well that they seem almost to have fully recovered. Clozapine may improve some negative symptoms and relieve deficiencies in memory and attention. It is the only drug that has been proved effective for patients who do not respond to the older drugs. It does not raise prolactin levels. It has little effect on body movements and may even improve symptoms of tardive dyskinesia in some patients. Unfortunately, clozapine has many other side effects, including dizziness, drowsiness, drooling, lowered blood pressure, weight gain, and occasionally seizures. The greatest danger is agranulocytosis, a potentially deadly decrease in the capacity to manufacture white blood cells. With careful monitoring, it occurs in less than 1% of patients and can be corrected if it is discovered early. The death rate has been very low—about one in 10,000—but the need for periodic blood testing makes clozapine expensive and cumbersome to use.

Risperidone (Risperdal), already one of the most widely prescribed antipsychotic drugs, has some of the virtues of clozapine without the risk of agranulocytosis. Like clozapine, it may be useful in the treatment of positive and negative symptoms as well as thinking deficiencies. Its most common side effects are dizziness, fatigue, a dry mouth, a rapid heart beat, and lowered blood pressure. Unlike clozapine, risperidone raises prolactin levels and has some modest effect on body movements.

Olanzapine (Zyprexa) has recently outperformed the traditional medication haloperidol (Haldol) in two large controlled experiments. Like risperidone, it appears to be effective for both positive and negative symptoms, and researchers are now studying its effects on thinking. Patients often prefer it because of its unusually low rate of side effects (the most common are drowsiness, constipation, and weight gain). It affects body movements slightly, does not significantly raise prolactin levels, and is unlikely to cause seizures. Little is known about its long-term effectiveness.

Quetiapine (Seroquel) is useful for both positive and negative symptoms and has few significant side effects. It does not raise prolactin levels and has almost no effect on body movements. Some animals given high doses of quetiapine have developed cataracts. Although it is not clear that this can occur in human beings at therapeutic doses, the manufacturer recommends regular eye examinations for patients taking the drug.

Ziprasidone (Zeldox) is expected to be available soon as a prescription drug. It has little effect on sexual functions or body movements and does not cause weight gain. The main side effects are headache, nausea, constipation, and insomnia.

The development of new antipsychotic drugs has been stimulated by advances in our knowledge of the brain's chemical transmitters and the receptor sites on neurons where they lodge to regulate the passage of nerve impulses. All the older drugs relieve positive symptoms by preventing the neurotransmitter dopamine from acting at D2 nerve receptors in the limbic region of the brain, which governs emotional responses. They disturb body movements by affecting the same type of receptor in the extrapyramidal system. The new drugs work differently, each in its own way. Some block D2 receptors chiefly in the limbic region. Others may act at D1, D3, or D4 receptors and influence patterns of interaction among receptors for other transmitters, including norepinephrine, serotonin, and glutamate. Some authorities believe that malfunctioning of neurotransmitter systems in the prefrontal cortex, the seat of planning and social judgment, is the ultimate cause of negative schizophrenic symptoms. Low activity in that region may cause positive symptoms by weakening inhibitions against excessive dopamine activity in the limbic system. New drugs that seem to relieve negative symptoms may be acting indirectly on the prefrontal region by altering the balance of neurotransmitters elsewhere in the brain. Their relative lack of extrapyramidal activity presumably explains why they cause fewer abnormal body movements.

When schizophrenic symptoms first appear, drug treatment is often put off because the nature of the illness is unclear or because the patient cannot be persuaded to seek help. A year's delay between the first psychotic symptoms and the first use of antipsychotic drugs is common. Recent studies suggest that delay makes for slower recovery from the first episode and a poorer long-term prognosis. The alienating and isolating effects of prolonged psychotic episodes make it increasingly difficult to recover a normal personal and social life after each one. And each psychotic episode may heighten the brain's vulnerability to further psychosis, in the same way that an epileptic seizure can further irritate its focus (originating point) in the brain and raise the likelihood of later seizures. For these reasons, many authorities are now putting special emphasis on the need to detect and treat schizophrenia early. Psychiatrists have often been reluctant to prescribe antipsychotic drugs immediately because of their concern about side effects, but the new drugs should change that attitude.

Cognitive and behavioral support

Although most schizophrenic patients need antipsychotic medication to benefit from any other help, the drugs by themselves are far from sufficient; psychiatric care and social rehabilitation are just as important. Depending on the severity of their symptoms, patients may need help in understanding the illness, taking their drugs regularly, responding to signs of relapse, securing housing, jobs, and medical care, even caring for their basic physical needs and coping with everyday social situations and personal relations.

Behavioral techniques, including social skills training, are one widely used form of help. Schizophrenic patients are coached, prompted and corrected as they rehearse behavior and observe others as models. They are shown how to cash checks, prepare for interviews, sustain a conversation, and even clean and dress themselves. Research has shown that social skills training can be effective. In two recent meta-analyses (combined statistical analyses of many studies), this training has been found to reduce relapse rates for up to a year. But the results are difficult to transfer to real life, and they often dissipate over time.

Some mental health professionals are now trying to teach what could be called thinking and emotional skills. Patients are lectured and coached on how to monitor their thoughts, overcome tendencies to withdraw, paranoia, and loss of concentration, and cope with guilt, sadness, feelings of humiliation, and aggressive impulses. They may also work to improve memory, planning, and decision-making. A cognitive-behavioral program for hospitalized patients, integrated psychological therapy, uses word problems and games to practice conversation and the interpretation of social situations. Cognitive training can be time-consuming and expensive, and there is some question whether its effects carry over into daily life. Some believe that thinking exercises have limited potential for the damaged brains of schizophrenic patients. In one recent study, patients given integrated psychological therapy showed improvement on tests of attention after 18 months, but their capacity for complex thinking remained low, and they still lacked the skills needed for independent living.

Another cognitive approach emphasizes the content of thoughts rather than the process of thinking. Patients are taught to evaluate and correct their delusional ideas and hallucinatory perceptions. The therapist finds out when the most disabling psychotic symptoms occur, how seriously they interfere with the patient's life, and how the patient copes with them. The patient practices these methods and is helped to develop new ones. What little evidence there is suggests that this technique may be somewhat effective for delusions but does not affect hallucinations or the more common negative symptoms.

FOR FURTHER READING

Patricia Backlar. The Family Face of Schizophrenia: Practical Counsel from America's Leading Experts. *New York: Jeremy P. Tarcher/Putnam, 1994.*

John Michael Kane. Schizophrenia. *New England Journal of Medicine 334:34–41 (January 4, 1996).*

Kim T. Mueser and Susan Gingerich. Coping With Schizophrenia: A Guide for Families. *Oakland, CA: New Harbinger Publications, 1994.*

David L. Penn and Kim T. Mueser. Research update on the psychosocial treatment of schizophrenia. *American Journal of Psychiatry 153:607–617 (May 1996).*

This glossary of psychology terms is included to provide you with a convenient and ready reference as you encounter general terms in your study of psychology and personal growth and behavior that are unfamiliar or require a review. It is not intended to be comprehensive, but taken together with the many definitions included in the articles themselves, it should prove to be quite useful.

abnormal behavior Behavior that contributes to maladaptiveness, is considered deviant by the culture, or that leads to personal psychological distress.

absolute threshold The minimum amount of physical energy required to produce a sensation.

accommodation Process in cognitive development; involves altering or reorganizing the mental picture to make room for a new experience or idea.

acculturation The process of becoming part of a new cultural environment.

acetylcholine A neurotransmitter involved in memory.

achievement drive The need to attain self-esteem, success, or status. Society's expectations strongly influence the achievement motive.

achievement style The way people behave in achievement situations; achievement styles include the direct, instrumental, and relational styles.

acquired immune deficiency syndrome (AIDS) A fatal disease of the immune system.

acquisition In conditioning, forming associations in first learning a task.

actor-observer bias Tendency to attribute the behavior of other people to internal causes and our own behavior to external causes.

acupuncture Oriental practice involving the insertion of needles into the body to control pain.

adaptation The process of responding to changes in the environment by altering responses to keep a person's behavior appropriate to environmental demands.

adjustment How we react to stress; some change that we make in response to the demands placed upon us.

adrenal glands Endocrine glands involved in stress and energy regulation.

adrenaline A hormone produced by the adrenal glands that is involved in physiological arousal; adrenaline is also called epinephrine.

affective flattening Individuals with schizophrenia who do not exhibit any emotional arousal.

aggression Behavior intended to harm a member of the same or another species.

agoraphobia Anxiety disorder in which an individual is excessively afraid of places or situations from which it would be difficult or embarrassing to escape.

alarm reaction The first stage of Hans Selye's general adaptation syndrome. The alarm reaction is the immediate response to stress; adrenaline is released and digestion slows. The alarm reaction prepares the body for an emergency.

all-or-none law The principle that states that a neuron only fires when a stimulus is above a certain minimum strength (threshold), and when it fires, it does so at full strength.

alogia Individuals with schizophrenia that show a reduction in speech.

alpha Brain-wave activity that indicates that a person is relaxed and resting quietly; 8–12 Hz.

altered state of consciousness (ASC) A state of consciousness in which there is a redirection of attention, a change in the aspects of the world that occupy a person's thoughts, and a change in the stimuli to which a person responds.

ambivalent attachment Type of infant-parent attachment in which the infant seeks contact but resists once the contact is made.

amphetamine A strong stimulant; increases arousal of the central nervous system.

amygdala A part of the limbic system involved in fear, aggression, and other social behaviors.

anal stage Psychosexual stage during which, according to Sigmund Freud, the child experiences the first restrictions on his or her impulses.

analytical psychology The personality theory of Carl Jung.

anorexia nervosa Eating disorder in which an individual becomes severely underweight because of self-imposed restrictions on eating.

antisocial personality disorder Personality disorder in which individuals who engage in antisocial behavior experience no guilt or anxiety about their actions; sometimes called sociopathy or psychopathy.

anxiety disorder Fairly long-lasting disruption of a person's ability to deal with stress; often accompanied by feelings of fear and apprehension.

applied psychology The area of psychology that is most immediately concerned with helping to solve practical problems; includes clinical and counseling psychology as well as industrial, environmental, and legal psychology.

approach-approach conflict Occurs when we are attracted to two equally desirable goals that are incompatible.

approach-avoidance conflict When we are faced with a single goal that has positive and negative aspects.

aptitude test Any test designed to predict what a person with the proper training can accomplish in the future.

archetypes In Carl Jung's personality theory, unconscious universal ideas shared by all humans.

arousal theory Theory that focuses on the energy (arousal) aspect of motivation; it states that we are motivated to initiate behaviors that help to regulate overall arousal level.

asocial phase Phase in attachment development in which the neonate does not distinguish people from objects.

assertiveness training Training that helps individuals stand up for their rights while not denying rights of other people.

assimilation Process in cognitive development; occurs when something new is taken into the child's mental picture.

associationism A theory of learning suggesting that once two stimuli are presented together, one of them will remind a person of the other. Ideas are learned by association with sensory experiences and are not innate.

attachment Process in which the individual shows behaviors that promote proximity with a specific object or person.

attention Process of focusing on particular stimuli in the environment.

attention deficit disorder Hyperactivity; inability to concentrate.

attitude Learned disposition that actively guides us toward specific behaviors; attitudes consist of feelings, beliefs, and behavioral tendencies.

attribution The cognitive process of determining the motives of someone's behavior, and whether they are internal or external.

autism A personality disorder in which a child does not respond socially to people.

autokinetic effect Perception of movement of a stationary spot of light in a darkened room.

autonomic nervous system The part of the peripheral nervous system that carries messages from the central nervous system to the endocrine glands, the smooth muscles controlling the heart, and the primarily involuntary muscles controlling internal processes; includes the sympathetic and parasympathetic nervous systems.

aversion therapy A counterconditioning therapy in which unwanted responses are paired with unpleasant consequences.

avoidance conditioning Learning situation in which a subject avoids a stimulus by learning to respond appropriately before the stimulus begins.

avoidant attachment Type of infant-parent attachment in which the infant avoids the parent.

avolition Individuals with schizophrenia who lack motivation to follow through on an activity.

backward conditioning A procedure in classical conditioning in which the US is presented and terminated before the termination of the CS; very ineffective procedure.

basic research Research conducted to obtain information for its own sake.

behavior Anything you do or think, including various bodily reactions. Behavior includes physical and mental responses.

behavior genetics How genes influence behavior.

behavior modification Another term for behavior therapy; the modification of behavior through psychological techniques; often the application of conditioning principles to alter behavior.

behaviorism The school of thought founded by John Watson; it studied only observable behavior.

belongingness and love needs Third level of motives in Maslow's hierarchy; includes love and affection, friends, and social contact.

biological motives Motives that have a definite physiological basis and are biologically necessary for survival of the individual or species.

biological response system Systems of the body that are important in behavioral responding; includes the senses, muscles, endocrine system, and the nervous system.

biological therapy Treatment of behavior problems through biological techniques; major biological therapies include drug therapy, psychosurgery, and electroconvulsive therapy.

bipolar disorder Mood disorder characterized by extreme mood swings from sad depression to joyful mania; sometimes called manic-depression.

blinding technique In an experiment, a control for bias in which the assignment of a subject to the experimental or control group is unknown to the subject or experimenter or both (a double-blind experiment).

body dysmorphic disorder Somatoform disorder characterized by a preoccupation with an imaginary defect in the physical appearance of a physically healthy person.

body language Communication through position and movement of the body.

bottom-up processing The psychoanalytic process of understanding communication by listening to words, then interpreting phrases, and finally understanding ideas.

brief psychodynamic therapy A therapy developed for individuals with strong egos to resolve a core conflict.

bulimia nervosa Eating disorder in which an individual eats large amounts of calorie-rich food in a short time and then purges the food by vomiting or using laxatives.

bystander effect Phenomenon in an emergency situation in which a person is more likely to help when alone than when in a group of people.

California Psychological Inventory (CPI) An objective personality test used to study normal populations.

Cannon-Bard theory of emotion Theory of emotion that states that the emotional feeling and the physiological arousal occur at the same time.

cardinal traits In Gordon Allport's personality theory, the traits of an individual that are so dominant that they are expressed in everything the person does; few people possess cardinal traits.

catatonic schizophrenia A type of schizophrenia that is characterized by periods of complete immobility and the apparent absence of will to move or speak.

causal attribution Process of determining whether a person's behavior is due to internal or external motives.

central nervous system The part of the human nervous system that interprets and stores messages from the sense organs, decides what behavior to exhibit, and sends appropriate messages to the muscles and glands; includes the brain and spinal cord.

central tendency In statistics, measures of central tendency give a number that represents the entire group or sample.

central traits In Gordon Allport's personality theory, the traits of an individual that form the core of the personality; they are developed through experience.

cerebellum The part of the hindbrain that is involved in balance and muscle coordination.

cerebral cortex The outermost layer of the cerebrum of the brain where higher mental functions occur. The cerebral cortex is divided into sections, or lobes, which control various activities.

cerebrum (cerebral hemisphere) Largest part of the forebrain involved in cognitive functions; the cerebrum consists of two hemispheres connected by the corpus callosum.

chromosome Bodies in the cell nucleus that contain the genes.

chunking Process of combining stimuli in order to increase memory capacity.

classical conditioning The form of learning in which a stimulus is associated with another stimulus that causes a particular response. Sometimes called Pavlovian conditioning or respondent conditioning.

clinical psychology Subfield in which psychologists assess psychological problems and treat people with behavior problems using psychological techniques (called psychotherapy).

cognition Mental processes, such as perception, attention, memory, language, thinking, and problem solving; cognition involves the acquisition, storage, retrieval, and utilization of knowledge.

cognitive behavior therapy A form of behavior therapy that identifies self-defeating attitudes and thoughts in a subject, and then helps the subject to replace these with positive, supportive thoughts.

cognitive development Changes over time in mental processes such as thinking, memory, language, and problem solving.

cognitive dissonance Leon Festinger's theory of attitude change that states that, when people hold two psychologically inconsistent ideas, they experience tension that forces them to reconcile the conflicting ideas.

cognitive expectancy The condition in which an individual learns that certain behaviors lead to particular goals; cognitive expectancy motivates the individual to exhibit goal-directed behaviors.

cognitive learning Type of learning that theorizes that the learner utilizes cognitive structures in memory to make decisions about behaviors.

cognitive psychology The area of psychology that includes the study of mental activities involved in perception, memory, language, thought, and problem solving.

cognitive restructuring The modification of the client's thoughts and perceptions that are contributing to his or her maladjustments.

cognitive therapy Therapy developed by Aaron Beck in which an individual's negative, self-defeating thoughts are restructured in a positive way.

cognitive-motivational-relational theory of emotion A theory of emotion proposed by Richard Lazarus that includes cognitive appraisal, motivational goals, and relationships between an individual and the environment.

collective unconscious Carl Jung's representation of the thoughts shared by all humans.

collectivistic cultures Cultures in which the greatest emphasis is on the loyalty of each individual to the group.

comparative psychology Subfield in which experimental psychologists study and compare the behavior of different species of animals.

compulsions Rituals performed excessively such as checking doors or washing hands to reduce anxiety.

concept formation (concept learning) The development of the ability to respond to common features of categories of objects or events.

concrete operations period Stage in cognitive development, from 7 to 11 years, in which the child's ability to solve problems with reasoning greatly increases.

conditioned response (CR) The response or behavior that occurs when the conditioned stimulus is presented (after the CS has been associated with the US).

conditioned stimulus (CS) An originally neutral stimulus that is associated with an unconditioned stimulus and takes on the latter's capability of eliciting a particular reaction.

conditioned taste aversion (CTA) An aversion to particular tastes associated with stomach distress; usually considered a unique form of classical conditioning because of the extremely long interstimulus intervals involved.

conditioning A term applied to two types of learning (classical and operant). Conditioning refers to the scientific aspect of the type of learning.

conflict Situation that occurs when we experience incompatible demands or desires; the outcome when one individual or group perceives that another individual or group has caused or will cause harm.

conformity Type of social influence in which an individual changes his or her behavior to fit social norms or expectations.

connectionism Recent approach to problem solving; the development of neural connections allows us to think and solve problems.

conscientiousness The dimension in the five-factor personality theory that includes traits such as practical, cautious, serious, reliable, careful, and ambitious; also called dependability.

conscious Being aware of experiencing sensations, thoughts, and feelings at any given point in time.

conscious mind In Sigmund Freud's psychoanalytic theory of personality, the part of personality that we are aware of in everyday life.

consciousness The processing of information at various levels of awareness; state in which a person is aware of sensations, thoughts, and feelings.

consensus In causal attribution, the extent to which other people react as the subject does in a particular situation.

conservation The ability to recognize that something stays the same even if it takes on a different form; Piaget tested conservation of mass, number, length, and volume.

consistency In causal attribution, the extent to which the subject always behaves in the same way in a situation.

consolidation The biological neural process of making memories permanent; possibly short-term memory is electrically coded and long-term memory is chemically coded.

contingency model A theory that specific types of situations need particular types of leaders.

continuum of preparedness Martin Seligman's proposal that animals are biologically prepared to learn certain responses more readily than they are prepared to learn others.

control group Subjects in an experiment who do not receive the independent variable; the control group determines the effectiveness of the independent variable.

conventional morality Level II in Lawrence Kohlberg's theory, in which moral reasoning is based on conformity and social standards.

convergence Binocular depth cue in which we detect distance by interpreting the kinesthetic sensations produced by the muscles of the eyeballs.

conversion disorder Somatoform disorder in which a person displays obvious disturbance in the nervous system without a physical basis for the problem.

correlation Statistical technique to determine the degree of relationship that exists between two variables.

counterconditioning A behavior therapy in which an unwanted response is replaced by conditioning a new response that is incompatible with it.

creativity A process of coming up with new or unusual responses to familiar circumstances.

critical period hypothesis Period of time during development in which particular learning or experiences normally occur; if learning does not occur, the individual has a difficult time learning it later.

culture-bound The idea that a test's usefulness is limited to the culture in which it was written and utilized.

cumulative response curve Graphed curve that results when responses for a subject are added to one another over time; if subjects respond once every 5 minutes, they will have a cumulative response curve value of 12 after an hour.

curiosity motive Motive that causes the individual to seek out a certain amount of novelty.

cyclothymia disorder A moderately severe problem with numerous periods of hypomanic episodes and depressive symptoms.

death instinct (also called Thanatos) Freud's term for an instinct that is destructive to the individual or species; aggression is a major expression of death instinct.

decay Theory of forgetting in which sensory impressions leave memory traces that fade away with time.

defense mechanisms Psychological techniques to help protect ourselves from stress and anxiety, to resolve conflicts, and to preserve our self-esteem.

delayed conditioning A procedure in classical conditioning in which the presentation of the CS precedes the onset of the US and the termination of the CS is delayed until the US is presented; most effective procedure.

delusion The holding of obviously false beliefs; for example, imagining someone is trying to kill you.

dependent variable In psychology, the behavior or response that is measured; it is dependent on the independent variable.

depersonalization disorder Dissociative disorder in which the individual escapes from his or her own personality by believing that he or she does not exist or that his or her environment is not real.

depolarization Any change in which the internal electrical charge becomes more positive.

depression A temporary emotional state that normal individuals experience or a persistent state that may be considered a psychological disorder. Characterized by sadness and low self-esteem.

descriptive statistics Techniques that help summarize large amounts of data information.

developmental psychology Study of physical and mental growth and behavioral changes in individuals from conception to death.

Diagnostic and Statistic Manual of Mental Disorders (DSM) Published by the American Psychiatric Association in 1952, and revised in 1968, 1980, 1987, and 1994, this manual was provided to develop a set of diagnoses of abnormal behavior patterns.

diffusion of responsibility Finding that groups tend to inhibit helping behavior; responsibility is shared equally by members of the group so that no one individual feels a strong commitment.

disorganized schizophrenia A type of schizophrenia that is characterized by a severe personality disintegration; the individual often displays bizarre behavior.

displacement Defense mechanism by which the individual directs his or her aggression or hostility toward a person or object other than the one it should be directed toward; in Freud's dream theory, the process of reassigning emotional feelings from one object to another one.

dissociative disorder Psychological disorder that involves a disturbance in the memory, consciousness, or identity of an individual; types include multiple personality disorder, depersonalization disorder, psychogenic amnesia, and psychogenic fugue.

dissociative fugue Individuals who have lost their memory, relocated to a new geographical area, and started a new life as someone else.

dissociative identity disorder (multiple personality disorder) Dissociative disorder in which several personalities are present in the same individual.

distinctiveness In causal attribution, the extent to which the subject reacts the same way in other situations.

Down syndrome Form of mental retardation caused by having three number 21 chromosomes (trisomy 21).

dream analysis Psychoanalytic technique in which a patient's dreams are reviewed and analyzed to discover true feelings.

drive Motivational concept used to describe the internal forces that push an organism toward a goal; sometimes identified as psychological arousal arising from a physiological need.

dyssomnia Sleep disorder in which the chief symptom is a disturbance in the amount and quality of sleep; they include insomnia and hypersomnia.

dysthymic disorder Mood disorder in which the person suffers moderate depression much of the time for at least two years.

ego Sigmund Freud's term for an individual's sense of reality.

egocentric Seeing the world only from your perspective.

eidetic imagery Photographic memory; ability to recall great detail accurately after briefly viewing something.

Electra complex The Freudian idea that the young girl feels inferior to boys because she lacks a penis.

electroconvulsive therapy (ECT) A type of biological therapy in which electricity is applied to the brain in order to relieve severe depression.

emotion A response to a stimulus that involves physiological arousal, subjective feeling, cognitive interpretation, and overt behavior.

empiricism The view that behavior is learned through experience.

encoding The process of putting information into the memory system.

encounter group As in a sensitivity training group, a therapy where people become aware of themselves in meeting others.

endorphins Several neuropeptides that function as neurotransmitters. The opiate-like endorphins are involved in pain, reinforcement, and memory.

engineering psychology Area of psychology that is concerned with how work is performed, design of equipment, and work environment; also called human factors psychology.

engram The physical memory trace or neural circuit that holds memory; also called memory trace.

episodic memory Highest memory system; includes information about personal experiences.

Eros Sigmund Freud's term for an instinct that helps the individual or species survive; also called life instinct.

esteem needs Fourth level of motives in Abraham Maslow's hierarchy; includes high evaluation of oneself, self-respect, self-esteem, and respect of others.

eustress Stress that results from pleasant and satisfying experiences; earning a high grade or achieving success produces eustress.

excitement phase First phase in the human sexual response cycle; the beginning of sexual arousal.

experimental group Subjects in an experiment who receive the independent variable.

experimental psychology Subfield in which psychologists research the fundamental causes of behavior. Many experimental psychologists conduct experiments in basic research.

experimenter bias Source of potential error in an experiment from the action or expectancy of the experimenter; might influence the experimental results in ways that mask the true outcome.

external locus of control In Julian Rotter's personality theory, the perception that reinforcement is independent of a person's behavior.

extraversion The dimension in the five-factor personality theory that includes traits such as sociability, talkativeness, boldness, fun-lovingness, adventurousness, and assertiveness; also called surgency. The personality concept of Carl Jung in which the personal energy of the individual is directed externally.

factor analysis A statistical procedure used to determine the relationship among variables.

false memories Memories believed to be real, but the events never occurred.

fast mapping A process by which children can utilize a word after a single exposure.

fetal alcohol syndrome (FAS) Condition in which defects in the newborn child are caused by the mother's excessive alcohol intake.

five-factor model of personality tracts A trait theory of personality that includes the factors of extraversion, agreeableness, conscientiousness, emotional stability, and openness.

fixed action pattern (FAP) Unlearned, inherited, stereotyped behaviors that are shown by all members of a species; term used in ethology.

fixed interval (FI) schedule Schedule of reinforcement where the subject receives reinforcement for a correct response given after a specified time interval.

fixed ratio (FR) schedule Schedule of reinforcement in which the subject is reinforced after a certain number of responses.

flashbulb memory Memory of an event that is so important that significant details are vividly remembered for life.

forgetting In memory, not being able to retrieve the original learning. The part of the original learning that cannot be retrieved is said to be forgotten.

formal operations period Period in cognitive development; at 11 years, the adolescent begins abstract thinking and reasoning. This period continues throughout the rest of life.

free association Psychoanalytic technique in which the patient says everything that comes to mind.

free recall A verbal learning procedure in which the order of presentation of the stimuli is varied and the subject can learn the items in any order.

frequency theory of hearing Theory of hearing that states that the frequency of vibrations at the basilar membrane determines the frequency of firing of neurons carrying impulses to the brain.

frustration A cause of stress that results from the blocking of a person's goal-oriented behavior.

frustration-drive theory of aggression Theory of aggression that states that it is caused by frustration.

functionalism School of thought that studied the functional value of consciousness and behavior.

fundamental attribution error Attribution bias in which people overestimate the role of internal disposition and underestimate the role of external situation.

gate-control theory of pain Theory of pain that proposes that there is a gate that allows pain impulses to travel from the spinal cord to the brain.

gender-identity disorder (GID) Incongruence between assigned sex and gender identity.

gender-identity/role Term that incorporates gender identity (the private perception of one's sex) and gender role (the public expression of one's gender identity).

gene The basic unit of heredity; the gene is composed of deoxyribonucleic acid (DNA).

general adaptation syndrome (GAS) Hans Selye's theory of how the body responds to stress over time. GAS includes alarm reaction, resistance, and exhaustion.

generalized anxiety disorder Anxiety disorder in which the individual lives in a state of constant severe tension, continuous fear, and apprehension.

genetics The study of heredity; genetics is the science of discovering how traits are passed along generations.

genotype The complete set of genes inherited by an individual from his or her parents.

Gestalt psychology A school of thought that studied whole or complete perceptions.

Gestalt therapy Insight therapy designed to help people become more aware of themselves in the here and now and to take responsibility for their own actions.

grandiose delusion Distortion of reality; one's belief that he or she is extremely important or powerful.

group therapy Treatment of several patients at the same time.

groupthink When group members are so committed to, and optimistic about, the group that they feel it is invulnerable; they become so concerned with maintaining consensus that criticism is muted.

growth The normal quantitative changes that occur in the physical and psychological aspects of a healthy child with the passage of time.

GSR (galvanic skin response) A measure of autonomic nervous system activity; a slight electric current is passed over the skin, and the more nervous a subject is, the easier the current will flow.

hallucinations A sensory impression reported when no external stimulus exists to justify the report; often hallucinations are a symptom of mental illness.

hallucinogens Psychedelic drugs that result in hallucinations at high doses, and other effects on behavior and perception in mild doses.

halo effect The finding that once we form a general impression of someone, we tend to interpret additional information about the person in a consistent manner.

haptic Relating to or based on the sense of touch. Also, a predilection for the sense of touch.

Hawthorne effect The finding that behavior can be influenced just by participation in a research study.

health psychology Field of psychology that studies psychological influences on people's health, including how they stay healthy, why they become ill, and how their behavior relates to their state of health.

heuristic Problem-solving strategy; a person tests solutions most likely to be correct.

hierarchy of needs Abraham Maslow's list of motives in humans, arranged from the biological to the uniquely human.

higher order conditioning Learning to make associations with stimuli that have been learned previously.

hippocampus Brain structure in the limbic system that is important in learning and memory.

homeostasis The state of equilibrium that maintains a balance in the internal body environment.

hormones Chemicals produced by the endocrine glands that regulate activity of certain bodily processes.

humanistic psychology Psychological school of thought that believes that people are unique beings who cannot be broken down into parts.

hyperphagia Disorder in which the individual continues to eat until he or she is obese; can be caused by damage to ventromedial hypothalamus.

hypersomnia Sleep disorder in which an individual falls asleep at inappropriate times; narcolepsy is a form of hypersomnia.

hypnosis Altered state of consciousness characterized by heightened suggestibility.

hypochondriasis Somatoform disorder in which the individual is obsessed with fears of having a serious medical disease.

hypothalamus Part of the brain's limbic system; involved in motivational behaviors, including eating, drinking, and sex.

hypothesis In the scientific method, an educated guess or prediction about future observable events.

iconic memory Visual information that is encoded into the sensory memory store.

id Sigmund Freud's representation of the basic instinctual drives; the id always seeks pleasure.

identification The process in which children adopt the attitudes, values, and behaviors of their parents.

identity diffusion In Marcia's adolescent identity theory, the status of individuals who have failed to make a commitment to values and roles.

illusion An incorrect perception that occurs when sensation is distorted.

imitation The copying of another's behavior; learned through the process of observation.

impression formation Developing an evaluation of another person from your perceptions; first, or initial, impressions are often very important.

imprinting A form of early learning in which birds follow a moving stimulus (often the mother); may be similar to attachment in mammals.

independent variable The condition in an experiment that is controlled and manipulated by the experimenter; it is a stimulus that will cause a response.

indiscriminate attachment phase Stage of attachment in which babies prefer humans to nonhumans, but do not discriminate among individual people.

individuation Carl Jung's concept of the process leading to the unification of all parts of the personality.

inferential statistics Techniques that help researchers make generalizations about a finding based on a limited number of subjects.

inferiority complex Adler's personality concept that states that because children are dependent on adults and cannot meet the standards set for themselves they feel inferior.

inhibition Restraint of an impulse, desire, activity, or drive.

insight A sudden grasping of the means necessary to achieve a goal; important in the Gestalt approach to problem solving.

insight therapy Therapy based on the assumption that behavior is abnormal because people do not adequately understand the motivation causing their behavior.

instinct Highly stereotyped behavior common to all members of a species that often appears in virtually complete form in the absence of any obvious opportunities to learn it.

instrumental conditioning Operant conditioning.

intelligence Capacity to learn and behave adaptively.

intelligence quotient (IQ) An index of a person's performance on an intelligence test relative to others in the culture; ratio of a person's mental age to chronological age.

interference Theory of forgetting in which information that was learned before (proactive interference) or after (retroactive interference) causes the learner to be unable to remember the material of interest.

internal locus of control In Rotter's personality theory, the perception that reinforcement is contingent upon behavior.

interstimulus interval Time interval between two stimuli; in classical conditioning, it is the elapsed time between the CS and the US.

intrinsic motivation Motivation inside the individual; we do something because we receive satisfaction from it.

introspection Method in which a subject gives a self-report of his or her immediate experience.

introversion The personality concept of Carl Jung in which the personal energy of the individual is directed inward; characterized by introspection, seriousness, inhibition, and restraint.

James-Lange theory of emotion Theory of emotion that states that the physiological arousal and behavior come before the subjective experience of an emotion.

just noticeable difference (JND) Difference threshold: minimum amount of energy required to produce a difference in sensation.

kinesthesis The sense of bodily movement.

labeling of arousal Experiments suggest that an individual experiencing physical arousal that cannot be explained will interpret those feelings in terms of the situation she or he is in and will use environmental and contextual cues.

language acquisition device (LAD) Hypothesized biological structure that accounts for the relative ease of acquiring language, according to Noam Chomsky.

latent dream content In Sigmund Freud's dream theory, the true thoughts in the unconsciousness; the true meaning of the dream.

latent learning Learning that occurs when an individual acquires knowledge of something but does not show it until motivated to do so.

law of effect Edward Thorndike's law that if a response produces satisfaction it will be repeated; reinforcement.

learned helplessness Condition in which a person learns that his or her behavior has no effect on his or her environment; when an individual gives up and stops trying.

learned social motives Social motives that are learned; include achievement and affiliation.

learning The relatively permanent change in behavior or behavioral ability of an individual that occurs as a result of experience.

learning styles The preferences students have for learning; theories of learning styles include personality differences, styles of information processing, and instructional preferences.

life instinct (also called Eros) Sigmund Freud's term for an instinct that helps the individual or species survive; sex is the major expression of life instinct.

life structure In Daniel Levinson's theory of adult personality development, the underlying pattern of an individual's life at any particular time; seasonal cycles include preadulthood, early adulthood, middle adulthood, and late adulthood.

linguistic relativity hypothesis Proposal that the perception of reality differs according to the language of the observer.

locus of control Julian Rotter's theory in which a person's beliefs about reinforcement are classified as internal or external.

long-term memory The permanent memory where rehearsed information is stored.

love An emotion characterized by knowing, liking, and becoming intimate with someone.

low-ball procedure The compliance technique of presenting an attractive proposal to someone and then switching it to a more unattractive proposal.

magic number 7 The finding that most people can remember about seven items of information for a short time (in short-term memory).

magnetic resonance imaging (MRI) A method of studying brain activity using magnetic field imaging.

major depressive disorder Severe mood disorder in which a person experiences one or more major depressive episodes; sometimes referred to simply as depression.

maladjustment Condition that occurs when a person utilizes inappropriate abilities to respond to demands placed upon him or her.

manic depressive reaction A form of mental illness marked by alternations of extreme phases of elation (manic phase) and depression.

manifest dream content In Sigmund Freud's dream theory, what is remembered about a dream upon waking; a disguised representation of the unconscious wishes.

massed practice Learning as much material as possible in long continuous stretches.

maturation The genetically controlled process of growth that results in orderly changes in behavior.

mean The arithmetic average, in which the sum of scores is divided by the number of scores.

median The middle score in a group of scores that are arranged from lowest to highest.

meditation The practice of some form of relaxed concentration while ignoring other sensory stimuli.

memory The process of storing information so that it can be retrieved and used later.

memory attributes The critical features of an event that are used when the experience is encoded or retrieved.

mental age The age level on which a person is capable of performing; used in determining intelligence.

mental set Condition in which a person's thinking becomes so standardized that he or she approaches new problems in fixed ways.

Minnesota Multiphasic Personality Inventory (MMPI-2) An objective personality test that was originally devised to identify personality disorders.

mnemonic technique Method of improving memory by combining and relating chunks of information.

modeling A process of learning by imitation in a therapeutic situation.

mood disorder Psychological disorder in which a person experiences a severe disruption in mood or emotional balance.

moral development Development of individuals as they adopt their society's standards of right and wrong; development of awareness of ethical behavior.

motivated forgetting (repression) Theory that suggests that people want to forget unpleasant events.

motivation The forces that initiate and direct behavior, and the variables that determine the intensity and persistence of the behavior.

motivator needs In Federick Herzberg's theory, the factors that lead to job satisfaction; they include responsibility, the nature of the work, advancement, and recognition.

motive Anything that arouses the individual and directs his or her behavior toward some goal. Three categories of motives include biological, stimulus, and learned social.

Müller-Lyer illusion A well-known illusion, in which two horizontal lines have end lines either going in or out; the line with the end lines going in appears longer.

multiple approach-avoidance conflict Conflict that occurs when an individual has two or more goals, both of which have positive and negative aspects.

multiple attachment phase Later attachment stage in which the baby begins to form attachments to people other than the primary caretaker.

multiple intelligences Howard Gardner's theory that there exists several different kinds of intelligence.

Myers-Briggs Type Indicator (MBTI) Objective personality test based on Carl Jung's type theory.

narcotic analgesics Drugs that have an effect on the body similar to morphine; these relieve pain and suppress coughing.

naturalistic observation Research method in which behavior of people or animals in their normal environment is accurately recorded.

Necker cube A visual illusion. The Necker cube is a drawing of a cube designed so that it is difficult to determine which side is toward you.

negative reinforcement Removing something unpleasant to increase the probability that the preceding behavior will be repeated.

NEO Personality Inventory (NEO-PI) An objective personality test developed by Paul Costa Jr. and Robert McCrae to measure the five major factors in personality; consists of 181 questions.

neodissociation theory Idea that consciousness can be split into several streams of thought that are partially independent of each other.

neuron A specialized cell that functions to conduct messages throughout the body.

neurosis A Freudian term that was used to describe abnormal behavior caused by anxiety; it has been eliminated from *DSM-IV*.

neutral stimulus A stimulus that does not cause the response of interest; the individual may show some response to the stimulus but not the associated behavior.

norm A sample of scores representative of a population.

normal curve When scores of a large number of random cases are plotted on a graph, they often fall into a bell-shaped curve; as many cases on the curve are above the mean as below it.

observational learning In social learning theory, learning by observing someone else behave; people observe and imitate in learning socialization.

obsessions Fears that involve the inability to control impulses.

obsessive compulsive disorder Anxiety disorder in which the individual has repetitive thoughts (obsessions) that lead to constant urges (compulsions) to engage in meaningless rituals.

object permanence The ability to realize that objects continue to exist even if we can no longer see them.

Oedipus complex The Freudian idea that the young boy has sexual feelings for his mother and is jealous of his father and must identify with his father to resolve the conflict.

olfaction The smell sense.

openness The dimension in the five-factor personality theory that includes traits such as imagination, creativity, perception, knowledge, artistic ability, curiosity, and analytical ability; also called culture or intellect.

operant conditioning Form of learning in which behavior followed by reinforcement (satisfaction) increases in frequency.

opponent-process theory Theory that when one emotion is experienced, the other is suppressed.

optimum level of arousal Motivation theory that states that the individual will seek a level of arousal that is comfortable.

organic mental disorders Psychological disorders that involve physical damage to the nervous system; can be caused by disease or by an accident.

organizational psychology Area of industrial psychology that focuses on worker attitudes and motivation; derived primarily from personality and social psychology.

orgasm The climax of intense sexual excitement; release from building sexual tension, usually accompanied by ejaculation in men.

paired-associate learning A verbal learning procedure in which the subject is presented with a series of pairs of items to be remembered.

panic disorder Anxiety disorder characterized by the occurrence of specific periods of intense fear.

paranoid schizophrenia A type of schizophrenia in which the individual often has delusions of grandeur and persecution, thinking that someone is out to get him or her.

partial reinforcement Any schedule of reinforcement in which reinforcement follows only some of the correct responses.

partial reinforcement effect The finding that partial reinforcement produces a response that takes longer to extinguish than continuous reinforcement.

pattern recognition Memory process in which information attended to is compared with information already permanently stored in memory.

Pavlovian conditioning A bond or association between a neutral stimulus and a response; this type of learning is called classical conditioning.

perception The active process in which the sensory information that is carried through the nervous system to the brain is organized and interpreted; the interpretation of sensation.

persecutory delusion A delusion in which the individual has a distortion of reality; the belief that other people are out to get one.

person perception The process of using the information we gather in forming impressions of people to make evaluations of others.

personal unconscious Carl Jung's representation of the individual's repressed thoughts and memories.

personality disorder Psychological disorder in which there are problems in the basic personality structure of the individual.

phantom-limb pain Phenomenon in which people who have lost an arm or leg feel pain in the missing limb.

phobias Acute excessive fears of specific situations or objects that have no convincing basis in reality.

physiological needs First level of motives in Abraham Maslow's hierarchy; includes the biological needs of hunger, thirst, sex, exercise, and rest.

placebo An inert or inactive substance given to control subjects to test for bias effects.

plateau phase Second phase in the human sexual response cycle, during which the physiological arousal becomes more intense.

pleasure principle In Freudian theory, the idea that the instinctual drives of the id unconsciously and impulsively seek immediate pleasure.

positive reinforcement Presenting a subject something pleasant to increase the probability that the preceding behavior will be repeated.

postconventional morality Level III in Lawrence Kohlberg's theory, in which moral reasoning is based on personal standards and beliefs; highest level of moral thinking.

posttraumatic stress disorder (PTSD) Condition that can occur when a person experiences a severely distressing event; characterized by constant memories of the event, avoidance of anything associated with it, and general arousal.

Prägnanz (law of) Gestalt psychology law that states that people have a tendency to group stimuli according to rules, and that people do this whenever possible.

preconscious mind In Sigmund Freud's psychoanalytic theory of personality, the part of personality that contains information that we have learned but that we are not thinking about at the present time.

preconventional morality Level I of Lawrence Kohlberg's theory, in which moral reasoning is largely due to the expectation of rewards and punishments.

prejudice An unjustified fixed, usually negative, way of thinking about a person or object.

Premack principle Principle that states that, of any two responses, the one that is more likely to occur can be used to reinforce the response that is less likely to occur.

preoperational thought period Period in cognitive development; from two to seven years, the period during which the child learns to represent the environment with objects and symbols.

primacy effect Phenomenon where items are remembered because they come at the beginning of a list.

primary appraisal Activity of determining whether a new stimulus event is positive, neutral, or negative; first step in appraisal of stress.

primary narcissism A Freudian term that refers to the oral phase before the ego has developed; the individual constantly seeks pleasure.

primary reinforcement Reinforcement that is effective without having been associated with other reinforcers; sometimes called unconditioned reinforcement.

probability (p) In inferential statistics, the likelihood that the difference between the experimental and control groups is due to the independent variable.

procedural memory The most basic type of long-term memory; involves the formation of associations between stimuli and responses.

projection Defense mechanism in which a person attributes his or her unacceptable characteristics or motives to others rather than himself or herself.

projective personality test A personality test that presents ambiguous stimuli to which subjects are expected to respond with projections of their own personality.

proximity Closeness in time and space. In perception, it is the Gestalt perceptual principle in which stimuli next to one another are included together.

psyche According to Carl Jung, the thoughts and feelings (conscious and unconscious) of an individual.

psychoactive drug A drug that produces changes in behavior and cognition through modification of conscious awareness.

psychoanalysis The school of thought founded by Sigmund Freud that stressed unconscious motivation. In therapy, a patient's unconscious motivation is intensively explored in order to bring repressed conflicts up to consciousness; psychoanalysis usually takes a long time to accomplish.

psychobiology (also called biological psychology or physiological psychology) The subfield of experimental psychology concerned with the influence of heredity and the biological response systems on behavior.

psychogenic amnesia A dissociative disorder in which an individual loses his or her sense of identity.

psychogenic fugue A dissociative disorder in which an individual loses his or her sense of identity and goes to a new geographic location, forgetting all of the unpleasant emotions connected with the old life.

psychographics A technique used in consumer psychology to identify the attitudes of buyers and their preferences for particular products.

psycholinguistics The psychological study of how people convert the sounds of a language into meaningful symbols that can be used to communicate with others.

psychological dependence Situation in which a person craves a drug even though it is not biologically needed by the body.

psychological disorder A diagnosis of abnormal behavior; syndrome of abnormal adjustment, classified in *DSM*.

psychological types Carl Jung's term for different personality profiles; Jung combined two attitudes and four functions to produce eight psychological types.

psychopharmacology Study of effects of psychoactive drugs on behavior.

psychophysics An area of psychology in which researchers compare the physical energy of a stimulus with the sensation reported.

psychosexual stages Sigmund Freud's theoretical stages in personality development.

psychosomatic disorders A variety of body reactions that are closely related to psychological events.

psychotherapy Treatment of behavioral disorders through psychological techniques; major psychotherapies include insight therapy, behavior therapy, and group therapy.

psychotic disorders The more severe categories of abnormal behavior.

puberty Sexual maturation; the time at which the individual is able to perform sexually and to reproduce.

punishment Any event that decreases the likelihood that the behavior preceding it will be repeated.

quantitative trait loci (QTLs) Genes that collectively contribute to a trait for high intelligence.

rational-emotive therapy A cognitive behavior modification technique in which a person is taught to identify irrational, self-defeating beliefs and then to overcome them.

reaction formation Defense mechanism in which a person masks an unconsciously distressing or unacceptable trait by assuming an opposite attitude or behavior pattern.

reality principle In Freudian theory, the idea that the drives of the ego try to find socially acceptable ways to gratify the id.

reciprocal determinism The concept proposed by Albert Bandura that the behavior, the individual, and the situation interact and influence each other.

reciprocal inhibition Concept of Joseph Wolpe that states that it is possible to break the bond between anxiety-provoking stimuli and responses manifesting anxiety by facing those stimuli in a state antagonistic to anxiety.

reflex An automatic movement that occurs in direct response to a stimulus.

regression Defense mechanism in which a person retreats to an earlier, more immature form of behavior.

reinforcement Any event that increases the probability that the behavior that precedes it will be repeated; also called a reinforcer; similar to a reward.

reinforcement therapy A behavior therapy in which reinforcement is used to modify behavior. Techniques in reinforcement therapy include shaping, extinction, and token economy.

releaser (sign stimulus) Specific environmental cues that stimulate a stereotyped behavior to occur; releasers cause fixed action patterns.

repression Defense mechanism in which painful memories and unacceptable thoughts and motives are conveniently forgotten so that they will not have to be dealt with.

residual schizophrenia Type of schizophrenia in which the individual currently does not have symptoms but has had a schizophrenic episode in the past.

resistance Psychoanalytic term used when a patient avoids a painful area of conflict.

resolution phase The last phase in the human sexual response cycle; the time after orgasm when the body gradually returns to the unaroused state.

Restricted Environmental Stimulation Technique (REST) Research technique in which environmental stimuli available to an individual are reduced drastically; formerly called sensory deprivation.

retroactive interference Interference caused by information learned after the material of interest.

retrograde amnesia Forgetting information recently learned because of a disruptive stimulus such as an electric shock.

reversible figure In perception, a situation in which the figure and ground seem to reverse themselves; an illusion in which objects alternate as the main figure.

risky-shift The tendency for groups to make riskier decisions than individuals.

Rorschach Inkblot Test A projective personality test in which subjects are asked to discuss what they see in cards containing blots of ink.

safety needs Second level of motives in Abraham Maslow's hierarchy; includes security, stability, dependency, protection, freedom from fear and anxiety, and the need for structure and order.

Schachter-Singer theory of emotion Theory of emotion that states that we interpret our arousal according to our environment and label our emotions accordingly.

scheme A unit of knowledge that the person possesses; used in Jean Piaget's cognitive development theory.

schizophrenia Severe psychotic disorder that is characterized by disruptions in thinking, perception, and emotion.

scientific method An attitude and procedure that scientists use to conduct research. The steps include stating the problem, forming the hypothesis, collecting the information, evaluating the information, and drawing conclusions.

secondary appraisal In appraisal of stress, this is the evaluation that an individual's abilities and resources are sufficient to meet the demands of a stressful event.

secondary reinforcement Reinforcement that is effective only after it has been associated with a primary reinforcer; also called conditioned reinforcement.

secondary traits In Gordon Allport's personality theory, the less important situation-specific traits that help round out personality; they include attitudes, skills, and behavior patterns.

secure attachment Type of infant-parent attachment in which the infant actively seeks contact with the parent.

self-actualization A humanistic term describing the state in which all of an individual's capacities are developed fully. Fifth and highest level of motives in Abraham Maslow's hierarchy, this level, the realization of one's potential, is rarely reached.

self-efficacy An individual's sense of self-worth and success in adjusting to the world.

self-evaluation maintenance model (SEM) Tesser's theory of how we maintain a positive self-image despite the success of others close to us.

self-handicapping strategy A strategy that people use to prepare for failure; people behave in ways that produce obstacles to success so that when they do fail they can place the blame on the obstacle.

self-serving bias An attribution bias in which an individual attributes success to his or her own behavior and failure to external environmental causes.

semantic memory Type of long-term memory that can use cognitive activities, such as everyday knowledge.

sensation The passive process in which stimuli are received by sense receptors and transformed into neural impulses that can be carried through the nervous system; first stage in becoming aware of environment.

sensitivity training group (T-group) Therapy group that has the goal of making participants more aware of themselves and their ideas.

sensorimotor period Period in cognitive development; the first two years, during which the infant learns to coordinate sensory experiences with motor activities.

sensory adaptation Tendency of the sense organs to adjust to continuous stimulation by reducing their functioning; a stimulus that once caused sensation and no longer does.

sensory deprivation Situation in which normal environmental sensory stimuli available to an individual are reduced drastically; also called REST (Restricted Environmental Stimulation Technique).

serial learning A verbal learning procedure in which the stimuli are always presented in the same order, and the subject has to learn them in the order in which they are presented.

sex roles The set of behaviors and attitudes that are determined to be appropriate for one sex or the other in a society.

shaping In operant conditioning, the gradual process of reinforcing behaviors that get closer to some final desired behavior. Shaping is also called successive approximation.

signal detection theory Research approach in which the subject's behavior in detecting a threshold is treated as a form of decision making.

similarity Gestalt principle in which similar stimuli are perceived as a unit.

simple phobia Excessive irrational fear that does not fall into other specific categories, such as fear of dogs, insects, snakes, or closed-in places.

simultaneous conditioning A procedure in classical conditioning in which the CS and US are presented at exactly the same time.

Sixteen Personality Factor Questionnaire (16PF) Raymond Cattell's personality test to measure source traits.

Skinner box B. F. Skinner's animal cage with a lever that triggers reinforcement for a subject.

sleep terror disorder (pavor nocturnus) Nonrapid-eye-movement (NREM) sleep disorder in which the person (usually a child) wakes up screaming and terrified, but cannot recall why.

sleepwalking (somnambulism) NREM sleep disorder in which the person walks in his or her sleep.

social cognition The process of understanding other people and ourselves by forming and utilizing information about the social world.

social cognitive theory Albert Bandura's approach to personality that proposes that individuals use observation, imitation, and cognition to develop personality.

social comparison Theory proposed by Leon Festinger that we tend to compare our behavior to others to ensure that we are conforming.

social exchange theory Theory of interpersonal relationships that states that people evaluate the costs and rewards of their relationships and act accordingly.

social facilitation Phenomenon in which the presence of others increases dominant behavior patterns in an individual; Richard Zajonc's theory states that the presence of others enhances the emission of the dominant response of the individual.

social influence Influence designed to change the attitudes or behavior of other people; includes conformity, compliance, and obedience.

social learning theory An approach to social psychology that emphasizes observation and modeling; states that reinforcement is involved in motivation rather than in learning, and proposes that aggression is a form of learned behavior.

social phobia Excessive irrational fear and embarrassment when interacting with other people. Social phobias may include fear of assertive behavior, fear of making mistakes, or fear of public speaking.

social psychology The study of how an individual's behavior, thoughts, and feelings are influenced by other people.

sociobiology Study of the genetic basis of social behavior.

sociocultural Emphasizes the importance of culture, gender, and ethnicity in how we think, feel, and act.

somatic nervous system The part of the peripheral nervous system that carries messages from the sense organs and relays information that directs the voluntary movements of the skeletal muscles.

somatization disorder Somatoform disorder in which a person has medical complaints without physical cause.

somatoform disorders Psychological disorders characterized by physical symptoms for which there are no obvious physical causes.

specific attachment phase Stage at about six months of age, in which the baby becomes attached to a specific person.

split-brain research Popular name for Roger Sperry's research on the syndrome of hemisphere deconnection; research on individuals with the corpus callosum severed. Normal functioning breaks down in split-brain subjects when different information is presented to each hemisphere.

SQ5R A technique to improve learning and memory. Components include survey, question, read, record, recite, review, and reflect.

stage of exhaustion Third stage in Hans Selye's general adaptation syndrome. As the body continues to resist stress, it depletes its energy resources and the person becomes exhausted.

stage of resistance Second stage in Hans Selye's general adaptation syndrome. When stress is prolonged, the body builds some resistance to the effects of stress.

standardization The process of obtaining a representative sample of scores in the population so that a particular score can be interpreted correctly.

Stanford-Binet Intelligence Scale An intelligence test first revised by Lewis Terman at Stanford University in 1916; still a popular test used today.

state-dependent learning Situation in which what is learned in one state can only be remembered when the person is in that state of mind.

statistically significant In inferential statistics, a finding that the independent variable did influence greatly the outcome of the experimental and control group.

stereotype An exaggerated and rigid mental image of a particular class of persons or objects.

stimulus A unit of the environment that causes a response in an individual; a physical or chemical agent acting on an appropriate sense receptor.

stimulus discrimination Responding to relevant stimuli.

stimulus generalization Responding to stimuli similar to the stimulus that had caused the response.

stimulus motives Motivating factors that are internal and unlearned, but do not appear to have a physiological basis; stimulus motives cause an individual to seek out sensory stimulation through interaction with the environment.

stimulus trace The perceptual persistence of a stimulus after it is no longer present.

strange situation procedure A measure of attachment developed by Mary Ainsworth that consists of eight phases during which the infant is increasingly stressed.

stress Anything that produces demands on us to adjust and threatens our well-being.

Strong Interest Inventory An objective personality test that compares people's personalities to groups that achieve success in certain occupations.

structuralism First school of thought in psychology; it studied conscious experience to discover the structure of the mind.

subject bias Source of potential error in an experiment from the action or expectancy of a subject; a subject might influence the experimental results in ways that mask the true outcome.

subjective organization Long-term memory procedures in which the individual provides a personal method of organizing information to be memorized.

sublimation Defense mechanism; a person redirects his or her socially undesirable urges into socially acceptable behavior.

successive approximation Shaping; in operant conditioning, the gradual process of reinforcing behaviors that get closer to some final desired behavior.

sudden infant death syndrome (SIDS) Situation in which a seemingly healthy infant dies suddenly in its sleep; also called crib death.

superego Sigmund Freud's representation of conscience.

surface traits In Raymond Cattell's personality theory, the observable characteristics of a person's behavior and personality.

symbolization In Sigmund Freud's dream theory, the process of converting the latent content of a dream into manifest symbols.

systematic desensitization Application of counterconditioning, in which the individual overcomes anxiety by learning to relax in the presence of stimuli that had once made him or her unbearably nervous.

task-oriented coping Adjustment responses in which the person evaluates a stressful situation objectively and then formulates a plan with which to solve the problem.

test of significance An inferential statistical technique used to determine whether the difference in scores between the experimental and control groups is really due to the effects of the independent variable or to random chance. If the probability of an outcome is extremely low, we say that outcome is significant.

Thanatos Sigmund Freud's term for a destructive instinct such as aggression; also called death instinct.

Thematic Apperception Test (TAT) Projective personality test in which subjects are shown pictures of people in everyday settings; subjects must make up a story about the people portrayed.

theory of social impact Latané's theory of social behavior; it states that each member of a group shares the responsibility equally.

Theory X Douglas McGregor's theory that states that the worker dislikes work and must be forced to do it.

Theory Y Douglas McGregor's theory that states that work is natural and can be a source of satisfaction, and, when it is, the worker can be highly committed and motivated.

therapy In psychology, the treatment of behavior problems; two major types of therapy include psychotherapy and biological therapy.

time and motion studies In engineering psychology, studies that analyze the time it takes to perform an action and the movements that go into the action.

tip-of-the-tongue phenomenon A phenomenon in which the closer a person comes to recalling something, the more accurately he or she can remember details, such as the number of syllables or letters.

token economy A behavior therapy in which desired behaviors are reinforced immediately with tokens that can be exchanged at a later time for desired rewards, such as food or recreational privileges.

trace conditioning A procedure in classical conditioning in which the CS is a discrete event that is presented and terminated before the US is presented.

trait A distinctive and stable attribute in people.

trait anxiety Anxiety that is long-lasting; a relatively stable personality characteristic.

transference Psychoanalytic term used when a patient projects his feelings onto the therapist.

transsexualism A condition in which a person feels trapped in the body of the wrong sex.

trial and error learning Trying various behaviors in a situation until the solution is found.

triangular theory of love Robert Sternberg's theory that states that love consists of intimacy, passion, and decision/commitment.

triarchic theory of intelligence Robert Sternberg's theory of intelligence that states that it consists of three parts: componential, experiential, and contextual subtheories.

Type-A behavior Behavior shown by a particular type of individual; a personality pattern of behavior that can lead to stress and heart disease.

unconditional positive regard Part of Carl Rogers's personality theory; occurs when we accept someone regardless of what he or she does or says.

unconditioned response (UR) An automatic reaction elicited by a stimulus.

unconditioned stimulus (US) Any stimulus that elicits an automatic or reflexive reaction in an individual; it does not have to be learned in the present situation.

unconscious mind In Sigmund Freud's psychoanalytic theory of personality, the part of personality that is unavailable to us; Freud suggests that instincts and unpleasant memories are stored in the unconscious mind.

undifferentiated schizophrenia Type of schizophrenia that does not fit into any particular category, or fits into more than one category.

validity The degree to which you actually measure what you intend to measure.

variability In statistics, variability measures the range of the scores.

variable interval (VI) schedule Schedule of reinforcement in which the subject is reinforced for the first response given after a certain time interval, with the interval being different for each trial.

variable ratio (VR) schedule Schedule of reinforcement in which the subject is given reinforcement after a varying number of responses; the number of responses required for reinforcement is different for every trial.

vestibular sense Sense that helps us keep our balance.

visuo-spatial sketch pad Responsible for visual images involved in geographical orientation and spatial task.

vulnerability-stress model Theory of schizophrenia that states that some people have a biological tendency to develop schizophrenia if they are stressed enough by their environment.

Weber's Law Ernst Weber's law that states that the difference threshold depends on the ratio of the intensity of one stimulus to another rather than on an absolute difference.

Wechsler Adult Intelligence Scale (WAIS) An intelligence test for adults, first published by David Wechsler in 1955; it contains verbal and performance subscales.

Wechsler Intelligence Scale for Children (WISC-III) Similar to the Wechsler Adult Intelligence Scale, except that it is designed for children ages 6 through 16, and helps diagnose certain childhood disorders, such as dyslexia and other learning disabilities.

Wechsler Preschool and Primary Scale of Intelligence (WPPSI-R) Designed for children between the ages of 4 and 7; helps diagnose certain childhood disorders, such as dyslexia and other learning disabilities.

withdrawal Unpleasant physical reactions that a drug-dependent user experiences when he or she stops taking the drug.

within-subject experiment An experimental design in which each subject is given all treatments, including the control condition; subjects serve in both experimental and control groups.

working memory The memory store, with a capacity of about 7 items and enduring for up to 30 seconds, that handles current information.

Yerkes-Dodson Law Popular idea that performance is best when arousal is at a medium level.

Sources for the Glossary:

The majority of terms in this glossary are from Psychology: A ConnecText, 4th Edition, Terry F. Pettijohn. ©1999 Dushkin/ McGraw-Hill, Guilford, CT 06437. The remaining terms were developed by the Annual Editions staff.

AE Article Review Form

We encourage you to photocopy and use this page as a tool to assess how the articles in **Annual Editions** expand on the information in your textbook. By reflecting on the articles you will gain enhanced text information. You can also access this useful form on a product's book support Web site at *http://www.dushkin.com/online/*.

NAME: _____ DATE: _____

TITLE AND NUMBER OF ARTICLE: _____

BRIEFLY STATE THE MAIN IDEA OF THIS ARTICLE: _____

LIST THREE IMPORTANT FACTS THAT THE AUTHOR USES TO SUPPORT THE MAIN IDEA:

WHAT INFORMATION OR IDEAS DISCUSSED IN THIS ARTICLE ARE ALSO DISCUSSED IN YOUR TEXTBOOK OR OTHER READINGS THAT YOU HAVE DONE? LIST THE TEXTBOOK CHAPTERS AND PAGE NUMBERS:

LIST ANY EXAMPLES OF BIAS OR FAULTY REASONING THAT YOU FOUND IN THE ARTICLE:

LIST ANY NEW TERMS/CONCEPTS THAT WERE DISCUSSED IN THE ARTICLE, AND WRITE A SHORT DEFINITION:

ANNUAL EDITIONS revisions depend on two major opinion sources: one is our Advisory Board, listed in the front of this volume, which works with us in scanning the thousands of articles published in the public press each year; the other is you—the person actually using the book. Please help us and the users of the next edition by completing the prepaid article rating form on this page and returning it to us. Thank you for your help!

ANNUAL EDITIONS: Psychology 00/01

ARTICLE RATING FORM

Here is an opportunity for you to have direct input into the next revision of this volume. We would like you to rate each of the 47 articles listed below, using the following scale:

1. Excellent: should definitely be retained
2. Above average: should probably be retained
3. Below average: should probably be deleted
4. Poor: should definitely be deleted

Your ratings will play a vital part in the next revision. So please mail this prepaid form to us just as soon as you complete it. Thanks for your help!

We Want Your Advice

RATING

ARTICLE

1. Science and Pseudoscience
2. Research in the Psychological Laboratory: Truth or Triviality?
3. How Are Psychologists Portrayed on Screen?
4. Nature, Nurture: Not Mutually Exclusive
5. What We Learn from Twins: The Mirror of Your Soul
6. Optimizing Expression of the Common Human Genome for Child Development
7. The Split Brain Revisited
8. The Senses
9. Deaf Defying
10. The Importance of Taste
11. Night Life
12. Learning Begins Even before Babies Are Born, Scientists Show
13. What Constitutes "Appropriate" Punishment?
14. Losing Your Mind?
15. Traumatic Memory Is Special
16. Child Psychologist: Jean Piaget
17. Cognitive Development in Social and Cultural Context
18. Multiple Intelligence Disorder
19. Penetrating the Barriers to Teaching Higher Thinking
20. Face It!
21. Emotion in the Second Half of Life
22. Psychology: A Study Finds That among Professions, the Secret Service Is Best at Distinguishing between Lies and Truth

RATING

ARTICLE

23. The Biology of Joy
24. The Moral Development of Children
25. The Seven Stages of Man
26. Fetal Psychology
27. Do Parents Really Matter? Kid Stuff
28. Rethinking Puberty: The Development of Sexual Attraction
29. Live to 100? No Thanks
30. Who Are the Freudians?
31. The Stability of Personality: Observations and Evaluations
32. Making Sense of Self-Esteem
33. Social Anxiety
34. Friendships and Adaptation across the Life Span
35. What Makes a Leader?
36. Reducing Prejudice: Combating Intergroup Biases
37. Psychologist Links Video Games, Violence
38. Chronic Anxiety: How to Stop Living on the Edge
39. How Stress Attacks You
40. Dysthymia: Treating Mild Depression's Major Effects
41. The Clustering and Contagion of Suicide
42. Obsessive-Compulsive Disorder—Part I
43. Obsessive-Compulsive Disorder—Part II
44. What You Can Change and What You Cannot Change
45. Think Like a Shrink
46. The Quest for a Cure
47. New Treatments for Schizophrenia—Part I

(Continued on next page)

ANNUAL EDITIONS: PSYCHOLOGY 00/01

BUSINESS REPLY MAIL
FIRST-CLASS MAIL PERMIT NO. 84 GUILFORD CT

POSTAGE WILL BE PAID BY ADDRESSEE

Dushkin/McGraw-Hill
Sluice Dock
Guilford, CT 06437-9989

IIII....II...I...I...III...IIII.II..I.I.I.I.I...I.I.I..I.I.I

ABOUT YOU

Name _____   Date _____

Are you a teacher? ☐ A student? ☐

Your school's name _____

Department _____

Address _____   City _____   State ____ Zip ____

School telephone # _____

YOUR COMMENTS ARE IMPORTANT TO US !

Please fill in the following information:
For which course did you use this book?
_____

Did you use a text with this *ANNUAL EDITION*? ☐ yes ☐ no
What was the title of the text?
_____

What are your general reactions to the *Annual Editions* concept?
_____

Have you read any particular articles recently that you think should be included in the next edition?
_____

Are there any articles you feel should be replaced in the next edition? Why?
_____

Are there any World Wide Web sites you feel should be included in the next edition? Please annotate.
_____

May we contact you for editorial input? ☐ yes ☐ no
May we quote your comments? ☐ yes ☐ no